Employee Development

About the author

Rosemary Harrison is a graduate (History Honours) of Kings College, London University. She obtained the Diploma of the Institute of Personnel Management (now the Institute of Personnel and Development) in 1969 with distinctions, and was elected Fellow of the Institute in 1985. Since 1989 she has been Lecturer in Human Resource Management at Durham University Business School, where she is also a Director of its Human Resource Development Unit. Previously Senior Lecturer in Personnel Management and Organisational Behaviour at the then Newcastle Polytechnic and a training officer in the health service, she has also carried out consultancy assignments in many British private- and public-sector organizations.

Her publications include: *Equality at Work* (Pergamon, 1986); *Training and Development* (IPM, 1988); 'Employee Development at Barratt', in *Case Studies in Personnel*, (edited by Winstanley and Woodall, IPM, 1992); *Developing Human Resources for Productivity* (International Labour Office, Geneva, 1992); and *Strategic Human Resource Management* (with G Anderson, Addison-Wesley International, 1993).

She was a specialist adviser in Training and Development to the Council for National Academic Awards from 1989 to the Council's dissolution. Other external academic roles include Chief External Examiner (MA in Managing Human Resources) at Kingston Business School; Visiting Lecturer at Newcastle University; and Visiting Lecturer at the Foundation for Corporate Education in the Netherlands.

She lives in Durham with her family.

Management Studies 2 Series

The IPD examination system provides a unique route into professional personnel practice. After the Professional Management Foundation Programme, the IPD Stage 2 syllabus covers the core subject areas of Employee Resourcing, Development and Relations. Management Studies 2 Series forms the essential reading for all students at this level.

Other titles in the series:

Case Studies in Personnel
Diana Winstanley and Jean Woodall

Employee Relations
David Farnham

Employee Resourcing
Derek Torrington, Laura Hall, Isabel Haylor and Judith Myers

Passing Your IPM Exams
Elaine Crosthwaite

MANAGEMENT STUDIES 2

Employee Development

Rosemary Harrison

Institute of Personnel and Development

For my family: Malcolm, Piers and Dominic

First published in 1992

Reprinted 1993 (twice), 1995

Phototypeset by The Comp-Room, Aylesbury
and printed in Great Britain
by the Cromwell Press, Broughton Gifford, Wiltshire

British Library Cataloguing in Publication Data

Harrison, Rosemary
Employee Development. – (Management
Studies Series)
I. Title II. Series
658.3

ISBN 0-85292-487-9

INSTITUTE OF PERSONNEL
AND DEVELOPMENT

IPD House, Camp Road, London SW19 4UX
Tel: 0181 971 9000 Fax: 0181 263 3333
Registered office as above. Registered Charity No. 1038333
A company limited by guarantee. Registered in England No. 2931892

Contents

PART FOUR
Promoting individual and organizational growth

APPENDICES

List of figures

Acknowledgements

I am grateful to all the individuals and organizations who allowed me to write about them or to quote from their publications; also to Alan Rutter, University of Northumbria at Newcastle upon Tyne Business School, who collaborated with me in producing for my 1988 text material which reappears here in Chapter 9 in the section on 'Managing Training and Development Resources'.

All real-life case study material relates only to situations current at the dates given in the text, and comments on all such information are my own; they do not represent the views of any other individual or organization. In particular, British Rail wish it to be known that the views conveyed on pages 427–9 are those of the two named co-authors only and not necessarily those of the organization, and that in the ensuing period many changes have taken place in the fundamental model underpinning BR's management development programmes and processes. Peter Phillips at BP points out that the material on pages 275–6 is now mainly of historical interest since in the wake of recent major changes at BP important new initiatives have been taken in their management development and competency work. Laurence Jackson has recently produced further information on innovative work still being done on competences at Manchester Airport (pages 276–8). And Volvo Car UK Limited (pages 461–2) have made major progress with their 1990 initiatives, especially in relation to the manager/employee feedback system.

Much of the material in Part 1 of the book is vulnerable to change, and Ron Johnson and Chris Hayes in particular emphasize that the situations described in their quoted work (Chapter 4) are in a continuous state of flux.

Material from J. W. Gilley and S. A. Eggland, *Principles of Human Resource Development*, copyright 1989 by the Addison Wesley Publishing Company, is reprinted with permission of the publisher.

Material from C. Fombrun, N. M. Tichy and M. A. Devanna, *Strategic Human Resource Management*, copyright © 1984 by John Wiley and Sons, Inc., New York, is reprinted with permission of the publisher.

Quotations from the *Daily Telegraph* article '*A Sixth Sense for Business*' (page 37) by Paul Marston, 31 May, 1991, is copyright The Telegraph plc, 1991.

Preface

The purpose of this book is twofold: to produce, through a revision and extension of my 1988 book *Training and Development,* a text for Institute of Personnel and Development (IPD) students and for students on other degree and postgraduate courses, such as BA Business Studies, MA in Human Resource Management and MBA, where Employee Development constitutes a significant area of study; and, equally important, to simulate and help practitioners who, through the medium of a text interspersed with practical activities and case studies, may wish to reinforce and extend their understanding of employee development in the workplace.

The book falls into four parts. Part One looks at key issues in employee development and sets the scene by explaining the national education and training framework and by making some international comparisons in order to provide the wider context that is now essential not only for those concerned with national training activity, but for every manager who has a concern to develop people in their organization.

Part Two takes as its main theme the development of the 'learning organization'. It highlights: the importance of training and development as major contributors to organizational growth and success; the political nature of developmental activity; the theory and reality of employee development responsibilities, roles and skills in organizations; and the ways of improving the status of training and the competences of those involved in managing and organizing the function. It discusses the concept of the organization as a learning system where each individual has a major part to play in ensuring the continuous development of all its members while also steadily improving organizational performance.

Part Three focuses on the training and learning that need to take place in order to achieve this business-led development of people. Advice is given on how to plan and manage learning events, with special emphasis on how to tackle the crucial areas of costing, assessment of needs and the design, delivery and evaluation of learning events.

Part Four concentrates on ways of developing a high-quality, high-performing and flexible workforce, looking at those processes and areas of activity that can have the most direct impact on productivity, flexibility, quality, and strategic and innovative capability at organizational as well as at individual levels.

Although in Chapters 2 and 3 the topics examined are taken to a level of complexity more appropriate for students following an optional course or specialist module in those areas, there is in general no attempt to adopt a stepped approach to subject matter; it is not feasible to do so, and it would work against the essential structure and readability of the book for non-students.

The treatment of two key areas merits explanation here:

National Vocational Education and Training System (NVET)

This subject covers a vast and constantly changing area of information and analysis. An understanding of the whole subject must therefore be derived less from text books, whose content will tend to date rapidly, than from newspaper articles, journals and various reports and working papers.

Students have in fact always found difficulty with the subject, tending to avoid it in examinations unless they have specialist experience or knowledge. This is regrettable, because the national framework for education and training offers so many opportunities as well as constraints to individual organizations; and national policy and strategies explain so much about the attitudes behind employee development at local and organizational levels.

The approach taken in this book is to give a factual explanation of current national vocational education and training policy and framework in Chapter 2; to evaluate that system in Chapter 3; and to develop understanding and critical ability further by examining some international comparisons and pressures in Chapter 4. By using a conceptual framework of vision, mission, strategy and implementation for this analysis, these chapters about national human resource development set the scene for discussion later in the book of employee development policy and strategies within organizations, and for the conclusions reached in the final chapter. Furthermore, by making explicit in Part

One the need for integration between national educational, training and development policies and systems, the necessity for such integration within every organization should become evident.

Training and development of special groups and to meet special contigencies

The considerations here are very similar to those discussed above. The heading disguises a multiplicity of topics, and it would be impossible to treat them all in any meaningful way, even if more space were available for the task. Harry Barrington and Margaret Reid's *Training Interventions* (1986; fourth edition, 1994) does an excellent job in this respect, and is essential reading. The aim of Chapter 18 is to complement that textbook by identifying some of the most commonly encountered areas of need, whether by type of employee (such as supervisory training and development) or type of concern (such as training and development for equal opportunities), and then by showing how, through the application of a common methodology, relevant learning can be ensured.

That kind of treatment is consistent with the focus of this book as a whole; it is a text primarily intended for students and novice practitioners and its aim is not, therefore, to tackle every possible area of specialist training. (Such technical knowledge and expertise can, in any case, more appropriately be obtained in or through the place of work.) It is intended rather to help readers gain a practical understanding of the main employee development strategies and processes whereby the needs of the organization and the individual can be brought together and pursued in an integrated and productive way.

Until very recently it was common, in a book about employee development, to be preoccupied with functional and technical matters; to focus on how to achieve a systematic approach to training, and on how to design and deliver the different kinds of training that were commonly carried out in organizations at different levels and for different groups. Now, however, as Chapter 1 makes clear, the concern is changing. The issues that increasingly engage the attention are to do with the contribution that employee development can make to the 'bottom line', its relationship to business needs and the part it can play in building up a flexible, committed and high-performing workforce. The topics of major perceived importance are therefore: achieving a business-led employee development strategy; measuring and evaluating outcomes of training and development activity; helping to change the organization's culture; achieving total quality and a customer orientation; developing a 'learning organization'; reducing skill shortages; and gaining and maintaining a competitive edge in an international, not merely a national context. All these themes, referred to only in passing in my 1988 book, must occupy considerable space in this one, written for the 1990s and, hopefully, beyond.

The core skills that were emphasized in 1988 – observation and reflection, analysis, creativity, decision-making and problem-solving, and evaluation – remain as crucial now as they were then to anyone with responsibility for promoting employee development in the organization. Possession of these skills, and an understanding both of major current training and development issues and of key strategies and techniques, should enable those with employee development responsibilities to perform effectively in a rapidly widening field of operation, gaining more specialized skills and knowledge as the need for these becomes apparent.

This book, therefore, like the last, tries to stimulate readers to develop those core skills. It actively involves them in a wide range of practical 'experiences' (most in the form of real-life case studies and consultancy projects) to which they are invited to respond both analytically and creatively. Considerable use is made of material from the professional journals of the Institute of Personnel and Development, since they form an easily accessible and invaluable source of secondary practical experience for students and practitioners. To help extend learning, exercises are given both within and at the end of most chapters. The end-of-chapter exercises are taken from, or related to, IPD Stage 2 Examination papers, but are also useful in a wider practical context. They require you to seek and use additional information, building on data covered in the chapter but also referring to some of the references given at the end of the chapter.

The only exception to this interactive approach is in Part One, where it is necessary to cover a considerable amount of factual information in order that necessary levels of understanding and evaluative ability can be achieved. This means that the chapters are longer than elsewhere, and case study material is of an illustrative nature rather than acting as a focus for practical work.

Terminology

Every attempt has been made to avoid sexist language. In organizational terminology, the word 'manager' refers to anyone who has managerial responsibilities, and therefore takes in supervisory positions; terms like 'employees', 'people', or 'team' have been preferred to words like 'staff' or 'workers', whilst the words 'boss' and 'subordinate' appear only in quoted extracts, since they are inappropriate in a book which places so much stress on a joint approach to work planning, review, and diagnosis of needs, and on the right of everyone to development, whatever their formal status in the organization.

Confusion often exists about the meaning of terms like 'learning', 'training', 'education' and 'development', and full definitions are given in Chapters 1 and 7. The word 'training' is used throughout most of the book as a shorthand for planned instructional activities, and sometimes (the context will make clear when) for wider developmental activities and processes. 'Development' is used to cover all learning experiences. When used in conjunction with 'training' it is in order to distinguish wider learning experiences from narrowly focused planned, job-related events. The phrase 'learning event' applies to any planned learning experience, no matter how simple or complex, how brief or how extended in time, whereby people's behaviour and performance is to be developed and/or changed.

These points emphasize the overall purpose of the book; it is concerned with *everyone* who holds responsibility for training and developing people in the organization. Wherever possible its terminology reflects this concern.

Part One

Employee Development: The National and International Context

Chapter 1

Employee development: the key issues

Learning Objectives

After reading this chapter you will:

1 appreciate the difference and the interrelationship between development, education and training;
2 understand the meaning of key terms such as 'policy' and 'strategy', and the need to integrate employee development with wider employee resourcing and other business policies and strategies;
3 understand the need for changed attitudes towards the development of people;
4 appreciate what some of the fundamental employee development issues are at national and organizational levels;
5 appreciate the need for employee development to make a convincing contribution to the achievement of organizational as well as individual goals.

What is Meant by Employee Development?

It is important first to clarify some fundamental terms: 'development', 'education' and 'training'. They are often used as if they were synonymous, and even in this book they will be used fairly loosely, usually as a convenient shorthand to indicate a variety of organizational learning activities. But the terms do have quite distinct meanings, and looking at some definitions helps to clarify what 'development' is really about.

Here are some dictionary definitions (Oxford, 1978):

- DEVELOP: to unfold more fully, bring out all that is potentially contained in
- EDUCATE: to bring up so as to form habits, manners, intellectual and physical aptitudes

- TRAIN: to instruct and discipline in or for some particular art, profession, occupation or practice; to make proficient by such instruction and practice

We can see from these definitions why the overall term 'employee development' (or 'human resource development' or its equivalent) is being used increasingly in organizations today in preference to the more limited term 'training'. Development is the all-important primary process, through which individual and organizational growth can through time achieve its fullest potential. Education is a major contributor to that developmental process, because it directly and continuously affects the formation not only of knowledge and abilities, but also of character and of culture, aspirations and achievements. Training is the shorter-term, systematic process through which an individual is helped to master defined tasks or areas of skill and knowledge to predetermined standards. There needs to be a coherent and well-planned integration of training, education and continuous development in the organization if real growth at individual and organizational levels is to be achieved and sustained.

What, then, is employee development? We can define it thus:

> Employee development as part of the organization's overall human resource strategy means the skilful provision and organization of learning experiences in the workplace in order that performance can be improved, that work goals can be achieved and that, through enhancing the skills, knowledge, learning ability and enthusiasm of people at every level, there can be continuous organizational as well as individual growth. Employee development must, therefore, be part of a wider strategy for the business, aligned with the organization's corporate mission and goals.

The term 'business' in this context refers to any kind of employing organization, public or private sector, service, process or product-driven.

Employee Development, Employee Resourcing and Overall Business Strategy

Employee development should always take place within a wider framework of employee resourcing policy and strategy and, beyond that, of the overall policy of the organization. The critical linkages between the three strategic areas will be explained in detail in Chapters 11 and 21. At this point, however, terminology again needs explaining: what is the difference between 'employee resourcing', 'personnel management', and 'human resource management'? For detailed clarification, see Torrington et al. (1991), Chapter 1. But for our present purposes we can safely assume that all such phrases have a similar meaning; they represent that function of management that is concerned with how best to plan, utilize, manage and develop the workforce of an organization in order to ensure the achievement of its corporate goals with the commitment of its people. Employee development is, therefore, an area within the overall function of employee resourcing, although, because of its importance and complexity, it is often studied as a subject in its own right for the purposes of professional examinations.

What is meant by terms such as policy, strategy and implementation?

Pearson (1991, pp. 4-6) observes that even in some of the most respected literature on business strategy (e.g. Chandler, 1962; Johnson and Scholes, 1989) there is a regrettable tendency to treat a number of different terms as if they are synonymous. Here are some definitions which will be adhered to throughout this book. For simplicity, they are expressed in the context of the organization, but their essential meaning remains the same when they are used in a wider context, as later in this chapter.

- Vision: This is the certainty about the kind of organization it should be. Top management must have a clear and unwavering vision, and the determination and leadership, the creativity and skills, to drive their organization forward to realize that vision. It was these qualities that distinguished Chief Executive Colin Marshall in his successful fight to turn British Airways around from being virtually bankrupt in 1981 to realizing, within only five years, his vision of it as the world's leading airline.
- Mission: The mission statement expresses the vision in words which then become guidelines for strategy. It explains the organization's *raison d'être* and is 'the most generalized type of objective' (Johnson and Scholes, 1989, p. 134). Colin Marshall's mission statement for British Airways in the 1980s was that it should become 'the Harrods of the airways of the world'. A mission statement is more or

less essential as the foundation for strategy and plans, and the structure that supports them.

- Policy: At the macro level, policy is simply an elaboration of the organization's mission. Where there is no mission statement, then the organization's overall policy represents an explanation of its mission. General policy is that which is concerned with long-term goals and values. By establishing overall purpose and direction and expressing the enduring values of the organization (Leontiades, 1980) it sets the limits within which strategy must be formulated.
- Strategy: Peter Wickens (1987) described strategy as, quite simply, getting the organization 'from here to there'. Once vision has been given concrete expression in a mission or policy for the organization, then comes the process of evaluating alternative ways in which that mission could be achieved through time. Which route or strategy should be adopted? Only after a thorough, fully informed analysis of strengths, weaknesses, opportunities and threats, both internal and external, using a process that should involve getting ideas from people throughout the organization who have relevant knowledge and views to offer, can valid decisions be made about overall business strategy and related strategic objectives.
- Implementation: Implementation of strategy requires a framework, plans and resources. The framework means the structure of policies and institutions whereby the plans of action can be delivered. It must facilitate the achievement of strategic objectives, and ensure the monitoring and control of the operations of those responsible for implementing strategy. The policies, at this micro level, specify the targets they must establish to achieve the wider strategic objectives, and the programmes, plans and resources whereby action will be achieved.

The cultural and structural context

There are many strategies to achieve employee development, but all take place within the context of an organization's culture and structure.

The culture relating to people in the organization is typified by the way they are to be treated and managed, the value attached to them and 'the way things are done here'. The corporate philosophy about people and the values, attitudes and styles of leadership, management and social interactions to which they give rise establish the framework within which specific employee development policies and strategies are formulated (see, for example, Deal and Kennedy, 1982; Benson, 1987; Fellbom, 1987; Thomas, 1985; Upton, 1987).

An organization's culture is intricately related to its structure, since it is structure that determines formal roles, responsibilities and tasks, together with the systems and procedures by which people work, and the formal extent of and limitations to their autonomy. Structure, in turn, both influences and is influenced by employee development policy and practices. Issues of organizational culture and structure will be explored in more detail later in the book, particularly in Chapters 5, 6, 11 and 21.

The employee resourcing context

Within the framework of the organization's primary philosophy, values and culture regarding people, and the structure that significantly governs their behaviour and interactions, employee resourcing strategy defines the ways in which the organization's workforce should be planned, managed and developed in order to move the organization forward and achieve its corporate goals. The terms 'human resource management' and 'personnel management' when they appear in this book have the same meaning. Every area of employee resourcing policy and activity has its direct influence on people's development.

- Human resource planning determines how many people should be employed, how, when and where they are employed, and how they will be utilized. The framework established here is the critical one within which employee development policy, strategy and plans must be formulated.
- Recruitment and selection are the processes through which people move into the organization. If well chosen, this human material should prove to have the abilities and desire to respond positively and fruitfully to developmental initiatives.

However, ineffective recruitment and selection will almost always defeat attempts to instill skills and knowledge and unlock potential.

- Leadership provides the vision and values that drive employee development in an organization.
- Teamwork, like leadership, will either provide continuing developmental opportunities that will maximize the organization's investment in people, or will erect barriers that may lead to rapid

depreciation in that most expensive of its resources.

- Appraisal is the process at the heart of development, but attempts to use it also as a major method of control may defeat its developmental objectives.
- Learning activities and opportunities appropriate to the needs of individuals, groups and the organization can be, where relevant, formally structured, but should also form a part of daily operations in the workplace so that a process of continuous development and improvement can take place. Continuous development, principally through the integration of learning and work, has as its major objective the achievement of operational goals and the steady growth of the ability to learn at every level, from the individual to the organization as a whole. Whereas the main concern in training is to help people to acquire skills related to a particular task or tasks, continuous development is primarily concerned with uncovering and utilizing potential, and in developing those core skills to which the Preface refers: observation and reflection, analysis, creativity, decision-making and problem-solving, and evaluation.
- Incentive and reward systems will either help to encourage people to develop or, as *A Challenge to Complacency* observed (Coopers and Lybrand, 1985), will be so few and/or so irrelevant to areas like training that individual as well as organizational motivation to develop will be low.
- Protective measures, whether against discrimination or in matters of health, safety and welfare, will again either remove barriers to individual and organizational growth or put such obstacles in their path that little can be achieved.
- Termination policies and procedures should ensure that, when people leave the organization, positive steps are taken to help them, facilitating their continued development after that exit point is reached, rather than leaving them with little hope or aspirations.

These, then, are the major employee resourcing processes which constitute the 'umbrella' for the development of people in an organization (see Rothwell, 1984). In Chapters 11 and 21 we shall explore in more detail how the integration of employee development with wider employee resourcing strategies can best be achieved in order to ensure plans that make a significant contribution to the achievement of business goals as well as to the satisfaction of individual needs.

The Need for Changed Attitudes and Levels of Investment in People

The rationale for this book remains in 1992 the same as for its predecessor in 1988; to produce or reinforce positive attitudes which should lead to a belief in the need for substantial investment in human resource development in organizations, and in the payback that can be achieved from that investment; and to offer help in building up the necessary expertise. Such a rationale seems justified by a wide range of evidence.

In 1985 a major report on training in British organizations, *A Challenge to Complacency* (Coopers and Lybrand) was published. The report offered evidence of a disturbingly low level of investment in training in both public- and private-sector organizations. The main reason for this widespread failure to perform a function which (see especially *Competence and Competition*, Institute of Manpower Studies, 1984) is so crucial to the achievement of organizational goals was seen by the authors to be a mixture of complacent, ill-informed and sceptical attitudes to training at all organizational levels, including those of personnel practitioners themselves. Developing positive attitudes was emphasized as a crucial task, and the report made many suggestions about how to influence attitudes to training. For the purposes of this book the following are particularly important:

- Exhortations and encouragements to invest in human resource development
- A more systematic approach to the organization of the training function and greater expertise in training practitioners
- More rigorous costing and evaluation of training, in order to demonstrate to managers its cost benefit and cost-effectiveness to the organization
- Case studies showing how training can contribute to the achievement of individual and corporate goals – and how failure to train can inhibit progress.

Since 1985 there has been increasing concern about the inadequacy and ineffectiveness of national education and training, with a multiplicity of initiatives being established and a new national training framework being introduced. Claims are sometimes made that a positive change is occurring too in the attitudes and behaviour of employers towards employee development, but the evidence for this is uncertain. In May 1991 the journal *Personnel Management* reported a survey of senior managers in 254 of Britain's top companies, showing that only 45 per cent felt that employees in their own firms were well trained, while 94 per cent put the blame for this on the poor attitude of managers towards the need for training. About a third criticized trainers' over-academic approaches and ineffective performance. Only 29 per cent blamed a lack of training services. In a report by the Employment Institute (1991), a similar perception emerged: that Britain's problem was 'not just insufficient training but also . . . inefficient training', a major weakness being employers' failure to think strategically about their skill needs and how to utilize skilled workers. Detailed training decisions were, it claimed, too often left in the hands of line managers, resulting in an inadequate integration of those decisions in firms' general strategic decision-making. Finally, too little was being done in companies to measure the outcome of training, so that a culture existed where 'training is not thought of as an investment'.

Two similar reports over the past few years have produced evidence of the damaging failure of employers to invest adequately in the development of people. A Warwick University Paper (IRRU, 1990) showed that over 50 per cent of employers surveyed had no plans, either in recruitment or in training and development, to introduce measures to deal with demographic changes in the labour market, even though existing older workers were typified as being 'closed to new concepts', 'lacking in motivation' and 'not adaptable'.

An article entitled 'Skill Shortages Set to Worsen' in *Personnel Management Plus* (November 1990) quotes another report, by Manpower, showing that although skills shortages affect almost half of Britain's employers, with the situation likely to worsen in the future, and although a high level of concern was expressed about the problem, more than half of the 1,400 personnel executives surveyed had no specific plans to resolve the issue. Only 12 per cent aimed to offer training, while 11 per cent said they would make use of temporary staff.

The same negative picture emerges in major academic texts (see, for example, Keep, 1989 a and b), in professional journals, in national surveys and in government white papers. Although there is evidence of an increasing interest in techniques to improve human resource management, there is little to indicate a coherent or strategic direction to these attempts (Storey, 1992), or to show that the diagnosis of the key training and development problems and their causes put forward in 1985 has lost its validity. This explains why in essence the focus of this book remains the same as that of the earlier 1988 text.

National and International Challenges in the 1990s and Beyond

As we move into the last decade in the twentieth century human resource development in Britain faces major challenges on the international stage: entry into the single European market; increasing exposure to competition on a global, not simply on a European, scale; continued skills shortages of a kind critical to economic growth; and a huge demographic downturn in relation to 16–19-year-olds, with the numbers dropping by 25 per cent between 1988 and 1995 alone, with a significant commensurate upturn in the availability of older people for work, and a preponderance of ageing workforces.

The implications are clear: strategic, carefully planned and sustained training and development will be essential if valued workers are to be attracted to, and retained in, British private- and public-sector employment, and if, especially, able young people are to see in British organizations not only valued financial rewards, but also meaningful long-term career structures and prospects.

Britain's national vocational educational and training policies and strategies have so far proved woefully unequal to the vital task of building up a skilled and flexible labour force, as will be seen in Chapters 2, 3 and 4. However, certain major employers such as Ford, Lucas, Rover and ICI have introduced comprehensive and expensive development programmes, intended as a long-term investment to upgrade the skills, develop the potential and increase the commitment and flexibility of their entire workforces. The response to these programmes is promising, but it remains to be seen how far other employers, particularly in smaller companies, will move towards such wide-ranging development programmes for their people, rather than focusing their investment only on those employees who are seen to be of immediately critical importance to the organization.

Comprehensive and high-quality management training and development is of major importance in all of this, since inadequately skilled and poorly educated managers are unlikely to see the need for anything but a similarly low and narrow level of skills for other employees (see Chapter 19).

Improving Training and Development Expertise

With that last comment in mind, it is relevant to return to the theme raised at the start of this chapter: in a situation where there is widespread complacency and ignorance about employee development, and where external pressures are not in general providing strong enough triggers to organizations to make a high-level and continuous investment in it, much of the onus of convincing them of the value of investment in the development of people is on the specialist practitioners. Yet *A Challenge to Complacency* (Coopers and Lybrand, 1985), like other reports (e.g. Manpower Services Commission, 1987; Training Services Agency, 1977), showed too many personnel and training specialists to be apathetic, acquiescent in their generally low level of responsibility and status and their reactive, restricted role, and lacking in professional expertise. In those organizations where positive attitudes to human resource development did exist they appeared to derive not so much from the efforts and credibility of training personnel as from a situation where failure to train had an immediate and critical impact (e.g. service sectors with close customer-staff contact), or from a general ethos of caring for, developing and retaining staff. As we have already seen (see pages 9–10), there is evidence that these areas of inadequacy amongst practitioners still give major cause for concern, and in this connection the work of the National Lead Body for Training and Development is welcome, despite some reservations, for the effort it is devoting to providing national standards of training and development competence and associated methods of assessment which can act as a framework for national qualifications and also for best practice in organizations (see Chapters 2, 6 and 10).

The Need for a Business-led Employee Development Function

In *Training and Development* I ended Chapter 1 with the question 'Will the investment be made?' Now it is appropriate to end on a somewhat different note. Of course it is vital that a greatly increased investment *is* made in developing people, both nationally and within organizations. However, the size of the investment is less important than its focus and effectiveness. An instructive illustration of this is the

Investors in People initiative launched by the Training and Enterprise Education Division of the Department of Employment (see Appendix 1).

The Investors in People Campaign

The Investors in People (IIP) campaign made its first awards in 1991. It aims to promote investment in the development of people in organizations. However, the focus is not on employee development *per se*, but on employee development of a strategic, business-led kind. Organizations must show that their plans for developing people are tied to their business plans; that they are derived from a systematic analysis of needs at organizational as well as at individual levels; that employee development as a function is well integrated with all the other key functions of the business; and that development activities are monitored and evaluated, and show convincing evidence of contributing significantly to business results.

Another important aspect of the IIP campaign is that it offers accredited status to successful organizations. Assessment is carried out by trained assessors, through local Training and Enterprise Councils, and it is so rigorous that some fear that few organizations will put themselves forward. Various tactics are being suggested to attract more employers to seek IIP status, but the significance of insisting, in a national initiative, on employee development which is business-led, works in collaboration with other business functions and can offer convincing evidence of its major contribution to the achievement of business goals should not be underestimated. It reinforces a growing understanding that these are vital themes if the function is to make any impact on national as well as organizational and individual growth and prosperity.

Finally, a hopeful example from a sector where it is often thought that, because of lack of available expertise and financial underpinning, it is very hard to encourage or achieve any major investment in developing people: small firms.

Channel 4 prize goes to Liverpool
(*Personnel Management*, January 1991)

A firm which dates back to 1748 and boasts it is the oldest manufacturer in Liverpool won the Channel 4 Business Daily award for the company showing the most measurable benefit from training.

R. S. Clare, which employs 62 people making road-marking material and lubricants, based its training on the findings of an attitude survey of every employee. This showed that managers' skills needed to be developed, particularly the ability of middle managers to communicate.

It spent £30,000 on training courses in a year, after which a further survey showed that two-thirds of the workforce found an improvement in managers' communication and delegation skills and in general morale.

In 1989 productivity in one division increased by nearly 93 per cent and pre-tax profits went up by nearly a half.

Of course one would be right to ask what evidence there is that the productivity and profitability increases were due to the investment in training, and whether the initiative will prove of lasting benefit. None the less, it is significant that a small firm decided to find out what its major immediate training needs were; that it did this by surveying the opinions of its workforce; that it then made a sizeable investment in training; and that it monitored and measured the results of that investment. If all employers took these apparently simple steps, there is no doubt that employee development, of a kind beneficial to the organization as well as to individuals, would take an immense step forward.

References

BENSON J. 'Nabisco's winning strategy'. *Personnel Management*. May 1987. pp. 36-9

CHANDLER A. *Strategy and Structure: Chapters in the history of American industrial enterprise*. Cambridge, Mass., MIT Press. 1962

COOPER AND LYBRAND ASSOCIATES. *A challenge to complacency: Changing attitudes to training*. A report to the Manpower Services Commission and the National Economic Development Office. Sheffield, MSC. 1985

CRABB S. 'The way to cable change'. *Personnel Management*. June 1990. pp. 50-3

DEAL T AND KENNEDY A. *Corporate Cultures: rites and rituals of corporate life*. Maidenhead, Addison Wesley. 1982

EMPLOYMENT INSTITUTE. *Training – the problem for employers*, (Mayhew K). London, Employment Institute. 1991

FELLBOM E. 'Swedish stamp on the customer service message'. *Personnel Management*. June 1987. pp. 36-8

INDUSTRIAL RELATIONS RESEARCH UNIT. 'The impact of age upon employment'. *Warwick Papers in Industrial Relations No. 33*. Coventry, Warwick University, IRRU. 1990

INSTITUTE OF MANPOWER STUDIES. *Competence and Competition: training and education in the Federal Republic of Germany, the United States and Japan*. London, Manpower Services Commission/National Economic Development Office. 1984

JOHNSON G AND SCHOLES K. *Exploring Corporate Strategy: Text and cases*, 2nd ed. Hemel Hempstead, Prentice-Hall. 1989

KEEP E. 'A training scandal?' In *Personnel Management in Britain* (Sisson K, ed.). Oxford, Blackwell. 1989

KEEP E. 'Corporate training strategies: the vital component?' in *New Perspectives on Human Resource Management*'. (Storey J, ed.). London, Wiley. 1989

LEONTIADES M. *Strategies for Diversification and Change*. Boston, Little, Brown. 1980

MANPOWER SERVICES COMMISSION. *Developing Trainers: MSC support for training of trainers and staff development*. Sheffield, MSC. 1987

'A NEW TRAINING INITIATIVE – A Programme for Action'. Government white paper. London, HMSO. 1981

OXFORD ENGLISH DICTIONARY. Oxford, Clarendon Press. 1978

PEARSON R. *The Human Resource: Managing people and work in the 1990s*. London, McGraw-Hill. 1991

PERSONNEL MANAGEMENT. 'Channel 4 prize goes to Liverpool'. *Personnel Management*, January 1991. p. 10

PERSONNEL MANAGEMENT. 'Failure of training due largely to management indifference'. *Personnel Management*. May 1991. p. 4

PERSONNEL MANAGEMENT PLUS. 'Skill shortages set to worsen'. *Personnel Management Plus*. November 1990. p. 8

ROTHWELL S. 'Integrating the elements of a company employment policy'. *Personnel Management*. November 1984. pp. 31-3

STOREY J. 'HRM in action: The truth is out at last'. *Personnel Management*. August 1991. pp. 24-7

THOMAS M. 'In search of culture: Holy grail or gravy train?' *Personnel Management*. September 1985. pp. 24-7

TORRINGTON D, HALL L, HAYLOR I AND MYERS J. *Employee Resourcing*. (Management Studies 2 Series). London, Institute of Personnel Management. 1991

TRAINING SERVICES AGENCY. *An Approach to the Training of Staff with Training Officer Roles*. Sheffield, TSA. 1977

UPTON R. 'The bottom line: Bejam's ingredients for success'. *Personnel Management*. April 1987. pp. 34-9

WICKENS, P. *The Road to Nissan*. London, Macmillan. 1987

Further useful reading

FULLERTON H AND PRICE C. 'Culture change in the NHS'. *Personnel Management*. March 1991. pp. 50-3

PAYNE R. 'Taking stock of corporate culture'. *Personnel Management*. July 1991. pp. 26-9

PETTIGREW A M, SPARROW P AND HENDRY C. 'The forces that trigger training'. *Personnel Management*. December 1988. pp. 28-32

Chapter 2

The framework for national vocational education and training

Learning objectives

After reading this chapter you will:

1 understand the vision, policy and current strategy for national vocational education and training (NVET) in the UK;
2 be able to identify the framework and initiatives at national , sectoral and local level whereby NVET strategy is to be implemented;
3 understand some of the ways in which individual organizations can benefit from NVET strategy and intitiatives, and can contribute towards their successful implementation.

This chapter aims to help you achieve a sound general understanding of NVET policy and strategy and the system that has been set up to implement them. You will then be able to form your own views about the strengths and weaknesses of the system, testing those views against the more evaluative material in Chapter 3. Advice on how to keep abreast of current developments is given in the section on References.

Key Terms and Issues

In Chapter 1, we clarified the meanings of terms relevant to policy-making and strategic implementation:

- *Vision:* The certainty about the kind of organization it should be
- *Mission:* The statement expressing the vision in words which then become guidelines for strategy
- *Policy:* An elaboration of the organization's mission
- *Strategy:* The route chosen to achieve its mission
- *Implementation:* The framework of policies, plans, structures and resources whereby strategy can be carried out

Now let us relate these terms to a discussion of national vocational education and training (NVET).

> NVET seeks to reconcile the educational and training needs of the individual, the employer and the economy in such a way as to increase the competitiveness of organizations and of British industry as a whole, while at the same time ensuring that individuals can develop in ways that will enable them to lead meaningful, satisfying lives.

Achieving a shared vision, and agreeing on how it is to be implemented, often seems impossible given the varied interests of the key parties. Ron Johnson, Chairman of the Institute of Personnel Management's National Committee for Training and Development said (June 1990):

> There [does] not appear to be a coherent national strategy on the acknowledged-to-be-key areas of education, training and development. This state of affairs persists despite an avalanche of sensible and respectable research reports, strategic papers and polemics coming thick and fast in the last decade. What they all lack, however, is either thoughts on the implementation of policies or consensus on implementation in a real, practical sense.

National Vocational Education and Training: The Current Vision, Mission, and Strategy

Vision

The current vision of NVET is that, since the country's main source of wealth lies in its people, everyone without discrimination should have the opportunity and incentive to continue learning throughout life, thereby achieving continuous growth for themselves and for the nation, and giving the economy the skills it needs to achieve and maintain its competitive edge. The vision is typified in the following statement:

> The education and training system in this country has been revolutionised over the last decade. The reforms that have been put in place will help ensure that everyone has the opportunity and incentive to continue learning throughout life, and that the economy has the skills it needs to meet and beat the best in the world. (Employment Department Group, 1991, p. 28)

Mission/Policy

The national mission/policy which has arisen from this vision of NVET is to achieve a voluntary and committed partnership at local, sectoral and national levels between Government, business, training and education organizations, individuals and the broader community. 'Only by working together can we realise our vision for the future.' (Ibid.)

In 1991 seven aims were established for NVET policy (see Figure 1).

Figure 1
The seven aims of NVET policy

1. To ensure that high quality further education or training becomes the norm for all 16- and 17-year-olds who can benefit from it.
2. To increase the all-round levels of attainment by young people.
3. To increase the proportion of young people acquiring higher levels of skill.
4. To ensure that people are more committed to develop their own skills throughout working life, and more willing to invest their own time, money and effort in doing so.
5. To help the long-term unemployed and those at other kinds of disadvantage to make their full contribution to the economy.
6. To ensure that trainers and teachers remain responsive to the needs of individuals and business, working closely with business and widening individual choice.
7. To encourage and increase employer commitment to training by having effective enterprise plans that complement work.

White paper *Education and Training for the 21st Century*, 1991
(by permission of the Department of Employment)

Strategy

The Government's strategy since 1989 is based on principles of decentralization, diversity, innovation and excellence (Training Agency, 1989). It arose from a determination to defeat the weaknesses that, up to that point, had characterized the national training system:

- **Training had consistently been tackled at national rather than local level.** Central planning since 1964 had failed to serve national or local interests, as evidenced by 'remote training programmes which have rarely taken account of the character and needs of local industry.' (Field, 1990)
- **Programmes had been bureacratic and inflexible.** 'Training has been dictated by the rulebook. No matter how relevant or innovative the training proposal, its fate was decided by whether or not someone at Training Agency head office had the forethought to allow for this in the manual.' (Ibid.)
- **Training and enterprise provision was determined by national guidance.** Responsibility for training was laid at the door of Government.
- **Training was often done, or promoted, for training's sake.** (Ibid.)

The strategy established in 1989 was about having:

1 a locally based system;
2 an employer-led partnership;
3 an integrated approach to training, vocational education and enterprise development, focused on economic growth;
4 an accent on performance;
5 an enterprise organization at local level.

Six national strategic objectives whereby national policy aims could be achieved were established for the 1990s. They formed the base reference points for strategy and planning of Training and Enterprise Councils (TECs) at local level (see Appendix 1). They are about organizations and individuals working together to invest in the quality and level of education and training that would meet their mutual needs, and about the delivery of high-quality and flexible education and training.

National Vocational Education and Training: Framework and Plans for the Implementation of Strategy

Strategy often fails at the stage of implementation, and we have already seen that criticism levelled at NVET. We will examine implementation under two main headings: the local, sectoral and national framework and the plans that have been established to improve the UK's investment and outputs in training; and the new framework and plans for vocational standards and qualifications. The chapter will conclude by examining the changes now taking place in the education system in order to better integrate education and training under a single national strategy and framework.

The training framework and plans

Local level

In order to implement national strategy, a framework of voluntary and collaborative action was set up from 1989 onwards at national, sectoral and local levels. The whole weight of the system was planned to rest on a local structure dominated by Training and Enterprise Councils (TECs). According to the 1989 white paper *Employment in the 1990s*, TECs were to be the cornerstone of the framework at local level in England and Wales. By 1991 there were 83 TECs, intended to be 'strong, employer-led partnerships working to improve local skills and help local business become more competitive'. (Employment Department Group, 1991, Executive Summary)*

TECs represent a major transfer of responsibilities from the Area Manpower Boards, whose main task had been to administer and monitor youth training schemes. They were tripartite bodies, and therefore had difficulty in exerting pressure on employers. They had no funds to disburse, and had a tendency to become involved in 'political' discussions. Generally, they were not successful in creating a local partnership framework for training. TECs, on the other hand, are legally autonomous bodies which control the public funds allocated to them, can raise private funds and are dominated in their membership by senior executives from local private-sector organizations. They are based on a combination of the US Private Industry Councils and the German Chambers of Commerce (see Chapter 4).

* Differences in the education system and funding arrangements in Scotland mean that some of the more detailed points in the strategic guidelines given to TECs are not directly relevant to the Scottish Local Enterprise Companies (LECs); also Scottish Enterprise, Highland and Island Enterprise and their local enterprise companies have wider responsibilities than TECs in relation to the objective of encouraging enterprise and helping small businesses to grow. Responsibility for training in Wales is to be transferred from the Secretary of State for Employment to the Secretary of State for Wales from April 1992.

TECs have to examine the local labour market, identify key skill needs and opportunities for business growth and mobilize public and private funds to develop effective ways of responding to those needs in collaborative local activity.

> The fundamental aim of every TEC will be to foster economic growth and contribute to the regeneration of the community it serves . . . Managing existing programmes is only the start. The TEC will be a catalyst for change within its community. (Training Agency, 1989, p. 1)

Every TEC must produce a business plan with local strategic objectives which must link in to the six national strategic priorities (see Appendix 2). These business plans have to be submitted to the Secretary of State in order to obtain national funding as described below. TECs have to be very detailed in the plans they submit, showing for every area of activity:

- A description of the activity
- The target group
- Output measures and targets against which to assess achievements
- The method whereby quality standards will be set for the activity, including monitoring and evaluation arrangements

TECs operate under a performance contract with the Training, Enterprise and Education Division of the Department of Employment, and have executive responsibility for almost £3 billion of public expenditure (£20 million, on average, per TEC). The contract specifies standards of management and performance, and TECs exceeding their targets will receive a bonus, while those which underachieve will have to revise their strategies and plans in order to make good that deficiency. TECs' performance against national objectives will be closely monitored by the National Training Task Force (see below). Thus:

> TECs are to be measured and controlled through their business plans, and their performance against targets.

The TECs are responsible for the various programmes previously run by the Training Agency, and must improve these in terms of quality, relevance and delivery. TECs' local initiative funding may be applied to any of these programmes, or it may be used for new programme development activities. (TECs can carry some, but not excessive, balances of money forward to the following financial year.) The four programme heads (Training Agency, 1989) are:

- **Opportunities for young people.** The aim is that every young person will have access to relevant education or training leading to recognized vocational qualifications and to a job. TECs must decide, working closely with local education and training institutions, how best to achieve this aim and ensure a smooth transition from education to work. Each TEC must contract sufficient training places to meet the Government's guarantee of a place for every young person, but can tailor existing programmes (including the length and occupational mix of training) and develop new initiatives.
- **Opportunities for the unemployed.** The TECs are to plan and deliver Employment Training, with the goal of increasing employer investment and improving the quality, relevance and accessibility of the programme. Key criteria of success will be the number of people who achieve National Vocational Qualifications and how many are placed in meaningful jobs.
- **Promoting training for the employed.** This will be done by providing advice on training needs and how to meet and resource them; enhancing access to information about training; encouraging use of cost-effective and flexible methods; organizing groups of employers with common training needs so that they can invest collectively in learning resources and facilities; designing customized training programmes to prepare new recruits for jobs in skill shortage occupations; and arranging assessment of organizations seeking Investor in People status (see Appendix 1).
- **Business growth.** TECs work with the Small Firms Service, Local Enterprise Agencies and other organizations in the small business support network to help new enterprises and expanding businesses, by assessing the kind of services they need and advising on how best to meet those needs, and by disbursing funds for business growth and enterprise initiatives. (See, for example, how Barratt, the construction firm, was successful in attracting £74,000 of pump-priming funding for its new, business-led Sales Training Programme, in Harrison, 1992.)

To ensure that they are employer-driven, at least two-thirds of TEC members are employers at top management level from the private sector; the other third includes senior figures from local education, training and economic development activities, and from voluntary bodies and trade unions. Employer members are at chief executive level, and under an appeals procedure introduced in 1991 very senior personnel professionals may in special cases also join TEC Boards. Existing business organizations like Chambers of Commerce and the CBI often form the nucleus of a TEC, which is thereby able to build on existing local communications and training networks.

Other local bodies that can give help to organizations and individuals include Chambers of Commerce (some of whom will have formed the basis of the local TECs), professional bodies such as the Institute of Personnel Management (IPM), Institute of Training and Development (ITD) and British Institute of Management (BIM), and the network of local educational institutions. Other, and wider, local enterprise funding can be obtained through the Enterprise Initiative and the Inner Cities Initiative, both of which operate collaboratively with the TEC programmes, but which have separate sources of funding and are run by the Department of Trade and Industry. The European Commission is also a source of funding for a variety of initiatives (see *Personnel Management Plus*, 1991).

Now let us see how a local TEC is carrying out its complex functions, to the benefit of the local area.

Sheffield TEC (1990)

(With acknowledgements to R Field and *Personnel Management*)

Sheffield underwent major industrial upheaval during the 1970s and 1980s as steel experienced a dramatic downturn. Unemployment soared, and is still higher than the regional and national average. The city is an Urban Programme area, and although there is an economic regeneration strategy, this can only be realized if a Sheffield TEC tackles skills shortages and nurtures business growth.

The TEC's mission is 'to improve the economic prosperity and quality of life for all in Sheffield through a training and enterprise partnership and investment in people'. There are 11 strategic objectives underpinning this mission, many specifically directed at delivery issues. In a major consultation exercise involving 3,800 organizations and individuals, the following needs were identified:

- Demand for more foundation training
- Training leading to recognized standards and qualifications
- Vocational training linked to jobs
- Greater coherence of training provision and the identification of clear career routes
- Increased employer investment in training and training strategies
- Equality for disadvantaged groups

To tackle these needs the TEC decided to operate on three fronts:

- **Quality.** The TEC and its providers are to achieve the recognized British quality standard (BS5750) by 1993. Competitive tendering will be introduced, and local kitemarking of training consultants will be promoted by the TEC, through a list of 'approved' consultants issued to local businesses.
- **Relevance.** Those needs identified in the consultative exercise will guide future activities. Employment Training and Youth Training will be geared in content and length to the specific needs of an enterprise, with length dependent on achieving a certain standard, usually a recognized qualification. The funding of both enterprise and training providers will be increasingly output-related, linked to achievement of outputs such as jobs and vocational qualifications. A requirement for TEC support (especially funding) will be the construction of a company human resource development plan.
- **Delivery.** Various initiatives are being sponsored or promoted by the TEC which make provision of learning accessible in terms of time, place and method to those who need it.

The Sheffield TEC board is a city-wide partnership of employers, trade unionists and representatives of education and local government. Furthermore, action teams and task forces comprising over 2,000 individuals have been established to tackle specific issues ranging from quality to equal opportunities. A recent issue concerned local engineering companies which had been turning away orders. The TEC funded a study into this, and its report went to its engineering task force. The findings were that companies could not attract back skilled workers who had gone into other industries, and that school leavers were not attracted into engineering. Solutions included an improvement in education–industry links by, for example, incorporating engineering into the secondary school syllabus from the first year; and the upgrading of existing semi-skilled employees to craft standards.

Thus Sheffield TEC is taking the lead in providing a local response to local needs, showing how investment in relevant and high-quality training can become a major contributor to business enterprise and growth.

From this example we can make two observations about TECs:

> TECs constitute a radical innovation in the UK training system. They are intended to ensure an NVET system that is driven by local needs, is based on an active partnership of local interests, and is geared to making a major impact on business growth in every TEC area.
>
> TECs represent a major source of expertise, funding and other support for local organizations. Since they are at the centre of a powerful local training and enterprise network, they are well placed to help local organizations wishing or needing to invest, or increase their investment, in employee development.

Sectoral level

At sectoral level the main parties are about 170 non-statutory Industry Training Organizations (NSTOs). These were established, in the main on a voluntary basis, when most of the Industrial Training Boards were abolished. They are intended to advise on and encourage investment in training in their industrial sectors. Like the TECs they are independent and employer-led. Their main role is to identify and monitor key skill needs and training requirements in their sectors. Most of them are also Lead Bodies responsible for developing and maintaining standards of competence as a basis for related National Vocational Qualifications. NSTOs will be discussed further in Chapter 3.

National level

Since 1990 the Department of Employment is responsible for training, enterprise and education functions at national level, while the Training, Enterprise and Education Division (TEED) handles the performance contracts of the TECs. The Department of Education is responsible for policy and planning in the educational sector, but the lines between the two departments are often unclear, leading to many problems in policy-making and implementation. This issue will be discussed in Chapter 3.

The availability of accurate, comprehensive and meaningful data about manpower is essential if national policy and local strategies and plans related to NVET are to be valid. The Development Framework set up by the Department of Employment aims to help TECs to improve the quality of training by stimulating new developments of national importance and disseminating them widely; to offer them the opportunity to undertake individually and collaboratively research projects meeting national and local needs; and to foster an overall strategic approach to research and evaluation.

> TECs are expected to promote and sponsor research, especially into training and development, that will either help their locality or will, even though not related directly to their particular locality, have spin-offs relevant to local initiatives.

A 12-member body, the National Training Task Force, was set up in 1989 to assist the Secretary of State for Employment to develop the TEC network. In 1991 its brief was extended to cover assessment of TECs' performance against local and national policy and objectives; to advise the Secretary of State on the strategic policy objectives of TECs; and to oversee the development of the Investors in People initiative (see page 13). These responsibilities are being handled by three committees led by some of the most senior private-sector business people in the country. (*Personnel Management*, 1991)

The framework and plans for national vocational standards and qualifications

Vocational qualifications are those that relate directly to a person's competence in employment. By 1986 less than a third of the UK labour force held vocational qualifications, compared to two-thirds in Germany (Keep, 1989, p. 181) and significantly less than in other competitor countries. Fundamental reform of the whole national vocational qualification system is another of the cornerstones of the new NVET framework.

The National Council for Vocational Qualifications (NCVQ) was set up in 1986 by the Government following the white paper *Working Together – Education and Training*. That white paper endorsed the recommendations of the *Review of Vocational Qualifications in England and Wales* produced by the CBI and TUC in the same year. The Council is an independent body, sponsored jointly by the Secretaries of State for Employment, for Education and Science, for Northern Ireland and for Wales. Its main role is to produce a national framework incorporating vocational qualifications that meet national standards of occupational competence within a simple structure of five levels. Links have been established with all the awarding bodies in the UK (currently around 250 examining bodies and 150 industrial training bodies), and with the European Commission. The longer-term aim is to have a harmonized European system of vocational qualifications, with consistency of standards across Europe in all occupations and professions.

National Vocational Qualifications

> A National Vocational Qualification (NVQ) represents a statement of competence confirming that the individual can perform to a specified standard in a range of work-related activities, and also possesses the skills, knowledge and understanding which makes possible such performance in the workplace. Through NVQs there will for the first time in the UK be agreed national standards of competence across every recognized occupational area.

NVQs are not awarded by the NCVQ but by various examining bodies such as BTEC, the City and Guilds, the RSA and Pitmans, whose courses incorporate standards, on a scale from one to five, laid down by the various industry Lead Bodies. The courses have been accredited by the NCVQ, and certificates will carry both the NVQ stamp and that of the examining body.

Support for NVQs from the various industries and professions stems from the fact that their representatives form the membership of the 150 Lead Bodies that are producing Lead Body Standards for different occupations and professions (see below). Given that the NCVQ's membership is also employer-dominated, it can fairly be claimed that it is employers and the professions, not some central government body insensitive to employers' needs, who 'drive' the NVQ movement and who give its products their seal of approval.

Lead Body Standards have been developed by a lengthy analytical and consultative process, involving the breaking down of a job first into general areas of competence, each comprising abilities and skills, and then into more detailed elements of competence.

Each qualification approved by NCVQ is assigned to one of five levels within the NVQ framework. The levels indicate the degree of competence achieved. Levels 1 and 2 ('basic' and 'standard' levels) typify the kind of competence needed in many routine jobs and occuptions of a predictable character. They are below the level of any occupational standards operating in France or Germany, but the argument is that attaining Level 1 will encourage movement on to Level 2, and that

Level 2 will offer a foundation for further training. Levels 3 and 4 range though existing craft, technician and lower-level professional areas of skill, while Level 5 is intended to equate in most cases with the higher-level professional qualifications – although there is much debate about this among the professions. Some qualifications will be easier to integrate into the NVQ system than others, because many professions have a highly structured system for gaining qualifications, some of which include competences while others are more educationally based.

The government set objectives in 1991 whereby by 1997 80 per cent of all young people should hold an NVQ at Level 2 by the age of 18, with 50 per cent qualified by the year 2000 to at least Level 3 or equivalent. It was also suggested that 50 per cent of the employed workforce should be qualified to at least Level 3 by the year 2000 (see pp. 34). Many feel that these levels are too low.

> NVQs have been described as the 'currency of the labour market', which are being strengthened in order to increase the power of the economy, and the NCVQ will only accredit qualifications which, by conforming to Lead Body Standards, meet employment needs. 'With an NVQ an employer knows what he's getting because it's precisely what he asked for.' (Department of Employment, 1988)

Accreditation of Prior Learning (APL)

Since performance in the workplace or activities which realistically simulate it will be part of NVQs, assessment of workplace competence will have to be widely used, in ways and by assessors agreed between colleges, training organizations and employers. This has clear implications for appraisal schemes and also for the identification of training needs and the design of training courses in order to ensure that they both meet job-related needs and can achieve NVQ accreditation.

The Introduction of NVQs at United Glass (1991)
(With acknowledgement to A Arkin and *Personnel Management*)

United Glass and Glass Training Ltd, the Industry Training Organisation for the glass and allied industries, have collaborated to offer trained Grade 1 and 2 glass operators at United Glass the chance to gain NVQ awards. The process involves assessment of their existing skills, knowledge and performance in the workplace by assessors who have been trained and certified by Glass Training Ltd. The assessment process is also useful as a way of identifying gaps in individuals' competence which can then be remedied by training.

After some initial suspicion and scepticism among managers as well as operators, 'the machine operators have come to value the recognition which they are now receiving for skills they have had in some cases for as long as 25 years. This is especially true of those who have no other formal qualifications.' The accreditation process is now being extended to other skill groups, as managers and operatives see the relevance of the qualification to day-to-day work. 'This process is based on a recognition that people learn not only in the classroom but also at work and in other areas of their lives.'

From this study we can see how an organization can improve the performance and qualifications of sectors of its workforce by using APL and NVQs. APL recognizes existing areas and levels of competence that people have achieved in their jobs, and gives credit for it in terms of units of a qualification.

Credit accumulation and transfer

This is a comprehensive and flexible system that enables people to achieve a level of competence through various methods of training and work experience, at various centres and over varying periods of time and thereby also to acquire vocational qualifications. It is intended to design all qualifications in such a way that they can be offered on a modular basis and tested by judging someone's competence in the job. This is similar to the highly successful French vocational training and education schemes (see Chapter 4).

A unit of competence is a measure of an outcome of learning, and each NVQ is made up of a number of units. Credits will be given for the acquisition of units of competence. Through the credit accumulation and transfer system a workplace supervisor with training responsibilities might be able to gain one or two units of a training profession NVQ mainly through having his or her workplace performance assessed as meeting the standards laid down in those units, without immediately having to complete an entire course of study. He or she would then be seen as competent in those specific areas of activity, and could add to them or not as they chose.

Each unit builds up the credit balance of an individual's 'competence account'. Ways are being explored to express all existing qualifications in terms of units; units certificated by different awarding bodies could then be accumulated within the common system, and units common to two or more qualifications could perhaps be transferred in order to avoid repetition in training and assessment.

Individuals can continually register their achievement in an NVQ Record of Competence which will be opened when an individual embarks on a programme or seeks certification for the first time. This record moves with the individual, providing a recognized record of competence throughout the individual's life.

To summarize, since 1989 the Government has established in relation to national, local and individual training a vision, mission, strategy and framework for implementation. That framework rests on two main initiatives: the TEC system and the reform of NVQs to achieve a standardized system operating at five levels.

Now let us look at one of the major imperatives if NVET in the UK is to overcome its past weaknesses: an improved vocational education sytem, fully integrated with the framework for the planning and delivery of training at national, sectoral and local levels.

Achieving an Integrated National Vocational Education and Training System

The vocational education system in Britain now bears poor comparison with the systems of its competitors, as the following illustration shows.

Vocation in a Void
(With acknowledgements to A Smithers)

Professor Alan Smithers (1991), Professor of Education at Manchester University, points out that education after 16 is highly problematic, despite the fact that about four in five of our young people continue in some form of education and training after the end of compulsory schooling; that in international comparisons of educational attainment our 18-year-olds come in the top three with Hong Kong and Japan; and that our graduates are universally acknowledged to be of high quality.

Only about half of our 18-year-olds aim to achieve any kind of qualification. Less than a quarter are on A level courses. Only half of that quarter obtain three A levels (and only 8 per cent of those are comprehensive school children). Most 14-year-olds are near the bottom of the international attainment league, and there is widespread truancy and alienation.

Most sixth formers only tackle three subjects, too few go on to study Mathematics and Science in higher education, and there is no clear practical/technical ladder to complement the academic/theoretical. 'Vocational qualifications are essentially a route for people who have failed something academic. They are seen as second best and lack esteem . . . [It is not] surprising, in the circumstances, that our workforce is seriously underqualified compared with those of our European neighbours.'

Vision

The current vision is of every child receiving foundation learning that is best suited to their abilities, their aspirations and the range of employment opportunities likely to be available to them on leaving school. The vision is also about all adults being engaged in a lifelong process of learning.

Mission/policy

The mission is to achieve a complete integration of vocational education and training, ending what *A Strategy for Skills* (Employment Department Group, 1990) calls the 'obsolete' divisions between academic and vocational learning. There is to be a coherent 'cradle to grave' framework whereby young people receive relevant vocational preparation and qualifications at school, continue this process until the age of 18, whether or not they leave school at 16, and as adults, whether in or out of employment, are then enabled and motivated to improve their formal vocational attainments in line with the economy's needs.

Strategy

The strategy during the last decade of the twentieth century focuses on:

- Progressively introducing the National Curriculum in schools and ultimately linking it to the National Vocational Qualification system
- Improving vocational education in schools in order to clarify the system and expand choice, and to promote parity of esteem between academic and vocational qualifications
- Creating a new post-16 vocational education and training sector

Vocational Education: The Framework and Plans for Implementation of Strategy

Wide-ranging initiatives are taking place across the whole spectrum of education, from primary school level to university, to achieve certain national training targets. These targets were launched in July 1991 with the support of the Government, the CBI and the TUC (see Figure 2). They replaced less challenging government targets set two years before. TECs and Local Enterprise Companies are to take the lead in ensuring that they are achieved at the local level, and the National Training Task Force will oversee progress at national level.

Progressive introduction of the National Curriculum in schools

The introduction of the National Curriculum into schools is intended to be the leading instrument of vocational education reform. This major move signalled the Government's determination to standardize the outcomes of educational activity, and to do so in ways that could ultimately be related to NVQ levels.

The Education Reform Act, 1988, announced that by 1994 all children in state schools at the ages of 5, 7, 11, 14 and 16 would have to meet standard assessment targets of a National Curriculum covering three core subjects and seven foundation subjects. (In fact it is unlikely that the National Curriculum will ultimately contain ten attainment levels in each of ten subjects, because of a widespread view that this is not the most sensible way to measure progress in most National Curriculum subjects).

The reforms have to begin at the primary level. Recent surveys have led to widespread concern about standards of achievement in state primary schools, and the first National Curriculum tests of 7-year-olds (1991) suggested that a substantial minority are failing to master the

Figure 2

National Education and Training Targets

Foundation Learning

1 By 1997, at least 80 per cent of all young people should attain NVQ/SVQ Level 2 or its academic equivalent in their foundation education and training.
2 All young people who can benefit should be given an entitlement to structured training, work experience or education leading to NVQ Level 3 or its academic equivalent.
3 By 2000, at least half of the age group should attain NVQ Level 3 or its academic equivalent as a basis for further progression.
4 All education and training provision should be structured and designed to develop self-reliance, flexibility and broad competence as well as specific skills.

Lifetime Learning

1 By 1996, all employees should take part in training or development activities as the norm.
2 By 1996, at least half of the employed workforce should be aiming for qualifications or units towards them within the NVQ framework, preferably in the context of individual action plans and with support from employers.
3 By 2000, 50 per cent of the employed workforce should be qualified to NVQ Level 3 or its academic equivalent as a minimum.
4 By 1996 at least half of the medium-sized and larger organizations should qualify as Investors in People, assessed by the relevant TECs or LECs.

(*A Strategy for Skills*, Employment Department Group, 1991, pp. 11–12, reproduced by permission of the Department of Employment)

basic reading, writing and numerical skills (Clare, 1991a). In December 1991, Kenneth Clarke announced an inquiry into primary school teaching. If the country is to be assured of an adequately skilled workforce, then educational standards at the appropriate level must operate from primary school onwards.

The National Curriculum is to be applied to 14- and 16-year-olds in September 1992, and GCSE syllabuses must reflect this.

Improving vocational education in schools

> The major concern here is about the quantity, standards and relevance of its vocational education component, and about the high

> number of those who will leave school at 16 without any vocational qualification and go into employment where about half of them are unlikely to receive any further planned training or education. (McLeod, 1991)

Reform of GCSE and A levels

The aim is to develop coherent technical and vocational, as well as academic, pathways in a system currently dominated by the latter.

In 1985 GCE O levels and CSE were replaced by a single GCSE examination system aimed at offering the majority of 16-year-olds the chance to acquire an accreditation of their five years of secondary education. Children are now banded according to ability in each assessed area and assessments are mainly based on subject areas. Assessment uses a combination of continuous assignments and projects, and national examinations. This marks a significant move towards a system encouraging competence.

Reforms of the A level system are under way. A white paper, *Education and Training for the 21st Century*, in May 1991 announced plans for a new Advanced Diploma which will be available to young people who take two A levels or vocational qualifications, or a mixture of the two, and 'will become another route into higher education'. (Crequer, 1991) There was still, however, no intermediate diploma for those who could not achieve the advanced level of study, but could usefully study for at least a further year after 16.

One of the many problems facing the NVQ system is how to relate A levels to vocational qualifications, and it is here that the concept of 'core skills' becomes particularly important.

> The core skills of communication, problem-solving, personal skills, numeracy, information technology and modern language skills are to be embedded in all study programmes for 16–19-year-olds. The aim is to incorporate them into A and AS levels, vocational training courses and NVQs, with transfer between 'academic' and 'vocational' courses helped by a system of formal credits.

Improved technical and vocational education and qualifications

A major issue at the age of 14 and upwards is how to achieve higher standards of technical education and give technical subjects a higher profile. The announcement in 1986 of the Government's decision to apply the Technical and Vocational Education Initiative (TVEI) to all schools for the next ten years, together with the introduction of the Certificate of Pre-Vocational Education (CPVE) in 1984-5, typify attempts to help children acquire skills, knowledge and experiences which would be useful in adult life and work. In December 1991 a £25 million fund was announced by the Education Minister, whereby schools could bid for up to £500,000 to buy equipment and improve facilities in order to offer high-quality technical and vocational courses aimed particularly at pupils over 14. It was hoped that this scheme would broaden the impact of the city technology college network (Marston, 1991).

Incentives to make schools better managed and more responsive to customer needs

The Education Reform Act of 1988 gave schools the power in certain circumstances to opt out of local authority control, and by September 1991, 41 had done so. The intention was to cut through the red tape and give greater freedom to schools which show that they can manage effectively, thereby helping to ensure a greater responsiveness to customer needs (i.e. needs perceived not only by children, but by their parents and by employers). Following the 1990 Parents' Charter, the November 1991 Education Bill announced further changes to improve the secondary education system and emphasize the importance of its outcomes (Clare, 1991b):

- All schools, state and independent, must publish examination results, National Curriculum test scores, truancy rates and leavers' destinations in a standard form. The details will be summarized in local and national league tables.
- Every state school in England and Wales (27,000) will be monitored once every four years by teams of independent inspectors whose reports will be published. School governing bodies must tell parents how they propose to act on the inspectors' findings.
- All 16-year-olds must stay in school until the end of the summer term instead of leaving at Easter without taking their final exams.
- From September 1991 all parents will receive an annual written report on their children's progress.

Major managerial responsibilities have now been placed with school governors and heads, who must therefore be carefully chosen, and must develop sound business policies, strategic objectives and business plans, against which their performance and that of their schools can be measured.

By way of summarizing the kind of impact that could be made by some of these initiatives, let us look at a case study.

A sixth sense for business

(With acknowledgements to P Marston and the *Daily Telegraph*)

Deyes High School . . . is a former secondary modern in the modest Merseyside suburb of Maghull . . . By the mid-eighties . . . sixth-form staff [had become] increasingly concerned that the dominance of A levels . . . was discouraging intelligent but less academic fifth-formers from staying on . . . [Also] that some students, choosing A levels in the absence of a more suitable alternative, would inevitably fail . . . and that others, aiming for jobs at 18 . . . might have a better preparation for employment than two A levels.

In 1987 Deyes . . . started its own one-year pre-vocational programme . . . and succeeded in attracting 40 students. In 1989 the school became one of only 30 in England to launch a [two-year] BTEC National Diploma. [BTEC] is the vocational equivalent of A levels . . . but has hitherto been the preserve of further education colleges.

The Diploma in Business and Finance (chosen by Deyes to match local employment opportunities) contains 14 units . . . The work is based on 30 assignments requiring students to develop practical solutions to 'real life' business problems . . . Most of the marking is done by the Deyes teachers, subject to external monitoring . . .

When the course began, only two of the 17 [students who started] expressed an interest in higher education. Seven are now considering degree offers and another five are aiming for HNDs. Demand for the course rose . . . last year and 29 new takers are expected to start in September [1991]. With the pre-vocational course, BTEC has lifted the staying-on rate from 57 per cent to 83 per cent in four years.

The Headmaster, Leslie Jolley, said: 'We are giving opportunities for the whole ability range so that sixth-form life becomes the natural extension of life in the school.'

Creating a new post-16 education and training sector

Vocational training and educational provision for 16- and 17-year-old school leavers

All 16- and 17-year-old children who leave school and do not go into higher education are meant to join the Youth Training programme. In its revised (1990) form, this two-year initiative specifies a fixed period of time for 16- and 17-year-olds on the programme, in relation to both on-the-job and off-the-job training. However, courses can vary in length. The purpose is to encourage all able youngsters to aim for NVQs to A level standard or equivalent. TECs run the programme, with their funding from the Training, Education and Enterprise Division linked to performance targets in order to add impetus to the drive for young people to acquire NVQs.

Inner City Compacts, whereby school leavers are guaranteed job interviews if they meet certain performance targets, are also administered by TECs. By January 1990, 40 had been set up, with a further 20 to be established.

Finally, the 1991 Further and Higher Education Bill proposed to give all 16- and 17-year-olds who leave full-time education training credits worth £1,000 or more. (Currently the scheme is being piloted in 11 areas.) This is intended to enable them to purchase higher education of their choice. However, unless the Careers Service is operated effectively, and unless young people have received an effective education up to that point, 'choice' will be something they neither properly understand nor will be able to apply.

Post-16 further and higher education institutions

There are, as Keep (1986) observes, a bewildering number of providers of secondary and tertiary education: city technology colleges (15 approved over the past few years, five short of the original target, and with a questionable future, given their soaring costs and failure to attract substantial funding from major employers), sixth-form colleges, colleges of further education, polytechnics and universities.

The Government intends to create out of this confusion a unified framework for the provision of education and training for post-16-year-olds, applying to it the same principles of local autonomy, competition in an open market and responsiveness to customer needs that underpin reforms of the national training system and the secondary education sector.

Under the Education Reform Act (1988), polytechnics were given corporate status and freed from local authority control. Funding for polytechnics and the larger colleges was to come through a single funding council, the Polytechnic and College Funding Council (PCFC), and is largely dependent on numbers enrolled and types of courses offered. However, the Secretary of State has a firm grip on the PCFC, with 15 members appointed by him or her. The Secretary of State also has wide-ranging powers to confer or impose on the Council any additional powers thought fit. Thus if the system does not through time adequately cater for national needs in terms of its skills and qualification outputs, there is still the central power to force through further changes.

The white paper *Higher Education: a new framework* (May 1991) and the Further and Higher Education Bill (November 1991) announced another group of radical reforms:

- Universities, polytechnics and major colleges of higher education would by April 1994 all be brought together into a single structure for higher education, with power to award their own degrees, thus ending the binary line that has divided universities from other major higher education bodies for 25 years – a radical and widely welcomed move.
- New quality assurance measures would be introduced including external scrutiny by a quality audit unit developed in essence by the educational institutions.
- Remaining further education and sixth-form colleges would be given independent corporate status. While further education and sixth-form colleges are to be funded by the Government through a national council, an element of funding will depend on the numbers enrolled.

Another major step forward was taken in 1992 when all polytechnics legally assumed the status and title of 'universities'.

All higher education institutions, therefore, now need to be very responsive to market needs in order to operate successfully and so are run by governing bodies on which industrial, business and professional interests are increasingly dominant. Effective collaboration between these institutions and schools and local employers is particularly important in areas like profiling and assessment of pupils and students, careers guidance, and the design of sandwich courses and work experience. There will also have to be a major focus on open access and non-discrimination.

> Thus in post-16 vocational education and training there is increasingly, as with the TEC system, a decentralized framework, controlled largely by employers and the professions, and needing to be sensitive to local training and education demands.
>
> TECs, local education providers at secondary and tertiary levels and employers are required to work closely together in improving the quality, levels and relevance of vocational educational provision and attainment and TECs must achieve stated targets in all these areas.

Gateshead College: Part 1

(With acknowledgements to Pat Havord, Deputy Principal: Human Resources, Gateshead College, Tyne and Wear)

Gateshead Technical College, established in the mid-1950s, was located in an inner-city area on Tyneside where unemployment was high, but where there were important initiatives related to business growth and industrial development as the area moved away from dependence on traditional heavy industries to expansion into light engineering, high technology, the commercial and service sector and major changes in the public sector.

The College had served local needs with the usual kind of technical and educational vocational courses for many years. In 1990 after several years of intense local debate and political discussion, it was reorganized into a new tertiary college. This resulted in a new governing body, and a new principal and senior management team. Staff were recruited from the old Technical College and local schools.

One of the first objectives of the newly named Gateshead College was to establish a new corporate image, draw up mission and business strategy documents, and develop a new culture among its staff. Externally it was keen to make its actual and potential clients aware of the change and it devised, with the help of an outside consultant, a new image and marketing campaign. Internally it was vital to establish 'one staff', abolishing the old division between teaching and so-called non-teaching staff, and to promote a culture of continuous development.

A major initial exercise was to involve all staff in drawing up a mission statement which eventually included twelve commitments, used as the basis for future corporate planning. A functional organizational structure was introduced emphasizing accountability at middle management level. Human resource management became a corporate function, headed by a Deputy Principal, with staff development related to all employees one of its key policy areas. Marketing became another mainstream business function. A concerted effort to improve industrial relations was also undertaken.

A major organizational change programme was introduced: its focus was on culture change with great emphasis on team-building and team skills. The structure enabled team meetings to take place weekly and a development programme was put in place to support this. Communication channels became of vital importance, and many new ideas were generated and put into practice. At the same time a whole set of corporate goals and specific objectives was put into place and communicated throughout the College.

The College's products were expanded and improved and a new training consultancy division established. There was close collaboration between local schools, industry and commerce and the senior college staff, and external expertise in information systems, marketing, publicity and graphics was used. Accommodation was upgraded and a new logo and colours took precedence everywhere.

After four terms, the College recorded an increase in full-time enrolments of over 40 per cent with enrolments overall up well over 20 per cent. The College has undertaken a detailed market analysis and predicts ongoing future growth. Many of its secondary education courses attracted for the first time able boys and girls from independent as well as state schools – and not only those who were resitting GCSE or A level examinations, but those who had chosen to take post-16 academic and technical courses for the first time. Particular attention was paid in its business plan to improving access for adult learners, and equal opportunities have been built into both its planning and its operational processes and systems.

There are many aspects to the story of the College's first year that have not been covered here, including difficulties in the renegotiation of contracts with academic staff and predictable problems of balancing needs against resources. The purpose of this overview is, however, simply to demonstrate the many ways in which the old, bureaucratic, routinized institution has had to undergo profound change in order to transform it, and its people, into the kind of business-led 'company' that is informed about, and responsive to, the needs of its customers, and can meet those needs at required levels of effectiveness combined with efficiency. How it proposes to tackle the difficult question of ensuring that certain long-term educational aims are met, especially those related to research and to the continuous development of individuals rather than merely to immediate, job- and employment-related education and training, is another matter (see below, pages 285ff).

Exercises

1 Draft a short presentation to your local IPM branch on the subject of ONE of the following:

(a) College/employer liaison;
(b) sandwich courses;
(c) vocational guidance.

Incorporate ideas on the contribution the branch might make to promote the activity you select. (November 1989)

2 By 1991, further education will contain over 50 per cent 'employment interest governors'. What do you see as the main responsibilities which these governors must carry? What would you look for when identifying suitable people to be encouraged to take on the governor role? (May 1989)

3 What do you understand by the phrase 'workplace competence'? How would you like to see it reflected in:

(a) internal appraisal and assessment activity;
(b) National Vocational Qualifications? (November 1988)

References

ARKIN A. 'Giving credit to prior learning'. *Personnel Management*, April 1991a. pp. 41-3. (Includes case studies from an NHS Trust and British Gas.)
ARKIN A. 'A touch of glass'. *Personnel Management*. July 1991b. pp. 47-8
CLARE J. 'Clarke plans to simplify national curriculum'. *Daily Telegraph*, 21 September 1991a
CLARE J. 'No let up in pace of school reform'. *Daily Telegraph*, 1 November 1991b
CONFEDERATION OF BRITISH INDUSTRY and THE TRADE UNION CONGRESS. *Review of Vocational Qualifications in England and Wales: A Report by the Working Group*. London, HMSO, 1986
CREQUER N. 'Diplomas aimed to boost vocational studies'. *The Independent*, 30 March 1991
DEPARTMENT OF EMPLOYMENT. *Employment News*, No. 61, June 1988
'Education and Training for the 21st Century'. Government white paper. London, HMSO, 1991

EMPLOYMENT DEPARTMENT GROUP. *A Strategy for Skills: Guidance from the Secretary of State for Employment on training, vocational education and enterprise.* London, Department of Employment, November 1991

'Employment in the 1990s'. Government white paper. London, HMSO, 1989

FIELD R. 'Sheffield forges ahead on training'. *Personnel Management*, October 1990. pp. 66-9

HARRISON R. 'Employee development at Barratt'. In *Case Studies in Personnel* (Winstanley D and Woodall J, eds.), Ch. 10. London, Institute of Personnel Management. 1992

'Higher Education – A New Framework'. Government white paper. London, HMSO, 1991

JOHNSON R. 'Wanted: your input on training'. *Personnel Management Plus.* June 1990. p. 30

KEEP E. 'Can Britain build a coherent vocational training system?' *Personnel Management*, August 1986. pp. 28-31

KEEP E. 'A training scandal?' In *Personnel Management in Britain*, (Sisson K, ed.). Oxford, Blackwell. 1989

MANPOWER SERVICES COMMISSION/DEPARTMENT OF EDUCATION AND SCIENCE. *Review of Vocational Qualifications in England and Wales: A report by the Working Group.* London, HMSO. April 1986

MARSTON P. 'A sixth sense for business'. *Daily Telegraph*, 23 May 1991a

MARSTON P. 'Schools offered up to £1/2 million to boost science'. *Daily Telegraph*, 5 December 1991b

McCLEOD D. 'More pupils opt to stay in education'. *The Independent*, 26 April 1991

PERSONNEL MANAGEMENT. 'National Training Team reinforced'. *Personnel Management*, May 1991. p. 3

PERSONNEL MANAGEMENT PLUS. 'UK firms win EC funding for training'. *Personnel Management Plus*, December 1991. p. 6

SMITHERS A. 'Vocation in a void'. *Daily Telegraph*, 5 December 1991

TRAINING AGENCY. *Training and Enterprise Councils: A prospectus for the 1990s*. Sheffield, Moorfoot, TA. 1989

'Working Together – Education and Training'. Government white paper. London, HMSO. 1986

Further useful reading

'Access and Opportunity'. Government white paper. London, HMSO. 1991

ARKIN A. 'A tale of two TECs'. *Personnel Management Plus*, July 1991. pp. 20-1

BERKELEY J. 'A better pay-off from work experience'. *Personnel Management*, April 1988. pp. 56-61

DEPARTMENT OF EMPLOYMENT. *The Skills Decade.* London, Department of Employment. 1990

MACLURE S. *Missing Links: The challenge to further education.* London, Policy Studies Institute. 1991. (Excellent historical introduction.)

WOOD S. 'Work experience that works'. *Personnel Management*, November 1986. pp. 42-5

The information in Chapter 2 will need to be regularly updated, and the following are recommended as particularly helpful reading:

- The IPD's publication, *Management People*, contains reliable, accessible and up-to-date information.
- The 'quality' press – and especially the Sunday papers – for their regular articles and editorials on matters relating to the field of secondary and tertiary education, and national training.

The Times Educational Supplement and *The Times Higher Education Supplement* should also be consulted on a fairly regular basis, certainly by IPD students taking ED2 examinations.

Chapter 3

National vocational education and training: will the system work?

Learning Objectives

After reading this chapter you will:

1 understand the main trends in, and pressures upon, NVET policy and strategy in the UK in the past 30 years;
2 have carried out a critical analysis of the present system in order to identify its main strengths and weaknesses;
3 be able to assess the kind of framework for NVET most likely to be effective in the UK.

Let us take as our starting point a number of statements made in recent years about education and training in the UK.

- Very many 'training' initiatives have . . . been launched in recent years but they suffer from a lack of vision, or permanence, and cohesion, one with another. (Institute of Personnel Management, 1990)
- Commenting on national proposals in a piecemeal fashion is unsatisfactory because there does not appear to be a unifying national training policy from which these proposals could be said to flow. (Ibid.)
- The United Kingdom does not have a clearly articulated national strategic framework for training. (House of Lords Select Committee, 1990)

These criticisms were made in 1990. By 1991 what the Government claimed to be a new vision, policy and framework was in place; but was this claim of a new, more hopeful, start valid? In order to answer this question we need first to establish what happened during the years of effort to establish a meaningful NVET system, and then to evaluate the thinking and plans related to the system established at the start of the present decade.

National Training Policy and Strategy, Mid-1950s to Late 1980s

Introduction: policy or politics?

Our starting point is a quotation from the white paper, *Training for the Future* (1972), which stated the aims of national training to be both economic and social – to have the right workers in the right place at the right time, with the right skill, and to provide better opportunities to individuals to develop their skills and use their abilities to the full.

Duality of purpose is the first problem facing national training policy: how should it best achieve both economic and social ends? This raises another crucial question: how far has NVET in the past lacked any real vision and policy at all, being no more than a series of *ad hoc* reactions to continuing economic and social problems? Such an approach would explain the 'stop-start' pattern that has characterized government action in the area for so long. It is also consistent with the typical attitude towards training in too many UK organizations: a function left to chance, not seen as a strategic contributor to business results.

The pre-1964 *laissez-faire* era

Traditionally the attitude to training in the UK has been *laissez-faire* (Perry, 1975) with training generally perceived as an activity primarily to do with craft skills (Kenney and Reid, 1986, p. 273).

From the late 1880s onwards there were many inquiries into aspects of the UK's manpower policies and practices, reacting to public concern about the progress of our industrial competitors. Yet major educational reforms from the Butler Act of 1944 onwards only served to deepen the existing division between 'academic' and 'vocational/technical' education, to the detriment of the latter; and there was still no meaningful attempt to regulate industrial training.

As the post-war years developed in the UK into a long boom period there was no concern to improve industrial training even though investment in skills acquisition then would have built up valuable reserves for the future. Then in the late 1950s economic growth began to slow down, and the Conservative Government turned to central planning mechanisms to tackle the problem. The National Economic Development Council (NEDC) was set up in 1961, followed by the National Incomes Commission and a national incomes policy in 1962.

The focus was clearly on national manpower planning, and in 1962 Richard Stone, an economist at Cambridge, produced projections showing alarming increases needed in certain areas of skill – particularly in engineering, science and technology – if the UK economy was to move forward in the next decade. The 1950s had seen the rise of college sandwich courses for future technologists, but industry was failing to supply the industrial training places needed for those students. The apprenticeship system was also causing concern: the proportion of school leavers entering apprenticeships was declining, and the system itself was in urgent need of reform. As a result of the critical 1958 Carr Report *Training for Skills*, the Industrial Training Council was set up in 1958 to put pressure on industry in relation to the employment of young people. Its failure to bring about the training revolution needed was the final proof that the *laissez-faire* approach to industrial training could not be allowed to continue.

We can summarize this period as follows:

> Shortage of key skills, inadequacies in the quality and provision of industrial training and the continued slow-down of economic growth, together with the Government's continued preference for central planning and regulation during the Wilson years of 1964–70 all explain why legislation to regulate national training was introduced in the mid-sixties.

1964–71: the Industrial Training Board regulatory framework

In 1964 the Industrial Training Act established, through the Industrial Training Boards (ITBs) and the levy-grant system, a regulatory framework 'to make further provision for industrial and commercial training'. Its aims were dominated by three immediate economic considerations:

1. To ensure an adequate supply of properly trained manpower at all levels of industry;
2. To improve the quality and efficiency of industrial training;
3. To ensure that those two aims were carried out by sharing the costs evenly between industries.

The Wilson years saw the management of the economy floundering, with the pragmatism espoused by Wilson himself degenerating into what often appeared to be no more than 'a series of crisis expedients devoid of any real strategy to cope with the growing problems of the national economy' (Dutton, 1991). Much the same kind of criticism was made throughout that period about the national training system, which was seen by a growing number of employers and others as out of touch with the needs of business, bureaucratic, rigid and unable to solve the problems with which it was supposed to be dealing.

1972–79: central intervention and the rise of the Manpower Services Commission

After the Heath Government's initial attempt in 1970 to move away from the post-war consensus of central planning and intervention, it was forced into a humiliating U-turn as the economy remained stagnant, unemployment rose past the million mark for the first time in post-war history, and the unions proved more intractable than ever. In 1971 it launched a powerfully interventionist Industry Bill and a formal incomes policy.

Intervention once again extended to industrial training. The white paper of 1972, *Training for the Future*, stated that ITBs had failed to make enough impact on critical skills shortages, and that the levy-grant system was not providing adequate incentives to employers to invest in the kind of training needed by the economy. The 'quick fix' remedy was to set up a powerful new central body, the Manpower Services Commission (MSC), in 1973, 'to make such arrangements as it considers appropriate for assisting people to select, train for, obtain and retain employment, and for assisting employers to obtain suitable employees' ('Employment and Training', 1973). Its two operating arms were the Training Services Agency, co-ordinating the work of ITBs and stimulating training in areas not covered by them, and the Employment Services Agency, looking after a wide range of services related to employment and unemployment.

The years from 1974 to 1979 marked a period of political uncertainty, with the new Labour Government failing to achieve an overall parliamentary majority, and having to cut and trim its policies accordingly. Inflation soared, unemployment climbed steadily, and there were further setbacks to economic growth especially after the 1973 oil crisis. The MSC, initially intended to head a major drive whereby whole workforces would acquire new skills to meet the challenge of modernization and new technology, degenerated into a body desperately developing one work experience or training programme after another as unemployment (particularly youth unemployment) and critical skills shortages both worsened (Ainley and Carney, 1990). A commentator at the time (Lawrence, 1977) wrote:

> Much of the output of the Manpower Services Commission so far has been a response to Government requirements for short-term, even cosmetic, measures . . . Recent events have created particularly harsh manpower problems and our characteristic answer is to set up a new body. Will the MSC make a real, far-sighted contribution?

1979–82: a return to voluntarism

The answer to that question was to be no. With the advent of the Thatcher Government in 1979 came a determination to abandon the consensus politics that had dominated the post-war era, and that had coincided with a lower rate of growth for the UK economy than for most other industrial nations (Dutton, 1991). The market, not the state, was to decide the allocation of resources; full employment was, for the first time, no longer the overriding priority; and the unions were not considered to have any special claim to power – and in fact exercised an increasingly negligible influence over government policy.

Immediate enquiries into the state of the national training system were not, in this context, surprising: criticisms were in any case widespread. However, there were many warning voices, including that of the IPM, against wholesale abolition of the ITBs and a return to a voluntary system that had never worked. 'The facts and history of industrial life in this country underline the futility of a purely voluntary approach' (Kaufman, 1981). Nevertheless in 1981 16 of the 23 ITBs were axed, the statutory levy-grant system was abolished, and about 170 Non-Statutory Industry Training Organisations (NSTOs) were set up to disburse MSC training grants and persuade and advise industry to invest in training. Their operating costs (as well as those of the remaining ITBs) were to be met by firms in their industry. All of this was a clear expression of the Government's determination to make training mainly the responsibility of individuals and employers, cutting back dramatically on public expenditure and allowing market forces far freer play – a move fully consistent with Thatcher philosophy, though greeted with dismay by many.

However, another set of ideas about national education and training policy also underpinned the 1981 measures. In October 1975, Geoffrey

Holland, then head of the MSC, later Permanent Secretary at the Department of Employment, wrote of the need to envisage an integrated national training system with four components through which the individual should pass in his or her progress from school to retirement: full-time education, initial job training, training within employment and training of those not currently in employment.

> [National training] policy should see the nation's manpower . . . as functioning within a single system, rather than as affected by a series of random occurrences. It should be able to exert influence on the operation of the national system at key points. (Holland, 1975)

This logic did permeate the measures introduced in 1981, even though it could not prevail against the ineffective framework of implementation which was set up at that time. The white paper *A New Training Initiative: A programme for action* (1981) identified three main objectives: reform of occupational skills training and qualifications; a comprehensive scheme of vocational preparation for all young people under 18; and wider opportunities for adult training. Holland's 'cradle to grave' vision persisted throughout that decade, and lies behind the long-term policy and strategy that appears to have emerged from 1989 onwards.

> There can be little doubt that the advent of the New Training Initiative marked the development, at least in outline, of a comprehensive national training strategy. It is the delivery system that has become increasingly fragmented and less open to central direction (Keep, 1986).

1983–88: the return of central intervention

By 1983 the failure of the resumed voluntarist approach was all too apparent. With one or two exceptions the NSTOs had failed to have any real effect on either the volume or the standard of training in their industries (Coopers and Lybrand, 1985). Like the Industrial Training Council of 1958 (p. 47) they lacked teeth, and proved no substitute for statutory bodies. Meanwhile 'employers subjected to the enormous counter pressures of cash-flow and declining markets' (Kaufman, 1981) were failing to make any adequate investment in training for the skills so badly needed in the economy at large.

A recurrence of the old problems of high youth unemployment and skills shortages in critical areas, together with the widely publicized inadequacies of the educational system and increasing information about the links between training and industrial performance, all resulted in a partial return to central intervention: the establishment in 1983 of 55 centrally funded Area Manpower Boards to help implement the New Training Initiative. However, the Boards proved largely ineffective, and the Youth Training Scheme (YTS) in particular was seen by many to be a way of doctoring unemployment figures. While many programmes were excellent in design and content, the output of YTS as a whole in terms of employment rates and levels of vocational qualifications proved disappointing. An analysis of YTS published in 1986 by Youthaid, the independent youth employment charity, found that fewer than six out of ten school leavers obtained work, and that those who needed most help had the least chance of work.

In the next few years the pattern of problems and short-term reactions to them continued, but one trend was constant: the attempt to force the education system into providing more and better vocational preparation. Again, however, strategy foundered at the stage of implementation.

On the one hand the Department of Education and Science spearheaded its own educational reforms, most notably through the white paper *Better Schools* (1985) which led to the introduction of the Certificate of Pre-Vocational Education (CPVE), the establishment of city technology colleges, the introduction of a compulsory core curriculum and the devolution of budgetary control to some schools. Meanwhile the National Council for Vocational Qualifications (NCVQ) was trying to rationalize and simplify vocational courses and qualifications. Finally, in the field of further education the MSC was taking control of an increasingly large percentage of funding (from 8 per cent in 1985 to 16 per cent in 1986–7) in order to produce a better response to labour market needs. Amidst such a plethora of initiatives and institutions, failures were inevitable.

The failures of TVEI

Between 1983 and 1987 the Government spent more than £1 billion on the largest-ever investment in the British curriculum, the Technical and Vocational Education Initiative (TVEI), which was introduced in 1983–4 on a pilot basis, and extended to cover all secondary schools in 1986.

In May 1989 a report by Edinburgh University's Centre for Educational Sociology said that the scheme had failed to improve examination results or truancy rates, to persuade young people to stay at school after 16 or to improve their chances of finding a job. David Raffe, who carried out the research, said that the 1986 assessment of it as an outstanding success had been made before the first pupils had completed their four-year programme, so that there was no systematic evidence of its impact. (Clare, 1989)

In the same article, Clare observed that a 1989 study by school inspectors in Essex had found that the standards of work on TVEI were variable and insufficiently challenging.

In 1990 the Labour Party accused the Government of undermining TVEI by cutting funding. 'The cuts in TVEI reflect the black hole in government policy caused by almost total lack of coherence and co-ordination between the Department of Education and Science and the Department of Employment.' (Jack Straw in *Personnel Management Plus*, 1990a)

Meanwhile on the international stage, where global competition was increasing, substantial information was emerging about the very different educational and training systems, strategies and outcomes of our main competitor countries, and in particular about the high level of investment they made in education and training.

In the mid 1980s the *Competence and Competition* (Institute of Manpower Studies, 1984), *Challenge to Complacency* (Coopers and Lybrand, 1985), Handy (1987) and Constable/McCormick (1987) Reports received great publicity, and raised the general awareness that we were falling far behind our competitors in the skills profile of our workforce, and in the levels of educational and vocational attainment and qualifications of our young people. The movement towards the single European market increased this awareness. It was also clear that steps must be taken to invest heavily in the retraining and development of existing workers, given the known demographic trends whereby, up to at least 2025, there would be a dramatic reduction in all countries in the availability of young people for work, and a predominance of ageing workforces in most Western countries.

These international pressures, with all their implications for the UK economy and its workforce, clearly reinforced the Government's belief, in the years after 1981, that vocational education and training must primarily be about jobs. That belief underpinned the controversial white paper *Training for Employment* (1988), the 1988 Employment Reform Act and the continuing reform of the education system. The concept of any wider social purpose for education and training was given lip service but little else.

1989: the new deregulated framework: a fundamental change, or a resumption of 'stop-start'?

In 1989 came the white paper *Employment for the 1990s* which announced the current national framework and strategy. There were still, in a rapidly expanding economy, skill shortages in critical areas; furthermore employers' attitudes and beliefs had not changed sufficiently to ensure that, left to them, the necessary investment in training would take place. There was, therefore, once more a system of incentives, but this time resting on a framework of voluntary partnership driven by local employers. Six of the seven ITBs left were wound up, to be replaced by voluntary bodies. Meanwhile the once-powerful MSC shrank to the Training Commission; then to the Training Agency (TA) (1989), and finally, in 1990, to the Training, Enterprise and Education Division of the Department of Employment.

Did all of this mark a new vision and a long-term policy and strategy for NVET? The Government believed so:

> We stand at the crossroads. In one direction lie the behaviour and attitudes, the short-term planning and the easy options which have so bedevilled our performance in the past. In the other direction lie the new opportunities and challenges which TECs provide: a passport to a more enterprising and better skilled workforce, increased competitiveness and economic growth. (Training Agency, 1989, p. 19)

Others, like Kenny (1990) were sceptical:

> Politicians of all colours have always subordinated training to jobs – any jobs – and when jobs have been plentiful real interest in training has been scarce . . . With the formation of TECs the onus has been put back on the very employers who have so significantly failed us in the past.

NVET

The purpose of this exercise is to help you review and absorb the information presented in the chapter so far.

Activity in NVET between the mid-1950s and 1989 has been interpreted as merely a series of reactions to wider economic and social issues rather than as attempts to implement a positive, long-term NVET policy. Is this interpretation valid?

FEEDBACK NOTES

Between 1964 and 1981 there was no evidence of vision or of a long-term policy and overarching system of values, aims and beliefs related to NVET. Movements into and away from a regulatory framework all coincided with fluctuations in wider economic and social problems, and with changing governmental approaches to dealing with them.

However, from 1981 to 1989 it is possible to see the emergence of a clear, meaningful 'cradle to grave' vision of NVET together with the development of a consistent long-term policy. What was lacking was a workable system for achieving that policy.

Is the 1990s Vision and Mission of NVET Convincing?

By 1989 the intention was that there should be a decentralized, largely voluntary, structure for national training in future.

Vision

The vision for NVET is one of a nation of continuously developing young people and adults with the skills available in the right place and at the right time in order that sustained economic growth and competitiveness can be achieved.

This vision is controversial: while there is no doubt that preparing young people to be economic assets for the country must be *one* important function of education, the concern is that it could be becoming virtually the *only* meaningful function. Chitty (1990) says, 'Full-time post-16 education is too often regarded as an emergency alternative to employment', and Cowie (1988) remarks:

> We are in danger of producing a skilled but uneducated workforce with a weak understanding of society and not very adaptable . . . A good education develops the individual to the best of his or her abilities . . . [and] imparts understanding on the basis of which new skills can be acquired. Training looks for performance in a specific skill.

There is also the question of what role education should play for those young people and adults who cannot obtain employment, but still deserve opportunities to achieve some kind of meaningful life – one of the 'social' ends of NVET that seems too often to have been ignored by government policy.

Mission

The current mission for NVET is to achieve an adequate investment by a voluntary partnership of interested parties in a market-led vocational training system whose costs are borne by those who operate in the market – i.e. mainly by employers and individuals.

This mission raises a number of questions that go to the heart of concerns about NVET in the UK.

Are there adequate incentives for individuals?

For individuals, as the Coopers and Lybrand Report (1985) pointed out, there has been far less to encourage them to invest in training than in many competitor countries, notably Germany, where increased wages and career prospects are linked to training and qualifications, and young people are not distracted by high-pay temptations. In the UK:

> Nearly half our 16-year-olds leave school at once. There is a lively labour market for 16- and 17-year-olds, pay is often high, and training problematic. It is flying in the face of experience to think young people will renounce these offers and make use of their vouchers to buy virtuous training. (Cassells, 1991)

Some UK firms are beginning to make links between qualifications and pay, as the following exercise shows.

Sheerness Steel (1991)
(With acknowledgements to J Pickard and *Personnel Management*)

What are the benefits that this example shows can be gained by an employer investing heavily in the education and training of its workforce?

Sheerness Steel is a private, medium-sized company, which in 1981 was faced with the need to cut costs in order to remain competitive at a time of recession. As part of its cost-cutting drive, it stopped training apprentices and made a quarter of its workforce redundant.

In 1984 the recession began to lift, and Sheerness faced a skills crisis. It was a company that had never had a high profile in the development of people, but at this point its top management realized that it must build up a skilled workforce, not only to improve existing productivity levels, but in order to achieve a lasting competitive edge. The company therefore established an entirely new set of personnel policies with a wide-ranging vocational education and training programme at their core, working in close collaboration with local colleges.

What have been the results of this massive investment? By the end of 1989 production in the rod mill had gone up by 60 per cent, significantly due, it is believed, to faster and more efficient working, greater flexibility and increased skills. In the bar mill and the melt shop, productivity rates had improved by a similar amount. Meanwhile, man-hour productivity figures had also steadily improved and, after the introduction of a comprehensive health and safety programme, days lost due to accidents were more than halved. A quarter of all employees were studying for vocational qualifications and over a quarter already possessed them; the target was to have 75 per cent of all employees holding vocational qualifications by 1992.

By late 1991, when Sheerness Steel won the Compass/IPM award for outstanding achievement in resourcing, the results were still impressive and, in the company's view, were directly related to its drive to develop its people. Productivity had steadily increased from 609 billet tonnes per employee in 1983 to 1,064 in 1990, and 60 per cent of employees either held or were pursuing a vocational qualification.

The company has moved from a general recruitment policy, which left it competing in the general scrum for skills at the height of the skill shortage, to one of recruiting and developing high-quality young people, including apprentices, sixth-formers and graduates. (*Personnel Management*, 1991b.)

Sheerness had also set up an engineering group training centre with support from other employers and local authorities, and in 1991 it doubled its apprentice intake to counter demographic trends – despite a national tendency to reduce numbers of apprentices dramatically as a short-term response to continued recession and low growth.

Promotion at Sheerness is now dependent on an employee studying for or gaining a vocational qualification, and the company bonus scheme depends on six factors including educational achievement. 'Employees are encouraged to add to their qualifications at any stage of their career. This can include language training and information technology as well as skills directly related to their jobs. The company has an open learning centre.' (Ibid.)

FEEDBACK NOTES

Many of the benefits Sheerness Steel has obtained from its investment in workforce-wide education and training activities appear in the list given in *Employment News* (Department of Employment, 1988):

- Improved profitability and economic performance
- Development of a workforce more able to adapt to new situations, updating and modifying skills as needed through the system of credit accumulation and transfer
- Increased co-operation between employers, training organizations and awarding bodies
- Increased individual motivation and awareness of standards, through the real value of the qualifications the employer helps them to achieve
- Easier recruitment of competent staff because employers know what an NVQ stands for
- Clear goals set for continued learning and staff development, providing the opportunity for improvement in corporate performance

However, there is a long way to go before Sheerness's approach of encouraging and rewarding individual initiative in relation to vocational education becomes a general one.

Tax relief would, of course, make a difference to individual's motivation to acquire vocational qualifications. In April 1992 tax relief of 25 per cent was introduced for students paying for courses leading to NVQs/SVQs. This move, together with plans to extend Training Credits to adults, and for career development loans, encourage 'market-led' training investment by helping individuals who want to make a new career move or upgrade their skills, and companies which want to retrain the workforce or adapt to new technology.

> However, the question remains as to how far any of these incentives will actually make a significant difference to individuals' motivation to acquire skills and qualifications until the latter are tied to a universal reward system.

Are there adequate incentives for organizations to invest?

This is doubtful, for many reasons. There is still evidence of the complacency and failure of expertise in training and development that was apparent in the mid-1980s, and was highlighted in influential national reports. This complacency was reported in 1985 (Coopers and Lybrand) and again in a Hatfield Polytechnic survey (1991), showing that although the evidence of the need to improve our vocational education and training system is now much more widely available, and is taken more seriously, commitment to action lags behind.

Moreover the financial base of most organizations and the structure of industry generally in the UK is such that they are driven by short-termism. Large-scale domination of UK businesses by the financial sector and the accountancy profession (Handy, 1987) inhibits long-term strategic investment. This leads to the inevitable cycle of times of prosperity being characterized by high profits for shareholders, while in times of recession, just when the maintenance of skills and build-up for recovery is needed, cutbacks are made in order to avoid large cuts in profits, problems with shareholders, and the danger of hostile takeovers. Such takeovers are themselves inevitable when companies cannot grow steadily by re-investing retained profits at times of economic fluctuation and when they are pressurized by high interest rates and high dividend yields. Acquisitions satisfy shareholders' demands for growth (Yates, 1990).

It is the same vicious circle that explains much of the UK's failure to invest adequately in scientific research and development. The two forms of investment, in research and in human resource development, are in fact inextricably linked, as Yates (1990) points out:

> Failure to invest adequately means that as skills reduce, there is not the same capacity and competence to carry out research and development even were there financial resources available to do

so. Thus, inevitably, the economy goes into a downwards spiral as its true sources of engendering wealth decline.

The fear of poaching is another factor, and one which is valid as long as only the minority of organizations invest heavily in training. Surveys and reports still show that the majority do not have the capacity, or do not see the need, to offer long-term security of employment and a related internal career system, despite the much-publicized efforts of a few well-known organizations such as Ford, Rover, Lucas, Bosch, Nissan and other Japanese subsidiaries, and ICI. This being the case, many people, especially the upwardly mobile and those possessing valued skills, will move in and out of organizations searching for better terms, conditions and opportunities, and will be open to higher bids for their labour. Employers in turn will continue to remedy skills shortages far more by recruitment and reward strategies than by development.

Poaching and short-termism in training

1 **Upping the pay** (IPM, 1991a; with acknowledgements to *Personnel Management*)

Firms introducing new technology are failing to give a high priority to training despite being hampered by skill shortages . . . A survey has revealed that short-term solutions are adopted instead. The Economic and Social Research Council-funded project, involving interviews with the managing directors of over 50 Sheffield engineering companies, found that 54 per cent of firms had adopted new manufacturing technology in the last three years. 21 per cent . . . reported the need for more skilled labour, while 36 per cent found both that training costs had increased and that their training needs exceeded their in-house capacity. Major recruitment problems were also experienced, particularly in filling vacancies in semi-skilled and unskilled jobs. But training was not high on the agenda to overcome these shortages, with firms instead preferring short-term measures such as raising pay and increasing overtime.

2 **Training as an emergency measure** (IPM, 1991b; with acknowledgements to *Personnel Management*)

New technology firm Epitaxial Products International had no choice but to train almost its entire workforce, as there was no existing market from which to recruit experienced staff.

This story had a happy ending: the training of unskilled and inexperienced operators, mostly recruited locally, led to about 50 workers progressing from being unskilled to forming a competent workforce, and in two years sales have risen from nil to £250,000 per month. The company won the Channel 4 Business Daily Award for the most positive return on business investment.

However, the real nature of the 'skills market' is not one of a highly mobile population of workers touting their skills to the highest bidder. Dore (1987) shows that the very concepts that explain poaching also produce the voluntarist approach to training that sees skills provision ensured by the workings of a free labour market; were the whole labour market really to be 'free' in terms of the movement of people and skills, then the voluntary approach would work, because there would always be a natural balance between supply and demand. The flaw in the model is that although there are *some* highly mobile occupations and individuals, most employees are not continuously mobile, nor are they encouraged to be so by their employers, who in fact often induce them to stay by offering various longer-term incentives in order to get the benefits of low turnover and continuity of skilled performance.

Because there is not a universally mobile 'skills market' adequate investment in training cannot be ensured by simply relying on market forces. All that such reliance leads to is precisely the endless succession of skills problems that have bedevilled the UK economy since the 1950s. Some organizations hoard skills; some overinvest and then retain their skilled people by long-term internal development and reward policies and systems; others overinvest but are unable or unwilling to restructure in those ways and lose many of their skilled people to 'poachers'; the poachers do no investment unless poaching fails. Meanwhile few individuals have incentives to invest for themselves, for reasons already explored.

Summary

We have made the following points about the current vision and mission for NVET:

> The vision is a controversial one, because it sees the role of vocational education as serving immediate needs for the production of

a skilled labour force for the economy. Any longer-term or different purpose for vocational education is effectively ignored.

The mission ignores the fact that there still appear to be inadequate incentives for individuals and organizations to invest in vocational education and training to the extent needed by the economy. For the individual, doing so does not, in most cases, lead directly to rewards in terms of jobs, pay or career development. For organizations, there are a number of reasons for continued failure to invest:

- The prevalence of attitudes of complacency and of failure of expertise in training
- Short-termism
- Fear of poaching
- The lack of a universally mobile skills market

What is Current NVET Strategy, and Can It Be Implemented?

The criticism is often made that although there is now a clear vision and policy for NVET, the fatal weaknesses lie in the strategy and framework for implementation. There is certainly evidence to support that criticism when we look at plans for implementation at local, sectoral and national level.

Local level: TECs

While the strategy of getting local, employer-led bodies to head the drive for a better investment in training may well be valid, the problems come in implementing that strategy: in other words, in resourcing, operating and controlling those bodies.

Lack of commitment to training by TEC chairmen

Continued evidence about the lack of commitment by even the most influential employers to making a real investment in training came from an unexpected and worrying quarter. In early 1991 Hatfield Polytechnic's survey for the Employment Institute found that chairmen of TECs were failing to set a good example in their own companies. Only eight of the 31 surveyed were expecting to provide increased training for their own workforces in 1991, and almost a quarter of the companies led by TEC chairmen were expecting to take on fewer trainees than in 1990. The reason given was usually the need to get extra value for money from training in recessionary times.

The report also found that some TECs had little knowledge of the situation in their own areas. Only five TECs had introduced new initiatives because of the recession, and only two of these were directly related to the economic downturn. It remains to be seen how predictive these early signs are of TECs' long-term operational effectiveness.

Bureaucracy and resourcing

In August 1990 the leaking of a confidential minute of a meeting between the Employment Secretary and the chairmen of the then 10 TECs revealed concern among industrialists over cuts in the Government's training budget, and a watering down of targets (Johnston, 1990). One chairman said that the operation of the scheme 'bore little resemblance to the vision that had attracted businessmen to TECs in the first instance', and that the TEC movement was hungry for signals of the Government's commitment.

Priority 4 of *A Strategy for Skills* (Employment Department Group, 1991) stresses the need for TECs to fulfil their guarantee and aim for long-term unemployed people, those with disabilities and others with specific needs to obtain jobs and qualifications, and for increasing employers' involvement in and contributions to the Employment Training (ET) scheme. Implementation is different: in February 1991, it was announced that unemployed people over the age of 24 were to be excluded from the Government's main training scheme for adults, ET, owing to reductions in funding of more than 30 per cent and a rise in the numbers out of work. The age limit was most likely to be imposed in regions of high unemployment where the number of jobless was beginning to overwhelm the system even before the cash reductions were confirmed. 'It will be the first time for more than a decade that older long-term unemployed people will not qualify for a government-sponsored work experience or training scheme.' (Whitfield, 1991)

About 200 specialist trainers were made redundant after the renegotiation of Youth Training (YT) contracts with the Training Agency in May 1989. (*Personnel Management Plus*, 1990b) By May 1991, there was evidence indicating that more than half of the 66,000 training places for the unemployed provided by charities and voluntary organizations had been axed because of government cuts: more than three quarters of those places on ET and half of those YT places were for special needs cases and the disadvantaged (National Council for Voluntary Organisations survey, quoted by Clement, 1991). Meanwhile other training providers were offering fewer places to youngsters with special needs. In January 1992, it was announced that the Apex Trust, the widely acclaimed charity training ex-offenders, had been refused Government support to prevent its imminent collapse following confusion in funding arrangements. (The Trust went into receivership, but was turned round and obtained a rescue package from the private sector.) FullEmploy, the only training organization for ethnic minorities, had just gone into liquidation after the Home Office refused to lift a block on a £250,000 grant.

Meeting and balancing local and national needs

While local TECs may be able to offer much to small and medium-sized organizations, the large employers face a confusing picture: they will have to deal with as many TECs as they have sites in different regions, and with as many NSTOs as they have different sectoral groups. Allied to this is the fact that many of the existing TECs correspond to local authority rather than local economic boundaries, especially within large conurbations. This creates a number of tensions, as a national survey in 1990 (PA Cambridge) showed. The ability of TECs to improve supply to meet local needs in their areas was limited. They might also be unable to meet the training needs of local companies where labour was very mobile, and in their anxiety to deal with local needs they might overlook needs of national importance.

Results of early monitoring of the system

Despite all these strains on the system, in the early 1990s there was no sign of the Government changing course. 'Arguments about taking a voluntary approach or not are too simplistic,' said Sir Geoffrey Holland (*Personnel Management Plus*, 1991). He believed that progress could be made through large companies putting pressure on their suppliers, through consortium arrangements between neighbouring firms and through the leverage grants that TECs could use to pump-prime local initiatives. 'The key thing now is to get chief executives in industry and commerce committed to training and Investors in

People, which is why they are on TEC boards.'

Ron Johnson, then Vice-President, Training and Development at the IPM, was pessimistic. He doubted whether the framework of national standards would prove strong enough to ensure uniform effectiveness, and he pointed out that the US pattern on which TECs are modelled is known to be patchy in its success. He also felt that in terms of workload and funding, TECs were overburdened and had little room for developing new initiatives. Nearly 90 per cent of their public funding was earmarked for YT and ET programmes, already very underfunded, they were accountable not to the local community but to Central Government for that funding, and they also had a massive workload related to developing NVQs, where they had to deal with 180 Lead Bodies instead of the 10 or 20 common in other countries. 'The rhetoric [is] good but the mechanism [is] very, very poor, I fear for the TECs really,' he said (Neale, 1990).

The results of a first-year monitoring exercise by the Centre for Local Economic Strategies (1991) confirmed many fears. The review said that with 90 per cent of the TECs' budgets earmarked for government schemes, they were delivering low-grade 'make-work' programmes instead of tackling critical skill shortages or providing high-tech training. The review concluded that the national training system was being led by a volatile labour market, and that 'in linking the training system to the most short-term market imperatives, the opportunity to anticipate and respond to long-term structural skill needs is surrendered.' It also found that close links between TECs and their local communities were the exception, and that their private company status was a major barrier to the development of genuine local accountability.

In April 1992, a Warwick Business School survey (Gribben, 1992) revealed growing unease among TECs about their funding and their ability to fulfil their remit. The survey commented:

> Government policy has moved an alarming distance from the lofty ideals of a skills revolution in a remarkably short time. Its primary concern appears to be to reduce public expenditure on training despite there being no evidence of a commensurate increase in privately funded training.

The study said that rising unemployment would put the TECs under immense pressures to provide short-term palliatives, whereas the real need was to improve the quality of training and change employer attitudes to training responsibilities. It noted the structural weakness of the

TEC framework, the chronic lack of resources, and the Government's 'retreat' on the issue of national training. It concluded: '[The councils] cannot credibly be charged with the prime responsibility for taking forward a skills revolution.'

Sectoral level

It has already been noted that the Non-Statutory Industry Training Organisations (NSTOs) do not appear to have been effective. In February 1991 it was announced that the Department of Employment was conducting a study to try to raise their standards.

Thus far the conclusion seems inescapable: that the vision and mission for NVET, while meaningful, beg many controversial questions; and that the framework and initiatives at local and sectoral level seem unlikely to be able to implement strategy effectively and consistently.

National level

Here, the main preoccupation is the national framework of vocational qualifications. Bryan Nicholson, NCVQ Chairman, believes that it is the consensus and commitment to training which distinguishes 1990 from the early 1980s. 'You are getting policy which is agreed with, and delivery on the ground' (Hodges, 1990). In fact, the difficulties facing delivery of that policy are formidable. Apart from the need to have an effective national system for policy-making and control (see the end of this chapter) there are other problem areas.

Maintenance of vocational qualification standards

The system is popular in certain industries which previously had few recognized qualifications, for example the retail industry which at that time had about 33,000 people registered on NVQ courses. However, as Hughes pointed out in *The Independent* (1991), the main deficiency is in the numbers of people qualified at intermediate and craft levels, and there were in 1991 fewer people emerging with craft-level qualifications in engineering than there were a decade before. Furthermore, some fear that the NVQ system will deteriorate into a mass of standards set at the very low levels which have no equivalent across the rest of Europe.

There is also the fear that while useful harmonization is likely to occur at Levels 3 and 4, where currently there is much confusion among craft and technical qualifications and standards; at Level 5 there are such limitations in the descriptions and concepts relating to standards that professional bodies will not participate sufficiently. The IPD feels that there has been lack of attention to the variations in the job brought about by different work settings: there needs to be a focus on workplace knowledge, professional knowledge, political sensitivity and the personal strengths needed for the job (Pickard, 1991).

Assessment, maintenance, and control of standards

Rather than having assessment done by 400 or so interested parties as in the UK, Dore (1987) called for a 'national network of skill-testing centres which would provide a framework for all testing activities for lower-level skills which are bought and sold regularly in the market place; a separation of training and certification at higher levels of skills; and state subsidy and control primarily for the definition, testing and meaningful certification of standards of competence'.

Another issue is the need for a rigorous and standardized system for assessing workplace learning, and for accrediting prior learning in order to recognize the work achievement of older people and allow them to continue up the vocational training ladder. A particularly thorny issue is to do with the plan to relate GCSE to NVQs (see pp. 35 and 71).

Finally, there needs to be strategic, long-term planning, and the maintainance of standards through time: 'How will the standards be maintained? Can the providers of training deliver the goods? Can they provide reliable, valid assessment at an acceptable price in all our industries?' (Willmott, 1991) And who will take over the task of the Lead Bodies, most of whom have been established with a limited life and depend on project funding from the Government?

The dangers of bureaucratization and underresourcing

The fear of bureaucratization is exemplified by the Bradford and Bingley Building Society's threat to break away from the NVQ system because of the time and paperwork involved in assessing trainees for Level 2 NVQ. Building societies have also been critical of the high degree of simulation required, arising from the great variety of activities being included in the NVQ (*Personnel Management Plus*, 1991a).

Inadequate resourcing has already hit the work of the National Curriculum Council, and there is widespread concern in schools about the time and staff resources needed to perform effectively the tasks of testing, assessing, and profiling pupils on the scale and to the standards required.

Setting adequate targets for NVET

Finally, there is the criticism that targets set for NVET are too low. Yates (1990) sees the UK needing an estimated £1½–2 billion additional expenditure every year to achieve adequate vocational training for all and increased participation in higher education. He urges a national target of no able-bodied person being employed below the age of 19 unless they are undertaking vocational training on an organized basis with the aim of achieving internationally recognized qualifications (i.e. Level 3 or above). The target exceeds that set by the Government (see p. 34), but Yates stresses the need for it in order to ensure a flow of skilled craftsmen, 'supported by well-trained semi-skilled people who underpin the whole of the trained technical population, and professional engineers'.

The National Framework for Vocational Qualifications

Briefly outline the main difficulties facing the implementation of the national strategy to improve vocational qualifications.
(The information needed to reply to the question is contained in the preceding paragraphs.)

FEEDBACK NOTES

Apart from the need to have an effective national system for its co-ordination, the main difficulties include:

- Maintenance of vocational qualification standards
- Assessment of standards
- Bureaucratization and underresourcing
- Setting adequate targets for NVET

What Kind of System and Incentives Should There Be for NVET?

There are strong indicators that there should be a quite tightly regulated system, with considerable financial incentives.

The inevitability of short-termism, and a lack of overall balance

The 1991 Hatfield Polytechnic survey suggested that a recession would reveal the fundamental flaws of a voluntary training strategy, with TECs facing repeated government cutbacks in their training budgets and unable to avoid cutbacks in training similar to those seen in the last recession. The Government was urged to take a lead by formulating a long-term training strategy. The PA survey (1990) pointed to the problems of catering for national training needs, given the preoccupation of TECs with their brief of responding to local needs, and emphasized the importance of ensuring a comprehensive national training programme with a national framework for monitoring, evaluation and adjustment.

The inevitability of the poaching cycle

Yates (1990) observed that smaller companies, lacking financial and other resources and in a generally vulnerable position, could not be blamed for poaching, nor could larger companies for failing to 'act as charities and over-train'. 'It cannot be left to the simple matter of choice or voluntary participation.'

Unfavourable comparisons with EC systems

In its 1990 *Report on Vocational Training and Retraining* the House of Lords Select Committee on European Communities drew attention to the fact that the UK has far less legislative underpinning of its vocational training system and far fewer equitable methods of dealing with the funding of training, than most of its EC partners. *Personnel Management Plus* (1990c) said that a 'legal and financial framework is required to encourage employers to play their full part in the provision of training and development opportunities'.

The need to ensure adequate VET for 16–18-year-olds

Further legal measures were called for by Sir John Cassells, former Director-General of NEDO to require employers to provide training for all 16–18-year-olds, leading to recognized qualifications, and to place limits on young people's pay levels. He foresaw that without legislation 'the labour market will continue to operate as it has in the past'. Companies need to regard 18 as the normal age at which to recruit young people, and should make it clear to recruits that they expect them to have acquired relevant qualifications (Policy Studies Institute Report, 1990).

The need to ensure that the costs of learning are shared

In October 1990 the IPM strategy document on training called for the costs of learning to be shared between Government, employers and employees, since it is an investment in the future for all of them. 'It would not be unreasonable if the state paid for all off-the-job vocational and general education provided to young people, with the employer paying for on-the-job training, and the young person "paying" by accepting a trainee's instead of a worker's wage.' It also calls for employers and individuals to share the costs of adult learning, and for incentives for the self-employed and unemployed that go wider than the present tax allowances for those studying for NVQs.

> The Government's belief in 1989 was that the TEC framework would resolve problems of implementation and produce the change in attitudes that had so far failed to take place. Evidence in this chapter suggests that there is every likelihood that such a national policy and framework will be insecure as long as they are held in place by little more than the shifting philosophy, politics and reactions of successive governments, together with a reliance on voluntary, collaborative and effective effort in a decentralized structure which still contains inadequate incentives for individuals and for employers.

Will an Integrated and Effective NVET System be Achieved?

Finally, let us look at the current state of play in the educational sector, and at how far the reforms described in Chapter 2 seem likely to be successful, leading to a coherent, effective, integrated NVET system.

Quality of schooling

Here, the main problem is putting muscle into the rhetoric of reform. As Hughes points out in a compelling article in *The Independent* (1992), this means that as well as reform of the primary and secondary curriculum, there must also be increased resources to train teachers, update their skills and fundamentally alter many of their attitudes in relation to classroom management and curricular priorities. Teacher quality is a prime consideration, yet there is no sign of a policy on primary teacher training, and the whole scenario in relation to the appraisal of teachers is in confusion, with many threatening to black the initiative because of its implied threat to job security. Moreover, the Government has announced that 66 per cent of the responsibility for the initial training of secondary teachers will take place in 'training schools' in both state and private sectors, where senior staff will act as mentors. However, it is unclear how such staff are to be trained and appraised in their roles; and there are still no government guidelines on the transfer of funds from higher education institutions. A *Daily Telegraph* editorial (June 1992) expressed concern at these areas of ambiguity and at the Government's failure to give schools a clear leading role in their new 'partnerships' with education departments.

Reforms in the National Curriculum

Here, confusion reigns:

> How are the aims of the National Curriculum going to be matched with its controversial testing system, let alone GCSE and post-16 qualifications? . . . The School Examinations and Assessment Council is drastically restructuring GCSE and repeatedly redesigning National Curriculum tests, with little regard for the inevitable effect of those changes on the National Curriculum itself . . . [Meanwhile] . . . the National Curriculum Council is embarking on a review of the National Curriculum, asking teachers their needs and the problems they are encountering (Hughes, 1992).

Clearly the two bodies need to be amalgamated to achieve coherence and integration in the policy and structure for the National Curriculum and for assessment.

The issue goes wider than that: GCSEs and A levels have to be related to NVQs. Here, there are further concerns. One is that, if the NCVQ moves towards broadly based, occupational, as opposed to industry-specific, qualifications, NVQs will lose their direct relevance to the people on the shop floor and become 'an education instead of a training model' (Arkin, 1991). Another is that retaining A levels in their present form will preclude the broadening of the sixth-form curriculum and prevent parity of esteem for the new NVQs in the eyes of parents and employers – and NVQs will only acquire real value if they are demanded by employers and recognized by higher pay. Furthermore, there is still no help for those who need a less stringent course than A or AS level, and no credit for a one-year course of study. In Chapter 4 we shall see the reforms that certain influential educationalists and training experts believe are necessary if our educational system is to improve its outputs to something like the level of those in key competitor countries.

The structure for delivery

Here again, there is confusion. With the autonomy offered to schools and to institutions in the further and higher education sector, the role of local education authorities is unclear. Hughes (1992) predicts that there will soon be several authorities in which most secondary schools have opted out of local authority control, and observes that already budgetary control has been devolved to all schools. In the event of a mass opting-out, either new regional funding councils would have to be created to manage the distribution of funds to schools, or the local administration of schools would have to be transferred to directly elected school boards. In May 1992 Crequer reported that a third county – Warwickshire – was poised to join Cambridgeshire and Kent in 'proposing a mass opt-out of secondary schools from local authority control', and that the Department of Education:

> . . . has become concerned about a potential wave of mass opt-outs . . . It does not have a structure to cope with such a response and is already drawing up plans for new regional bodies to have an overseeing role.

Meanwhile, the shape of the planned new independent inspection service for schools is also unclear, with membership possibly comprising an uneasy partnership drawn from Her Majesty's Inspectorate, private consultancies and local inspectorates. As Hughes (1992) says, 'Is it wise to transform the structure of our education service so radically without having any clearly expressed goal in mind?'

The view at the top of the whole structure looks no better.

> The struggle between the government departments of education and employment for supremacy in the area of education and training for employment has bedevilled progress throughout most of this century, and never more so than in the last two decades. (Kenny, 1990)

In 1986 there did seem to be real hope for a workable national framework for VET. The MSC had assumed a central role, aiming for 'an integrated, national strategy for managing change in education and training across the entire age range – from school to the mature, even advanced, ages of adult working life.' (Keep, 1986, quoting Bryan Nicholson, then MSC Chairman) At the same time the Government was pursuing a policy of encouraging a switch away from the humanities and towards science and technological subjects; and there was speculation that at last there was going to be a formal merger between the Department of Education and the MSC to create a single Ministry of Education and Training. (Ibid.)

Then came an about-turn: the MSC disappeared in the restructuring of 1989; and changes in the method of funding secondary and tertiary education shifted the locus of control from local education authorities towards the state on the one hand, but also to the unpredictabilities of the market on the other. Despite major changes announced in 1991 to introduce a new post-16 vocational education and training sector by 1994 (see pp. 38–41), the Department of Education and Science and the Department of Employment remain separate bodies.

The TECs have to ensure that the present decentralized, deregulated system of secondary and tertiary education provides outcomes relevant to local needs. In 1990 the £105 million budget for work-related further education was transferred from the Department of Employment to TECs, and concern was expressed at their inexperience in this field. (*Personnel Management*, December 1990) A year later (*Personnel Management*, November 1991) Geoffrey Holland admitted that TEC boards still needed to develop a full understanding of their responsibilities in areas such as education, and to become more accountable to their local communities. He said that if things did not progress sufficiently within the next 12 months (i.e. by the end of 1992) 'we may have to move' – a worrying statement.

Summary

Looking at the educational sector, the conclusion is inescapable that policy and goals are confused, and that strategy is becoming ineffective because of problems in implementation. Looking across the wider scene of NVET, by 1992 the whole system was under severe strain. With no single, powerful government body covering vocational education and training, continued fragmentation and confusion of policy and delivery seems inevitable. What is needed is clear: a quite tightly regulated national vocational training system, with adequate financial incentives, integrated with a vocational educational system that has clear and relevant policy goals and a feasible strategy for their implementation. What is less clear is whether these desirable ends will be achieved.

Exercises

1 How might the TECs (or LECs) get local employers to:
   (a) understand the complex VET scene;
   (b) be accurate about what they do and don't do? (May, 1991)

2 'Training is all very well for large organizations, with their substantial resources, easy access to facilities and advanced technical knowledge; small organizations by definition cannot train adequately for future needs, and must recruit trained staff to compete.' Comment on this statement, and outline your preferred approaches by both large and small organizations to expected skills shortages. (November, 1989)

3 What are Training and Enterprise Councils? How do you anticipate that they will influence the future concerning:
   (a) government training schemes;
   (b) skills shortages;
   (c) further education? (May, 1989)

4 What criteria would you suggest to establish the effectiveness of a Non-Statutory Training Organization (NSTO)? What might the

Department of Employment do to ensure that NSTOs respect these criteria and wish to own them? (November, 1988)

References

AINLEY P AND CARNEY M. *Training for the Future: The rise and fall of the MSC.* London, Cassell. 1990

ARKIN A. 'A touch of glass'. *Personnel Management*, July 1991. p. 48

'Better Schools'. Government white paper. London, HMSO. 1985

CARR REPORT. *Training for Skills: Recruitment and training of young workers in industry.* National Joint Advisory Council. London, HMSO. 1958

CASSELLS J. 'A system in need of loving care'. *Personnel Management Plus*, June 1991. p. 10

CENTRE FOR LOCAL ECONOMIC STRATEGIES. *Challenging the TECs: the first year interim report of the CLES TECs and LECs monitoring project.* Manchester, CLES. 1991

CHITTY C (ed.). *Post-16 Education: Studies in access and achievement.* London, Kogan Page for University of London Institute of Education. 1990

CLARE J. 'No benefit from £16 bn vocational learning scheme'. *Daily Telegraph.* 26 August 1989

CLEMENT B. 'Voluntary training places halved'. *The Independent.* 15 May 1991

CONSTABLE J AND McCORMICK R. *The Making of British Managers: A report for the British Institute of Management and Confederation of British Industry into management training, education and development.* London, BIM. 1987

COOPERS AND LYBRAND ASSOCIATES. *A Challenge to Complacency: Changing attitudes to training.* Report to the Manpower Services Commission and the National Economic Development Office. Sheffield, MSC. 1985

COWIE A. 'Art of training for life', *Observer*, 24 January 1988

CREQUER N. 'Third county set to propose mass school opt-outs'. *The Independent*, 4 May 1992

DAILY TELEGRAPH. 'Patten's unwise concern'. 8 June 1992. p. 18

DEPARTMENT OF EMPLOYMENT. 'Qualified for success'. *Employment News. No. 161.* London, Department of Employment. January 1988

DORE R. *Taking Japan Seriously: A Confucian perspective on leading economic issues.* London, The Athlone Press. 1987

DUTTON D. *British Politics Since 1945: the rise and fall of consensus.* Historical Association Studies. Oxford, Blackwell. 1991

'Employment and Training: Government Proposals'. Government white paper. London, HMSO. 1973

EMPLOYMENT DEPARTMENT GROUP. *A Strategy for Skills: Guidance from the Secretary of State for Employment on Training, Vocational Education and Enterprise.* London, Department of Employment. 1991

'Employment for the 1990s'. Government white paper. London, HMSO. 1989

GRIBBEN R. 'TECs worried over funding and direction'. *Daily Telegraph*, 21 April 1992

HANDY REPORT. *The Making of Managers.* A report for the NEDC, the MSC and the BIM on management education, training and development in the USA, West Germany, France, Japan and the UK. London, National Economic Development Office. 1987

HATFIELD POLYTECHNIC. 'Can TECs Cope with Recession?' *Economic Report No. 9.* London, Employment Institute. 1991

HODGES C. 'New NCVQ Chairman plans higher profile'. *Personnel Management Plus*, November 1990. p. 7

HOLLAND G. 'Training for the Nation: The grand design'. *Personnel Management*, October 1975

HOUSE OF LORDS SELECT COMMITTEE. *Report on Vocational Training and Retraining*. October 1990

HOWARD M. *Paper to the National Economic Development Centre*. London, NEDC. January 1991

HUGHES C. 'Credits plan ''will fail to attract young people''.' *The Independent*, 28 May 1991

HUGHES C. 'Memo to John Patten: get on with it'. *The Independent*, 23 April 1992

INSTITUTE OF MANPOWER STUDIES. *Competence and Competition: Training and Education in the Federal Republic of Germany, the United States and Japan*. London, MSC/National Economic Development Office. 1984

INSTITUTE OF PERSONNEL MANAGEMENT. 'High-tech firms need more investment in new skills'. News section, *Personnel Management*, December 1991a. p. 10

INSTITUTE OF PERSONNEL MANAGEMENT. 'High-tech company grows its own skilled staff to beat labour shortage'. News section, *Personnel Management*, December 1991b. p. 12

INSTITUTE OF PERSONNEL MANAGEMENT. *A National Strategy for Education, Training and Development.* Consultative paper prepared by the National Committee for Training and Development. London, IPM. 1990

JOHNSTON P. 'Leaked minute reveals concern on training cuts'. *Daily Telegraph*, 8 August 1990

KAUFMAN M. 'Is there a future for training?' *National Association of Teachers in Further and Higher Education Journal*, May 1981. pp. 23–5

KEEP E. 'Can Britain build a coherent vocational training system?' *Personnel Management*, August 1986. pp. 28–31

KENNEY J AND REID M. *Training Interventions*. London, Institute of Personnel Management, 1986; third edition, by Reid, Barrington and Kenney. 1992

KENNY T. Book review. *Personnel Management*, August 1990. pp. 64–5

LAWRENCE J. 'Getting to grips with the British disease'. *Personnel Management*, January 1977

MACLURE S. *Missing Links: The challenge to further education.* London, Policy Studies Institute. 1990

NEALE F. 'Personnel Profile: Ron Johnson'. *IPM Digest*, June 1990. pp. 9–10

'A New Training Initiative'. Government white paper. London, HMSO. 1981

PA CAMBRIDGE ECONOMIC CONSULTANTS. *The Cambridge Regional Economic Review*. Department of Land Economy, University of Cambridge. 1990

PERRY P J C. *The evolution of British Manpower Policy*. London, British Association for Commercial and Industrial Education. 1975

PERSONNEL MANAGEMENT. 'Market-led approach will limit ability to tackle skills crisis'. *Personnel Management*, January 1991a. p. 11

PERSONNEL MANAGEMENT. 'Sheerness Steel wins IPM/Compass award for achievements in resourcing'. *Personnel Management*, October 1991b. p. 13

PERSONNEL MANAGEMENT PLUS. 'TVEI is being undermined by budget cuts, says opposition'. *Personnel Management Plus*, August 1990a. p. 5

PERSONNEL MANAGEMENT PLUS. 'Special needs providers hit by cutback in Youth Training budget'. *Personnel Management Plus*, September 1990b. p. 10

PERSONNEL MANAGEMENT PLUS. 'Case made for legislation on vocational training'. *Personnel Management Plus*, October 1990c. p. 45

PERSONNEL MANAGEMENT PLUS. 'Responsibility for work-related further education goes to TECs'. *Personnel Management Plus*, December 1990. p. 5

PERSONNEL MANAGEMENT PLUS. 'NVQ system is "too bureaucratic" '. *Personnel Management Plus*, May 1991a. p. 6

PERSONNEL MANAGEMENT PLUS. 'Holland says TECs must move'. *Personnel Management Plus*, November 1991b. p. 12

PICKARD J. 'Awards for employees who go through the mill'. *Personnel Management*, February 1990. pp. 36–41

PICKARD J. 'IPM claims new training standards fail to address essential points'. *Personnel Management Plus*, February 1991. p. 3

POLICY STUDIES INSTITUTE. *Britain's Real Skill Shortage*. London, Policy Studies Institute. May 1990

TRAINING AGENCY. *Training and Enterprise Councils: A prospectus for the 1990s*. Sheffield, Training Agency. 1989

'Training for Employment'. Government white paper. London, HMSO. 1988

'Training for the Future'. Government white paper. London, HMSO. 1972

WHITFIELD M. 'Age limit on training for the unemployed'. *The Independent*, 11 February 1991

WILLMOTT T. 'The standard response to training'. *Personnel Management*, July 1991. p. 6

YATES I R. In *Proc. Conference Board European Human Resources Conference*, London, 28 November 1990. London, Conference Board. 1990

YOUTHAID. *Leave it Out – Young People Leaving the Youth Training Scheme 1983–1986*. London, Youthaid. 1986

Further useful reading

KEEP E. 'A Training scandal'. In *Personnel Management in Britain* (Sisson K, ed.). Oxford, Blackwell. 1989

LINDLEY J. 'Training and competitiveness'. *Collection of papers from a private seminar, summer 1990*. London, NEDO. January 1991

MANCHESTER UNIVERSITY CONTINUING EDUCATION AND TRAINING RESEARCH UNIT. *Continuing Education and Training of the Long-term Unemployed in the UK.* Manchester, MUCETRU. 1990

REID W. 'Setting standards for the future'. *Personnel Management* August 1992. pp. 28–31

STEVENS J AND MACKAY T (eds). *Training and Competitiveness.* London, Kogan Page 1991

Chapter 4

International comparisons and pressures

Learning Objectives

After reading this chapter you will:

1 understand the key differences between NVET philosophies, policies and systems in our key competitor countries and in the UK;
2 be able to assess what lessons the UK should learn from these differences;
3 be able to assess what individual organizations in the UK can usefully and feasibly learn and apply from such comparisons;
4 understand the main implications of entry into the single European market for NVET policy and practice in the UK, and for the training function in British organizations.

In Chapters 2 and 3 we looked back at national training policy over the years and found little evidence that a decentralized, loosely regulated voluntary system can work, either in ensuring commitment from individuals and employers to invest adequately in the skills needed to promote economic productivity, growth and competitiveness, or in achieving a well-integrated, high-quality and effective NVET system.

We will now look at key features of NVET systems in some of our international competitor countries. Comparisons are difficult because of the many economic, cultural, industrial and educational differences between countries. France and Germany are comparable in size to the UK, but the history of union-employer relationships in Germany, for example, is quite different, and helps to explain much of the success of the national training system and strategy. Reliable and meaningful comparative data is also difficult to obtain, and areas of emphasis and methods of evaluation vary significantly from country to country.

None the less, there are still valuable insights to be obtained from some comparisons and contrasts. We will first take an international overview, and then examine the systems of individual countries in some detail, paying most attention to Germany, France and Japan, where there are particularly important lessons for the UK. We will then look at the main implications for training and development of entry into the single European market and conclude with some guidelines for the UK and for individual organizations.

Some Key Differences Between Countries

National investment in education

In 1989 less than 33 per cent of the labour force in Britain had vocational qualifications, whereas in Germany the figure was around 65 per cent and in France around 40 per cent. Furthermore in 1986 only 15 per cent of young French people left full-time education without completing a vocational course, and more than 70 per cent of 16–18-year-olds were staying on in full-time education compared to just over 30 per cent in the UK. (Steedman, 1990) In France, technical subjects can start at 13 or 14, as they can in Belgium, Luxembourg, Ireland and the Netherlands. In Greece, vocational education can start at 15. In the UK, on the other hand, the vocational education which starts at 14 is still considered to be poorly resourced and ineffectively integrated with mainstream academic pathways (see Chapters 2 and 3).

In the UK, the cost of industrial training is borne in the main by employers, and this goes far to explain the consistently inadequate investment made in training (see Chapter 3). In Sweden the State pays for the integrated upper secondary school, and in Italy, France, Belgium, Luxembourg and the Netherlands the State pays for full-time training. In both France and Germany apprentices receive only a modest income (Johnson, 1984a), whereas in Britain, as noted in Chapter 3, starting wages at 16 can be high and are not tied to vocational qualifications, thus acting as a disincentive for young people to aim for such qualifications.

After the Second World War Japan, Germany and the Netherlands rebuilt their educational systems and students in their schools today lead the world in advanced mathematics, science and other technical subjects. (*Newsweek*, 1991) The way that the money is spent matters more than the amount: Germany and Japan spend about 50 per cent less than the USA, yet consistently rank higher. Countries that value educators and education tend to keep students in school longer: in

South Korea, for example, 55 per cent of students go on to college.

Teachers in Germany are extremely well paid, and many have the rank of civil servant, with job tenure and attractive fringe benefits. Teacher training is rigorous and operates at a very high academic standard, with every type of school requiring its own kind of training course. It is therefore not surprising that some of the best brains in Germany move into teaching, and that supply heavily outweighs demand. In Japan, too, teacher salaries are high, and the profession holds high status.

The USA tends to invest more money in buildings and administration, with relatively less going on teacher salaries. There is increasing concern at poor standards of teaching and attainment in the American secondary education system, and the Bush administration launched the 'America 2000' reforms in the early 1990s, calling for an overhaul of mathematics and science instruction. There is a similar picture in the UK: the pay and status of the teaching profession have, for many years, been far too low to attract sufficient high-ability recruits. This, coupled with a secondary education system that has not focused adequately on science and technology, has led to a critical undersupply of teachers in those subjects.

Emphasis on full-time education and training for 16–18-year-olds, and on effective vocational preparation

Although the school-leaving age across Europe ranges between 14 to 16, there is already a major emphasis on extending full-time education and training to the age of 18 in Sweden, Belgium, Luxembourg, Greece, and Ireland. There is a similar emphasis in France, but there both full-time vocational and apprenticeship training are important for the age group. In Germany and the Netherlands, part-time attendance at a school or college is compulsory up to the age of 18. In Denmark the emphasis is on young school leavers moving into the apprenticeship system, as it is in Germany where, however, the term covers most jobs that 16-year-olds can be employed to do.

On the other hand in Britain, as we saw in Chapter 3, attempts have only just begun to develop a unified sector of vocational education and training for the 16–18-year-old age group, and in 1990 only 53 per cent of children were staying on at school or college. Although the proportion of those aged 16 and 17 in education and training combined rose to 78 per cent in that year, much of that proportion would be on YT programmes where there were low rates of completion and of attainment of vocational qualifications.

Assessment of occupational standards

In most competitor countries, including Japan, occupational training is tied to the attainment of national standards, and examinations are rigorously controlled by independent bodies or by partnership bodies of employers, unions and educationalists. In Britain, there is some slow progress towards a national vocational qualification system, and the assessment of standards is still being left to around 400 examining and industrial training bodies, all of which are also involved in the design of the courses and often in their delivery. There is no proposal for any independent national system of assessment of standards.

Coverage of industrial training

Each year, Germany trains twice as many mechanics, electricians, construction workers per head of the workforce as the UK, and even more office and distributive trade workers. (Prais and Wagner, 1981; Prais, 1985) In the UK, management and supervisory training now get the highest level of investment, followed by technical and professional training, and then blue-collar worker training. Clerical training is very poor in both quantity and quality compared to France and Germany (Steedman, 1987), and there are relatively poor opportunities for women. This uneven distribution of the training investment in the UK means that there is a serious shortage of skills in the middle and lower ranks of the workforce, and this impedes many organizations' ability to implement technological change and more flexible work patterns.

Training for manual workers in Britain has been almost entirely in the form of apprenticeship, with the cost, after the demise of the ITBs, borne by employers. Unsurprisingly, therefore, between 1964 (when there were 240,000 apprentices in British manufacturing industry) and 1986 (when there were 63,700), there has been a huge decline, with numbers of craftsmen and technicians in basic training in engineering alone estimated to have fallen from 26,141 in 1978 to 13,564 in 1989. (Coughlan, 1991) Young people not on apprenticeship schemes received little or no training until YT programmes were introduced, but only in the early 1990s were significant moves made to focus those programmes on outputs and on meeting local needs (see Chapter 2).

A recent study (Northcott, 1991) shows just how far behind the UK is in terms of its education and training compared to competitor countries, and how urgent is the need to improve the situation. The need is greater because of the changes that will take place over the next 20 years. 'Higher-level jobs will continue to grow fast – professional, scientific, technical, managerial, administration jobs have already grown from 13 per cent of all jobs to 32 per cent in the last 40 years – while the workforce will be ageing, with large inflows of new workers no longer possible because of the demographic downturn (Cassells, 1991). So investment will have to increase dramatically, and training and development will have to be undertaken at all levels, if higher-level jobs are to be performed adequately, and existing workers are to be retrained to meet new work demands.

We can see from this summary that some of the key differences between NVET in the UK and in leading competitor countries are in the areas of:

- National investment in education
- Emphasis on full-time education and training for 16–18-year-olds, and on effective vocational preparation
- Assessment of occupational standards
- Coverage of industrial training

Now let us look at some distinctive features of NVET in key competitor countries, which attribute much of their ability to achieve and sustain a leading edge in world markets to their high investment in the development of their human assets.

Germany (old Federal Republic)

Germany is one of the major industrial countries, fourth in the world in terms of overall economic performance, and second in world trade (Bertelsmann, 1989). In 1974 the then Federal Republic was hit by worldwide recession. The most pressing problems now are a slowing down of economic growth, rising unemployment, general inflationary pressures and, of course, all the economic and labour market pressures created or intensified by reunification. High labour costs mean that 'an increasing number of companies is relocating plant in cheaper countries'. (*Daily Telegraph*, 1992). It will be important to see what, if any, difference such pressures cause in patterns of investment in vocational education and training.

The environment for training 'is set by a strong formalized tradition of training backed by legislation, monitored for content and with recognized qualifications'. (Coopers and Lybrand, 1985) The whole system of vocational education and training is very carefully and rigorously regulated, and carried out by a partnership of the State and employers. The Federal Government is responsible for the training regulations, the Länder governments are responsible for schools, regional Chambers of Commerce and Industry are responsible for overseeing the dual system, and employers are obliged to belong to these bodies. Businesses see it as their responsibility to train young people in order to develop a national pool of labour.

Employers and unions are social partners whose alliance has underpinned the stability of the whole economic system. Recently there have been signs of strains in this alliance, as trade unions have begun, in response to signs of recession, to demand inflationary wage increases 'that bear no relation to productivity gains' (*Daily Telegraph*, 1992). Be that as it may, the unions have always played an active role in helping to decide on the structure and content of training provision, and on manpower plans. 'They represent all workers in an entire branch of industry, and are party-politically and denominationally neutral as well as having the power to withdraw from firms the right to undertake initial training.' (Coopers and Lybrand, 1985)

The Federal Institute for Employment gives young people and adults subsidies and loans for vocational training if needed and also promotes further vocational training and retraining in other skills. This particularly helps the unemployed to adapt their skills to rapidly changing demands on the labour market. The Institute also carries out research into the labour market and vocational training opportunities as an aid to governmental decision-making.

Secondary and tertiary education system

The German reverence for trade crafts is at the heart of its three-track high-school system, considered to be the best in the world. School attendance is compulsory on a full-time basis from the age of 6 to 15, and from the age of 11 about a third of children attend a *Gymnasium* (high school) from which most go on to university. The remaining two thirds attend vocational and technical schools. The principle is enshrined in law that no young person should begin their working life without vocational training, and those under 18 who receive no other form of education are therefore legally bound to attend vocational school. In recent years demand for vocational training has outstripped supply and various initiatives have been introduced to help all children to obtain relevant vocational qualifications.

The three-track system is flexible, allowing qualified vocational and technical students to switch to the *Gymnasium* at any point, while on the other hand some *Gymnasium* students enrol in vocational programmes even after getting into university.

The major pillar of the tertiary education system is the universities, including some technical universities and other specialized institutions of higher education. The average student spends six years at university, emerging with high-level academic or technical qualifications.

For those who leave school at 15 or 16, 'rigorous two- or three-year [apprenticeship] programmes are accepted as the normal entry route to employment and only approved employers can take on school leavers as trainees'. (Coopers and Lybrand, 1985) Apprenticeship training must, by law, be paralleled for three years by education and training at least one day a week, often two, in a vocational school (or, exceptionally, at a centre on the premises of the employer). There, work is carried out according to a prescribed syllabus in which practical on-the-job learning is combined with theoretical instruction. This 'dual' system of training aims 'to provide through a systematic training programme a broadly conceived basic preparation for an occupation and the necessary technical abilities and knowledge to engage in a skilled form of occupational activity'. (Vocational Education and Training Act, 1969)

'Apprenticeship' has a far wider meaning in Germany than in Britain: traineeships relate to all (about 400) officially recognized occupations. Apprenticeship training in firms must, by law, be under the supervision of an appropriately qualified person, usually a *Meister* (a master tradesman), and this system helps to explain the exceptional quality of the skilled trades in Germany. Trainees have a legal contract with their employers, usually for three years, with a training wage which increases annually. The contract is registered with a supervising authority, usually a Chamber of Commerce, that administers qualifying examinations.

Apprenticeship syllabuses are set out in training regulations issued by the Federal Government and occupational examinations are held by the self-governing business organizations designated by the State.

Those who do well in their skilled worker tests and examinations may proceed in further education and training towards technician level or *Meister* qualification. (Johnson, 1984a)

Adult education and development

In Germany continuous education and development is a fundamental concept in order to cope with increasing and ever-changing work demands. Adult education centres, dating back to the end of the nineteenth century, are seen as part of an overall system of further education. They are usually operated communally or by local governments or registered associations, with the Länder contributing funds.

Training programmes for adults in employment tend to be organized half in company time, half in employees' time. Large firms like BMW run major adult development programmes – BMW itself was running a programme involving half of its 45,000 employees in 1984, with the aim of meeting the company's need for a more highly qualified, flexible workforce. The push was for impact on output and results, for obtaining individual commitment to innovation, and for high-quality performance.

In 1985 the Federal Government, the Federal Institute for Employment and the two sides of industry began a broad qualification offensive, aimed at expanding further vocational training in order to preserve and improve the employment prospects of workers, cut unemployment and reduce the shortage of skilled workers. Three quarters of unemployed participants who finish courses successfully find work within half a year, and facilities provided by the State, local authorities, churches, unions, political parties and business organizations are used by over ten million people – more than the whole general school population.

Here is a case study showing what can be done by a British organization basing its approach to vocational education and training on the German dual system model.

Dual system of education and training at Hoechst UK
(With acknowledgements to *Personnel Management*)

Hoescht is a Frankfurt-based chemical conglomerate with an excellent record of vocational training. In 1991 Hoechst UK introduced its own 'dual system' of education and training for British management trainees, basing it on the German management apprenticeship system.

Hoescht is very committed to youth training, but by 1991 the supply of YTS youngsters had dried up, and the company decided to refocus on A level entrants who wanted an alternative to university. Two courses were run in 1991, the first in Frankfurt with five British management trainees. Four of the group, who studied alongside German trainees, were due to finish the modular *Industrie Kaufmeister* course in 18 months, and the fifth in the average time of two years. All scored high in their final examinations.

The second group, of 12 trainees, were based in the UK, and will 'combine practical experience at the three Hoechst sites in the UK with either BTEC or a Diploma in Management course at Thames Valley College or Kingston Polytechnic. Trainees will also learn German at the company's own language laboratory and do business games. They may also spend some time in Frankfurt.' (*Personnel Management*, 1991)

Japan

Cultural pressures also significantly drive training provision in Japan. Japanese firms work continuously to involve employees in the business, taking a long-term, coherent and wide-ranging developmental strategy which includes job rotation and transfer, multi-task working, and participation in quality circles and zero defect groups. Larger firms link quality checks to training for subcontractors. More will be said about this system in Chapters 19 and 21.

Secondary and tertiary education

The differences between the Japanese and British educational systems are profound. In Japan, there is little pre-vocational or vocational training in schools. The purpose of the education system is to lay a broad, non-specialized foundation of knowledge and attitudes to underpin future training, and to set very high standards of educational attainment upon which employers can then build with organization-specific training and development.

Science and technology subjects start in elementary school, where 25 per cent of time goes to science and mathematics. The standard of teaching and attainment in these subjects is exceptional, with a focus on problem-solving and application of knowledge and skills. Central control over the education system is tight. The Ministry of Education 'dictates everything from curricula to the emphasis on rote memorization in math, history and language'. (*Newsweek*, 1991)

Full-time upper secondary education is almost universal, with 96 per cent of young people staying at school up to the age of 18 or 19. Most of that education is general and a decreasing proportion vocational. Forty-two per cent of males and 34 per cent of females enter higher education. (Keep, 1989)

The Japanese education system has a rigidly structured, test-centred national curriculum that 'is superb at producing a capable and efficient work force to keep production booming'; on the other hand 'such regimentation notoriously discourages children from learning to think for themselves' and puts extreme pressures on students. (*Newsweek*, 1991)

Adult training and development

Employers train and develop new recruits in their own training schools and on the job. After a brief period of initial training, all workers (and there is little distinction between blue- and white-collar workers in Japan) are then given as wide a range of experience as is feasible. As employees' years of service increase, so does their carefully organized experience, with broad on-the-job training being supplemented with short in-service off-the-job training periods which, through the years, give a theoretical background to blue-collar workers' wide-ranging experience. Short courses give a wide coverage of topics concerned with management problems, thus giving a widening perspective and understanding.

Because of this continuous development process, their high level of basic education and the encouragement they receive to learn and use standard problem-solving techniques, Japanese workers quickly gain an intellectual understanding of the structure of the machines and products they are dealing with and of the production process. They can thus deal remarkably well with any changes that occur and can usually themselves suggest and determine with their supervisor how to improve efficiency.

Working practices like these are widespread, with an estimated half of even the smallest companies, with less than 50 employees, adopting them for their essential skilled personnel (Koike, 1988). Even in these smallest companies, poaching is not a major problem; it has been estimated that only 20 per cent of such companies look on this approach as an ultimately positive measure rather than one to be adopted out of necessity. (Ibid.)

There is a national skill-testing and qualification system used mainly by smaller companies, which provides a coherent structure for individuals to obtain appropriate training and recognized qualifications. (Coopers and Lybrand, 1985)

In Japan, the culture is for employees to continue learning at work and also to continue education outside work and at their own expense. All big Japanese firms have their own education and training colleges, and some of them – Hitachi and NTT – are international showpieces.

> Every Fujitsu employee reaching the age of 45 goes into the company college for an intensive three months' reassessment to find out what job he or she ought to be doing next. It is expensive, but the firm argues that the individual benefits, those who stand in during their absence benefit, and as a result Fujitsu – and Japan – benefit. (Hayes et al., 1984)

France

France offers the nearest parallel to the British experience, with the difference that the French have resolved their skills shortage and vocational education problems, while we still struggle to deal with ours. The following account is based largely on Steedman (1990).

As in Germany, employers and trade unions work with the authorities in determining the content of vocational training. The educational system in France is, however, dominated by education ministries, and there is therefore a strong tendency towards more general education, with apprentices, as in the UK, impatient with academic subjects which do not seem to help them to do better on the job. (Johnson, 1984a) In the 1960s France had even greater problems of skills shortages and educational levels than Britain now faces. There was also, as in the UK, a widespread reluctance on the part of employers to take a lead in the vocational training of young people. In the ensuing two decades the pace of technological and skills change in the economy was vast, yet France managed to equip her workforce to cope effectively with all the demands that faced it, and in the 1980s 40 per cent of the French working population had acquired at least the CAP (equivalent of a City and Guilds craft certificate and several GCSE passes), an increase of 25 per cent. Thus France, in a ten-year period when Britain made almost no progress in increasing the level of vocational and technical qualifications of its labour force, reached a halfway position between Britain (26 per cent) and Germany (64 per cent).

Steedman (1990) explains that the key to the French success has been its use of targets for vocational attainment, set by successive governments in the 1960s and 1970s, using full-time education to provide courses leading to the combined craft and general education CAP certificates. By 1986 only 15 per cent of young French people left full-time education without completing a course leading to the CAP, and more than 70 per cent of 16–18-year-olds were staying on in full-time schooling, compared to just over 30 per cent as late as 1990 in Britain.

> The most important reason for this difference is that the French system offers something for everybody in this age group . . . A coherent range of qualifications – including theoretical technical courses, applied technology courses and applied vocational courses – means that practically the whole ability range can gain nationally recognized qualifications which are frequently rewarded by higher pay, since collective agreements in France usually link pay to vocational and technical qualifications. The qualifications system has recently been modernized by the crucial addition of a set of vocational A levels which are based on the craft level CAP but can still lead to higher education. (Steedman, 1990)

In Britain in the same decade, 'huge opportunities have been wasted'. Although many young school leavers went through YT programmes, the number emerging with vocational qualifications was slight.

Apprenticeship

Apprenticeship in France is results-orientated, with practical and written tests throughout, and vocational certificates (covering about 300 trades) obtained either through full-time vocational education or through apprenticeship. Vocational certificates entitle the young person to the wages of a basic-level skilled worker. Vocational training is modular, with credits awarded for each module taken, whether or not an entire certificated course is eventually taken or passed.

As in Germany, employers and unions work with the authorities to determine the content of training, and in the trade testing procedures in the apprenticeship system (Johnson, 1984a). As in Germany too, trainees only receive a modest income while undertaking their apprenticeship, which is regulated by negotiated agreements involving employers and unions. The apprenticeship system is regulated by law and partially funded by a remissable apprenticeship tax.

Training in employment

The French have a training tax, set at a minimum level of expenditure (1·4 per cent of total payroll) to be invested in training by qualified trainers, but it has been felt that it leads to irrelevant training, and, as was the case with the now defunct British levy-grant system, that the tax does not perform any central role in the French level of success in building up a skilled, highly qualified workforce. (Coopers and Lybrand, 1985)

Sweden

Sweden pays great attention to full-time education for young people, and to adult education and development.

Secondary and tertiary education

'The general aim of the Swedish integrated upper secondary school is to give students a more uniform starting point for their subsequent educational and vocational activities.' (Johnson, 1984a) About 85 per cent of young people enter upper secondary school at 16 to take one of about 25 'lines' of study which are related to labour market forecasts, and Sweden aims to provide full-time courses for all of its 16-year-olds. Throughout upper secondary school there is a focus on integration of academic, practical and technical work, and there is a strong careers guidance system in operation. Employers generally accept that they should provide training for young people at completion of secondary school studies; it usually takes a further year of training to attain skilled worker level.

Adult training and development

There is a high priority on adult training and development in Sweden, with 2·07 per cent of GNP being spent on training programmes and grants for trainees, four times as much as in the USA. The Government pays tuition fees in full, and good wages to all trainees, and, commensurately, far less is paid out in cash benefits for the unemployed. The adult training drive is very effective, with 70 per cent of trainees finding work within six months of finishing special training courses covering a wide range of vocational skills and knowledge at 100 government-funded centres throughout the country. (*Newsweek*, 1991)

USA

National training system

The ethos of individual initiative and of the innate value of education and training means that individuals invest highly in it. The system is less formalized than in Germany, with the pressure on employers coming more from individuals wanting training or prepared to undertake it on their own intitiative.

> Employer-provided training tends to be arranged in short units as and when required, and employers generally make an effort to fit training in around production, thus minimising the costs of lost output. (Coopers and Lybrand, 1985)

In 1983 a framework of locally based Private Industry Councils (PICs) was set up, responsible for the local implementation of the Job Training Partnership Act, which involves distributing funds for training redundant and disadvantaged unemployed workers. PICs work with local government agencies and training providers to assess local skill requirements, choose and evaluate training programmes, and arrange work placements. They have funds, and their committees have a majority of local business representatives. PICs have met with mixed success, but none the less have provided a major model for the British TEC system.

Although in the USA certain major companies see training and development as a key to longer-term competitive performance, encompassing all sections of their labour forces, this is by no means a universal picture. Germany, France and Japan offer better models for good practice.

What Lessons Can be Learnt from International Comparisons?

How do our competitor countries differ from the UK?

1 **All the countries surveyed in this chapter have a culture that values 'overtraining'**. In the US 'overtraining' means richness and diversity of competence which can be brought to bear on innovation and change; in Germany it reinforces the confidence born of the long cherished aim of technical excellence; and in Japan it is the basis of the twin aims of perfection and the ability to learn so as to assume any new work role successfully. (Hayes et al., 1984) Only in the UK is overtraining generally regarded by employers as wasteful and foolish, an attitude partially caused and certainly excacerbated by the problems of short-termism.

2 **The high value placed on education and training means that in most of our competitor countries they attract a high level of investment, shared between the key parties.** German employers voluntarily bear most of the cost and effort involved, working closely with unions and the authorities to provide a high-quality, rigorously administered and controlled, NVET system. In Japan, the costs are shared by the education system and the employers, with only limited state-sponsored public-sector provision. In France, collective agreements usually link pay to vocational and technical qualifications, and small means-tested allowances are available to pupils in secondary and tertiary education.

3 **In most competitor countries there is a major emphasis on standards and on independent control systems.** It is widely assumed that young people who do not have a degree will be vocationally qualified. In France the use of targets of vocational attainment and the introduction of a coherent range of academic, technical and applied vocational courses into secondary schools has achieved an exceptional improvement in levels of skill and vocational qualifications there. In Germany the aim is that no one without a satisfactorily completed apprenticeship should enter the labour market. By 1984 over 90 per cent of young German people achieved that. It is also illegal in Germany, as it is not in the UK, to stop youth training before it has gone full term, or to stop the off-the-job element

during the training period; and in most EC countries except Britain youth wages are low until a significant level of vocational qualification has been achieved.

4 **In our major competitor countries there is a far higher commitment to adult training, retraining, and continuous development, both in and out of employment.** Johnson (1984b) points out that although the provision of adult education and training in Europe has arisen for the most part in unplanned ways, as it has in the UK, the distinction between education and training is often not as marked, and the distinction between vocational and non-vocational education and training is even less so. Furthermore the need for continuing education and training in order to ensure advancement and adaptation is now widely accepted. In Germany and France, local Chambers of Commerce make training available for employed workers, and in most countries there are now arrangements to train the unemployed – often also to help those likely to become unemployed.

From these and many other differences between NVET in the UK and in leading competitor countries, the main lesson to be learnt is clearly, that further reforms are urgently needed.

Reforms needed in the educational system

In October 1991 an independent commission of leading educationalists in the UK, including Prof. A H Halsey, an influential Labour Party supporter, and Prof. S J Prais, produced an 18-point plan to bring British schooling up to Continental standards (Clare, 1991). They observed that in Britain the organization of education meant that children of average and below average ability could not reach levels of educational attainment now common throughout Europe (see Figure 3).

Reforms needed in youth training

The following points are based mainly on comments made by Johnson (1984a) after he examined patterns of youth training in the UK, France, Germany and Sweden. They remain valid today.

Figure 3

Changes needed to bring British education up to continental standards

Proposals by Halsey and Prais

- 11-year-olds should not enter secondary education until they have a basic competency in literacy and numeracy.
- Pupils should be able to choose an academic, technical or vocational path in secondary schools.
- All 14-year-olds should reach minimum standards across a range of subjects.
- A levels should be broadened so that most pupils on an academic or technical path should study four or five subjects.

Additional proposals by Steedman (1990):

- Adequate national targets of vocational attainment.
- A range of technical and vocational qualifications to be accredited by the GCSE boards working with BTEC and NVQ.
- Offering financial help, where needed, to increase staying-on rates at school after 16. At present, those who stay on after that age forego the chance of earnings – often surprisingly high – or of a YT allowance.
- Employers to be discouraged, especially by TECs, from recruiting unqualified 16-year-olds and paying them attractive wages. Preference should be given to better-qualified 18-year-olds.

- **Need for training up to skilled worker level.** All young people who leave school must have the opportunity to be trained up to skilled worker level, under a national system where there are agreed definitions of competence and how it can be assessed in a practical sense.
- **Need for a legal framework, and programmes to achieve recognized occupational standards.**

> 'Without a legal framework, without further work on occupational training competence and without programmes which enable young people to achieve recognized standards of practical ability, it is difficult to see how a skilled workforce can be developed in the future.

- **Need for political will.** As we concluded in Chapter 3, it is unlikely that anything less than a well-regulated system, coupled with adequate financial incentives for employers and individuals, will achieve that political will amongst employers, unions and Government in the UK.
- **Need for training for flexibility.** When future patterns of demand for skills are so unpredictable, flexibility of skills at an early age is vital. It also gives young people a wider career choice. In Germany attempts are being made to establish a basic vocational training year in apprenticeships, and in France there is a twin focus on broadening general education and developing core transferable competences in training programmes. 'Studies have shown that over a 10 year period up to half the skilled workers in Germany move into alternative occupations – generally without undue difficulty.'

Reforms needed in adult training and development

With regard to adult training, both in and out of employment, despite the fanfare of changes introduced in the MSC's *Towards an Adult Training Strategy* (1983), including the establishment of the Open Tech, programmes for training the unemployed, and, in 1986, the launch of the Open College, training for adults is still patchy and inadequate.

As Johnson (1984b) observes:

> A mere description of the systems used in various countries fails to convey adequately one essential message. On the Continent, adult education and training is taken seriously by individuals, employers, trade unions and governments alike . . . The vital ingredient is the commitment of top people . . . You can find all the best methods here; the question is, do we have the will to use them to the full to enable our people to cope with change, to manage their lives and to create their future?

Implications of Joining the Single European Market

There is one final area of importance to examine in this chapter: the education and training implications for the UK of joining the single European market.

> We can identify two kinds of implications: those related to the need to conform with Community requirements; and those related to helping the individual organization manage its move into a wider European context.

The EC is taking many steps to improve training provision in the 12 member states at national level, and programmes are being guided and supported by collective initiatives at EC level. The information that follows has been extracted from Mill (1990).

Mill explains that there are seven areas on which the European Commission is concentrating action until 1992. Funded programmes operate in each of these areas:

- Improving the quality of education systems
- Language and culture
- Higher education
- Initial and continuing vocational training
- Technology
- Youth training
- Free movement and recognition of qualifications

Thus, for example, there is a special programme for small and medium-sized enterprises under the 'initial and continuing vocational training' heading, and an organization wishing to mount an innovatory initiative in that area might well be able to obtain financial support from the EC to support it.

The European Social Fund 'is a principal source of community funding for these ongoing vocational training programmes', aiming both to improve young people's employment prospects and to help combat long-term unemployment and aid regional development. In 1988 the UK and Ireland received the highest levels of assistance from EC funding, mainly in relation to YT programmes.

> The Social Charter states that 'every European Community worker must be able to have access to vocational training throughout their working life', and its action programme gives a high priority to vocational training. All member states are to aim for continual vocational training systems that will enable all working people to improve their skills or acquire new skills, especially in the light of technological development.

The aim underpins the British determination to reform and improve its own vocational training system, with clear targets to be achieved by the year 2000 (see p. 19).

Most occupations which in the UK are known as 'professions' are controlled in other EC countries too, and the basic effect of an EC directive of December 1989 will be to allow a qualified professional (one who has had at least three years' university-level training) to practise in any member state they choose, without the need to requalify.

Furthermore, as Johnson (1991) points out, if an individual wishes to set up a business, offer services as a self-employed person or obtain a job in the EC, they may need a particular vocational qualification. The position regarding all such 'regulated' occupations below the professional level is much less clear, and for the large percentage of occupations that are not 'regulated' at all, the task of harmonization is immense.

> What is obvious from examining the complex current situation is that Britain has no choice but to press urgently ahead with the task of achieving a national vocational qualification system covering all levels of profession and occupation.

Individual organizations too must take action if they are to maintain a competitive edge in Europe. Mill (1990) sees the following needs having training implications for most organizations:

- The need to understand new regulations and changes to old ones, and to be aware of EC developments affecting the organization
- The need for language skills and cultural awareness as organizations develop contacts with other member states
- The need to understand education and training qualifications of member states, to 'know how to recruit from the European pool, and be aware of the pay and benefits being offered by their competitors in other parts of the community'
- The need to equip people at all levels of the organization with the skills, knowledge and attitudes needed 'to face the new competition from other member states and to take new market opportunities'

The main effect of the single European market will be to remove barriers to free trade throughout the EC and therefore expose most organizations to the effects of global competition.

Employee Training and development at Banco Bilbao, Vizcaya, Spain
(based on Portela, 1989)

What changes did attempts to improve the banks' ability to compete in the Single Market make to the training function in the following case?

Banco Bilbao Vizcaya (BBV) was formed in 1988 by the merger of two major Spanish banks. Spain had entered the EC in 1986, and the merger took place in an attempt to improve both banks' ability to compete in the single European market.

The new bank had a number of challenges to face:

- Increased competition for key staff, particularly because of the entry of foreign banks into Spain
- A resultant need for better incentive and reward strategies – taxation is at a high level in Spain, so offering more competitive salaries could not, of itself, guarantee improved recruitment and performance; new ways of creating staff loyalty and commitment would need to be achieved
- Reduction in manning levels because of tightening financial margins
- Retraining of bank employees to improve their commercial skills and attitudes; to achieve higher levels of service and quality; and to ensure flexibility in relation to modernization
- Developing a high-calibre management team, able to respond effectively to competitiveness in the market and achieve specific results

> Training was seen as the lever of change in preparing staff and senior management for the new market. After 1987, BBV's four-year plan covered the following areas: new business specialization; management ability; products and services; operational administration; and corporate identity. The latter was particularly crucial since the corporate cultures of the two banks were completely different prior to the merger.
>
> The aims of the training initiatives were: to bring a new reality to the company; to orient both senior management and administrative staff to a client and quality focus; to increase the overall profit-orientation through management by objectives; to introduce new technology effectively; and to build effective leadership and the ability to manage change. (Portela, 1989)

FEEDBACK NOTES

In this case study the kind of changes needed in the training function typify those facing an increasing number of organizations after 1992. Steven Mann, Senior Vice President and Managing Director of Zenger-Miller International, USA, observed (1989) that organizations will need to have a valid corporate strategy, and to greatly improve quality, service, innovation, cost reduction and productivity. This, in turn, means effective teamwork at all levels, decentralized decision-making, and new, more customer-led work processes. The training function will see the following changes (Mann, 1989):

- Greater importance and responsibility of the function
- Greater involvement in strategy
- Greater volumes of training
- More training further down in the organization
- More objective-oriented training
- More management involvement in training
- More internally run training
- More emphasis on practical skills

Thus the implications of entry to the single market for the training function in most organizations are considerable: in direct terms, most organizations will need to improve the vocational qualifications and skills of their workforces in order to comply with EC regulations and to achieve a better competitive edge in widening markets.

The wide-ranging impact of the single market will also mean that most organizations should, like BBV in Spain, use training as one of their main levers to enable them to operate effectively, attract and retain employees from a wider pool of labour, and ensure the high calibre of managers needed.

Exercises

1 What are the employee development implications for employers of the advent of the single European market? What should your organization be doing now with these things in mind? (November, 1989)

2 From your knowledge of international comparisons related to NVET practices, what sort of goals and policies should employers be

installing in their organizations, even if they are not currently directly competing in international markets? Why?

3. From information you can obtain about the UK apprenticeship system, what are its weaknesses compared to apprenticeship in major competitor countries; and what is being done to tackle these weaknesses by your local TECs and other concerned bodies?

References

BERTELSMANN J. *Facts about Germany*. Lexicon Verlag. 1989

CASSELLS J. 'Preparing ourselves for the year 2010'. *Personnel Management Plus*, March 1991. p. 10

CLARE J. 'European methods urged to improve school standards'. *Daily Telegraph*, 23 October 1991

COOPERS AND LYBRAND ASSOCIATES. *A Challenge to Complacency: Changing attitudes to training*. A report to the Manpower Services Commission and the National Economic Development Office, Sheffield, MSC. 1985

COUGHLAN D. 'The disappearing trainees'. *Daily Telegraph*, 9 May 1991

DAILY TELEGRAPH. 'Germany loses momentum'. *Daily Telegraph*, 17 January 1992

HAYES C, ANDERSON A AND FONDA N. 'International competition and the role of competence'. *Personnel Management*, September 1984. pp. 36-8

JOHNSON R. 'Youth training in Europe'. *Personnel Management*, July 1984a. pp. 24-6

JOHNSON R. 'Adult training in Europe'. *Personnel Management*, August 1984b. pp. 24-7

JOHNSON R. 'Europe finds its true vocation'. *Personnel Management*, August 1991. p. 17

KEEP E. 'A training scandal?' In *Personnel Management in Britain* (Sisson K, ed.) Oxford, Blackwell. 1989

KOIKE K. *Industrial Relations in Modern Japan*. London, Macmillan. 1988

MANN S. 'Training for Europe – new programme demands: a consultant's perspective'. In *Proc. EFMD Economist Unit Conference: 1992 and beyond – practical approaches to the human resource and management development issues, Brussels, 2–3 March 1989*. London, Economist Unit. 1989

MANPOWER SERVICES COMMISSION. *Towards an Adult Training Strategy*, Sheffield, MSC. 1983

MILL C. 'A co-ordinated approach to vocational training'. *Personnel Management*, September 1990. pp. 29-30

NEWSWEEK. 'The best schools in the world'. *Newsweek*, 2 December 1991. pp. 38-50

NORTHCOTT J AND PSI RESEARCH TEAM. *Britain in 2010*. London, Policy Studies Institute. 1991

PERSONNEL MANAGEMENT. 'German apprenticeship scheme introduced for sixth-formers by Hoechst'. *Personnel Management*, May 1991. p. 9

PORTELA M. 'Managing human resources for 1992 – the Banco Bilbao Vizcaya experience. In *Proc. EFMD/Economist Unit Conference: 1992 and beyond – practical approaches to the human resource and management development issues, Brussels, 2-3 March 1989*. London, Economist Unit. 1989

PRAIS S J. 'What can we learn from the German system of education and vocational training?' In *Education and Economic Performance* (Worswick G D N, ed.). London, Gower. 1985. pp. 40–51

PRAIS S J AND WAGNER K. 'Some practical aspects of human capital investment; training standards in five occupations in Britain and Germany'. *International Institute of Economic and Social Research Review*, November 1981. pp. 48-65

STEEDMAN H. 'Vocational training in France and Britain: Office work'. *Discussion Paper No. 14, National Institute of Economic and Social Research*. London, NIESR. 1987

STEEDMAN H. 'Speaking practically, the French have it'. *The Independent*, 5 September 1990

Further useful reading

REID M AND BARRINGTON H. *Training Interventions*. 4th edn. London, Institute of Personnel and Development. 1994

INSTITUTE OF PERSONNEL MANAGEMENT AND INCOMES DATA SERVICES. *European Management Guides Series: Training and Development*. London, IPM. 1992

MILL C. 'How the European Community works'. *Personnel Management Plus*, July 1990. p. 17

STEVENS J AND MacKAY R (eds.). *Training and Competitiveness*. London, Kogan Page. 1991

Part Two

Employee Development: Embedding it in the Organization

Chapter 5

The politics of employee development

Learning Objectives

After reading this chapter you will:

1 understand what is meant by 'the politics of employee development';
2 know how to analyse the context of an organization by reference to its primary culture, structure and power sources;
3 be able to diagnose the main political issues in a typical training situation, and outline a strategy for dealing with them.

The Politics of Employee Development

Politics, or 'the art of the possible', is what employee development is often all about. In Chapter 3 we saw how NVET in the UK has for decades been the creature of political activity that at government level has been preoccupied with other concerns.

The same subordination of training and development to other concerns which are thought, in terms of 'the business', to be more important, characterizes many organizations. It is not surprising that the function carries little weight where no strong case is made for it and there is little attempt to convince powerful parties in the organization that it is worth a significant level of investment. Furthermore, specialist training functions are quite often headed by managers who are at a relatively low level in the organization, or whose expertise and attitudes do not give them credibility in the eyes of those whose support they need: line managers, unions, the workforce and directors. As we have seen in Chapters 1 and 3, there is much evidence to show that comments made in 1985 still have validity today:

> Few employers think training sufficiently central to their business for it to be a main component in their corporate strategy; the great majority did not see it as an issue of major importance . . .
>
> Other manifestations of the generally low level of importance attached to training include decisions on training delegated to line managers who often have short-term horizons when considering returns on investment . . . [and] the relatively low status of training managers. (Coopers and Lybrand, 1985)

If employee development is to make its optimum contribution to organizational goals, those responsible for the function at different levels must examine their own role, position, resources, skills and organizational context, and identify what it is possible and necessary to achieve. Then an appropriate strategy must be adopted. In this sense the management of employee development is like a military activity, with a set of goals, an overall strategy for achieving them, and short-term tactics for different contingencies. Political skill is crucial to success, not just for the specialist but for all those in the organization who have a major responsibility for the development of people. (For an illustration of this point, see Harrison, 1992.)

So how can support for training and development be obtained? There are a range of external and internal 'triggers' that raise needs related to development of people (Pettigrew et al. 1988) including:

- **Business strategy.** As we shall see in Chapters 11 and 21, and as has already been noted in Chapter 1, the organization's business strategy at both corporate and unit level will give rise to a range of needs with immediate and longer-term implications for the training and development of the workforce. Careful analysis of those needs, and agreement with management on plans to meet them, will be one of the most important ways of ensuring support for employee development. (See Harrison, 1992, for a case study example.)
- **Internal values and systems.** There must be a commitment to employee development among powerful parties in the organization who can then influence the rest of the organization.
- **Internal labour market needs.** These include, for example, the need for a multi-skilled workforce; the need for new skills related to technological innovation; the need for a reduction in labour turnover by improved induction, training and development; and the need for employee development strategies that will attract and retain scarce and valued personnel.

- **External labour market shortages.** Although much publicity has been given to the higher profile training is bound to achieve in the face of predictable shortages in the labour market, particularly caused by the demographic downturn that has already commenced, we have already seen (pp. 59–60) that, in the UK at least, the typical response to this is to turn to recruitment and pay rather than to training. It is up to personnel and training practitioners to convince managers of the limitations these approaches often carry compared to the long- and short-term benefits that effective training and development can offer.
- **External support agencies.** As we saw in Chapter 2, there are a number of external agencies which can give powerful support to employee development initiatives within the organization.

Real, lasting support for employee development activities, however, only comes with one thing – success – so an essential part of the 'politics' of employee development is choosing the areas of priority where the function will make the most noticeable impact on the organization's effectiveness, then succeeding in those areas and ensuring that the success is broadcast in order to build on it. In other words:

> Find out what they want. Give it to them; and be seen to give it to them.

But what about failure? We all make mistakes, and attempting to deny them outright is rarely a convincing strategy. How does the skilled politician deal with failure?

Explaining failure

How do you deal with your failure in a particular task or area of work when it has to be discussed with your manager, or with a powerful colleague, or admitted to those working for you? Please describe three or four of your typical methods of dealing with your failures in such discussions.

FEEDBACK NOTES

You have probably mentioned at least one of the following techniques. There are so many ways of coping with failure that this is by no means an exhaustive list: just a few of the most common methods.

1 I admit the failure, and try to show that I have learnt from it and that it will not recur.

2 I try to cover up, blaming other people, events, problems, etc.

3 I minimize the seriousness of the failure, and try to show that there were compensating successes.

4 I try to show that it was not actually failure at all, but part of a plan, and the true benefits are shortly, or in the longer term, going to emerge. I deflect attention to the plan and its benefits, so that it becomes the focus of the discussion.

As you can see by watching the behaviour of politicians, political success is more often than not a matter of practising the last two tactics rather than either of the first two. Politics, after all, is about achieving one's aims and to be seen to fail too often and too badly is one sure way of never achieving anything. However, it is important to remember that tactics relate to situations. Sometimes the general climate will be such that honest admission of failure, together with convincing evidence that it will not recur, will be the best policy. However, in other types of situation or of organization (and generally, too, the higher up the organization you are) surviving failure will be much more difficult, and you will have to find very compelling reasons for discounting it and for asking people to continue to give you the support and resources you need. At the end of this chapter we will tackle an exercise which will require you to look in some detail at this difficult area of dealing with failure. For the time being, let us note that:

> Politics is the art of achieving your aims and of surviving. Strategies for both achieving and for survival are essential.

The Organizational Context of Employee Development

So far, we have discussed politics in a general way, and have reached the conclusion that the essence of politics in training is to get support, to be seen to be successful, and to know how to survive failure. But we have also observed that politics is always rooted in a particular situation or organization.

> Success in politics involves understanding the context in which you have to operate and adapting to it.

You will probably have met at least one manager who came to their present job with an excellent record of success, but somehow that success has not been repeated. On analysis, some factor or factors in the two situations or contexts will be different, and failure to identify and respond to that difference can be fatal. So now we need to consider the particular context of training: its specific situation. We will examine three important aspects of context: culture, structure, and power.

There are, or course, many other factors which the manager must consider when drawing up plans for training and development. There are also other, more complex and insightful, ways of analysing the political reality of organizational life (see Silverman, 1970; Pfeffer, 1981) and the different meanings which people attach to it (see Morgan, 1986). However, in this chapter we use only the simplest possible approach which is compatible with developing a practical understanding of organizational politics. It is in the culture, structure and power system of the organization that politics is embedded. If, therefore, we are unable to analyse these three aspects, we will have no chance of success in handling the politics of employee development.

Organizational cultures and structures

Try to give your own definitions of these terms. If you are familiar with organization theory, that should not be difficult, but if you are not, have a guess anyway: think about phrases like 'the culture of our country' or 'the structure of the family', because they contain some clues.

1 When we refer to the **culture** of an organization, we mean in general terms:____

____

2 When we refer to the **structure** of an organization we mean in general terms:____

____

FEEDBACK NOTES

If you have anything similar to the following, then you are clearly familiar with what we are going to discuss. If you have not, then hopefully your queries will be answered in the next few pages. You should also read Torrington et al, 1991, Chapters 8 and 9 for a fuller exposition of organizational structure and culture.

When we refer to the **culture** of an organization we mean in general terms the set of norms, ideas, beliefs about 'how things ought to be done' in the organization or in a particular part of it. Sometimes the word 'climate' is used instead; it has the same sort of meaning as 'culture'.

When we refer to the **structure** of an organization we mean the network of roles and relationships whereby activities are allocated to the different levels, parts and people of the organization. It refers to the way the organization is designed, or 'shaped'. We can envisage structure as the 'skeleton' of an organization.

The culture of the organization is critical to the achievement of its mission and goals, as we saw in Chapter 1. We shall look more closely at the links between employee development and the creation and reinforcement of organizational cultures in Chapter 21, but Payne's comment (1991) is useful to note at this point:

> A corporation that can create a strong culture has employees who believe in its products, its customers and its processes. They sell it willingly because it is part of their own identity (Ibid, p. 21)

Organizational structure has long been a focus of research and an acknowledged primary influence on organizational behaviour and performance. Child (1984) has written an exceptionally clear and practical book on how to analyse structure and how to select what is appropriate for the particular organization; Mintzberg (1983) has developed one of the most widely known and theoretically rigorous models for the analysis of structure; and Drucker (1988) contains an up-to-date critique of the whole area.

Culture and structure do not exist in isolation from one another. They are tightly interrelated, and Harrison (1972) developed a widely-used 'culture-structure' model, which is the subject of an illuminating chapter by Handy (1985). Handy observed that every organization has its own distinctive culture, which both gives rise to and in turn arises from (amongst other things) its particular structure. Many organizations, especially larger ones, contain more than one culture and structure so that what Handy called a 'differentiated' culture/structure system prevails. These writers identified at least four main types of culture to be found among and often within organizations, each associated with a particular structure.

Although Handy has subsequently moved away from this fairly straightforward set of concepts to raise complex questions about the kinds of structure that an increasing number of organizations may have to design given the discontinuous types of changes now facing them in the turbulent environments with which they have to contend, the fourfold model is still a sound enough introductory guide to understanding our own organizations.

The power culture and web structure

This is the culture of centralized power. It is most often found in small entrepreneurial firms, and at the top of large bureaucratic organizations. Control is exercised by one person, or by a small set of people, from whom rays of power and influence spread out, connected by functional or specialist strings. The structure to which such a culture gives rise is therefore web-like.

Essentially such organizations, or parts of them, are political. Decisions are taken largely on the outcome of the balance of power rather than according to set procedures or on purely 'rational' grounds. People who succeed in this kind of organization are those who want and can handle power, politically skilled, risk-takers rather than concerned with security. Since all key decisions are made only by one or a few people, such organizations move very quickly and react well to threats: they 'think on their feet'. Success means getting the results desired by the central power point; means tend to count for relatively little. Organizational life is highly competitive, and survival, even at the centre, is always difficult. In the end, the quality of those at the centre is their key to succes and when a key figure goes, or is displaced, the whole balance of power in the system may change radically.

Those concerned with, or responsible for, employee development in such a system have to produce the kinds of success desired by the central power source, and to relate training objectives and plans to needs recognized as important by that source – by no means an easy task.

The role culture and pyramid structure

This is the culture of bureaucracy. Its prevailing belief is that an organization should have its purpose and overall plan defined at the top, and then rest for its strength on a clearly defined hierarchy of functions or specialisms. Co-ordination of the many descending levels of departments is carried out at the top by a narrow band of senior management, advised by specialist functions. Rules and procedures govern every role and position in this pyramid, temple or hierarchy. They also govern communications and the conduct of disputes.

Precedents dominate decision-making, and the whole organization tends to be security-orientated with a tendency to rigidity rather than to innovation. Role cultures and structures are slow to see and accept the need to change, and change itself is usually a lengthy and difficult process, with job definitions, rules, established methods and ways of working and behaving pulling people back to the past rather than forward into the future. At the same time, the role structure is probably the most widely used way of organizing large numbers of people around a common goal, not only in work organizations but in states and religions; one has only to think of China, Germany, the former Soviet Union, and the Catholic Church to realize the enduring organizational power of the bureaucratic model, as well as the dangers inherent in its misuse.

For whoever carries responsibility for employee development in such a system, the position to which he or she is allocated will be the major intitial source of power. The higher the position, the more power to influence the system. However, even if the formal position is fairly low or peripheral, all is not lost; the person who knows their way round and through the rules, the files, the procedures and the whole political system can use them very successfully to achieve their ends.

The greatest danger is that, in this segmented and inward-looking system, open-minded, objective and 'professional' vision can become 'departmentalized'. How many managers have you met who have become absorbed in the goals and interests of their little empire, rather than striving for the benefit of the whole? And given the type of culture that prevails, is such behaviour surprising?

The task culture and net structure

Task cultures (also known as 'organic' or 'matrix' systems) bring people together because there is a job or project to be done, irrespective of personal power or formal position. The emphasis is on the team rather than the individual, because the culture is one of teams brought together to work on projects as they come in, which are disbanded when the job is done, with new teams being formed as new projects arise. The structure can be pictured as a net, with some of the strands thicker and more permanent than the rest. Much of the power lies at the permanent knots of that net.

Task cultures and net structures are flexible and skilled, but Handy (1985) claims that they do not often produce economies of scale or depth of expertise, and that control, especially day-to-day control, needs special interpersonal and managerial skills. To be successful in such a structure, people need to be expert at their task, concerned with the project above all else, and ready to give it all the time, skill and effort that it requires. They must also be team-centred and able to cope with little supervision or control from above.

Whoever is responsible for the development of people in such a system will probably be concerned in the main with helping to build up teamwork and team skills (because expertise is often bought in rather than home-grown), with the provision of training to meet specific needs as they arise, and when, where and by whom it is needed; and with encouraging continuous development through the integration of learning with work and through self-development.

Success will be a matter of being expert in tasks, but speed of reaction, flexibility, sensitivity and creativity are often more important than depth of expertise. Working in a task culture is challenging and stimulating, but few find it easy, because it requires constant effort to keep up-to-date in one's expertise, to move through a number of different teams as time goes on, and always to remain committed to the matter in hand, no matter how stressful the demands.

When resources become limited in this kind of organization (or part of an organization, because most bureaucracies, for example, contain a number of task cultures and net structures within the main system) and money and people have to be rationed, the norms of the culture begin to be challenged. Often there is a shift towards either a power or a role culture, and sometimes this can lead to a permanent change, and to a new structure. It is a possibility of which specialist functions should always be aware, and in the last few years many training managers have lost their departments, even their jobs, through not planning for such a contingency.

The person culture and galaxy structure

This is not so much a type of organization (although some partnerships operate on this basis) as a way of describing those clusters of individuals one finds in most organizations, who see their job and the resources available to them mainly as a means of serving their own interests. Often these cultures exist where there is one person who has a unique contribution to make on the basis of specialist skills or knowledge, and so they become the 'star' around whom everything and everyone tend to revolve.

Anyone trying to promote development of people in such a system can find it a hard task. Often 'star' individuals not only need development themselves, but are also exercising a stifling effect on the development of their staff. However, because they have unique skills, they can usually get other jobs without too much difficulty, or they may have protected tenure. In either case, they will probably fail to acknowledge any expertise as greater or more compelling than their own, and attempts at personal persuasion are unlikely to succeed. However, appealing to that expertise may be one way of at least using them to develop others; few can resist the plea to help those less gifted or knowledgeable than themselves by passing on some of their wisdom and experience, whether in a lecture, a more informal discussion, project work or some other form of learning.

Another way of looking at person cultures is to see them as dominated by a belief in people's potential, and therefore characterized by a strong focus on the development of people, and on delegating to individuals as much responsibility for decision-making and resources as is feasible, given their own capacity for autonomy. The skill of management in such a culture is continually to hold in balance this belief, with its concern for appreciating and responding to individual needs and aspirations and continuously developing abilities and potential, with the responsibility of ensuring that work targets and commitment to organizational objectives are also achieved.

The culture and structure of your organization

Take your own organization, or a department or section of it (or, if this is difficult for any reason, then some organization with which you are familiar) and analyse it in terms of its primary structure and culture.

(Maximum recommended length: approximately 1,500 words)

Start your analysis with an introduction, of not more than two or three paragraphs, in which you briefly explain what your organization is and whether your chosen frame of reference is the whole organization or a particular branch, section, or department of it. You should also indicate how far your organization, or your chosen part of it, is considered to be successful and any particular problems and/or opportunities it faces in operating.

Then pay particular attention to the following points, illustrating your analysis with practical examples and explanations wherever possible:

- The kind of culture and structure you think top management *intends and believes* to exist, and the kind of culture and structure you feel *actually* exists
- How far the culture and structure promote or hinder the achievement of organizational goals at various levels
- The kind of people who 'get on' in the system, and the reasons for their success
- The kind of people who are unsuccessful in the system, and the reasons for their failure
- How far people's needs, aspirations and development are matters of *real* concern to the organization
- The pressures and opportunities facing employee development because of the culture and structure of the organization

FEEDBACK NOTES

There are no set answers to this exercise: the results are bound to be different for each person who attempts it. However, if you are a student tackling it wholly or partly as a class exercise, then your tutor could split the class up into groups in order for group members to exchange information arising from their analyses. A full class session thereafter could then obtain from each group the most interesting outcomes from those group discussions. The sorts of issues that can be examined include:

- Where people come from the same, or similar, organizations, are their perceptions of the culture and structure in which they work the same, or different? Why? (For example, someone working in the Personnel Department of a local authority may be aware that the authority as a whole is rigid and bureaucratic. However, if their own department is organized more as a net structure where the management culture is one of teamwork, participative decision-making, and achieving a dynamic, pro-active role for the personnel function, then their daily perceptions of the organization will be very different from those of someone else working in a more centralized part of that same authority.)

- What about personnel and training staff in the various organizations? Have they leading roles in the organization? If not, why not? If they are effective, what are the reasons for this?
- How has political skill, or lack of it, affected the performance and credibility of personnel and training staff?
- How far is development of people in the different organizations that have been analysed a major responsibility of the personnel departments or of training specialists or departments? Or is it primarily the responsibility of line management?
- What sorts of attitudes and policies are there about employee development in the various organizations, and how do these relate to the cultures and structures of those organizations?

In this section we have been looking at different sorts of cultures and structures between and within organizations, and we have seen that one easy and useful way to classify them is by using a fourfold system.

> There are at least four main types of culture, each with its typical associated structure. It is essential for anyone seeking to promote the development of people in an organization to identify the primary culture and structure to which they must relate, and to adapt their strategy accordingly.

A questionnaire designed by Harrison (1972) and reproduced in Handy (1985) offers a simple but effective way of achieving practical insights into the culture and structure of an organization.

Culture and structure are two of the three factors relating to the political context of training with which this chapter is concerned. The third is power.

Power in organizations

> Power is a property that exists in any organization . . . Politics is the way power is put into action. (Torrington and Weightman, 1985)

It is essential for anyone trying to promote the development of people in an organization to understand the basis of power in that organization, and to know how to acquire and use power in order to achieve their objectives.

There are innumerable studies of power in organizations. One of the most compelling is the social action analysis contained in Silverman's (1970) complex but fascinating book. French and Raven (1959), Pfeffer (1981) and Handy (1985) offer particularly absorbing discussions. The following exercise is based in part on their work.

Types of power in organizations

Here are six types of power commonly met in organizations. Please explain what you think each means. Don't worry if you cannot work them all out; it is just a way of opening up our discussion.

- Physical power
- Resource power
- Position, or legal, power
- Expert power
- Personal power
- Negative power

FEEDBACK NOTES

Now let's check on definitions.

Physical power means the kind of power that derives from physical strength, appearance or presence. Often someone's mere presence in a workplace is enough to galvanize everyone into action. So when we think about physical power, we should consider not just the effect *actual* power can have, but also the ways in which the *potential* of such power can influence people.

Resource power means the power derived from control of resources valued by those you wish to influence. The resources can be anything: money, promotion, a bigger carpet in the office. What matters is that they are wanted, valued. Many of those who are responsible for developing others have few direct resources of their own, and so one of their first tasks must be to discover who holds the resources that they need, and how to obtain them.

Position power means the power inherent in a particular role. We have already seen the importance of position as a source of power in a role culture, and its implications for those trying to develop people in such a system.

Expert power is, as we have seen, highly valued in a task culture, although less reliable in a role culture (where the 'expert' can quite quickly be cut down to size by rules and procedures, time lags, and the many convoluted decision-making mechanisms).

Personal power, deriving solely from the individual's character and personality, is a type of power seen at its most obvious, probably, in power cultures, where it is often used to reinforce all the other power sources of the person or group at the centre. However, it is an important quality for someone like a training practitioner to possess if working in a task culture, where interactions are often difficult and sensitive to manage. When confronted with a person culture, personal power may be the only way of influencing the 'stars'.

Negative power is the power, possessed by us all, to withdraw our energy, effort and commitment. Sometimes the results are not as we had hoped: unless we are in a job, or have a skill, that is vital, and is difficult to replace, then withdrawal of effort may have no real impact even when a large number of people join together in the withdrawal. However, developing people depends for its success on getting the full commitment and enthusiasm of everyone, from the manager who provides, or may withhold, crucial information about the learning needs of staff, to the individual placed in a learning situation but not necessarily motivated to learn from it, especially if he or she sees no meaningful rewards at the end of the process. Inability to understand and deal with the exercise of negative power is a major weakness in anyone responsible for developing learning in the organization.

> There are many power sources in an organization. It is important to identify the type of power possessed by oneself and by others. Knowing how to use and relate to different types of power is a major political skill.

So far in this chapter we have looked at three aspects of organizational life that relate centrally to the politics of employee development: the culture, structure and power system surrounding the function. We have recognized that to be successful in the employee development function a high level of political skill may be required, and that the ability to analyse and understand organizational politics is an important part of that skill. Now let's try an exercise, to put some of these ideas into practice.

The management training problem

Read the case study carefully, and then answer the questions on it. It can be tackled as a self-learning activity, or as coursework or as a class activity with students and tutor agreeing on how it should be done.

You are a training officer, aged 26, working in the Personnel Department of a large private-sector service organization in the Midlands. You were recruited three years ago, after working for two years as a training officer in a local authority where most of your work involved administration of a YT scheme. You have a degree in Business Studies, and in your present post you are responsible for the administration of various long-established management and supervisory educational and training courses, and for organizing short courses, mainly of a technical nature.

You have no formal personnel or training qualifications, although you would like to acquire some. There are several other personnel staff, one of whom is a training officer specializing in technical training.

You report to the Personnel Director, Roger Mason, a middle-aged man, IPM-qualified, and considered by top management to be effective. He has been with the organization for 15 years. He is not so highly regarded by many other staff in the organization, who see the personnel function as a very bureaucratic department, absorbed in paperwork and procedures rather than offering real help to anyone. Mason's main interest and workload lie in employee relations. He is currently heavily involved in drawing up an equal opportunities policy for the organization. He has always tended to 'manage by exception', which translates in his case into 'only start to worry when things go wrong'. Staff are reluctant to ask him, or each other, for help, as they are afraid that this may be construed as a sign of incompetence on their part; most stick rigidly to their job descriptions. You do not much like working in the department, but are hoping that once you have a little more experience you will get another post and move on. You intend to specialize in training.

Just after you joined the organization, Mason told you to 'do something about educating our junior and middle managers'. He said top management felt that the performance of these groups, and of supervisors below them, was not always as good as it could be (although he gave you no specific evidence on this score). Furthermore, the younger people at least, many of whom were in technical functions, would be moving up in the next few years, and it was felt that they needed a greater awareness of what general management involved. Something had to be done, and he would like some courses organized, although nothing too expensive.

You knew little about management training, but it seemed to you that education was a very important part of people's development; it broadened their minds and gave them new knowledge and techniques. You therefore suggested that about six managers at various levels and from different departments in the organization should be sent on a Diploma of Business Administration (DBA) course at the local polytechnic each year. The two-year part-time course involved attendance one afternoon and evening a week, with subjects like Organizational Behaviour, Quantitative Methods, Management Practice, Finance, and Marketing. Students also had to tackle a work-based project in their second year.

Mason liked the idea, particularly as it didn't involve his department in anything more than calling for nominees and organizing their attendance. Sixteen managers have subsequently gone on the course, at the rate of around five a year. All were chosen by Mason from nominations made by the superior officers of the staff concerned. He did not explain to you the criteria for nomination or selection.

This year Mason has been asked by top management for some information about the management programme to go into the Annual Report. Last week he came to you in a panic, asking you to provide the information for him in two weeks' time.

You have therefore been going round departments talking to all those who have been through the courses or are still following them. The courses seem popular with the staff from departments like management services, sales and marketing, all of whom tend to be in their twenties or thirties with degrees or equivalent qualifications. They find the course content intellectually stimulating, and some are able to apply newly learnt techniques to their jobs, although the majority find that there is no real support for or interest in this in their departments. However, the remark made by one of them to you typifies the general feelings of this group:

> I won't be here for ever, so I'll be able to use the learning in the next job I get; in the meantime, it's certainly made me more aware of the deficiencies of this place – especially how out of date my boss is! Pity you couldn't persuade *him* to do one of these courses!

The nine staff from this group who have gone through the DBA, or are currently studying for it, have all done well in coursework and final examinations, and have particularly enjoyed the project work.

Unfortunately the seven staff from technical departments are neither so satisfied nor so successful. Their ages range from the mid-thirties to the mid-forties, and all have technical qualifications, one a degree. Some of them have managerial responsibilities, others do not. All find the course hard, some because so much of the content is completely outside their experience and others because, to quote one:

> We've been doing our jobs perfectly well up to now; why are we being pushed on to these college courses? We're not going to get more pay or promotion, and there's nothing new in any of it except that Organizational Behaviour stuff, and that's just common sense, anyway – a lot of jargon, but that's all it really is.

One of the technical staff dropped out after two months and although three others passed the examinations last year, one did not, and has to resit this year. Most feel that the DBA is pointless for them. It does not help them with their daily problems, and they resent the fact that while 'whizz kids from sales and marketing have got it made' they themselves cannot even get cover when they are away each week, and they already have such a mass of work to do that piling up 'all this homework business' was just an impossible burden.

You have had a preliminary chat with Mason about these reactions, and he is rather concerned, especially about the technical people and their managers, with whom he has never had particularly good relationships. He has asked you to see him tomorrow to discuss the situation, and to decide what should be said about the programme in the Annual Report.

Why will your discussion need to be handled with considerable political skill? What are the main 'political' issues? Outline how you propose to deal with the discussion, and what you hope and intend to get out of it.

FEEDBACK NOTES

You will have to explain the failures in the programme to Mason in a way that will not only leave your own credibility intact but also help him, in turn, to present a positive rather than a negative picture in the Annual Report.

1 You should clarify the outcomes sought from the discussion. Your major concern should be that, in future, training needs are accurately assessed, training objectives and plans are agreed and understood and training has the commitment of all the interested parties. The design of courses should in future motivate and help learners to gain results that are of value to the organization and to the individual. You will also want to leave the meeting with Mason's active support. Aiming for these outcomes will give purpose and direction to your discussion.

2 You should put failure into context and look for successes. Your best strategy will be to stress the benefits that have arisen from the programme so far (and there are quite a number) and, while admitting failures, to put them into context. The programme has, after all, run for three years, so some failures are inevitable. Furthermore, major activities such as this not infrequently uncover problems that were probably always there, and could have come to the surface at any time; for example the gap between older and younger staff, and between specialists and generalists.

These are essentially organizational problems, which must be viewed in that wider context. What rewards does the organization offer its older managers and supervisors for the effort of going through a tough examination course, for example? How far does its salary and career structure support such initiatives? What explanation was offered to staff initially about their enrolment on the DBA? Why is there inadequate support for many of the staff when they try to put their new learning into practice? (For a clear discussion of such problems, see Fairbairn, 1991.)

3 You should get support for training from both learners and managers. Having looked at the successes of the programme, and emphasized the need for a wider perspective on some of the problems which have come to light during the three years, you can then suggest that joint discussions, between training, managerial and supervisory staff, even joint planning and design of courses, would be a positive way forward. Other, more work-related, developmental initiatives may be relevant now, rather than just concentrating on educational courses, and the ideas of the staff and their managers will be essential here. Such work-based activities would also be relevant and motivating for older staff and those in technical positions. Involving their managers in discussions would also be a way of getting those managers more interested in the whole idea of developing their staff, and thus of reducing the problems that some staff experienced when they tried to apply learning from the DBA course to their jobs.

4 You should consider culture, structure and power factors. The situation we have described is very common in a large bureaucratic organization like this one, with a culture in the Personnel Department that does not encourage a systematic or creative approach to employee development, nor one which stresses its relationship to business needs. Of course you yourself should have queried the need for the focus on managerial training and development in the first place: what was the evidence that there were deficiencies here? Or that training was the best response to those deficiencies? And of course you should have looked at other ways of responding to Mason's instructions: what about training and development through work-based activities, rather than, or as well as, an educational programme? And there should have been careful monitoring of the selection and progress of staff on the course, together with an evaluation at the end of each course, and later, when staff got back into their jobs. And what about pre-course briefing, and post-course debriefing, for the staff?

In other words, there are very many things you *should* have done in this hypothetical case, but obviously inexperience and your junior position in the Personnel Department help to explain why you did not do them.

No doubt by now you would be well aware of your own deficiencies. In the discussion, however, you should avoid too much breast-beating, or you could find yourself being made a scapegoat, rather than managing to do anything constructive about the situation. You should aim instead to agree with Mason on establishing positive links between training and line management staff, and on developing simple but effective procedures for the diagnosis of learning needs, and for the selection and monitoring of staff on training and educational programmes. You should also point to the value of trying to take a wider perspective on employee development in the organization.

That was quite a complex exercise. Don't worry if you missed some of the more specialized points that I have covered in the Feedback Notes – it is the general political strategy that is important:

- Be clear about the outcomes you seek from the discussion.
- Consider culture, structure and power factors.
- Put failure into context and identify successes.
- Get support for training and development initiatives.

Only one more factor needs emphasis in this chapter: the need for a clear vision about the place employee development should have in the particular organization. As we saw in Chapter 3, lack of vision leads to lack of a clear, convincing policy and strategy, and this is as true at organizational as at national and international levels.

Exercises

1 In an organization of your choice, identify a particular training/development situation where political skills are needed in order to produce effective outcomes. Why are 'politics' important in the situation and what course of action would you suggest in this instance?

2 Given the need to cope effectively with 'the politics of employee development' how can those with significant training and development responsibilities be helped to acquire political skills?

3 Analyse the main issues relevant to employee development put for-

ward in ONE of the following (full titles in the References section):

Payne (1991)
Pettigrew et al. (1988)
Drucker (1988)

References

CHILD J. *Organization: A guide to problems and practice*, 2nd ed. London, Harper and Row. 1984

COOPERS AND LYBRAND ASSOCIATES. *A Challenge to Complacency: Changing attitudes to training*. A report to the Manpower Services Commission and the National Economic Development Office. Sheffield, MSC. 1985

DRUCKER P. 'The coming of the new organization'. *Harvard Business Review*, January/February 1988. pp. 45-53

FAIRBAIRN J. 'Plugging the gap in training needs analysis'. *Personnel Management*, February 1991, pp. 43-5

FRENCH J R P AND RAVEN B H. 'The bases of social power'. In *Studies in Social Power* (Cartwright D, ed.). Ann Arbor, University of Michigan Press. 1959

HANDY C B. *Understanding Organizations*, 3rd ed. Harmondsworth, Penguin. 1985

HANDY C B. *The Age of Unreason*. London, Business Books. 1989

HARRISON Roger. 'Understanding your organization's character'. *Harvard Business Review*, May/June 1972. pp. 119-28

HARRISON Rosemary. 'Employee development at Barratt'. In *Case Studies in Personnel* (Winstanley D and Woodall J, eds.). Ch. 10. London, Institute of Personnel Management. 1992

MINTZBERG H. *Structure in Fives: Designing effective organizations*. Englewood Cliffs, New Jersey, Prentice Hall. 1983

MORGAN G. *Riding the Waves of Change: Developing managerial competences for a turbulent world*. San Francisco, Jossey-Bass. 1988

MORGAN G. *Images of Organization*. London, Sage. 1986

PAYNE R. 'Taking stock of corporate culture'. *Personnel Management*, July 1991. pp. 26-9

PETTIGREW A M, SWALLOW P AND HENDRY C. 'The forces that trigger training'. *Personnel Management*, December 1988. pp. 28-32

PFEFFER J. *Power in Organizations*. Marshfield, Massachusetts, Pitman. 1981

SILVERMAN D. *The Theory of Organizations*. London, Heinemann Educational Books (Studies in Sociology). 1970

TORRINGTON D, HALL L, HAYLOR I AND MYERS J. *Employee Resourcing*. Management Studies 2 Series. London, Institute of Personnel Management. 1991

TORRINGTON D AND WEIGHTMAN J. *The Business of Management*, London, Prentice Hall. 1985

Further useful reading

DEAL T AND KENNEDY A. *Corporate Cultures: Rites and rituals of corporate life*. Maidenhead, Addison Wesley. 1982

FULLERTON H AND PRICE C. 'Culture change in the NHS'. *Personnel Management*, March 1991. pp. 50-3

THOMAS M. 'In search of culture: Holy grail or gravy train?' *Personnel Management*, September 1985. pp. 24-7

TOFFLER A. *The Third Wave*. London, Collins. 1980

WILLIAMS A, DOBSON P AND WALTERS M. *Changing Culture: New organizational approaches*. London, Institute of Personnel Management. 1989

Chapter 6

Employee development roles, responsibilities and tasks

Learning Objectives

After reading this chapter you will:

1 understand the main levels of responsibility for employee development in organizations, and the main functions involved at those levels;
2 understand the main types of employee development roles and tasks, the key theories relating to them, and the main influences on their formation and reinforcement;
3 be able to produce guidelines for improving the status of employee development in a particular organizational context.

Organizational Responsibilities for Employee Development

There are four levels of responsibility for employee development in most organizations: top management, line management, the individual and specialist practitioners.

Top management

Top management carries the responsibility for communicating a clear vision about what employee development means in the organization, and the part it is to play in organizational performance and growth. Without very positive values about people from the top of the organization, accompanied by a commitment to invest significant resources in employee development, the function can never become fully integrated into the business.

> Integrated Human Resource Development means simply that, if you want to develop thriving human resources who will be

> skilled, flexible, innovative, co-operative and above all productive, you must manage the environment in which they live. (Webster, 1990)

Since the organizational environment in which people live is created and sustained above all by top management, the primary responsibility for employee development must lie at that level. Let us look at an example. It is based on a real company, but at the request of its present owners, all means of identifying it have been removed.

Etewel

In 1990 Etewel was acquired by friendly takeover as a very successful family-owned consumer food company employing 3,000 people across the country. It had a management turnover of only about 5 per cent per annum, and was a very dynamic, market-sensitive, fast-reactive business.

Etewel's workforce was a major asset. Etewel attributed its level of excellence mainly to a long-standing policy of high investment in employee development which had enabled the company:

1 to attract and retain good people at a time of demographic downturn and considerable competition in the local labour market;

2 to develop a flexible, high-quality, innovative workforce;

3 to achieve the sustained motivation and stimulation of its people, particularly at management level where, because of low turnover, there were few promotion opportunities.

The investment in employee development was consistent with Etewel's overall philosophy about people, stemming from the strong values of the Chief Executive, who encouraged an open style and care for people while setting high goals in the pursuit of excellence. They were summarized thus:

Together we succeed through:

- A dynamic, supportive and positive environment
- Respect for the individual
- The fostering of creativity, initiative and the removal of blocks to change
- An imaginative training and development programme which supports initiatives and allows space for self-development
- Care for the community

Etewel seeks a wider dimension than organisational success or personal gain, and is committed to care for the wider community.

In practical terms, these values translated into a wide range of processes to attract, retain and develop people, including :

- Personal development plans and regular personal development workshops
- Planned induction, providing broad-based initial experience
- Regular reviews of managers' performance
- In-company management development courses aimed at embedding the Etewel culture in participants, 'developing a mission' in participants and stimulating and supporting the exercise of initiative in ways of value to the company
- Cross-functional internal appointments at executive levels, leading to open career paths for managers

Management development was supported by line managers, who were chosen as exemplars of effective management. All employees had competitive salaries that were surveyed regularly.

The results of the major investment in employee development had been convincing: the company had successfully maintained high standards of recruitment and low average employee turnover right up to the point of acquisition in November, 1989. It had attracted people with value to offer the organization, met their expectations, retained them, and got their full commitment. There had been no significant cost in functional terms: there was only one training specialist, and the training courses and the development work *in situ* had been done by line managers, who themselves had received training as trainers.

There were many reasons for the success of employee development at Etewel, but above all it was explained by the fact that the whole investment in people was driven by the commitment and beliefs of the Chief Executive and that it fitted the firm's primary values, mission and culture.

Webster (1990) found the same kind of values at Kwik-Fit, a company distinguished both by its high standards of quality and customer service and by its policy of integrated and continuous development of the whole workforce. Discussing its philosophy and systems for the continuous development and improvement of its workforce, he observed:

> Vision arises not from a dry analysis of assiduously gathered information but . . . from the values of individual human beings . . .

> As the values permeate the organisation and its people, they produce an environment in which the vision takes root and flourishes. But it cannot be left to chance; the environment must be managed . . . Values and vision give the organisation direction . . .
> . . . This integrated approach grew naturally from the values and beliefs of Tom Farmer [the Chief Executive Officer] and from his own understanding of what would work . . . Top management must learn to understand that every action they take either produces healthy growth in the workforce or it inhibits it. They must review the systems, the organisation structure, the physical layout and the human resource policies . . . with the specific purpose of creating through them the environment in which people may thrive (Ibid, p. 47).

Line management

Line managers carry the fundamental responsibility for ensuring that people are enabled to perform their jobs effectively and efficiently, and to enjoy continuous learning opportunities through which their abilities and potential can be developed. This responsibility means that managers, whether alone or with the help of specialist staff, must:

1 create a work environment, policy and systems at their management level that encourage and support the acquisition of the skills, knowledge and attitudes people need in order to perform well in their jobs;
2 regularly review work targets, appraise performance and assess potential in order to help people to improve in their jobs and develop in ways that will be beneficial to the organization as well as motivating to themselves;
3 regularly monitor and evaluate the results of formal and informal learning in the workplace.

These responsibilities require values, expertise and resources, especially time, that many managers may not possess. Leicester (1989), reporting on an ongoing research programme established in 1984 and based primarily at the University of Sussex, quoted data showing that:

> Those organizations whose managers are trained in interpersonal skills and who have explicit responsibility for managing people are more inclined to ensure that their workforce is fully trained, not just once, not just for the job, or for the job as currently defined – but continuously prepared for a work performance that

> is a regular contribution to corporate success. In this sense training begets training: only a fully trained management will create and continue to maintain a properly trained workforce.

There are four requirements if managers are to carry out such responsibilities:

- Job descriptions must focus on human resource management and development as crucial tasks of all managers.
- Competence and motivation in relation to those tasks must be seen as a prerequisite for selection to management positions.
- Managers must, where appraisal shows this to be necessary, receive training and development in those skills that will help them to be good developers of people – notably skills of appraisal, assessment, counselling and coaching.
- Reward systems must recognize the central importance of the development of people in managers' performance.

Such steps, of course, must be backed by a top management whose values, style and vision demonstrate the importance they attach to employee development, and who make it a formal responsibility of line managers, with appropriate rewards for good performance. And so we return to the first point:

> It is vital for top management to support employee development in the organization fully, and to be committed to providing all the necessary resources and systems to make it an integral part of organizational strategy and performance.

Are these steps realistic? Yes – and essential if employee development is to enter the organization's bloodstream. An article by Wille (1990) describes a number of different organizations, all successful in their business performance, who have created conditions for total employee growth. Two extracts from the article are particularly illuminating, showing different approaches to instilling in managers the awareness of the need to develop their people, and to measuring their performance in this area of responsibility:

> ICI has no one corporate development plan . . . but a key corporate objective is to lay down standards of knowledge, skills and attainment worldwide . . . Development of people tends to merge with culture development, as in the programme 'Understanding ICI' . . .

> Success in management development will be evaluated by such ratios as numbers of managers to non-managers (fewer is better, so that employees' responsibility is diffused), by the level of internal promotions, by the extent that personal development plans get fulfilled, by the limitation on external recruitment and by progress in developing subordinates (Wille, p. 35).

> Rothmans and Nissan are both keen to pervade their organizations with developmental activity, and with a strong sense of team working and employee involvement . . . Activities designed to 'empower' people include daily team meetings involving everybody, appraisal for all, responsibility exercised at the lowest possible level, and a sense of the next person in line as the customer. Managers are there to release people's energies (Wille, p. 36).

None of these activities involves heavy financial costs; they could be practised by small, medium-sized or large organizations. What they do require, however, is what we have already stressed: a particular vision of what employee development means in the organization; a set of values about people that guarantees a long-term commitment to their development; and top management's determination to ensure that every manager of people in the organization will accept development of people as one of their key responsibilities, involving tasks in which their own performance will be assessed and rewarded (see also Chapter 21).

The individual

As a member of the organizational team, every individual has a responsibility to consider their own learning needs in relation to their daily work, forthcoming changes and their career aspirations. Self-directed learning and self-development are increasingly important for everyone, whether in or out of employment. Furthermore, if the organization does not take the initiative in offering opportunities for individual development, then these may be the only ways whereby people can realize their potential.

Individuals should take an active role in articulating their needs, and should seek to make a positive contribution to the decisions on how needs may be met; in this way planning, execution and evaluation of their development can become a genuinely two-way process. Only thus can individuals hope to influence those who carry developmental roles (especially, of course, their own managers at whatever level), and so put pressure on managers to aim for a marriage rather than a divorce of individual and organizational training and development goals.

Unfortunately there are often no incentives for individuals to press for training, since the rewards, material or otherwise, are so few in most organizations, as also for the unemployed (see pp. 56–7).

Specialist staff

An organization may have a specialist function with responsibility for employee development: sometimes the personnel function carries it out; sometimes training departments are established, either within or independent of the personnel department; and sometimes training and development are part of some other area of activity. No matter how employee development is organized in a specialist department, however, the fundamental task remains the same: to ensure that all managers are aware of their responsibility for such development and to help them in carrying out that responsibility. (Singer, 1977) There are a variety of roles that specialist staff can carry out. Let us look now at some of these roles.

Types of Employee Development Roles

What do we mean by 'role'? The *Oxford Illustrated Dictionary* (Coulson et al. 1975) definition is 'actor's part; one's part or function'. This is a useful way of thinking about 'role' because of the emphasis on playing a part, on interracting in a particular way with others, as well as on functions to be performed. It is also illuminating because it contains the concept of dynamism: every actor differs in his or her interpretation of a given part, and makes of it something unique as well as fulfilling its formal requirements. These related ideas of a given and a developed role are emphasized in much of the research about training roles published in recent years (see, especially, Kenney and Reid, 1986, pp. 40–9).

Let us now look at two perspectives on training roles and tasks:

- Pettigrew's fivefold model
- The Lead Body Standards

Pettigrew's fivefold model of training roles

Pettigrew et al. (1982) have produced probably the best-known typology of training roles, using five categories which are not mutually exclusive. The roles were identified in a sample of training officers in the chemical industry in the UK, but they are of wider relevance in helping to understand the different functions and tasks that training and development practitioners can assume or be expected to perform in different organizational settings.

The change agent

This role is concerned with the definition of organizational problems and helping others to resolve them through changing the organizational culture. Kenney and Reid (1986) see this as a difficult and not always legitimate role for training. It is, however, a legitimate and even necessary role for employee development if we accept that the function needs to be one that is integral to the business strategy of the organization and must be embedded in the organization's mission and culture.

The provider

> The provider offers training services and systems which are primarily oriented to the maintenance and improvement of organisational performance rather than to changing the organisation in any major ways. (Pettigrew et al., 1982, p. 8).

The passive provider

Again, this is a role concerned with the maintenance of performance, not with the changing of the organization, but differs from the 'provider' role because of lack of expertise (especially of political skills) in putting across and developing that role with conviction. Therefore it often operates at a very low level of activity and influence in the organization.

The training manager

In this role the focus is on the managerial aspect of training, being primarily concerned with its planning, organization, direction and control. The training manager may have responsibility for a group of training staff, or may simply be responsible for co-ordinating the provision of training courses and other services. We shall look at this role in detail in Chapters 9 and 10.

The role in transition

This describes a role that is in the process of changing from that of 'provider' to that of 'change agent'. The work therefore currently includes elements of both sorts of activity, being concerned with developing a wider vision of the training role, and trying to make a more proactive contribution to organizational performance and growth.

The Lead Body Standards

The Training and Development Lead Body (TDLB) was established in 1989, helped by the Training Agency, to set occupational standards and provide the basis for vocational qualifications for all those with a training and development responsibility. The standards apply to anyone in a training and development role, whether practitioner or line manager, at whatever level, and whether full-time or part-time.

In January, 1991, as part of the movement to develop standards for all professions and occupations and relate them to NVQs (see pp. 28–9, 65–7), the TDLB published provisional national standards for training and development, based on definitions of key roles and the outcomes to be expected from them. Following national consultation, the final version of the Lead Body Standards was published in 1992, together with the first three in a series of NVQs for anyone with a training and development responsibility. The intention was that accreditation of major national qualifications related to training and development would be made through key awarding bodies during that year.

Let us have a look at the Standards, and carry out an exercise that will familiarize you with them and help you to examine them critically.

National lead body standards for training and development

In the information below and in Appendix 3 you will find an explanation of the Lead Body Standards for Training and Development. What are six or seven of the main uses for such standards? And how far do they adequately identify and explain the roles of those with key responsibilities for training and development in an organization and offer meaningful standards against which their performance can be assessed?

The TDLB defines the Key Purpose of Training and Development as: To develop human potential to assist organizations and individuals to achieve their objectives (Training and Development Lead Body, 1992a p. 2)

The TDLB has identified four typical training and development roles:

- To manage human resource development strategy
- To manage training operations
- To meet training needs in general
- To meet specialized training needs

(Training and Development Lead Body, 1992b, p. 4)

It has also identified five related functional areas of competence

- Identifying training and development needs
- Designing training and development strategies and plans
- Providing learning opportunities, resources and support
- Evaluating the effectiveness of training and development
- Supporting training and development advances and practice

(Training and Development Lead Body, 1992a, p. 3)

An Occupational Standard describes what is expected of an individual performing a particular occupational role, by defining the outcomes expected of someone who performs competently. Occupational Standards have been produced by bodies of experts who have examined at length a wide range of existing best practice. The Standards are also intended to lead towards best practice in the future and will be revised as necessary to take account of changes and improvements in best practice.

Every standard comprises three components:

- An element of competence
- Its associated performance criteria
- A range indicator which defines the range of applications the element has – i.e. the types of relationships, resources, methods, processes and locations for which achievement of the specified outcomes is required

FEEDBACK NOTES

Let's take the easy question first! Occupational standards in training and development can be used:

- As a basis for job descriptions
- As a guide to recruitment and selection
- To identify training needs
- To develop training programmes
- As a basis for appraisal and assessment
- As a benchmark for development
- To form vocational qualifications.

Now the more difficult question. There has been a great deal of controversy about the Standards. The debate about how far they adequately describe roles and can or should act as guides for assessing performance in those roles is wide-ranging, and the main issues are outlined below.

The basis on which the Standards have been drawn up

The standards have been derived from what is called functional analysis – that is to say, training and development is defined by reference to five functions (listed in the exercise above), with each function subdivided into areas of competence, then into Units of Competence (Standards), and finally into Elements of Competence which lead into Criteria of Performance. The functional approach aims to create a 'logical hierarchy' of activities, each of which contains subsets of skills needed in order to perform to identified standards.

You will notice that this is a very different approach to that used by Pettigrew et al. (1982). They did not go into detail about tasks, because to them tasks will be determined by the particular organizational context. Instead they used role analysis to describe the kinds of relationship training practitioners can have to other key parties in their organization.

The Lead Body Standards tell us nothing about relationships between parties, even though it is those relationships that to a significant extent determine the way roles finally develop. Instead they produce what is claimed to be an all-inclusive list of training and development functions. The functions and their subdivisions constitute a checklist against which particular training and development practitioners or managers can identify what they at their organizational level actually do. In theory, they can then identify what specific tasks and standards they should be achieving, and be measured by reference to criteria relating to those standards.

The Association for Management Education Development has criticized this functional approach as one-sided, saying:

> It is reductionist and atomistic; everything a trainer or developer is expected to do is broken down into small units for training purposes. (Transform, 1991)

The inference is that in real life, such neat and tidy definitions do not adequately indicate what the trainer or developer should do or how best to do it: the whole is greater than merely the sum of its parts, and effective employee development is about something more than simply carrying out up to 102 prescribed elements of activity to a set of generalized standards (see also Chapter 12).

The need to recognize contextual and other factors

In fact, there has to be a balance. There are certain common tasks and skills involved in developing people, as there are in all professions and occupations; some can be closely defined, others require the exercise of imagination, creativity and political sensitivity – qualities which are not quantifiable, but which are essential to the success of much that the trainer and developer do. The IPM's comments are relevant here. While welcoming the Standards for the way in which they direct attention to the importance of certain functions and techniques, and to the need for assessing performance against agreed criteria, the Institute criticized them for failure to recognize the variations needed in ways of performing jobs and tasks brought about by different work settings. (Pickard, 1991)

The failure to recognize the distinction between training and development

The key purpose on which all the Standards rest not only fails to recognize the difference between training and development, treating them as if they were one and the same process; it also lacks a clear focus. 'Developing human potential to assist organizations and individuals to achieve their objectives' is such a broad and generalized statement as to give few practical insights. Note particularly the lack of clarity about whether development should be short-term or long-term; focused primarily on achieving business goals or primarily on meeting individual interests; expected to lead to improved performance or to less quantifiable outcomes; and so on.

Concluding points

There is undoubtedly a need for certain core occupational standards in the training and development field. Such standards will be particularly useful if they help managers and practitioners to examine critically what they do and how they do it, especially in relation to:

- Identifying training and development needs
- Designing training and development strategies and plans
- Providing learning opportunities, resources and support
- Evaluating the effectiveness of training and development

The Coopers and Lybrand Report (1985) found that there was a general lack of expertise in crucial areas like planning and organizing training, cost-benefit analysis and evaluation, and these are some of the key areas identified in the Lead Body Standards. In 1990 a survey of training managers in 59 of the UK's largest employers (Laurie International, 1990) found that training was generally considered to be poorly managed.

> Better processes and systems to manage training and development are required, as well as clarity about the nature, requirements and role of learning in achieving business objectives. (*Personnel Management Plus*, 1990)

Effectively carrying out the functions identified in the Lead Body document would not solve all of these problems, but it would make a very significant contribution to their resolution.

However, success in the field of employee development requires more than functional expertise. It also needs an understanding of the particular organization and the knowledge and skills needed to deal with its culture and its politics, the ability to see and use to advantage external support agencies, and the achievement of personal, professional and organizational status that will give the credibility needed in the particular situation in which the practitioner has to operate.

Moreover, minimum rather than optimum outcomes will be achieved, if 'development' roles are only perceived to relate to designing activities that can be systematically derived and measured. What is vital is that roles should also be concerned with developing the organization as a learning system where, as at Kwik-Fit, Nissan and Rothmans, people are encouraged and enabled to be creative, flexible and committed fully to contributing to organizational goals and growth.

Finally, as we noted earlier in this chapter, for employee development to take root fully in the organization the crucial role is that of top management, which needs to hold and communicate the kind of vision and values that will support and maintain full and continuous development of people.

Major Influences on Employee Development Roles and Responsibilities

When an actor plays a part, it is the interplay of their given role and the way they develop it that explains the uniqueness of their performance in it. Relating this concept to training, we can say that:

> Formal and informal factors influence the parts, or roles, that people play, and so also influence training and development roles in a particular organizational context.

Factors influencing training and development roles

Please describe, by reference to Pettigrew's fivefold model, the role held by the person who carries the main formal responsibility for employee development in your own organization, or in some organization with which you are familiar. (It may, for example, be the Personnel Director or Manager, or the Training Manager, or a designated line manager.) Produce a list of the main factors, formal and informal, which you think influence that person's role.

FEEDBACK NOTES

You can assess your response to this exercise by referring to the comments that follow, which expand on and conclude our discussion of training responsibilities and roles.

The environment of the organization

This refers to the world outside the organization, and all the opportunities and constraints, threats and challenges that it presents. Training policy in an organization which is fighting for survival in an increasingly competitive business market will have no choice but to be completely business-led; appropriate roles will certainly include the provider, probably the training manager, and possibly the change agent or role in transition. On the other hand in a stable organization facing few internal or external changes, training may largely be a matter of continuing to carry out long-established routines with little questioning of their relevance either to the organization or to the individual: in that event the most likely roles are the passive provider and the training manager.

However, in many hitherto bureaucratized private- and public-sector organizations (e.g. the National Health Service), employee development has become a function of critical importance in order to cope with the demands of a rapidly changing, turbulent environment. In such organizations passive providers are having to become expert providers or perish. There is also an increase in training manager roles, and a new emphasis on employee development rather than on training. In such organizations, as we shall see in Chapters 11 and 21, organization-wide role, task and culture changes require virtually all sectors of the workforce to become more flexible, more orientated to customer care, and more concerned with the quality and effectiveness of service provision. At regional level in the NHS a wave of new 'organization development' positions have been created to stimulate and facilitate the effective management of these change processes, so at that level the importance of the change agent role has been formally acknowledged.

The political environment is also an important influence on training and development roles too. In the 1960s the biggest promoter of change for training in organizations, for better or for worse, was the advent of Industrial Training Boards (ITBs). They led to a widespread requirement for an increase in the amount and kind of training tasks that had to be performed and this often led to greater position power for the training function and an increase in training manager roles. However, given the widely perceived organizational irrelevance of much of the work of ITBs, their virtual abolition in the early 1980s was predictably followed in many cases by a rapid decline in the power of training departments and of training itself as a function.

The establishment in the last years of that decade of employer-led TECs, strongly tied to their local communities, may not prove an effective way of promoting the necessary levels of investment in skills development (see Chapter 3), but TECs and other local bodies do offer certain valuable incentives and resources which can help to further the cause of employee development in the organization. One external initiative in which many companies are now actively interested is the Investors in People campaign (see Appendix 1). The intention is that it should do much to promote a strategic, business-led role for employee development. This is a role which does not quite fit into either the fivefold model or the Lead Body framework, but it is arguably the most rapidly growing and important for the function, given the unpredictable future that faces so many private- and public-sector organizations today. It is fully examined in Chapter 11.

Business goals and strategy

Business goals and strategy must have a fundamental influence on determining employee development policy and plans, and therefore also on the kind of roles and tasks which those responsible for implementation of policy should perform (see Chapter 11).

Organizational structure and culture

Sometimes, and almost always in large-scale organizations, there will be what Handy (1985) calls a 'differentiated' structure, with elements of bureaucracy in the routinized areas of activity, but with, say, more of a team-centred, matrix structure in areas requiring flexibility and innovative activity. As we saw in Chapter 5, the structure and culture in which those with employee development responsibilities have to operate have major effects not only on their roles but also on their choice of strategies.

One very important structural issue is the place and operation of the personnel function in the organization. As Mumford (1971) points out, 'The historical development of the personnel function . . . may or may not have included training.' He goes on to observe that a similar and important factor will be 'the number of other specialists such as work study, O&M, medical services, already reporting to a manager'. Another key issue is, of course, the nature of the organization's culture, values and political system – an issue with which we dealt in Chapter 5.

Technology

This refers to the way in which work and work processes are organized, the type of technology used, and, in particular, the technology available for training and development. As we shall see in Chapter 16, there are many important changes taking place in training technology, especially with the growing focus on computer-based training and open and distance learning, and these too affect training and development roles and tasks (see, for example, Harrison, 1992).

The workforce

The size, behavioural patterns, performance, occupational structure and learning needs of the workforce will all influence the training and development tasks to be done, and therefore the overall role of employee development in the organization.

Figure 4 shows the well-known model of the organization as a system.

Figure 4
The organization as a system

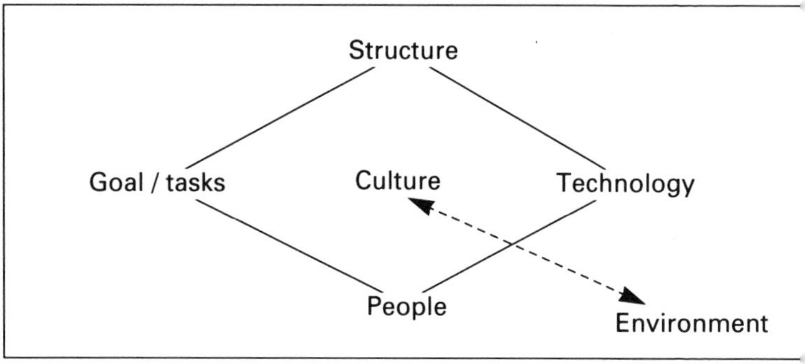

You can see how environment, goal and tasks, structure and culture, technology and people all interact and help to determine the kind of roles held by those with employee development responsibilities.

We can therefore say that:

> Key influences on employee development roles and tasks in an organization are the particular environment of the organization,

its business goals and strategy, its structure and culture, and its technology and workforce.

Improving the Status of Employee Development in the Organization

What, then, is to be done, both to ensure that training responsibilities at all levels are accepted and carried out, and that meaningful and proactive training roles are widespread rather than rare in organizations? There are four particularly crucial areas of skill for the training manager or anyone responsible for training in the organization, and these must be mastered if attitudes to training are to be changed, and if training is to make its maximum impact on performance: boundary management, a systematic approach, cost-benefit analysis and evaluation.

Boundary management

Anyone with employee development responsibilities is in constant interaction with others in the organization. This network of relationships, together with the vision, mission, technical and personal skills of the trainer/developer will directly affect the role the function finally comes to play in the organization. The inept, unskilled manager has little chance of improving the role of training, and may indeed find that, as a consequence of repeated failure to seize opportunities and to prove the value of training, the role becomes further reduced. Likewise the influential line manager who shows colleagues and team how little he or she values training and development will often foster a climate of scepticism that will be hard for anyone else to change.

These conclusions are supported by evidence gathered by Pettigrew and his team, who wrote (1982):

> The change agents, roles in transition, and managers were more aware of the issue of boundary management, had formulated a strategy which more often than not involved at least articulating a mission and sets of operational objectives, and were attempting to implement a broader range of transactions, through a wider set of relationships, than either the providers or passive providers.

They went on to discuss an issue raised in Chapter 5: the importance for those with employee development responsibilities of identifying their own power resources and power bases, and from those to decide what strategies are most likely to be successful in influencing others in the organization to support them in the role they seek to occupy, and the area and level of operations they see as essential for employee development.

A systematic approach

Coopers and Lybrand (1985) saw a systematic approach to training and development as significantly lacking in many organizations. This does not mean that developmental initiatives should never be spontaneous, or that there should be a rigid and bureaucratic approach to training. Nor does it deny that a learning event may often itself trigger off new needs for further learning that would have been impossible to predict before that event. And it does not reject the argument of those who, like Webster (1990), believe that employee development must be continuous and open-ended, with the organizational environment designed to facilitate this never-ending process.

However, in most organizations there is a very long way to go, both culturally and in terms of top-level understanding and commitment, before an open-ended approach can be achieved. In many, it will never happen. So it is necessary to ensure that what at least can be shown to be essential to the success of the organization's business strategy is done, and that means a convincing explanation of the level of investment the organization must make in training and developing its workforce. An assessment must therefore be made of known and agreed priority needs at all levels. A plan for training and development can then be formulated which can guide top management in its decisions about the investment of resources through time, about the agreed corporate goals and strategy for employee development, and about the key roles necessary to ensure effective implementation of strategy.

Within the context of the individual manager's department, there should be the same agreement on what overall needs exist, however they may be defined and over whatever timespan they are to be met. The manager can then put forward a reasoned case for the resources to meet those needs.

Cost-benefit analysis

For the same reasons it is essential to be able to identify clearly and meaningfully the main costs – however they are expressed – of employee development to the organization; the past, current and anticipated future outcomes that justify those costs; and, where additional pressure to invest is needed, the estimated costs of failure to train and develop. Without this information, it is impossible to make valid decisions about whether to increase or reduce expenditure and allocation of other resources, or to alter strategy in order to achieve a better balance of costs and benefits, or to change existing attitudes towards employee development where this is clearly essential.

Cost-benefit analysis will involve financial calculations, but not exclusively. It will involve discussion of quantitative but also of qualitative outcomes and methods of measurement, and it should encompass a consideration of strategies to do with 'growing people', as at Kwik-Fit (see pp. 128–9) as much as of strategies to do with 'training for skills'. The crucial issue is to assess what kind and level of investment is needed in order to produce the kind of outcomes that will be seen as valuable and valued by the key parties. More on this will follow in Chapters 9 and 11.

Evaluation

Evaluation of employee development strategy and plans is essential. It must be expressed in a language that managers can understand, and it must establish the main outcomes that are being achieved in relation to the objectives originally sought and the value of those outcomes in terms that are meaningful to the parties. Evaluation must feed into ongoing planning and action, not be a paper exercise. It should therefore be done only when needed, in a form that is relevant to its purpose, and by those best suited to carry it out (see Chapter 17).

In Chapters 7 and 8, as we explore the meaning of the organization as a 'learning system', we shall see how by building concepts of learning into the everyday language and behaviour of the organization, attitudes to employee development should begin to change. The everyday experience of training and development in too many organizations is still that it is a low-level, peripheral function, concerned mainly with packaged activities, usually in the shape of courses, where the specialists themselves may be poorly trained, lacking in expertise, and acquiescing in the organization's unfavourable definition of their role.

Changing the status of employee development in the organization is to do with technically and politically expert practitioners who speak the language of the business and fully understand the organization in which they have to operate; line managers who recognize their key role in employee development and are helped and encouraged to take it seriously; and the existence of an organizational culture which acknowledges the crucial role employee development has to play in attracting, retaining, motivating and rewarding the kind of workforce that the organization needs in order to achieve its mission and goals (see Chapters 11 and 21).

Improving the status of employee development in the organization

Take an organization with which you are familiar, where training and development have low status and credibility. Produce an analysis of the reasons for this situation, and outline a strategy whereby the role and status of the function could be significantly improved.

FEEDBACK NOTES

The exercise will generate many different responses. The analysis should take account of our checklist of factors influencing employee development roles and tasks: the organizational environment, its business goals and strategy, its structure and culture, and its technology and workforce.

Reading Pettigrew et al. (1982), pp. 13–15, will help you to do a full analysis of issues related to boundary management; and special reference should also be made to the need for a systematic approach, for expertise in cost-benefit analysis, and for a meaningful and productive evaluation of activities and strategy.

Your analysis should lead to two or three key objectives that will result in significant improvement in the role and status of employee development in your organization, and your strategy should be carefully chosen to enable those objectives to be achieved over a given timespan.

Exercises

1 'When personnel managers publicly criticize line management for their lack of intereset in training, it contributes to the low opinion and regard with which the personnel function is held.' Do you

agree? What measures would you like taken inside your organization to promote among line management a greater commitment to employee development? (May 1991)

2 A new line manager is about to be appointed in your organization to head a department where significant personnel problems (both interpersonal and trades union) have been apparent over the past three years. The new manager has not previously worked in the department. Prepare an induction programme for the person concerned, identifying the issues to be addressed and justifying the learning methods proposed. (November, 1988)
(Note for IPM students: Think creatively about this one, transferring to the context of the question ideas gained in reading this chapter; focus mainly on the 'issues' dimension, outlining learning methods but not tackling them in any real detail.)

References

COOPERS AND LYBRAND ASSOCIATES. *A Challenge to Complacency: Changing attitudes to training.* A report to the Manpower Services Commission and the National Economic Development Office. Sheffield, MSC. 1985

COULSON J, CARR C T, HUTCHINSON L AND EAGLE D (EDS.). *Oxford Illustrated Dictionary.* 2nd ed. Oxford, Oxford University Press. 1975

HANDY C B. *Understanding Organizations.* 3rd ed. Harmondsworth, Middlesex, Penguin Books. 1985

HARRISON R. 'Employee Development at Barratt'. In *Case Studies in Personnel* (Woodall D and Winstanley D, eds.). London, Institute of Personnel Management. 1992

KENNEY J AND REID M. *Training Interventions.* London, Institute of Personnel Management, 1986; third edition, by Reid, Barrington and Kenney. 1992

LAURIE INTERNATIONAL. Training and Development: *Top management issues for the next decade.* London, Laurie International Ltd. 1990

LEICESTER C. 'The key role of the line manager in employee development'. *Personnel Management*, March 1989. pp. 53-7

MUMFORD A. *The Manager and Training.* London, Times Management Library. 1971

PERSONNEL MANAGEMENT PLUS. 'Major change in management development needed in '90s'. *Personnel Management Plus*, August 1990. p. 2

PETTIGREW A M, JONES G R AND REASON P W. *Training and Development Roles in Their Organisational Setting.* Sheffield, Manpower Services Commission. 1982

PICKARD J. 'IPM claims new training standards fail to address essential points'. *Personnel Management Plus*, February 1991. p. 3

SINGER E. *Training in Industry and Commerce.* London, Institute of Personnel Management. 1977

TRAINING AND DEVELOPMENT LEAD BODY. *National Standards for Training and Development: An Executive Summary.* Nottingham, Department of Employment. 1992a

TRAINING AND DEVELOPMENT LEAD BODY. *National Standards for Training and Development: Guidelines for Implementation.* Nottingham, Department of Employment. 1992b

TRAINING AND DEVELOPMENT LEAD BODY. *National Standards for Training and Development.* Nottingham, Department of Employment. 1992c

TRANSFORM CONSULTANCY. *Developing the Developers.* Report for the Association for Management Education Development. London, AMED. 1991

WEBSTER B. 'Beyond the mechanics of HRD'. *Personnel Management*, March 1990. pp. 44-7

WILLE E. 'Should management development just be for managers?' *Personnel Management*, August 1990. pp. 34-6

Further useful reading

MANPOWER SERVICES COMMISSION AND INSTITUTE OF TRAINING AND DEVELOPMENT. *Trainer Task Inventory.* Sheffield, MSC. 1984

MANPOWER SERVICES COMMISSION AND INSTITUTE OF TRAINING AND DEVELOPMENT. *Guide to Trainer Effectiveness.* Sheffield, MSC. 1984

NADLER L. 'The variety of training roles'. *Industrial and Commercial Training*, Vol. 1, 1 November 1969. pp. 33-7

PINTO P R AND WALKER J W. 'What do training and development professionals really do?' *Training and Development Journal*, Vol. 32, 7 July 1978. pp. 58-64

TRAINING AND DEVELOPMENT LEAD BODY. *National Standards for Training and Development: Qualifications Structure.* Nottingham, Department of Employment. 1992

TRAINING OF TRAINERS COMMITTEE. *First Report: Training of Trainers.* Sheffield, Manpower Services Commission. 1978

WALTHER R H. 'ASTD members – their perceptions and training goals'. *Training and Development Journal.* Vol. 25, 3 March 1971. pp. 32-7

Chapter 7

The learning organization

Learning Objectives

After reading this chapter you will:

1 understand some major theories about the nature of the learning process, and appreciate their practical relationship to the organization of learning in the workplace;
2 appreciate the value of integrating work and learning, and the importance of a process of continuous development of people, operational tasks and the organization;
3 be able to explain the importance of identifying the overall objectives for learning in the organization, and the main strategies to achieve different kinds of 'learning organization'.

The Learning Process in Theory and Practice

Organizations and the people within them develop by learning. But what exactly does 'learning' mean? One well-known definition is: 'Learning is a relatively permanent change in behaviour that occurs as a result of practice or experience.' (Bass and Vaughan, 1967) In other words, we have 'learnt' something when we have acquired new or changed knowledge, skills or attitudes that stay with us, becoming part of our regular behaviour or performance. The 'relatively permanent change in behaviour' is brought about by practising something we have been taught, or taught ourselves, or experienced, until it has been fully absorbed.

Thinking about learning in this way leads to two major theories which feature throughout this book because they have important practical implications for the development of people and organizations. At this stage we only need an introduction to these theories, and an appreciation of how they relate to one another and to the wider context of organizational learning.

Kolb's theory

Kolb (1974) says that learning can be viewed as a circular and perpetual process, whose key stages are experience, observation of and reflection on that experience, analysis of the key learning points arising from it, and the consequent planning and trying out of new or changed behaviour. Often people go through this cycle almost instinctively, sometimes so skilfully that they produce increasingly successful behaviour in situations which initially caused them problems. But they also often make mistakes at one or more stages of the cycle so that the ultimate skills, knowledge or attitudes acquired do not lead to any improvement. This concept of the learning process is shown in Figure 5.

Figure 5
The learning process (Based on Kolb et al., 1974)

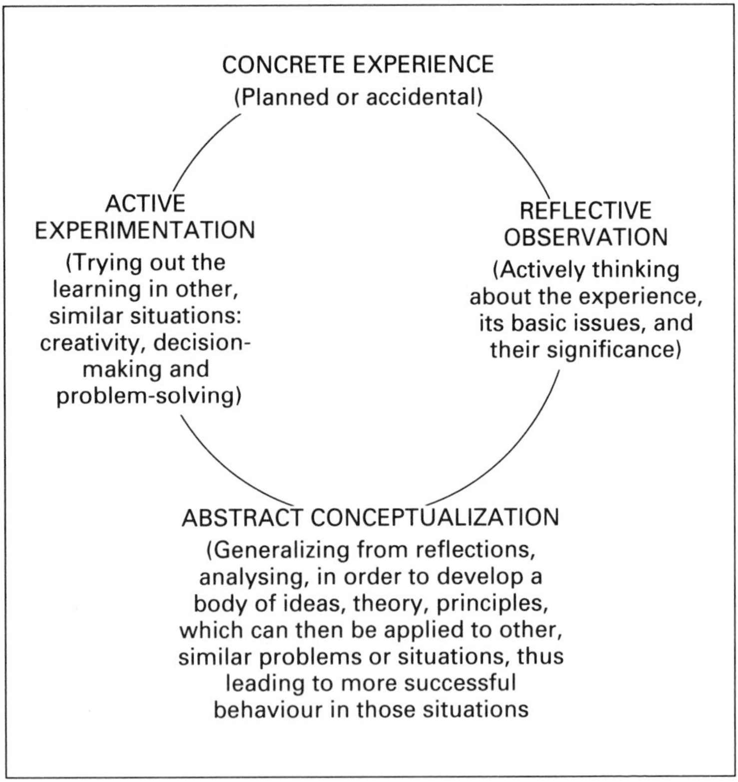
CONCRETE EXPERIENCE
(Planned or accidental)
REFLECTIVE OBSERVATION
(Actively thinking about the experience, its basic issues, and their significance)
ABSTRACT CONCEPTUALIZATION
(Generalizing from reflections, analysing, in order to develop a body of ideas, theory, principles, which can then be applied to other, similar problems or situations, thus leading to more successful behaviour in those situations
ACTIVE EXPERIMENTATION
(Trying out the learning in other, similar situations: creativity, decision-making and problem-solving)

Let's look at this theory more closely. When was the last time you felt you *really* learnt something? Take yourself back to that occasion, and try relating it to Kolb's concept of the learning process. Here is an everyday example.

Mary and her Manager

Mary came out of her manager's room groaning inwardly. He had called her in half an hour before, without warning, and she had walked into another veiled dressing down, and the usual failure to put across her defence in a convincing way, or to change his view of the event. Why did he always manage to throw her like this? She knew that their personalities were so different that the relationship was always going to be difficult, but there had to be some way of getting things on to a better footing. What could she do?

When she got into her office she sat down and **reflected** for quite a long time, not only about her most recent experience with him, but about all the other times when meetings or discussions between the two of them had gone badly. Then, as she thought it all through, she **observed** that it didn't happen the same way *every* time. Sometimes things went well: when she knew a meeting was coming up, and she could prepare for it thoroughly in advance, getting all her facts together, and anticipating every major criticism that could be made of her line of logic, until her arguments, proposals or conclusions were virtually watertight. On those occasions, because she had thought it through carefully, her own emotions tended to take a back seat, and the discussion with her manager became much more objective – she could take most of his endless questioning on board because she had played devil's advocate herself beforehand. But, she **reflected**, when she didn't know beforehand what the meeting was to be about she began to panic as soon as she got into the room. She felt no match for his dry, legalistic probing, his apparently sarcastic comments, or the rapid instructions and follow-up questions he would often throw at her. His formality and sharpness always made her feel that he was looking for failure, and expected it.

Slowly, she began to **analyse**. She started to relate her observations to some of her knowledge about personality and behaviour (she was studying for the IPM examinations!), and she began to see in her own behaviour all the signs of stress and destructive relief of tension that she had read about in her textbooks. So, what did the books say about constructive responses? What principles did they advocate, and what could she think up herself? She happened to have a copy of *Twenty Ways to Manage Better* (Leigh, 1984) in her bookcase, and opening it, she found a chapter on 'Coping with failure' that suddenly seemed to pull all her experiences together! Gradually she began to see a pattern in her successful meetings which conformed to the positive suggestions and principles she was reading about. A strategy was developing in her mind for coping better with those unexpected times when she had to go in for a new brief, or for a reprimand over some error she had made. She **decided** to make herself try the new strategy on the very next occasion, and see if it worked: she would **experiment**, in order to overcome her problems with her manager. Of course, it wouldn't work perfectly at first, but every new experience of such meetings that she encountered from now on represented opportunities for her to **evaluate** and perhaps again alter her strategy, until at last she had learnt how to overcome her problems.

Mary, in this learning process, had been using those core learning skills to which we have made regular reference in this book so far. They are crucial in any problem-solving situation:

- Observation/reflection
- Analysis
- Creativity
- Decision-making/experimentation
- Evaluation

I wonder whether that example is familiar to you? It is a factual one, and I am glad to say that Mary *did* succeed eventually, and by that circular learning process, repeated several times round, she did develop a new way of dealing with those awkward unexpected meetings, and now has a much better relationship with her manager. I hope that, in reading her story, you have also gained a better understanding of Kolb's learning theory, and begun to see how very practical and useful it is.

This 'continuous learning' process should not be dismissed simply as an interesting aspect of daily life, or be left to the individual to manage and possibly but not inevitably benefit from. If those with a responsibility for the development of people in the organization can 'manage' a variety of everyday work situations, as well as planned training activities, in ways that will foster the key skills involved in the learning cycle then those skills can be transferred to an ever-widening range of organizational problems and situations on a continuing basis. Not only individual but organizational performance will thus be developed. It is those five skills with which this book is primarily concerned, since they are core to the success of anyone with a responsibility for employee development in an organization.

Stimulus-response theory

Our second major theory about learning seems at first sight very different. It sees the mastery of the learning process in relation to four key factors:

1 **Drive.** For learning to occur there must first of all be a basic need which makes someone want to learn, and which acts as the continued spur to that activity. In other words, there must be a drive, or motivation, to learn.
2 **Stimulus.** A stimulus means a message which makes an impact on our senses because it relates to one or more of our primary or secondary drives. For learning to occur, people must be stimulated by the learning situation; methods of learning must be used which make a level of impact sufficient to enable and encourage the person to learn in that situation.
3 **Response.** In every learning situation the learner must acquire appropriate responses, i.e. skills, knowledge and attitudes, which will lead to improved performance and/or the development of potential.
4 **Reinforcement.** These responses must be reinforced by practice, experience and feedback of various kinds until they are fully learnt while unproductive responses are highlighted before they can become habitual.

(see Gagne, 1965)

This may seem an instrumental and over-simplified explanation of human learning. One is reminded of animal psychology and the so-called 'law of effect', and pictures come to mind of the dog, cat or pigeon being 'trained' to perform in particular ways by a process of instruction, reward and punishment. It also seems at odds with Kolb's 'experience-based' and learner-led theory.

But the differences are more apparent than real. Let us think more carefully about stimulus-response theory. What it actually stresses is the importance of factors that also emerge as important when considering the practical applications of Kolb's learning theory.

Needs and stimulation

There must be a need and a stimulus, if learning is to occur. The learning experience must either relate to a need of which people are already aware, and to which they attach importance, or it must itself create that need, by presenting to the learners a situation which they must master, a problem they have to resolve. Whether the need is something perceived in advance or simply arising with the particular experience is not significant; the point is that for learning to occur, there must be a state of arousal that leads to the active involvement of the learner.

At each stage of learning, there may be problems. Perhaps the kinds of learning experiences being provided are felt to be artificial or irrelevant; perhaps the learners lack time, encouragement or skill to reflect on and therefore learn from experience (whether it is a work project or some part of a structured training or educational programme); perhaps they lack or are not being helped to develop analytical skills which will lead to accurate diagnoses of situations; or perhaps they lack the ability to test out new learning. Whoever is responsible for the learning process, be it the individual directing their own learning or someone acting as the manager of a learning event, must know how to provide the right kind of stimulation, practice and feedback at the crucial stages of learning.

Objectives and planning

Setting objectives for learning, and planning for it to occur, are always essential processes. The setting of objectives may be the responsibility of the individual learner, the manager of a group at work or a personnel or training specialist. The objectives themselves may be generalized or highly specific, short- or long-term, relating to an individual, to a group, or to the whole organization. Moreover, the processes of objective-setting and planning will not always lead to a structured training situation, nor to all learning situations being led by a 'trainer', using only passive skills on the part of the learners. But there must be objectives: they represent the *raison d'être* for the creation and maintenance of learning situations in whatever form.

Learning strategies

Those responsible for managing individual and organizational learning must decide on the strategies that will best meet learning needs and objectives.

Often, integrating learning with work, so that the task in hand is also used deliberately as a vehicle for learning, will be a highly appropriate and cost-effective strategy. However, there are many other situations where important learning needs may require a carefully planned training programme or a series of well-designed developmental activities through which specified learning objectives can be achieved by designated learners over a set period of time.

There are an increasing number of organizations now where strategies like quality circles, briefing groups and team-building activities are planned as part of a strategy to develop the whole organization as well as individuals within it. Taken to its logical conclusion, such a strategy (for example in firms like Kwik-Fit, pp. 128–9) is an integral part of the overall culture of the company, whose structure and systems are designed to 'grow' flexible, creative people who take responsibility for problem-solving at the point where those problems first arise. It is a response to the perceived need to create the kind of organization and workforce that will achieve and sustain business success (see Chapter 21).

Reinforcement of learning

There is always a need for practice and feedback throughout the learning process, in order that learners can quickly and confidently acquire new learning, and test it out in their practical situations. Kolb's theory emphasizes this when it shows the stage of experimentation leading into further experience, which then generates the possibility of review, analysis and modification or repetition of the new learning. This leads to the next point.

Appraisal of development, both at organizational and individual levels

Appraisal, which should be regular, not at infrequent intervals, will ensure feedback and reinforcement of learning. Reviewing the way in which experiences are tackled, or seem likely to be tackled, will show what further kinds of experience are required. Thus analysis of learning must be carried out at organizational and individual levels if relevant outcomes of learning are to be achieved, and if appropriate learning strategies are to be developed. (Appraisal of individual performance is covered extensively in Chapter 14.)

So there is no essential contradiction between the two approaches to the learning process that we have been examining in this chapter.

Taken together, they offer valuable insights about the learning process and its relationship to individual and organizational growth.

Managing the Organization as a Continuous Learning System

In organizational life everyday experience is the most fundamental influence on people's learning. This experience consists not simply of the work that people do, but also of the way they interract with others in the organization, and the behaviour, attitudes and values of those others. It consists, therefore, of people's entire work environment. Three practical points arise from this realization of the impact of the environment on people's learning in the organization:

1 **Everyday experience should be carefully examined, because of its effects on learning.** We should be aware, whether as individuals, managers or training specialists, of the kind of experiences offered in the daily work environment, and of the learning that is occurring because of them. Some of that learning will have a positive effect on performance, but much of it may have adverse effects: people may be acquiring attitudes that conflict with work objectives, and may be developing serious errors or gaps in knowledge and skills.

2 **The organization should be viewed and managed as a continuous learning system.** Since everyday experience is a profound source of learning, it should be managed to take advantage of that fact. This means that line managers have a key role to play in finding ways of using the workplace as a primary source of positive learning for individuals and teams. Coaching, counselling and guidance will then become vital processes through which people can be helped to recognize and benefit from that experience.

3 **There must be a conscious decision to develop an organizational environment that will promote and sustain desired kinds of organizational learning.** Kolb (1974) says that learning should be an explicit organizational objective, 'pursued as consciously and deliberately as profit or productivity'. He stresses that there must be 'a climate seeing the value of such an approach . . . developed in the organization'. So we return to the need for a particular environment of attitudes, culture and systems in the organization.

The Colour Television Project
(Quoted from Barrington, 1986, with acknowledgements to H Barrington and *Personnel Review*)

What major insights about learning and work arise from reading the following case study?

When colour TV was first introduced on a major scale, it was appreciated that a new dimension was being added to advertising commercials. Six months before the actual start date, a senior marketing manager [in the organization in which I then served] was charged with collecting – from places such as film studios, colleges of art, and advertising agencies – as much know-how about colour as he could assimilate.

After one month, he had to present his findings to a collective meeting of marketing management. That meeting raised a large number of unanswered questions, and he and several others were charged with further investigations. Another meeting a month later produced more sharing of experience, more unanswered questions, more commitment to get answers, and so on. By the fourth month, discussions were tending to accept certain questions as 'only answerable via experience' and creative decisions were beginning to be taken on how the experience should be managed.

This was the learning system in action, members defining their needs and researching to collect data which was then shared with colleagues to produce decisions on change, all in the service of operational ends. Learning was integrated with work, and both the work and the people were developed via the one process.

FEEDBACK NOTES

There will be a wide range of insights, depending on those parts of the case study that particularly interest you. The following, however, are of particular importance when we are thinking about the 'learning organization':

- The organization can be a powerful learning system.
- Integration of learning with work is a valuable and cost-effective learning strategy.
- Continuous development in the workplace benefits the whole organization.
- Development is a fundamental management responsibility.

In this case study we can see how a number of individuals gradually developed into a continuous learning group, achieving, as they tackled an operational task, a steady improvement in skills of reflection, analysis, creativity and decision-making which not only helped them to deal effectively with the immediate work project, but which could then be applied to future projects.

Of course other strategies could have been used, and often are in similar situations. A specialist could have been brought in to tackle the whole colour TV project, and would no doubt have done the job effectively and in a much shorter time, but no one else would have developed much from such a strategy. Or the team could have been trained in the appropriate skills and knowledge, so that necessary learning would have been acquired and could then be applied to that and any future similar task; but that would have been a lengthy and expensive approach. The strategy actually adopted was cheap, effective, and achieved work and learning targets, as well as the development of a work team.

Now, let us look at another example.

Venture Pressings (based on Arkin, 1990)
(With acknowledgements to A Arkin and *Personnel Management Plus*)

In terms of a learning organization, what are the points of similarity and of difference between this case study and the Colour Television Project?

Venture Pressings is a company formed in February 1988 to make body panels for Jaguar cars. It is at the leading edge of technological innovation. Its human resource manager, Tony O'Leary, stresses that:

> Without the flexibility generated by our commitment to an investment in employee development, the efficiency needed to make the company succeed would not have been possible (Arkin, 1990).

In order to attract and retain a high-calibre workforce, the company offered continuous training, competitive rates of pay and a longer-term profit-sharing bonus plan. The response to the initial recruitment drive was overwhelming.

Crucial to guaranteeing flexibility of skills, mobility of labour and the company's right to determine staffing levels were the initial signing of a single-union agreement with the general workers' union GMB, and the provisions for pendulum arbitration aimed at preventing stoppages. Stoppages cannot, of course, be prevented by any agreement, if a workforce is determined to take that kind of action. However, the company has taken all the steps it could to reduce such a possibility, particularly by the nature of its selection procedures, which include psychometric and aptitude tests, are very rigorous, and seek to ensure 'that the people we employ are committed to the same aims and objectives as we are'. (Ibid.)

Thus there has been a determination to create and sustain a particular culture that will ensure a committed, flexible, multiskilled and high-calibre workforce. The company's training programmes reinforce this culture by developing attitudes and behaviour, as well as skills, that are consistent with those the company sees as essential to the achievement of its aims. The training budget (5 per cent of payroll in 1990) is far above the UK norm, and covers a 4–6-week induction period involving outdoor development as well as classroom learning, followed by the opportunity to acquire new skills, with rewards for doing so.

> Progression through ten incremental points in each of four salary bands is determined by skill acquisition, and individuals' performance on a modular training programme is monitored by way of development plans that are discussed twice a year with their team leaders.
>
> Training is delivered both on the shopfloor, by team leaders who themselves receive training as trainers, and in the company's dedicated training centre.

The size of the workforce in 1990 was 260, with an eventual target of 320, so Venture Pressings is a small company, yet it invests very heavily in the training and development of its entire workforce through a variety of processes that focus consistently on flexibility and teamwork.

> Production staff are divided into teams of 'cells' consisting of around 40 employees and headed by a team leader. Although cell members have specialist skills, they also have broader responsibilities and are expected to turn their hands to a range of tasks, even when this involves skilled craftsmen taking on unskilled or semi-skilled work.
>
> Where a particular area of expertise found in one cell is needed by another, team leaders negotiate ways of sharing this expertise . . . Effective communication is crucial to the success of the cellular system, and as well as taking part in weekly meetings to discuss their own work, the cell's and that of the company generally, workers also come in about ten minutes before the start of each working day for further discussions.

FEEDBACK NOTES

What is similar about these two case studies? Both are about continuous development; in both, the vehicle is tasks to be done in the workplace; in both, the focus is on teams rather than individuals; valuable and motivating individual development will occur, but within the context of the work team. So in both, a major objective is the development of the team.

What is different? In the case of the Colour Television Project the strategy of using the workplace as a learning vehicle centred upon a particular group of people, with the objective of combining work and learning; we do not know what is happening at any wider level, and it is the kind of strategy that individual managers might well be able to apply without the need for reinforcement by processes or systems outside their 'territory'. In this kind of example the departmental culture is therefore the most powerful environmental influence as far as learning and development are concerned.

At Venture Pressings, on the other hand, continuous learning and development, whether of individual or of team, is part of a wider, fully integrated human resource management strategy that permeates the entire organization, and that, in conjunction with other business strategies, is aimed at the achievement of corporate goals. Venture Pressings could well be a Japanese company – Nissan, Fujitsu, or Komatsu, for example. That integrated approach is typical of work systems and employment practices in those companies. At Venture Pressings, it is therefore the culture of the whole company that is the most powerful environmental influence on work, learning and development, and it is that culture which, for the company, is of primary importance. Selection, training and development, are all aimed not only at recruiting and retaining people with the skills needed, but at ensuring that employees will 'fit' the culture, and so sustain the company's success through time.

What, then, do these two examples tell us about the management of the organization as a learning system? There must be a conscious decision made about what kind of learning strategy an organization should pursue, and 'the learning organization' can make a profound and lasting impact on organizational growth.

Learning Strategies for Organizations

Although detailed decisions about corporate goals and strategy for employee development will require the kinds of analysis covered in

Chapters 9 and 11, it is important to consider here the kinds of learning strategies that the organization should adopt, given its general objectives for learning. (The headings that follow are taken from Mezirow, 1985.)

Instrumental learning

This means learning how to do the job better once a satisfactory basic standard of performance has been attained. If this is the main objective, the learning strategy, which might start with some initial formal training, could be to encourage the individual as they do their work to 'identify a problem, formulate a course of action, try it out, observe the effects and assess the results . . . It is best described as on-the-job training of an informal nature.' (Gilley and Eggland, 1989)

Dialogic learning

This means the process of understanding the culture of the organization and the way it achieves its goals, so that there is a growing identification of the goals, values, attitudes and patterns of bahaviour of the individual with those of the organization. If this is the objective, the organization should place particular emphasis on their selection and induction processes, as at Venture Pressings, and their management style, organization of people and work, and training, development and reward strategies should continually focus on and reward attitudes and patterns of behaviour that underpin the culture the organization sees as crucial to the achievement of its goals. For an example of how this can be done in practice, see Mumford and Buley (1988), whose article explains the way in which the Birmingham Midshires Building Society assessed and rewarded behaviour skills needed to sustain the new culture needed by the Society at a time of major change.

Self-reflective learning

This is the kind of learning that Gilley and Eggland (1989) describe as 'critical reflectivity'. It is the learning that occurs when individuals grow to understand themselves and their role within the organization better through a process of analysing and redefining their current perspectives. If people are to form new views about how they should relate to the organization, they must be encouraged to be self-critical, and acknowledge the need for continuous changes in their attitudes and roles if the organization is to survive in an uncertain world. This means that they must feel able to admit errors, and learn from them, as well as taking risks in trying out new values and patterns of behaviour. As Argyris (1982) points out, this can only be done by working in an environment that 'enables and empowers individuals to be responsible, productive and creative' and to see error as a positive learning vehicle, as well as 'acknowledging uncertainty and spanning information boundaries'.

Self-reflective learning is clearly essential in organizations facing uncertainty, as are instrumental and dialogic learning. In companies designed like Venture Pressings, all three types of learning are given continuing emphasis in order to build and maintain the kind of dynamic, highly skilled, flexible workforce that they need. Furthermore in such an environment continuous development will not need to be planned for as a separate strategy (see Institute of Personnel and Development, 1994) but will occur as a natural consequence of the way culture, people and work interact to promote all three types of learning 'essential in the full enhancement of human performance and potential'. (Gilley and Eggland, 1989)

So the Venture Pressings strategy is the relevant one to follow in order to create the 'learning organization' in the fullest sense of that phrase. However, that strategy is complex, embracing as it does all the major work systems and human resource policies of the organization, and is beyond the capacity of individual managers and their teams to achieve. It must be an integral part of the organization's corporate mission, policy and business strategy. It constitutes a major, long-term business investment that will not be possible for many organizations to achieve, and in many more will not have the belief and commitment of top management as a meaningful strategy to adopt (see Chapter 21).

None the less, there are now an increasing number of companies who are trying to apply a strategy similar to that pursued at Venture Pressings. For some, it is seen as essential because they are at the leading edge technologically and/or in a competitive market; others because they are embattled and need major changes in their workforce. An example of the latter is Rover, the British Aerospace subsidiary. In September 1991, Rover effectively offered its employees jobs for life in return for the adoption of Japanese-style working practices, including training in a range of skills so that anyone capable of doing a task could be asked to do it, and the introduction of team working. The company had to achieve a leaner, more efficient, more flexible workforce if it was to survive. (Maguir, 1991; Gribben, 1991)

The basic decisions to be made about managing the organization as a learning system are therefore whether to pursue a strategy to improve productivity; whether to aim to promote a particular kind of culture; or whether the objective is to design and develop an organization that, in all its human resource policies, its work and reward systems, and its culture, will ensure the attraction, retention and growth of an integrated workforce with the skills, attitudes and flexibility to achieve the organization's business goals no matter what the conditions of uncertainty and change in which it has to operate. We shall return to this theme in Chapter 21.

Exercises

1 What do you consider the main reasons why a person is or is not motivated to learn? What action would you recommend within your own organization to ensure a higher level of motivation towards learning within the Personnel Department? (November, 1988)

2 Read the articles by Webster (1990) and Wille (1990), and, having reviewed the material in this chapter, carry out an analysis of the kind of 'learning organization' your own place of work should ideally be, and what immediate steps could be taken to begin the necessary change processes.

References

ARGYRIS C. *Reasoning, Learning and Action.* San Francisco, Jossey-Bass. 1982

ARKIN A. 'Breaking with the past'. *Personnel Management Plus*, November 1990. pp. 16-17

BARRINGTON H A. 'Continuous development: Theory and reality', *Personnel Review*, Vol. 15, No. 1, 1986

BASS B M AND VAUGHAN J A. *Training in Industry: The management of learning.* London, Tavistock Publications (Behavioural Science in Industry Series). 1967

GAGNE R M. *Conditions of Learning.* Eastbourne, Holt Rhinehart and Winston. 1965

GILLEY J W AND EGGLAND S A. *Principles of Human Resource Development.* Maidenhead, Addison Wesley. 1989

GRIBBEN R. 'Rover plans 30 pc cut in drive to match Japanese'. *Daily Telegraph*, 6 November 1991

INSTITUTE OF PERSONNEL AND DEVELOPMENT. *Statement on Continuous Development: People and work.* 2nd ed. London, IPD. 1994

KOLB D A, RUBIN I M AND McINTYRE J M. *Organizational Psychology: An experiential approach.* Englewood Cliffs, New Jersey, Prentice Hall. 1974

LEIGH A. *Twenty Ways to Manage Better.* London, Institute of Personnel Management. 1984

MAGUIR K. 'Rover offers jobs for life in effort to counter Japanese'. *Daily Telegraph*, 18 September 1991

MEZIROW J A. 'A critical theory of self-directed learning'. In *Self-Directed Learning: From theory to practice* (Brookfield S, ed.). San Francisco, Jossey-Bass. 1985

MUMFORD J AND BULEY T. 'Rewarding behavioural skills as part of performance'. *Personnel Management*, December 1988. pp. 33-7

WEBSTER B. 'Beyond the mechanics of HRD'. *Personnel Management*, March 1990. pp. 44-7

WILLE E. 'Should management development just be for managers?' *Personnel Management*, August 1990. pp. 34-6

Further useful reading

BARRINGTON H A. *Learning about Management.* Maidenhead, McGraw-Hill. 1984

KNOWLES M S. 'Organizations as learning systems'. *Training and Development Journal*, Vol. 40, No. 1, January 1986. pp. 5-8

MARSICK V AND WATKINS K. 'Learning and development in the workplace'. In *Proc. ASTD Professor Conference.* St. Louis, American Society of Training and Development. 1986

REID M AND BARRINGTON H. *Training Interventions.* London, Institute of Personnel and Development. 1994; fourth edition

RICHARDSON J AND BENNETT B. 'Applying learning techniques to on-the-job development: Part 2'. In *Journal of European Industrial Training.* Vol. 8, No. 3. 1984

WOOD S (ed.). *Continuous Development: The path to improved performance.* London, Institute of Personnel Management. 1988 (a book of real-life case studies on continuous development in organizations in different countries)

Chapter 8

Auditing learning and developing the learners

Learning Objectives

After reading this chapter you will:

1 understand the importance of auditing learning in the organization, and be able to plan an audit;
2 be able to analyse your own and others' learning styles and skills;
3 understand how effective learners can be developed in the organization;
4 know how to promote continuous development and self-directed learning in the organization.

Auditing Learning in the Organization

In order to make the best use of the organization as a learning system, it is first necessary, as we saw in Chapter 7, to have a clear vision of the kind of learning system needed to achieve organizational goals and develop individual performance and potential.

Let us assume that this vision exists. The next task is to examine the current situation carefully, analysing the aims, processes and outputs of learning; in other words, to carry out a learning audit. The main areas of concern are:

1 **What are the current aims and policy related to employee learning and development?** What, if any, learning and development aims and policy exist here? Are they understood and communicated to everyone? Or are the growth of commitment, abilities and potential left to chance, or at the most to *ad hoc* interventions – a course here, a pep talk or word of criticism there?

2 **What learning is going on?** How do people learn their jobs, tasks, and attitudes? Who and what helps or hinders them in that learning

process? Are the right kinds of practice and experience offered, so that effective and permanent changes to behaviour and performance occur? What are people's views about their own learning?

3 **What planned development is going on?** How and by whom are people being developed, and to what ends? What, if any, formal development programmes exist, and are they tailored to meet the combined needs of individuals and of the organization? What opportunities are there for self-development, and for 'learning to learn', and how far are people equipped to understand, identify and benefit from such opportunities? Again, what are the views of the people themselves on these points?

4 **What organizational growth is being achieved?** How far, if at all, is organizational performance and growth being stimulated by the kind of learning strategies being pursued? (We saw examples of learning strategies in Chapter 7.)

5 **Are the necessary learning skills being developed in the organization?** Depending on the kind of learning to be achieved, do people have the right kind of skills and attitudes to manage and achieve such learning?

Auditing itself has been described as:

> A process that produces an official accounting and verification, most often conducted by third party evaluators. Auditing typically relies on samples of information that are critical to the organisation and its decision makers. (Murphy and Swanson, 1988)

However, it is important to be clear that in referring in this chapter to a learning audit we are not discussing the evaluation of specific learning events – that will be examined in Chapter 17. Certainly the information gathered in our audit will be helpful for that purpose, but:

> The aim of the audit itself is to supply a snapshot of what is going on across the organization in terms of learning, in order to compare what *is* happening to the aims and expectations of what *should be* happening and to identify the action needed in order to produce the kind of learning organization desired.

How can an audit be carried out? There is no set way, but two different approaches can be considered at this point.

The IPD's audit

First, let us take the IPD's recommendations for developing the kind of organization that will promote continuous development of its workforce. The IPD defines continuous development as 'lifelong, self-directed learning', and in its Code of Continuous Development (1994, see Appendix 4), seven areas of activity are listed, to which attention must be directed in order to establish what is happening about learning in the organization, and to help establish a culture and system of continuous development across the whole organization. If the purpose of the audit is indeed to explore the extent to which continuous development is occurring in the workforce, and to make relevant recommendations, then each of the seven areas could be analysed in turn in order to identify current perceived and intended outcomes in that area. An appropriate strategy and action plan could then be drawn up in order to develop the organization as a 'continuous learning system'.

The seven areas of activity are:

- Policies
- Roles
- Identification of learning opportunities
- Learner involvement
- The provision of learning resources
- Benefits
- Results

The six-step approach to auditing

Murphy and Swanson (1988) outline six steps:

1. Establish objectives for each category of audit.
2. Describe what the evaluator expects to find.
3. Determine data collection procedures.
4. Collect data samples.
5. Report what was found in relation to expectations.
6. Write and report conclusions.

Let us now try an exercise using this model.

Carrying out an audit of instrumental learning

Using Murphy and Swanson's six-step approach, produce a simple plan for an audit in an organization where training and instrumental learning are the main forms of learning to be audited (either because they are perceived as the most important forms of learning needed in the organization; or because for some reason there is a concern about learning in these areas). By training we mean the formal training, whether on or off the job, whereby people are helped to acquire the skills needed to perform their jobs to standard; and by instrumental learning we mean the ways in which people learn to do their jobs better so that they reach high standards of productivity – 'best described as on-the-job training of an informal nature' (Gilley and Eggland, 1989).

FEEDBACK NOTES

You will need to explain briefly the kind of organization in which the audit is to be carried out, and its overall perceived levels of productivity and performance. You should also explain why it is important to carry out an audit of training and instrumental learning in that organization at this particular time. You might then produce a plan that looks something like this (but if yours is different, don't worry – as long as you have put something relevant and practical under the six headings, along the lines of what follows, that should give you the guidelines for action that will produce a useful audit).

1 **Objectives of the audit**

- To assess how far formal on- and off-the-job training activities result in learners reaching required standards of performance; and what kind of activities lead to the steady improvement of their job performance thereafter, in each sector of the workforce
- To identify any other ways by which people learn to achieve effective standards and to improve their performance, across each sector of the workforce
- To identify any barriers to effective training and instrumental learning, across each sector of the workforce

2 **What the evaluator expects to find**
The evaluator would expect to find that people are helped to achieve effective standards of performance by most of the planned training activities that occur; and that their management and organization in the workplace are aimed at the improvement of job performance

thereafter, especially through briefing groups, quality circles and other approaches whereby they are encouraged to identify problems themselves, formulate courses of action to resolve them, experiment with these, and assess how far they actually improve job performance.

3 **Data collection procedures**
Data will be gathered over a three-month period, by a questionnaire going out to samples across the whole workforce, and by follow-up interviews on a selective basis. The procedures will ensure that the views and expectations of trainers, managers and learners about training and instrumental learning are identified, and that their suggestions for change are also gathered. (You should elaborate, in this section, about the samples you will use and your rationale for that choice, about the design of the questionnaire, and about the checklists to be used for interviews.)

You will need to explain here who is to collect the data, and how they will be selected and organized (if it is not yourself). It may be that external consultants are used; or that the task could be done by a student on secondment who is able to use it as a project for an educational course; or that it is done by someone within the organization. Great care must be taken about the selection of those who carry out the various parts of the audit exercise (see Chapter 17).

4 **Collection of data samples**
You will need to produce a carefully worked out time-schedule for this stage.

5 **Report on what was found in relation to expectations**
The findings must be clearly and logically set out. In this audit, it would be expected that they would cover a range of positive findings – for example, that most formal courses do result in a perceived improvement in people's ability to perform their jobs, as seen by job holders and their managers; and that although certain changes are needed in terms of content and delivery, the broad thrust of training activities is considered by most of the key parties – trainers, learners, their managers and top management – to be satisfactory, and worth the general cost of the provision, with tangible evidence available to support those perceptions.

There will however be negatives too. Let us look at some of the most typical in an audit of this kind:

- **Impact and costs of training activities.** In terms of impact on job performance, certain training activities may be found to be unsuccessful, and decisions will have to be made about whether to amend or discontinue those activities. In terms of costs, certain training activities may be considered reasonably successful but may not warrant the costs they incurred. (This is often the case with external courses which, after such an audit, may be discontinued in favour of piloting the same training in house, with an agreement to extend that latter strategy if the pilot proves successful.)

- **Incentives for good job performance and for a steady pattern of improvement in standards reached.** The audit may reveal that formal training activities are not having their desired results because those who go through them do not feel they are being adequately rewarded, and so have no motivation to apply new skills and knowledge. So reward systems, whether of finance, career development, or levels and kinds of responsibility and status, would need to be examined (see Fairbairn, 1991).
- **Lack of managerial support for risk-taking and learning from failure.** Instrumental learning involves people trying out different ways of improving their performance in a given job. If the emphasis of managers is on the avoidance of mistakes, or on 'one best way' of performing tasks, and if failure is heavily penalized rather than being used as a vehicle for questioning and helping people to learn and improve, then effective instrumental learning cannot occur. Instead, learners will tend to reach a particular level of performance and remain there. If this is all that is required of them, then the result may be seen as satisfactory; if, however, learners are expected to make steady improvements in their performance, then changes will need to be made in the learning environment.

6 **Conclusions**

You should note here the need for the final report to take a form that is clear, concise, as brief as possible, and expresses findings in a language that will be meaningful to those to whom the audit is to be made available. Conclusions in this kind of audit might include some or all of the following types of recommendation, depending on your findings, and assessed cost and feasibility of actions proposed against needs that have been defined:

- To continue to run most of the training activities, with a specified range of changes, and with more careful attention to the selection of trainees, and to arrangements for transfer of learning after the activities and continued monitoring of performance
- To discontinue a minority of activities, piloting other forms of learning, or different kinds of training course, if desirable, while carefully monitoring the costs and outcomes of any pilot events and comparing them with costs and outcomes of those they have replaced, and those anticipated
- To carry out the training and development of certain managers in order to improve their ability to diagnose learning needs, and to transfer the learning of their trainees on to the job; and to help learners steadily improve their performance thereafter

For a good example of the six-step auditing model applied to the supervisory training in an organization, see Murphy and Swanson (1988). For an acount of the auditing of management development in an organization, see Ashton et al. (1980).

Let us end this section with a case study. It shows a variety of purposes for audits, ranging from the identification of the attitudes people hold towards their jobs, their managers and their 'clients', how these have been acquired, and their impact on performance, to how far action taken to change attitudes as well as skills (i.e. to achieve both instrumental and dialogic learning) have been successful.

British Airways, 1981-91

The vision and mission: 1981

In 1981, when British Airways (BA) was effectively bankrupt for a combination of reasons but very much because of a disastrous and continuous loss of customers, the new Chief Executive, Colin Marshall, assessed the situation and determined on a new mission for the company: it was to become 'the Harrods of the airlines of the world'. BA could never be like Laker – a small-scale operation, relying on low-cost, tight-margin, low-price operations to give it the cutting edge. So it would go for the opposite.

The corporate strategy

The corporate strategy to achieve this mission was complex, but its immediate aim was to win back customers by changing the attitudes, behaviour and performance of customer-contact staff.

Cultural change

Having identified that the existing bureaucratic, inward-looking, rigid and complacent culture that prevailed in British Airways was particularly strong at the top of the management hierarchy, Marshal recruited a new top management team, whose values matched his own and were to underpin the new customer-orientated culture. A two-way audit was carried out by an external consultancy firm, covering customers' perceptions of service provided by BA, and customer-contact staff's perceptions of their jobs, their roles, and their relationships with customers and BA management.

The audit highlighted many weaknesses in the company's customer service, primarily due to poor human resource management in BA, and to related major behavioural and performance problems among the contact staff. A massive training and teamwork programme was mounted which, over the next two or three years, radically changed the culture of the company and the behaviour and performance of all its people.

Training and development initiatives

The programme was designed by Time Management International, a consultant firm who, working closely with BA's Training Department, launched a series of two-day 'Putting People First' courses for customer-contact staff across the world between 1983 and 1986. The courses aimed to improve staff's self-image, and to change their attitudes towards BA and its customers, in order to achieve the highest possible standards of customer care throughout the corporation.

The courses led into quality circle team initiatives resourced by 'management workshops', and the new ideas generated by these teams of supervisors and staff were extremely productive for the company, as well as reinforcing the enthusiasm, commitment and positive attitudes of its employees. The courses proved extremely successful in promoting a different style of behaviour in customer-contact staff.

At this point another two-way audit was carried out. This time it covered the mutual perceptions of contact staff and their managers, and it revealed exactly the same kind of tensions between staff and their managers as had existed between customers and contact staff. In response to these problems of management style and behaviour, a series of short 'Managing People First' courses were then directed at all management strata. These courses were key components of a comprehensive training and development programme that stretched across the world, managed increasingly, as time went on and internal skills developed, by BA's training personnel.

A review of progress in 1983 led to longer courses of training for managers, and for professional and technical staff, focusing on team-building and teamwork, objective-setting, and other competences to produce across all of BA a more target-centred, efficient and productive organization.

Appraisal

A new system was designed and introduced to underpin the changes in culture, behaviour and performance. It focused on specific targets of behaviour and performance. Standards relating to behavioural targets were expressed on behavioural rating scales, identifying the types of behaviour that were considered 'good' and those considered 'unacceptable'. Peer and subordinate views were used in rating managers' styles and ways of behaving.

Financial rewards

To further reinforce the changes there was a review of the salary and bonus packages offered to employees, resulting in the availability of substantial bonuses related to productivity in terms of *both* kinds of targets – behavioural and performance.

Organization structure

After the first wave of training programmes, it became increasingly obvious that the bureaucratic structure of the company must be changed, in favour of a leaner, flatter, more efficient design which would facilitate teamwork, flexibility, high quality of service, and customer orientation. This change of structure was tackled as a longer-term strategy.

Other business strategies

At the same time as the organization was being restructured to achieve decentralization of decision-making and the reduction of hierarchical levels, technological and other systems improvements were being made and the financial and marketing management of the company was being overhauled.

Within only three years of the inception of the new human resource strategy, customer service and all round quality had strikingly improved, customer numbers, profits and productivity were soaring – and the success was sustained. The emphasis since those early years of turning the company around has been on constant monitoring to check on the performance of the organization, the operation of its culture and the effectiveness and efficiency of its structure and management. For example, late in 1989 a new Personnel Director was appointed, and, again using the technique of an audit, he surveyed the human resource management function and its effectiveness throughout BA. This led to a radical reorganization of that function early in 1990, with a reduction in its size. The top human resource team was cut from 11 to six, and those senior people were redeployed, giving each of them key responsibilities in different parts of the business at unit level, as well as general strategic and co-ordinating functions. Many human resource management responsibilities were reallocated to line managers, and some line managers were brought in to replace specialist staff.

As the early 1990s have shown, BA has to operate in an exceptionally difficult and unpredictable environment, in terms both of commercial competition and government policy. It has placed great emphasis on building a flexible structure and workforce, with a strong, corporation-wide primary culture and a business-led approach to human resource management and development in its continuous efforts to sustain its leading position.

In the BA study we can see the purposes that the audit technique can serve in identifying learning needs and promoting and supporting organizational change. We can also see an organization that is trying to promote two of the three kinds of learning identified by Mezirow (1985) as crucial to the full development of people's abilities and potential: instrumental and dialogic. How far self-reflective learning is encouraged throughout the company is impossible to deduce from this account, but clearly there is a need, given BA's unpredictable future, for a continuing reappraisal of the meanings that people attach to their roles, and of the ways in which they behave and interact in those roles.

Developing the Learners

Learners and those who are promoting their learning need to understand the learning and development processes, and to possess appropriate learning styles and learning skills. Major theories about the learning process were covered in Chapter 7, and if the principles to which they direct attention are observed in different learning strategies and activities in the organization, then much will already have been achieved. However, it is also important to consider the styles of learning that people prefer or tend habitually to adopt.

Styles of learning and problem-solving

People have different styles of learning which influence not only how they learn in a particular situation, but also how they manage, solve problems, and make decisions in their work. Major research by Honey and Mumford (1986), using Kolb's (1974) ideas as a theoretical base, has indicated that predominant learning styles tend to fall into one of four categories, related to the four different learning processes described by Kolb. Their definitions are as follows:

1 **Activists**

> Activists involve themselves fully . . . in new experiences. They enjoy the here and now and are happy to be dominated by immediate experiences. They are open-minded, not sceptical, and this

> tends to make them enthusiastic about anything new . . . They revel in short-term crisis fire fighting. They often tackle problems by brainstorming . . . [They tend to be] bored with implementation and longer-term consolidation.

2 Reflectors

> The thorough collection and analysis of data about experiences and events is what counts so they tend to postpone reaching definitive conclusions for as long as possible . . . They prefer to take a back seat in meetings . . . [and] enjoy observing other people in action . . . When they act it is as part of a wide picture which includes the past as well as the present, and others' observations as well as their own.

3 Theorists

> They tend to be detached, analytical and dedicated to rational objectivity rather than anything subjective or ambiguous. Their approach to problems is consistently logical . . . They prefer to maximise certainty and feel uncomfortable with subjective judgements, lateral thinking and anything flippant.

4 Pragmatists

> Pragmatists are keen on trying out ideas, theories and techniques to see if they work in practice . . . They don't like 'beating around the bush' and tend to be impatient with ruminating and open-ended discussions. They are essentially practical, down-to-earth people who like making practical decisions and solving problems . . . Their philosophy is . . . 'If it *works* it's good.'

In any organization there will be a mix of activists, reflectors, pragmatists and theorists. There will also be people able to learn in more than one of those modes equally effectively and some, perhaps, who can adapt with ease to any type of learning situation. It is important to identify the different learning styles and approaches, so that there can be a matching of styles to needs, and so that those dominated by one particular style, yet having to operate in situations which require them to learn in a different way, can develop learning styles and skills to suit their present, and also perhaps their likely future, roles and tasks. For example, situations or decisions calling for an essentially practical approach may be handled inappropriately if left to people who are strong theorists; and a problem which must be sorted out quickly and in a pragmatic manner may suffer if left to someone who is markedly reflective and theoretical in their approach to decision-making.

Career planning (see Chapter 20) also needs to take learning styles into account. For example, if someone who is highly competent in a professional role but without any direct management experience decides, for career reasons, to seek promotion into general management, they will not only need to acquire a range of new knowledge, skills and attitudes; they will also have to learn to think on their feet, be pragmatic, and cope with a way of life which may give them little chance to reflect and theorize before deciding on action. Some, considering carefully the transformation of their learning styles required, may decide that the change is possible and seek ways of developing themselves in the less familiar learning modes. Others may decide it is not possible, and that whatever skills and knowledge they may be able to develop, they would not be able to handle the demands of the new role in terms of the approaches to learning and problem-solving it would require.

At this point, why not try to find out what kind of learner you are yourself? Honey and Mumford's questionnaire can be found in their book. It has been used by many managers and others, and the authors say that it is generally felt to have a high degree of validity, although they recommend that you should try it twice in a two- or three-week period, rather than just once, to get a reliable set of scores. Of course, the questionnaire is meant to be a thought-provoking mechanism rather than a stringently scientific measuring instrument, so do bear that in mind when you are assessing your results.

Interestingly Honey and Mumford have looked at the primary styles of various occupational groups, and found that trainers tend to have high activist tendencies (although they do stress that the samples are not large enough to be sure that this conclusion was generally valid!).

Developing effective learners in the workplace

Now let us relate our knowledge of Kolb's learning theory and these ideas about learning styles and skills to learners in our own organization. Consider the following statements:

> Our cyclical economy and the speed of technical change suggest that 'learning to learn' is the central training problem of our time. (Kenney et al., 1979)
>
> People can become self-directed learners, understanding their learning styles and developing the skills needed for effective

> learning. Thus they can manage their own learning processes instead of relying on the system, or hoping they will learn naturally. (Mumford, 1981)

These statements emphasize that if people are to learn continuously, and to take advantage of the rich resources offered by the organization as a learning system, they must be able to cope with the demands that change places on them in terms of new learning, and they must have a mastery of the learning process. How can this learning ability be fostered? How, for example, can those responsible for employee development in a large organization, with several thousand people in its workforce, hope to develop people as *learners*? As with any other complex tasks, we must simplify it by reducing it to its essentials.

The Institute of Personnel and Development's Code of Continuous Development (1994, see Appendix 4) outlines ways in which people can be helped, and can help themselves, to become effective learners. However, it is appropriate here to go into rather more detail about what the training specialist or anyone with responsibility for the development of people in the organization can do to help here. Six major activities are essential:

1 **Self-development of those responsible for the learning of others.** Whoever is trying to help people become effective learners must themselves have an adequate mastery of each of the four major types of learning skill, and so one of their first tasks should be to identify what kind of learner they are themselves at present, using Honey and Mumford's (1986) learning inventory, which takes about 20 minutes to complete and to score, or Kolb's (1974), which takes rather less time and offers a very interesting alternative. If both are used, illuminating comparisons can be drawn from the two sets of scores. They then need to work out an action plan to improve those learning skills which will enable them to function effectively along all four dimensions rather than just one or two (Honey and Mumford's book gives detailed guidance and examples to help here).

2 **Promote self-directed learning.** Self-directed learning and self-development are crucial areas of learning skill, and so those helping to develop people in organizations must explain and promote these processes. The appraisal interview offers a major opportunity for this, and will be examined in some detail in Chapter 14. However, since it is increasingly important for people to play an active part in

their own development, how can this process of self-directed learning be carried out?

There are two approaches to this. One is to urge individuals to take responsibility themselves for the process. They can do this by identifying their own learning needs related to their present work, to any changes likely to occur to it in the future, and to their career aspirations; and then following the advice given by Mumford (1981) and summarized below.

- review how far their learning opportunities are inhibited or encouraged by their own learning style (do past learning experiences indicate that they are dominated by one style of learning?), or by their manager, or by the organizational culture and structure in which they work;
- assess how far and with what effect the organization relies on structured learning experiences such as courses or specially constructed learning projects;
- review their core learning skills of observation and reflection, analysis, creativity and decision-making, and evaluation, and consider how to use them more effectively;
- review the work and other experiences in which they are involved in terms of the kind of learning opportunities they offer;
- look for potential helpers in the self-development process: colleagues, specialists, manager, mentor, spouse;
- draw up learning objectives and a plan of action;
- set aside some time each day (or each week) to answer the question 'What did you learn today?'

On the other hand, in many organizations now individuals are being encouraged or even required to draw up personal learning/development plans, either as a precursor to a training or development programme, or as part of a longer-term career development strategy (see p. 128 and Chapter 20). In a nationally funded development programme for clinical consultant directors run by the Northern Regional Health Authority in conjunction with Durham University Business School, personal development plans were generated at an initial three-day development workshop using a variety of self-assessment processes including outdoor development activities. These plans were a key source of information about the consultants' individual and common needs as perceived by themselves, their managers and members of their role sets in the workplace. The plans helped to drive a programme aimed at the provision of a tailor-made sequence of learning events – including action learning sets – that would help each of the consultants to understand fully their new director roles and perform confidently and effectively in them. They thus helped to promote instrumental, dialogic and self-reflective learning – the three domains of learning seen by Mezirow (1985) as crucial for the full development of people's potential.

3 **Promote a climate of awareness about the opportunities for continuous learning and development.** The person responsible for developing learners must be continually on the look-out for everyday opportunities which can be converted into conscious learning experiences for various groups or individuals. Personnel and training staff especially should have discussions with managers and other key personnel in the organization, over coffee or lunch, after meetings, during talks about people's training needs, even perhaps at specially arranged continuous development seminars. In a variety of simple ways they can begin to build up an awareness of what continuous development means, and how it can be achieved through the integration of work with learning as well as through the more elaborate, artificial and expensive formalized learning events to which some but by no means all in the organization may from time to time have access.

4 **Design training events to develop learning styles and skills.** If training is to be fully accessible to all who need it, then it should be designed in such a way as not only to avoid the discriminatory barriers forbidden by law, but also to accommodate whenever necessary a range of learning styles rather than appealing only to one type of learner – the activist or the reflector, for example.

On the other hand, training must help learners to acquire or develop those styles most suited to the tasks they have to carry out. A training managers' course, for example, should promote all four types of learning style, in order to produce people who are not predominately activists, but have a balance of skills across the four categories, thus enabling them to function effectively in the different situations in which training experts have to operate.

5 **Seek to identify and reduce organizational barriers to the development of appropriate learning styles and skills.** There needs to

be an awareness of the value the organization can derive from recognizing and encouraging a diversity of learning approaches, in terms of improvement in certain areas of behaviour and of performance.

For example, the preferred mode of learning in a particular organization may be by initial basic skills training and then simply by trial and error through time. There is no understanding, and therefore no support, for the view that people might develop full proficiency in their work more quickly and more efficiently by methods such as on-the-job coaching, educational courses, computerized learning packages, or secondments. The full implications of this single-minded approach need to be clearly explained by whoever is responsible for the training and development of personnel. While the approach may appear cheap and effective because it will probably result in most people learning to perform to at least an adequate level, indirect costs might be a high turnover of new recruits, high rates of wastage, poor quality, lost production time during the extended learning period and many demotivated, underperforming workers. The approach will also tend to lead to a lack of innovative skills and of flexible attitudes, with an emphasis on past practice rather than on discovering new and perhaps better ways of doing things.

In a real-life example Cuthbert (1984) describes how one of the first things done by Formica at a time when it needed to build up a high-quality and adaptive workforce, was team training and development, with a major focus on reflection by managers of the ways in which they managed, on observation of the human processes set in motion by different sorts of management style and organizational structure, on the acquisition of a wider band of knowledge about leadership and teamwork, and on experimentation with different approaches until work behaviour and performance showed real improvement. It was an extremely successful programme, incorporating all four of Kolb's (1974) learning modes and developing the range of associated learning styles.

6 **Influence appraisers to consider learning styles when examining performance, or in the selection process.** Finally, anyone trying to help people become more skilled learners should seek to influence those involved in all forms of assessment and appraisal, including selection, transfer, promotion and termination of employment (an easier task if there is a call for appraisal training in the organization, and/or if personnel and training are closely integrated functions). Criteria should be developed which relate to the learning, problem-

solving and decision-making styles and skills needed, and these criteria should help to guide judgements. In this way not only should judgements and decisions become more valid but, in the process of discussing this extra dimension, there should be an improvement in managers' understanding of how central a part learning style and skills play in people's behaviour and performance at work.

Developing learners is not an unrealistic objective. Honey and Mumford's Learning Styles Inventory (1986) has already been used:

- to select salesmen for the computer industry;
- to select graduate management trainees;
- to put together compatible project teams;
- to aid career counselling and guidance;
- as part of an in-company annual appraisal system;
- as part of a market research survey.

Planning a Continuous Development Programme

Now, let us apply the learning in this chapter to a practical task – a concrete experience – about which you can then reflect, in order to produce a set of concepts that you can apply to similar tasks in the future. I hope you learn something useful from it. It was a task actually undertaken in November 1986 by a group of 25 IPM students in the second year of their IPM Stage 2 course in Employee Development, of which I was then tutor.

EXERCISE

You are the Employee Development tutor on a Stage 2 part-time IPM course, with 25 students who know very little about continuous development, either in theory or in practice. Their average age is 28, and they come from both private- and public-sector organizations. You are going to run a two-day non-residential course at a local hotel, and you and they have agreed on its learning objectives.

The overall purpose of the workshop is to understand what continuous development is, in order to assess its benefits for individuals and organizations, and to be able to apply it in a practical situation. The major immediate need to which it relates is to help students tackle any continuous development question on their forthcoming IPM examination paper.

The specific learning objectives are that by the end of the workshop each student should:

1 know the IPM's Code of Continuous Development and understand the philosophy about learning in organizations that underpins it;

2 know about the main theories relating to continuous development;

3 know about the main elements of continuous development;

4 be able to draw up a continuous development programme relating to his or her individual needs;

5 be able to draw up a proposal for a continuous development programme for an organization;

6 be able to critically evaluate continuous development theory and practice.

Please design a programme for the workshop. Hours are approximately 9.00 a.m.–5.00 p.m. each day. (If you are a student, you could do this exercise as a class-based group exercise, or as an individual assignment.)

FEEDBACK NOTES

There are many ways of designing such a workshop, and reflection and analysis with colleagues or fellow students and tutors will undoubtedly prove the most effective way of producing something worthwhile. My own students designed a workshop which incorporated a major concrete experience (they chose as their main task to split into groups, each of which had to design a continuous development programme for a particular organization or department of their choice). It also included opportunities for reflection, observation, periods when the students would be able to learn about continuous development theory and then relate that to their practical task, and opportunities to experiment with what they were learning in a practical way before going back to their homes or workplaces and taking part in further experiences which would help the learning to be fully transferred.

Since continuous development was a major area of our syllabus, it represented a real work task. By designing it together (in class two weeks beforehand), then after the workshop evaluating it at our next class meeting, and relating the whole experience to learning theory and to theory on the design of training, we were all involved in a continuous learning experience where work and learning were integrated, and the work task was also our learning material.

It proved to be a very effective workshop at all those levels, and the longer-term effects on the students were quite striking. Students who completed diaries for a few months subsequently, charting the progress of self-directed personal development plans to improve their learning styles, gained insights into those styles and the ways in which they affected their behaviour and reactions to situations at work.

In some cases there were marked and very productive behavioural and work changes. On the Course itself too, the workshop and its consequential learning, seemed to mark a turning point: motivation and interest in learning then appeared to take a leap forward; the students showed an increasing determination and ability in mastering whatever learning problems faced them, and in consciously developing more than one primary learning style in order to further their various learning objectives. Understanding your own learning processes is not easy, but once you become interested in doing so, the first step towards continuous development has taken place.

Exercises

1 Imagine you are a member of a small team appointed by the IPM to review, update and reissue the Institute's *Statement on Continuous Development: People and work.* What are the main elements in the Statement which you would like to see retained and strengthened, and why? (May 1991)

2 To what extent do you think it is desirable for learners to know about theories of learning? What would you recommend to enable adult learners in your organization to develop their own learning plans? (November 1989)

3 What do you see as the responsibilities of the learner in a continuous development culture? Suggest ways whereby learners in your own organization might be helped to appreciate and observe these responsibilities. (May 1989)

References

ASHTON D, BRAIDEN E AND EASTERBY-SMITH M. *Auditing Management Development.* Aldershot, Gower. 1980

CUTHBERT D. 'Why working together means training together'. *Personnel Management*, October 1984. pp. 47-9

FAIRBAIRN J. 'Plugging the gap in training needs analysis'. *Personnel Management*, February 1991. pp. 43-5

GILLEY J W AND EGGLAND S A. *Principles of Human Resource Development.* Maidenhead, Addison Wesley. 1989

HONEY P AND MUMFORD A. *The Manual of Learning Styles.* 2nd ed. Maidenhead, Peter Honey. 1986

INSTITUTE OF PERSONNEL MANAGEMENT. *The IPM Statement on Continuous Development: People and work.* 2nd ed. London, IPM. 1987

KENNEY J, DONNELLY D AND REID M. *Manpower Training and Development.* 2nd ed. London, Institute of Personnel Management. 1979; now *Training Interventions*, third edition by Reid, Barrington and Kenney. 1992

KOLB D A, RUBIN I M AND McINTYRE J M. *Organizational Psychology: An experiential approach.* Englewood Cliffs, New Jersey, Prentice Hall. 1974

LAUERMANN E. 'Designing the critical path for the implementation of human resource strategy at BA'. In *Proc. Institute for International Research Conference on Developing A Fully Integrated Business-led Human Resources Strategy*, 3 October 1990. London, IIR Ltd. 1990

MEZIROW J A. 'A critical theory of self-directed learning'. In *Self-directed Learning: from Theory to Practice* (Brookfield S, ed.) San Francisco, Jossey-Bass. 1985

MUMFORD A. 'What did you learn today?' *Personnel Management*, August 1981. pp. 35-9

MURPHY B P AND SWANSON R A. 'Auditing training and development'. *Journal of European and International Training*, Vol. 12, No. 2, 1988. pp. 13-6

PERSONNEL MANAGEMENT. 'Focus shifts to line managers in BA human resource shake-up'. *Personnel Management*, March 1989. p. 5

THOMAS M. 'Coming to terms with the *customer*'. *Personnel Management*, February 1987. pp. 24–8

Further useful reading

HONEY P. 'Learning styles and self-development'. *Training and Development*, January 1984. pp. 9-11

MUMFORD A. 'Learning in action'. *Personnel Management*, July 1991. pp. 34-7

Chapter 9

Organizing and managing the employee development function

Learning Objectives

After reading this chapter you will:

1 understand the basic issues involved in carrying out the training manager role, and in organizing an employee development function;
2 understand the main activities involved in managing training and development resources;
3 be able to carry out a simple costing of training activities, and know how to draw up and monitor a training budget;
4 understand the main factors involved in establishing a training record system.

The Training Manager Role

As a starting point, we can expand the definition of the training manager role that was given in Chapter 6, so that it now encompasses the employee development function rather than just the specialist training section or department. The role:

> . . . is focused on the administration and management of the learning system within the organization through the planning, organizing, staffing, controlling and marketing of the Human Resource Development department. This role is better known as the 'manager of HRD'. (Gilley and Eggland, 1989, p. 97)

Gilley and Eggland emphasize the importance of this role as:

> . . . the only human resource development role that maintains both the opportunity and the position power to bring about needed changes within the organization regarding the importance of human resources and the role that the HRD department plays in the development of such resources. (Ibid., p. 98)

Two crucial activities involved in managing employee development are auditing learning in the organization and managing the organization as a learning system – and we looked at these in Chapter 8. The third major activity – managing the function and all its resources, including its personnel, is the subject of this and the following chapter, with the main focus in this chapter on organizing specialist staff and managing training resources. The fourth and final task, that of marketing training and development in the organization, is often ignored in textbooks, yet it is as essential as the other three. Gilley and Eggland's chapter on that task (Chapter 11) is detailed and illuminating, and deserves careful reading.

The Need for the Function to Achieve a Good 'Fit' with the System

The employee development function must be so organized that it can achieve interactions with the culture, structure, technology and people of the organization that will enable it to fulfil its mission and strategy satisfactorily. Pages 139–43 are worth rereading at this point, since they give a detailed explanation of the 'fit' of training roles and function.

EXERCISE

You have been appointed as an organization's first Training Manager – any type of organization of your choice. You have the responsibility for advising on training and development policy and planning for the organization. (You may assume that your manager is a member of the top management team.) You will also have to draw up training plans for various sectors of the organization. Finally, you will have to establish and hold responsibility for a central training budget. (You may decide whether or not, in this Exercise, there are also training budgets at divisional or unit levels of the organization.)

It is your first day, a Monday morning, and you are sitting in your small office, empty of everything except a desk, a chair, a telephone, and a filing cabinet. You have to meet your manager tomorrow with some initial ideas on how to plan and organize training and development in the organization. What sorts of issues and questions will you raise with him or her at that meeting?

FEEDBACK NOTES

Of course there are innumerable issues and questions that you could list. Those shown below, however, cover those which need to be raised most immediately.

1 **Environment of the organization.** Is the organization stable, or exposed to external pressures, threats or changes? How are these likely to affect the training function? What training links, if any, exist with people and institutions outside the organization? If any direct use is made of them, why, and with what results? Does anyone measure their effectiveness? Examples of such links are:

- Consultants
- Other external providers of training and education
- Non-statutory training authority advisors
- The local TECs
- Other local training institutions
- Careers officers
- Local schools

2 **Business goals and strategy.** What are the current business goals and longer-term strategic objectives that training and development is meant to serve? Is there an organizational training and development policy and strategy? What kind of training and development activities are carried out in the organization? Specifically, what if anything is done in the following areas, and by whom?

- Diagnosis and analysis of needs
- Analysis of jobs/tasks
- Appraisal of people
- Development of training and development plans
- Design and operation of training and development events
- Recording and evaluation of training and development

What are perceived to be the most important training and development tasks at present? Why?

3 **Organization structure and culture.** What is the primary structure of the organization – power, role, task or person? Is the organization decentralized or multi-sited? How is employee resourcing, including training and development, currently organized? What are the main roles in those functions – operational, administrative, standard-setting, strategic? What is intended to be the precise nature of the organizational links between yourself and other functions in the organization, especially employee resourcing/personnel?

What is your own intended formal role and what are your prescribed responsibilities? Are you to be given a free hand in planning and organizing training and development? What is the exact nature of your authority and discretion here? Are you able to recruit any staff to help you, should this prove necessary?

What formal or informal procedures related to training and development tasks and activities currently exist in the organization? To what extent would you be able to change current procedures? When staff are sent on training programmes or external activities, what is the nature and extent of the employee resourcing/personnel function's responsibility for those staff?

What is the general climate of opinion – the dominating values and beliefs – about training and development in the organization? Which managers and other key personnel in the organization particularly support training and development activities? Who, on the other hand, has no interest in them, or is likely to oppose various initiatives? Is training and development generally perceived as a crucial function in the organization? What criteria are used to judge its contribution? Will there be any problems in involving line managers in the diagnosis of training needs and in other aspects of training and development?

4 **Technology.** What are the main systems and processes of work organization? What kind of 'training technology' exists, or is available? What are the main media and methods of training and development that you could use, on and off the job? Is there any possibility of using open learning, computer-assisted learning, etc?

5 **Workforce.** What is the size of the workforce, and its occupational structure? What are perceived at present to be the main current and future training and development needs of different sectors of the workforce? What are the incentives and rewards for people in relation to training and development? How, generally, is the function of training and development perceived in different sectors of the workforce – positively or negatively? Why?

Thus we have established issues to raise and a range of possible questions to ask by reference to the checklist we developed in Chapter 6:

- Organizational environment
- Business goals and strategy
- Structure and culture
- Technology
- Workforce

Political factors will go far to determine the support you are given as you try to discover what needs really exist and how they can best and most feasibly be met. One major factor in this case will be the personality, attitudes and values of your manager in relation to training and development, and their reactions to you.

So in your first meeting with your manager, you must not only try to obtain certain crucial facts about training needs, You must also try to build up a mental picture of the organization, getting the 'feel' of it and establishing where there are constraints, problems and opportunities. Having obtained the necessary information, you should then develop a policy, strategy and plans for the function which will meet agreed needs both in the longer and the short term. We shall be examining how this task can be carried out, but for a case study that gives a detailed example of how to tackle what you have just done in this exercise, please see Harrison (1992).

Organizing an Employee Development Function

Stredl and Rothwell (1987) list four questions to be tackled in order to organize a training function effectively:

1 How will tasks, duties, and responsibilities be divided?

2 How much authority will be delegated, to whom and about what?

3 How many positions will report to the training manager?

4 How will jobs be grouped?

Thus in the previous exercise data gathered by the training manager on arriving in the organization should be carefully analysed in order to establish answers to these questions.

Organizing employee development in a decentralized system

One issue of crucial importance will be whether or not the organization is decentralized. Fowler points out (1992) that this can involve devolution and de-layering, and that 'what is devolved and which levels of management might be removed depend, among other things, on what the organization considers is important to retain at the centre'. He advises that the personnel department 'must analyse its role, relative to the needs, shape and style of the business, and evolve a solution which ensures its organisational integration'.

He makes the point that the personnel function may become basically an operational function, tackling a range of day-to-day personnel tasks on line managers' behalf, an administrative support function or a standard-setting and monitoring function. The third function could imply or lead to a strategic role at corporate level, whereas the first two are unlikely to do so. All have particular implications in relation to the four questions posed by Stredl and Rothwell.

It is essential to read Fowler's article for a full understanding of the implications of all of these points for the organization of training and development. In the UK there is certainly evidence that in recent years there has been an increasing trend towards decentralizing businesses to field levels, and that this trend has brought with it a decentralization of personnel (including training) responsibilities. (British Institute of Management/Aston University, 1989) To a significant extent, decentralization is beginning to be a feature of public-sector organizations as well as those in the private sector. Examples are the autonomy given to trust hospitals in the NHS and the devolution of a wide range of personnel responsibilities from national and regional levels to unit level with the advent of the purchaser/provider split between districts and units; and the hiving off of many civil service and local government functions to agencies or outside contractors.

One worrying feature of decentralization in local authorities is that it has resulted already in between 60 and 80 authorities de-layering management at the expense of the personnel function, pushing personnel off the top management team and absorbing it lower down. At Wandsworth, for example, personnel is part of the new corporate services division, together with public relations and the policy and education committee units. (*Personnel Management*, 1992b) The ultimate fear is that the financial problems of many authorities could make personnel increasingly vulnerable, to the point that it becomes marginalized. They will impact directly on the organization and influence of employee development, which usually operates under the wider personnel umbrella in local authorities (see also Kessler, 1990).

The BIM survey showed that while on the one hand decentralization was increasing, so, on the other hand, was centralization – of the policy, strategy and control function.

London Underground's plans to decentralize the personnel function
(With acknowledgements to *Personnel Management*)

In January 1992 it was announced that London Underground intended to keep just a small central personnel department, retaining responsibility for questions of corporate policy and standards, employee relations and management development. Most of the function would be devolved to the nine underground lines which are run as business units and already have their own personnel managers and support staff. Those personnel staff would be given wider responsibilities 'to enable them to act more like factory personnel managers'.

At the same time there would be 'a massive increase in training linked to the introduction of multi-skilling and flexible rostering'. In the past there had been a high frequency of last-minute withdrawals from training programmes for operational reasons, with adverse effects on the cost and impact of training. Personnel Director Roger Straker anticipated that, when the new proposals had been carried out, training would be better organized and given a higher priority.

Straker left the organization in 1992. The trend towards this kind of decentralization poses the same strategic and organizational challenges for training and development as it does for employee resourcing generally: those of 'tight-loose fit', discussed extensively in Legge (1989, p. 29). Basically those challenges are about how to strike a balance between a strong and unifying corporate business strategy and culture, and the special needs of divisions and units (Miller, 1987; Purcell, 1989). If the employee resourcing function and strategy of a business has to be differentiated from unit to unit to meet the needs of the units' different business strategies, then the end result may be that every unit will pursue its own personnel policies – including those to do with employee development – at the expense, perhaps, of any corporate strategy.

This, indeed, is exactly what appears to have happened at Shell UK, which 'has had to rethink its approach to decentralization after finding it led to worsening performance'. (Pickard, 1992, p. 10). It found that pushing decision-making down to business units diluted the traditional corporate culture, and resulted in the units 'given more independence, [becoming] too cut off from each other and from the expertise at the centre'. (Ibid.) Shell's solution has been to make business units more accountable to each other and more guided by a central company culture, while keeping the basic decentralized structure. Clearly, there are lessons here for the organization of training and development in a decentralized business.

Be that as it may, the organization of the training and development function will, because it is so often tied into the organization of the wider employee resourcing function, have little choice in the matter. Typical ways of coping with decentralization include: organizing most of the specialist staff to work permanently in or with the units, retaining only a small core staff at headquarters to make and co-ordinate employee development policy and strategy (as at London Underground); or, as at Barratt (Harrison, 1992), setting up a minimal specialist function operating on a 'walk and talk the job' basis; or having a small specialist function working collaboratively with line managers who themselves have been trained and developed to carry an increasing range of employee development functions – the model used at Etewel (p. 128) and at ICI. There are variations on these options, all of which are heavily dependent on the general role of the function in the organization (see Fowler, 1992, pp. 22–3).

General principles of organization for the employee development function

Let us look at ICI. It is an organization with a long and distinguished history of investing in the development of its people, and a training and development function that is seen to play a crucial role in organizational success and individual growth. Although it is a multinational company, the principles that, in 1991, it was following in organizing the function could apply with equal relevance to much smaller organizations. Before reading through this case study, have another look at pages 5–6, where we identified key processes relevant to policy making and implementation.

The organization of training and development at ICI, 1991
(By permission of ICI)

Vision and mission

At ICI, there is a strong vision and related mission for training and development in the company. It is outlined by the Chairman in his foreword to the *Group Training Manual*:

> If we are to achieve our Group Purpose we must ensure that all of us are equipped as best we can possibly be to face up to the changing environment in which we must keep our competitive edge finely honed in all sorts of ways. That means a continuing process of on-going education and training . . . During the recession of the early 80s, when pressure on profits and cash flow was extreme, many babies were thrown out with the bath water for understandable reasons of short-term crisis. Training was one such infant, and we must make certain that this mistake is not repeated, whatever the economic climate.

There is a specific training and development policy built into ICI's corporate business strategy.

Training and development strategy

The strategy for training and development is to ensure that line managers carry the primary responsibility for developing their people, and are fully committed to corporate training and development policy. There are four strategic objectives:

- To raise line managers' awareness of their responsibility for staff training and development
- To enable line managers to own training and development
- To develop line managers' skills in leading and managing people for performance
- To enable line managers to respond flexibly and effectively to an ever-changing business environment.

Implementation of strategy

Each manager holds clear, specific accountability for training and developing their staff. This is held to be vital for the successful achievement of business performance, and the aim is that it should be emphasized at the level of every discrete unit in the company. An ICI *Group Training Manual*, which is issued throughout the worldwide Group, includes a section on Responsibilities and Organisation for Training and Development of Staff. The key responsibilities are:

- Ensuring that those who work for them are equipped with the necessary knowledge, understanding and skills to do their current jobs competently
- Determining training and development needs, both present and future, setting priorities, allocating resources and reviewing results
- Ensuring that training activity is reinforced as an aspect of the process of managing performance.

Individual members of staff are responsible for their own development throughout their careers. This implies:

- Learning and applying the knowledge, understanding and skills necessary for the performance of their jobs
- Working with their managers to identify current and future learning, training and development needs and opportunities.

Each operating unit below ICI level is responsible for maintaining its statement of training policy, responsibilities and arrangements in line with Group policy and its own business and regional needs. Specialist training staff have a supportive role to facilitate and provide expertise where needed. They help line managers identify the contribution which the training policy can make to the business. In ICI Americas, for instance, the training function operates through a system of Account Managers who keep very close to the business needs of the different units they serve. There is a central ICI training budget, but also a training and development budget in every business unit.

Support is given to the training policy through other policies. The ICI-wide framework for Performance Management includes Performance Development as a key component, to ensure that individuals develop the skills and knowledge required for them to achieve their objectives and to develop their future potential within the business.

At ICI, leadership must be in deed as well as in word. There are high-priority in-house training programmes for the most senior staff in ICI which reinforce the cultural, strategic and organizational developments needed. Leadership in word and deed is expected from the Chief Executive of each business unit, and must lead to significant action. An extract from one CE's Training Policy Statement reads:

> The Board wishes to promote effective training and development at every level in the organization. Every employee has a right to expect and will be given the training necessary to achieve and maintain full competence in the job. A substantial proportion of training will be targeted towards the understanding and achievement of the organization's strategic objectives. All planned change will include a provision for appropriate and timely training of the staff involved . . .
>
> To secure practice of what is preached, this unit has clearly established implementation and control procedures with regular plans, reviews, reports, records, and performance evaluations, at the level of each unit and individual manager.

The learning organization

At ICI managers are helped to see that most learning takes place on the job, not on courses, and that they therefore have a primary responsibility to develop their people. They must record what they do in that respect and must link the components of:

- Strategic business objectives
- The individual's business role
- Performance planning
- Performance development
- Personal assessment
- Performance-related recognition and reward.

Managers are trained to be trainers and developers, and are appraised and rewarded for employee development just as they are for the execution of their other key managerial tasks.

The Training and Development function at ICI in 1991 thus appeared to have all the essential characteristics of a well-managed function:

- A clear vision, mission and strategy that is in line with overall business goals and strategy
- Strategic objectives that are carried through into detailed, practical plans for implementation of the policies that serve those objectives
- A form of organizational structure and company-wide procedures that ensure that the policies are carried out with the commitment and expertise of all who have been assigned training and development roles and responsibilities
- A system of monitoring, appraisal and rewards related to performance in those roles
- Good management and utilization of training and development resources.

Managing Training and Development Resources

There are three main categories of training and development resources:

1 **Internal and external resources.** These include:

- Personnel available within and outside the organization
- Physical resources, i.e. accommodation, equipment, training materials, etc. available both within the organization and through external sources
- Finance available for the training and development of the workforce, whether allocated to a central training budget, or to departmental training budgets, and whether available from within the organization or from external sources

2 **Time.** The time available to carry out any activities in training, including the management and development of training resources, will have a crucial effect on training policy and strategy, on managerial strategy and effectiveness, and on day-to-day training and managerial tactics.

3 **Natural learning resources.** These are everyday learning opportunities available in the organization in the normal course of work. We referred to these in Chapters 7 and 8, where there are guidelines to help identify natural learning resources and plan how best to use them.

In order to be able to manage such resources effectively, the training manager must:

1 **Observe and reflect on** the present situation. Look at the current training budget (or, if none is available, some equivalent figures that show the costs of running the training function and carrying out training activities) to establish what is done, and what it costs; identify the other training resources available – materials, equipment, accommodation, personnel; and look at how they are currently being organized and used.

2 **Analyse** this information by reference to contextual factors such as the organization's training policy and strategy (if there is one in place); to the organization's external environment, business goals, structure, workforce; and to the kind of training technology that could be utilized. This analysis will help to establish whether the department's resources are being used rationally to meet key training needs.

3 **Be creative.** Think of alternative ways of using resources, i.e. of deploying staff, choosing and using materials, equipment and accommodation, and investing money which would achieve training objectives to the required standard, but more effectively or efficiently.

4 **Make decisions.** Choose the most feasible, cost-efficient and cost-effective action.

5 **Monitor and evaluate.** Choose those methods that are both simple and effective enough for the purpose, and agree well in advance who is to carry out these processes, and when.

Thus good training management requires those same core skills to which we have already referred (see p. 152): observation and reflection; analysis; creativity; decision-making and experimentation; and evaluation.

Measuring the training investment

While the evaluation of employee development in the organization is less to do with financial and quantitative measurements than with looking at the overall impact of the function on business needs and on organizational capability and growth (see Chapters 17 and 21), the management of a training function will none the less involve a need to develop simple measures of training activities, and the ability to establish the cost benefit of specific learning events.

The first place where one expects to find a categorization of training activities, and of their costs, is in the budget. Budgeting in training can take three main forms. There may be a budget for the training department, money for training and development may be held in unit or departmental budgets for which line managers are responsible or, as at ICI, there may be both a corporate training budget and unit budgets.

Whoever is responsible for a training budget, it is essential that training resources and activities should be costed and managed in such a way that full value is obtained from available money. It is also important that where at first sight priority needs cannot be met within current budgets, a sound case should be put forward for obtaining more money or for meeting needs by the use of changed approaches.

There is no general format for the presentation of financial information about training, since the format must always depend on three factors:

1 **Why the information is needed.** This will determine what information is to be collected, and what focus to give the costings.

2 **For whom the information is needed.** This will determine the way the information is expressed, and the specific format to be used. If financial information is needed by the Accounts Department, it should follow the format and language used in their accounting system. If data on the costs and benefits of one training solution compared to another is needed by a busy line manager to help them decide which solution to choose, then the data must be expressed in language that is immediately understandable to the manager.

3 **When the information is needed, and what is available.** If a request comes in today for information needed tomorrow, then it may prove impossible to obtain all the data theoretically desirable. The format must be tailored to match whatever data can be produced in time, so that the overall presentation makes its proper impact even if it is not entirely comprehensive.

Three pieces of information are always essential:

- the overall annual cost of running the training function
- how to recover that cost
- how to identify and compare the costs involved in training and development alternatives

In relation to all three areas of information, two terms are fundamental:

- **Trainer day costs.** This refers to the daily costs involved in the basic running of a training function.
- **Training day costs.** This refers to the total costs involved in running a training function *and* in carrying out its specific training activities.

Calculating the annual running costs of a training function

Before we examine how to establish these costs, we will look at how to calculate the basic annual running costs of a training function. Figure 6 shows an approach that is simple and practical. In this example the basic running costs of a training department are identified. Such costs can also be identified where there is no specialist department, as will be shown later.

From Figure 6 we can see that a simple but acceptably accurate calculation of the basic annual costs involved in running a training department can be obtained by looking at three kinds of costs, those related to personnel, overheads and administration.

Personnel and overhead costs are fixed (that is to say, the organization must pay them, whether or not training activities are carried out) but administration costs are variable, because they depend on the type and extent of the training activities. If a forecasting exercise is being carried out, then administration costs can be estimated in one of two ways:

Figure 6

Example of basic annual running costs of a training department, employing two training officers and a secretary (in collaboration with A Rutter, University of Northumbria at Newcastle Business School)

Personnel	
Training staff salaries plus, say, 25% for employment costs (pension, NI and other payments)	£30,000
Support staff (administrative and clerical)	£10,000
Overheads	
Annual rent and rates (or some approximate calculation of these) related to training accommodation (1 training room; 2 offices); to heating, lighting and cleaning; and to other maintenance costs of training accommodation	£5,000
Administration	
Estimated/actual: telephone and postal costs; printing, photocopying, etc. costs; computer costs (e.g. cost of computer time, software, etc.)	£3,000
TOTAL BASIC ANNUAL RUNNING COSTS THEREFORE	£48,000

1 By taking an average of the total administration costs incurred during, say, the last two years' training activities, if those activities were similar to those planned for the forthcoming year. An inflation cost will have to be built into this calculation.

2 If there is an annual training plan then the training manager can look at the administration costs actually incurred by the activities involved in the previous year's plan and, knowing the kind of activities planned for the forthcoming year, assess how much more or less the related administration costs are likely to be. Again, an inflation cost will have to be built in.

If there is no specialist training department, and no training overheads, then the basic annual running costs of the training function can be calculated by reference to:

- Personnel costs: the number of days each manager spends in carrying out training and training-related activities for others, expressed as a proportion of their annual salary and employment costs
- Administration costs: identifiable administration costs caused by work on training and training-related activities, expressed in annual terms.

Figure 6 deals with *basic* costs, irrespective of the training provided (except in relation to administration costs, where in order to get any acceptable figure, we have to consider the sort of demands likely to be made. In our next examples these costs will be related to actual training activities.

Recovering the cost of running the training function

The next stage in recovering the cost of training is to find out the cost of a *trainer day* (see p. 198). Figure 7 continues with the example used in Figure 6, adding some more information. (This same approach can, of course, be used to calculate the trainer day costs of anyone who carries out training/development activities, whether or not they are training staff.)

Figure 7

Calculating the cost of a trainer day (in collaboration with A Rutter)

Days actually worked by the 2 training staff (i.e. once holidays, etc. have been deducted) = 240 each = total of 480 days		
Annual running cost of the training dept. (see Figure 6)		£48,000
So cost of each day the training staff are actually working	=	£48,000 / 480
Cost of one trainer day	=	£100

This very easy calculation tells us that, if it is to recover the annual cost of running its training department (£48,000), this particular organization would need to provide training for 480 days a year and charge

£100 per day for that training. So the basic running costs of a training department or function can be expressed as a trainer day cost, and this cost, as we have seen in Figure 7, can be calculated as follows:

$$\frac{\text{Annual running cost of the training function}}{\text{Number of days each staff is involved in training work}} = \text{Trainer day cost}$$

But how can a training department recover its identifiable costs on a more or less strict financial basis? A case study should provide a helpful illustration at this point.

Mintech Ltd: Part 1
(In collaboration with A Rutter)

Mintech Ltd has a Training Department employing two Training Officers (Mike and John) and a Clerk/Secretary.

Basic annual running cost of the department	= £30,000
Number of days worked by the Officers:	
Mike: 250 + John: 250	= 500
Trainer day cost	$= \frac{£30,000}{500}$
	= £60

The department is involved in two sorts of training activity, the direct costs of which are shown below:

Training people

The trainers keep a record of the number of days they spend on face-to-face training of people:

Mike: 30 days
John: 20 days
Total: 50 trainer days
Cost: 50 x £60 = £3,000

The trainers add up the number of days that staff spend participating in these courses = 300

Assisting people to attend external training

The trainers keep a record of the number of days they spend on work connected with external courses, ranging from analysis of needs through to evaluation of results:

Mike: 220 days
John: 230 days
Total: 450 trainer days
Cost: 450 x £60 = £27,000

The trainers add up the number of days that staff spend participating in these courses = 3,000

Amount to be recovered for internal training activities: £3,000 for 300 training days	Amount to be recovered for external training activities: £27,000 for 3,000 training days
Total cost of internal training day per person = £10	Total cost of external training day per person = £9
Additional costs (fees, travel, subsistence, accommodation, course materials, per person) per day = £1	Additional costs (fees, travel, subsistence, accommodation, course materials, per person) per day = £200

To recover its costs of £10 per person for everyone who undergoes internal training, and £9 per person for everyone who attends external training and to cover the additional costs involved, Mintech's Training Department can do one of two things:

1 If it has its own budget, then it must include in the budget estimate enough to cover all of these costs.

2 If there is no central training budget, but each department has its own budget from which training costs must be met, then it must 'charge' departments the appropriate amount, depending on how many people from each department will be attending external or internal training.

This case study shows us that in order to calculate how to recover the costs involved in running a training department and in carrying out its training activities, the training day cost must be calculated, as follows:

$$\frac{\text{Trainer day cost}}{\text{Number of training days}} = \text{Training day cost}$$

Note that the number of training days is simply arrived at by adding up all the days it has taken to train people throughout the organization, in one case internally, in the other case externally. So if 100 people each went on three days' external training in a year, then the total number of external training days would come to 300. We can conclude by saying that:

> The trainer day cost can be used to calculate the basic cost of running the training function, and the training day cost to calculate the charge to be made by the function for training if its running costs are to be recovered on a strict financial basis.

We have now seen how to provide two of the three crucial pieces of information that every manager of training, whether or not a training specialist, should possess: the overall costs of running a training function, and how to recover those costs.

Identifying and comparing the costs involved in training alternatives

Using the same Mintech example, we can look at a typical situation facing many personnel and training officers: staff requests to go on education or training courses. We will see how, by comparing the costs of internal and external supervisory training, a sound decision can be reached by someone who is concerned to achieve both relevant training and good management of resources.

Mintech Ltd: Part 2
(In collaboration with A Rutter)

Three supervisors from different departments have applied to the Training Department to go on a day-release supervisory studies course at the local college. It lasts for a year, involves absence of half a day per week plus an evening (on the same day) over three ten-week terms, and ends with an examination leading to a national supervisory skills qualification. Mike, one of the two Training Officers, first identifies the costs involved. To help him do this calculation, he uses the 'Training day cost' identified in the previous case study.

OPTION A: Sending supervisors on external training course leading to national supervisory qualification

FEES (£500 per person per year) £500 x 3	£1,500
TRAVEL AND SUBSISTENCE (£2 per person per day at college): £2 x 3 x 30 days	£180
MATERIALS (books and other items used by trainees on the course) £50 x 3	£150
ADMINISTRATIVE OVERHEAD COST External training day cost x number of days x number of trainees (£9, already calculated, x 30 x 3)	£810
TOTAL COST of sending three people on course	**£2,640**

Mike could, of course, have made out a more complicated list which would have included indirect as well as direct costs. This would have made the final figure much higher. The indirect costs would be the less tangible costs incurred by attending the external course: lost opportunity costs, reduction in the output or quality of service of their staff due to less effective staff management during the periods of their absence, lost salary and related employment costs due to the supervisors' reduction in hours worked 'on the job' during the period of the course, and so on.

In practice, however, such costs are rarely taken into account in situations like this, unless there are tangible payments occasioned by the supervisors' absence (for example, overtime payments due to their work having to be done by others). Of course, if Mike had needed to make a particularly powerful case against sending people away on an external course, he would do well to draw attention to these 'hidden' costs.

The next step is for Mike to think carefully about the external course. In his own mind the benefits the course will bring to the supervisors, their departments and Mintech as a whole are considerable, but from the figures he has produced it is clear that to send the three supervisors on it will be expensive, and it may not be possible to offer the same opportunity, in the current year, to any further supervisory applicants. What alternatives might there be? (At this point you may like to take over and do some creative thinking to generate a list of alternatives. For the purposes of this exercise, I am only developing one other option, but in fact several are possible.)

One such alternative is for the exact training needs of all Mintech's 16 supervisors to be identified through appraisal interviews and other methods, and for the Training Department to organize internal courses to meet common needs, while individual needs could be met on some other appropriate basis. Mike discusses this idea with his colleagues and they agree that three one-week courses run by the Training Department in its conference room would cover the necessary material well, and would be a real benefit to at least 12 instead of only three supervisors. But what will it cost?

OPTION B: Internal supervisory training course run by training staff

There would be three one-week courses, for a total membership of 12 supervisors, with four attending each course.

FEES	—
SUBSISTENCE	
Mid-morning and mid-afternoon refreshments for participants and trainer, @ 60p per head per day (60p x 12 people x 5 days)	£36
MATERIALS (£20 per trainee)	£240
ADMINISTRATIVE OVERHEAD COST	
Internal training day cost, 12 supervisors for	

5 days each (£10, previously calculated, x 5 x 12)	£600
Total cost of training 12 supervisors internally	**£876**
Cost of training 3 supervisors on these courses	**£219**

Mike was interested to note the cost per trainee involved in each of the options:

Option	Total cost £	Number trained	Cost per trainee £
A	2,640	3	880
B	876	12	73

Thus Mike was able to show clearly that the cost of the organization running its own supervisory courses, using its own staff, was very much less than sending three supervisors on an external course. He did this by identifying, in each case, the following costs:

- Fees
- Expenses
- Materials
- Administrative overhead costs

Through the various examples we have examined we have discovered how to identify the three crucial pieces of information noted at the start of this section:

- The basic annual cost of running the training department
- How to recover the running cost on a strict financial basis
- How to identify and compare costs involved in training alternatives

However, there is still one more activity that needs to be carried out in order to ensure that cost-effective decisions are made in relation to the use of training resources.

Cost-benefit analysis

Cost-benefit analysis is concerned with establishing the costs of an activity, and comparing these with the benefits it is likely to confer. It should take into account efficiency as well as effectiveness in establishing the benefits.

EXERCISE

When Mike has finished his calculations, it is obvious that running an internal supervisory training programme using Mintech's own training staff would be by far the cheapest course of action. But is it the most cost-beneficial? On what main issues should Mike seek information in order to make a final decision?

FEEDBACK NOTES

Important issues are raised by the two alternatives, not least the potential clash between the individuals' wish to improve their career prospects by obtaining a recognized qualification and the organization's wish to cut costs. The following list is not exhaustive, but it shows six major issues which should always be considered when weighing up training alternatives, together with a sample of the kind of questions to be raised under each heading.

1 **Budgeting.** Would either of the options be affordable in terms of Mintech's budget per department for training?

2 **Training policy and strategy.** Which of the options would be most consistent with Mintech's overall training and development policy and strategy, as well as with the training policies of the departments concerned?

3 **Training needs.** Have supervisors' training needs been carefully analysed, and if so by whom, and using what criteria? Is there any conflict between individual and departmental or organizational needs? Which alternative would best meet a balance of needs, and why? Have adequate discussions been held with the supervisors and their managers on these points?

4 **Training benefits and evaluation.** Which of the options is most likely to help the job performance, motivation, commitment, etc. of the supervisors and/or carry other benefits for the organization? And which will most help the individuals, both related to their everyday work and to their longer-term career development? What information can be obtained about the value of each of the options, either from past initiatives at Mintech or from other similar organizations which have been involved in any or all of such initiatives themselves?

5 **Transfer of learning.** What positive action will be taken to ensure

transfer of learning for the supervisors if they attend the external course? Would there be better transfer if they attended an internal course?

6 **Alternative courses of action.** Are there any other ways in which the same kind and level of results could be achieved? What about integration of work and learning through experiences like team briefings, quality circles, management by objectives? (Some firms offer financial incentives to their supervisors, either alone or coupled with those sorts of initiatives.) What would be the costs of doing nothing? Would that lead to reduced motivation on the part of the supervisors, lack of development of their ability and potential, longer learning time for new techniques, to poorer quality work, higher rates of absenteeism or sickness, and so on?

When Mike discussed the two options with his colleagues, and with the managers of all Mintech's supervisors, it became increasingly clear to everyone that the company's supervisors needed two distinct kinds of training and development. It was agreed that the Personnel Manager would recommend to the Director that there should be:

1 **A programme of development for new supervisors, or those shortly to be promoted to that level, and for others whose inclusion would bring clear benefits to the company and to themselves.** This would include opportunities for up to four people each year to attend the external course, or for a greater number to do the course by a special distance-learning package; and for such supervisors also to have planned work experience and guidance.

2 **An internal training programme for all Mintech supervisors.** This would not only meet areas of common need, but also help the supervisors to develop a common language and team identity through the mechanism of a shared and work-related learning experience. There would be initial costs involved in designing the first course, which would need to be added to the costs shown in Mike's calculations on Option B. However, the design cost would not recur, and the more courses they ran, the quicker that cost would be recovered.

The costs involved were affordable within departments' training budgets, and the Personnel Manager was confident that the Director would see that the cost of an in-company programme would be more than offset by the benefits it would bring. Procedures for monitoring the programmes and for evaluation would have to be built in at the start, and responsibility for those processes clearly allocated.

A strategy for managing training resources

What we have learnt above shows that planned learning events, especially training events, can be managed efficiently and effectively by adopting the following strategy:

1 **Accurate and meaningful costing.** The costs of learning activities must be estimated as accurately as possible, and expressed in a way that is meaningful to the managers of the organization concerned.

2 **Relevance to organizational training policy and needs.** Decisions about expenditure on training activities must be consistent with decisions about the overall training policy and strategy of the organization, and must meet real training needs and priorities.

3 **Consistency with other employee resourcing policies and processes.** Decisions about learning activities must also be consistent with other employee resourcing policies and processes, for example employee resource planning and utilization, staff appraisal, promotion and career development planning, financial and other reward strategies.

4 **Considered alternatives.** Alternative ways of using resources and of achieving learning objectives must always be considered and costed before final decisions are made.

5 **Cost-efficient and cost-effective decisions.** Compare costs and benefits of the alternatives that have been produced (including that of doing nothing). Make a decision which strikes the best balance between being cost-beneficial, generally feasible, and politically sensitive.

6 **Monitoring and evaluation.** All learning events must be carefully controlled, and their value as well as their validity assessed. This point will be covered fully in Chapter 17.

We have also seen how the very process of thinking through a range of alternative training and development possibilities can act as a catalyst, producing further initiatives to the benefit of the organization.

Establishing a record system

There is one more crucial activity involved in the management of resources: establishing a training record system.

I shall not attempt to explain in any detail how to set up a record system or design training records. There are excellent texts to give that practical help, some of which are included in the reading list. My concern is simply to outline the key factors to be taken into account when establishing a record system.

In training, as in any other personnel area, what the record system must ensure or show is that:

1 **Training activities can be identified and monitored.** It should be possible at any time to check how far, in what ways, at what cost, and with what results, training activities are being carried out in every part of the organization. The more collaborative the approach to training, the easier it will be to obtain and record that information. Training records must also be comprehensive, up to date, and accurate.

2 **Training and development of individuals is recorded.** Personal records need to be kept showing the numbers and kinds of people who have been trained and developed. They must also facilitate monitoring to ensure non-discrimination.

3 **The law relating to employment is being observed.** It must be possible at any time to identify how far, and in what ways, the law relating to employment is being observed. Records must therefore pay particular attention to areas of training activity related to dismissal, redundancy, discrimination, health and safety, and data protection, since in all of these areas failure to ensure that employees have the right knowledge and skills can result in employers as well as employees becoming liable for breaches of the relevant legislation. Discrimination issues are receiving increasing publicity at present, and the importance of records in that connection cannot be over-stressed. I have made the point elsewhere that:

> Records and up-to-date information should always be available to show exactly what steps have been taken to prevent discrimination in the workplace, and to prove how people have been treated at work. (Harrison, 1986)

4 **The record system itself complies with the law.** The record system must comply with legal requirements. The Data Protection Act must therefore be carefully observed.

5 **The record system is cost-beneficial.** The record system must be cost-efficient and cost-effective. It should be as simple as possible, using sophisticated systems and processes only where the ensuing benefits can be shown to justify fully the human, physical and financial resources and costs. Particular attention must be paid to questions like how detailed particular records should be; for how long records should be kept; who should keep records; and how often records should be updated.

6 **Training records are consistent with other personnel records.** Training records should follow a similar style to records maintained in other areas of the organization's personnel management. They should therefore whenever possible be drawn up using a format and technology that complements rather than confuses other personnel record-keeping and data analysis. As far as possible their content should also avoid overlap with the content of other personnel records.

7 **Confidentiality is observed.** Particular attention must be paid to confidentiality, and therefore to what information goes on record, who should have access to various records and how access can be protected.

These, then, are the seven key factors to be taken into account when establishing a record system. The main point to remember is that, together with the budget, it is an invaluable aid to the control of resources. However, like the budget, the criteria for determining what goes into records depends, in the end, on three factors:

- Why the information is needed
- For whom it is needed
- When it is needed, and what information is available

Summary

In this chapter, we have covered four topics:

- The training manager role
- The need for the function to 'fit' the organization
- Four key questions in organizing an employee development function
- Managing training and development resources and establishing a training record system

In Chapter 10 we will look at the fifth topic: selecting and managing employee development personnel.

Exercises

1 What would you want to explore, and what to negotiate, before signing an agreement with an external training provider under which the provider will mount a series of courses for your organization on your premises? (November 1989)

2 Outline the steps you would take and the factors you would take into consideration in preparing a cost-benefit analysis of the desirability of setting up a company management training centre.

3 Explain the stages whereby, in your own organization, the training and development budget is built up, and how expenditure of the budget is controlled. Produce any recommendations necessary to improve the system.

References

BRITISH INSTITUTE OF MANAGEMENT AND ASTON UNIVERSITY. *The Responsive Organization.* London, BIM. 1989

FOWLER A. 'How to structure a personnel department'. *Personnel Management Plus,* January 1992. pp. 22-3

GILLEY J W AND EGGLAND S A. *Principles of Human Resource Development.* Maidenhead, Addison Wesley. 1989.

HARRISON R. *Equality at Work.* Oxford, Pergamon Press (Super Series No. 506). 1986

HARRISON R. 'Employee development at Barratt'. In *Case Studies in Personnel* (Woodall D and Winstanley D, eds.), Ch. 10. London, Institute of Personnel Management. 1992

KESSLER I. 'Personnel management in local government: The new agenda'. *Personnel Management,* November 1990. pp. 40-4

LEGGE K. 'Human resource management: A critical analysis'. In *New Perspectives on Human Resource Management* (Storey J, ed.). London, Routledge. 1989

MILLER P. 'Strategic industrial relations and human resource management – distinction, definition and recognition'. *Journal of Management Studies*, Vol. 24, 1987. pp. 347-52

PERSONNEL MANAGEMENT. 'London Underground to decentralise personnel function in wake of job cuts'. *Personnel Management*, January 1992a. p. 5

PERSONNEL MANAGEMENT. 'London borough council abolishes top personnel post in reorganisation'. *Personnel Management*, March 1992b. p. 12

PICKARD J. 'Shell UK pulls responsibility back to centre'. *Personnel Management Plus*, April 1992. p. 1

PURCELL J. 'The impact of corporate strategy on human resource management'. In *New Perspectives on Human Resource Management* (Storey J, ed.). London, Routledge. 1989

STREDL H J AND ROTHWELL W J. *The ASTD Reference Guide to Professional Training Roles and Competencies*. Amherst, Massachusetts, HRD Press Inc. 1987

Further useful reading

COOPERS AND LYBRAND ASSOCIATES. *A Challenge to Complacency: Changing attitudes to training*. A report to the Manpower Services Commission and the National Economic Development Office. Sheffield, MSC. 1985

GUEST D AND KENNY T. (eds.). 'Setting up a personnel department'. In *A Textbook of Techniques and Strategies in Personnel Management*. London, Institute of Personnel Management. 1983

HACKETT P. *Personnel: The department at work*. London, Institute of Personnel Management. 1991

HARPER S (ed.). 'Establishing a personnel department'. In *Personnel Management Handbook*. London, Gower. 1987

INSTITUTE OF PERSONNEL MANAGEMENT. *Training: Bibliography 21*. London, IPM (Information and Advisory Services). 1986

KENRICK P. *Costing, Budgeting and Evaluating Training*. Luton, Local Government Training Board. 1984

PEPPER A D. *Managing the Training and Development Function*. Aldershot, Gower. 1984

PERSONNEL MANAGEMENT. 'Personnel Record Systems: Factsheet No. 2'. *Personnel Management*, February 1988

ROBINSON K. *A Handbook of Training Management*. 2nd ed. London, Kogan Page. 1985

TALBOT J R AND ELLIS C D. *Analysis and Costing of Company Training*. Aldershot, Gower. 1969

Chapter 10

Managing training and development personnel

Learning Objectives

After reading this chapter you will:

1 understand the key issues involved in managing those with training and development roles in the organization;
2 be able to identify the competences, skills, knowledge and attitudes needed to perform such roles effectively;
3 be able to draw up an action plan to assess the performance of those in such roles, and to develop their abilities and potential;
4 understand what is needed for the training manager to become a fully effective member of the organization, and the importance of their own continuous self-development.

Introduction

Throughout this chapter any references to 'training' should be read as a shorthand for training and other ways of achieving employee development in the organization.

Kenney and Reid (1986) contend that an effective training function is one with the following characteristics:

1 **Planned training.** This involves the need for a clear and relevant vision, mission and strategy for training and development in the organization, and feasible plans for the implementation of that strategy.

2 **Management responsibility.** The fundamental responsibility for the training and development of people must lie with line management. The roles and responsibility of specialist staff must be well defined and relevant to organizational needs and context.

3 **Appropriate structure.** As we saw in Chapter 9, the function must be so structured as to fit the system within which it has to operate.

4 **Expertise.** Those with training and development roles, whether line managers or specialist staff, must be able to perform them to the standards required, and must have the interpersonal and political skills and credibility to enable them to function effectively.

It is with the last point that this chapter is concerned.

Managing Specialist Training and Development Staff

Unless specialist staff are acceptable in the organization, committed and expert in their jobs, and flexible in skills and outlook, the function can soon decline into the role of 'passive provider' whose dangers Pettigrew (1982) has clearly illustrated. There are eight processes involved in the effective management of specialist training and development staff:

- Employee resource planning
- Job analysis
- Recruitment and selection
- Induction and basic training
- Staff appraisal
- Continuous development
- Career development
- Leadership and teamwork

Employee resource planning

There must be an employee resource plan for the training department, no matter how small that department may be. It is essential for the training manager to work out the kind, number and level of staff currently needed; and to identify what is likely to be needed in future in the light of the organization's anticipated needs for training and development. An informed assessment of the current staffing situation can then be carried out; new work and responsibilities can be allocated; and job and career development plans for training staff can be formulated.

Job analysis

Training and development roles and tasks in the organization must be analysed, and the skills, knowledge and attitudes they require, identified.

In Chapter 6 we examined the Lead Body Standards for Training and Development. Whatever criticisms may be made of the Lead Body Standards (see pp. 134–7), they must be taken fully into account when planning the recruitment, training and development of training staff. They constitute the official national standards relating to the function, and will in future provide the basis for vocational qualifications for those with training and development responsibility, whether they are line managers or specialists (see Appendix 3).

An inventory that can, with amendments, be used to cover the competences listed in the Lead Body Standards is given in the MSC/ITD publication *Trainer Task Inventory* (1984). The task or job inventory approach identifies tasks being done at a particular time, rather than prescribing what should or will be done, and so can be claimed to offer a more dynamic approach, with less potential for conflict, than the conventional job description.

After this information has been analysed, the competences, experience and motivation needed in job-holders should be identified. This will enable personnel specifications to be drawn up for every training position (see Chapters 12 and 13, and Torrington et al., 1991, pp. 182–3). It is particularly important at this stage to look at the kinds of professional knowledge, political sensitivity and personal strengths needed to operate in the specific context of each job (Pickard, 1991) and at what kind of person is likely to be fully effective in the crucial tasks of boundary management (see pp. 143–4).

Job descriptions and personnel specifications will aid the recruitment and selection processes. They will also provide valuable information to help in the planning of training and development and in the allocation of work for staff. It should be remembered that with some appointments it may be more important for the person to dictate the nature of the job rather than the reverse, and this will determine how tight or loose the job description and personnel specification should be. (For more on this topic, see Chapters 12 and 13.)

Recruitment and selection

With careful analysis of the employee resource needs of the function, and of the requirements identified in job descriptions and personnel specifications, the most appropriate sources of candidates for training and development jobs should be tapped, and valid selection and assessment methods determined. (Torrington et al., 1991, pp. 185–8)

Attention needs to be given to who carries out recruitment, shortlisting and selection. Many poor-quality training appointments are made because of lack of skill at this stage, or because those who have had the major say in selection have understood little about training jobs and the kinds of competence and motivation they require. Recruitment and selection are often highly political activities, and unfortunately the choice of who carries them out, or of who carries the most weight in the processes, may not be entirely under the control of the Personnel or Training Manager.

Induction and basic training

There must be proper induction of all new staff, in order to explain the different contexts in which they will have to operate, and the work and organization of the training function. Basic training may also need to be provided, and this can take many forms depending on the nature of the need. If there are no resources for such training, then the remedy lies at the recruitment and selection stage: pre-trained, experienced staff need to be brought in.

It is equally important to recruit staff who have values, attitudes and motivation to match the general culture of the training department and of the wider organization, and to enable them to cope with the kinds of demands and pressures they will have to face.

For many, if not all, positions it will be advisable to have a probationary period, during which new staff, having been given clear guidelines and objectives for performance, can be regularly appraised and receive coaching, guidance and other forms of help where needed. A valuable device is to appoint mentors for new members of staff, to act as counsellors and facilitators of learning during this important period. At the end of the probationary period, each side can make a decision whether the appointment is to be confirmed on a permanent basis, or is to be terminated. It is as important for the job holder to be given this opportunity to learn what the job and the organization are really like as it is for the organization to be sure that they have the right kind of recruit.

Staff appraisal

Appraisal is essential if staff are to learn their jobs effectively, perform well and develop their abilities and potential. Appraisal should lead to three outcomes:

- Feedback on performance – to give and receive feedback on their performance (remember that the training manager will not be aware of all the detail of how staff perform in their jobs, and the appraisal interview is therefore an important source of feedback for the manager too)
- Work planning – to take stock of work over a period of time and to draw up work objectives and plans for the forthcoming period
- Diagnosis of training and development needs – to discover training and development needs and expectations of staff, and to agree appropriate plans

These appraisal sessions must be genuine developmental and motivating experiences or none of the outcomes can be achieved (see Chapter 14). The MSC/ITD *Guide to Trainer Effectiveness* (1984) offers a clear and helpful approach to assessing and planning development for training staff. It looks at six key indicators of effectiveness in any training role:

- Role orientation and perception
- Competences
- Trainer characteristics and credibility
- Trainer work behaviour and style
- Outcomes of trainer activity
- Organizational factors

In the last two of its six modules it offers help in appraising and assessing staff along these dimensions, and ends with a format for action planning.

Continuous development

All personnel, including the training manager, must be actively committed to self-development on a continuous basis. There may be little time, money or opportunity for the formalized training and development of training staff, and self-development will therefore be the only way in which they can ensure continuous diagnosis of their learning needs, and explore ways of improving or changing their skills, knowledge and attitudes. Self-development is also important because through understanding and being committed to the process training staff will gain valuable insights into the relationship between the understanding and practice of learning styles and skills and the developmental process.

Within the first few weeks of appointment a new training manager could usefully hold a meeting with his or her staff to explore the characteristics of the organization in which they are to work as a learning system and to discuss their own developmental needs. One important outcome of such a meeting could be a commitment by all staff to drawing up personal development plans. The guides produced by the MSC/ITD can be helpful instruments here. Through a process of self-assessment and discussion, each member of staff can establish two or three personal developmental targets relevant to their individual learning needs, with a jointly agreed or self-generated plan to achieve those objectives over a given period.

In considering the continuous development of staff it is particularly important to focus on the boundary management skills that they need (pp. 143–4). Boundary management is largely a matter of processes rather than tasks, and so in any narrowly defined task-led approach to appraisal and development those processes could well be ignored, with potentially fatal results.

The importance of boundary management is shown in a decentralized organization, where Training Staff are either permanently seconded to business units or who need to work in close collaboration with those units from the base of a central training function. They will need to have:

1 a wide-ranging knowledge of 'the business' to give them credibility in the units, and to enable them to understand fully the units' training and development needs;

2 the skills, motivation and professional commitment to ensure that they neither identify so closely with business units as to 'view the central . . . function as an influence to be kept at bay' (Fowler, 1992), nor identify so closely with the central function as to lose credibility at unit level and become inflexible in their approach.

One way of helping training specialists to achieve an educated understanding of business language, functions and systems in parallel with their developing experience in their own place of work while also promoting their professional skills is to support their attendance on an external course that aims both to cater for their needs as managers of training and development, and to widen their business knowledge and skills (see, for example, Arkin, 1991).

Career development

There must be a strong focus on career planning and development for staff. Attention must be given not only to those who are likely to be moving up (whether in their present organization or another one), but also to those who may never leave their present job or present level. As Williams (1984) has pointed out, although the 'upward and onward' view of careers is still very prevalent, it

> . . . does not square with what organizations are able to offer today; promotion is for a still smaller minority than in the past. There needs, therefore, to be a shift away from the advancement orientated view of careers, and an increased emphasis on career development at the same organizational level or within the present job.

Davies and Deighan (1986) observe likewise that it is as important to be concerned for the development of the 'solid citizens' and apparent 'dead wood' in a department, as it is to have plans for the 'learners' and the 'high fliers' – more so, perhaps, since the solid citizens and the dead wood may be the people who constitute the majority, and in any event will have a strong attitudinal influence on newcomers to the department. Unless ways are found to stimulate and regenerate these people, they may increasingly pull down the whole department.

The requirement that every member of the department should have personal development plans will aid the processes of self-development and career development, and will give impetus to 'growing' a learning culture in the training and development department.

Achieving vocational qualifications will become an increasingly important part of the career development of training staff, and in this connection the training manager must consider the kind of workplace experience and formal education and training that will help staff to progress towards those qualifications (see, for example, Appendix 3). The accreditation of workplace experience and competence needs to be considered, as does the matter of how that experience and competence can be assessed.

Measures must also ensure that all managers have the skills and the attitudes needed to promote the effective development of people. This reinforces the point made by Leicester (1989):

> Those organisations whose managers are trained in interpersonal skills and who have explicit responsibility for managing people are more inclined to ensure that their workforce is fully trained . . . [and] continuously prepared for a work performance that is a regular contribution to corporate success (p. 57).

This is arguably the most important factor of all in recruiting, managing and developing those with training and development responsibilities. Unless training and development staff have skilled leadership and can act as an effective team both within the department and in the wider organization, their basic abilities and commitment, and their impact on the organization, will suffer. The Training Manager has two key questions to answer:

- What should his or her leadership style be – tight or loose, authoritarian or participative, task-centred or person-centred?
- How should the group of training staff be organized – as a close-knit team or a loosely knit collection of individuals, or somewhere in between the two extremes?

As with decisions about how the training function should be organized, so with decisions about how to lead it: the system within which it has to operate must be analysed. Two points are important to stress here, one relating to structure, the other to people.

If there is a devolved structure for the training department, with central staff being transferred out to or already working in units, then there is a danger of professional isolation for those staff; there is also a possibility that they will become so closely involved with the units in which they are working that they will lose their own team identity. Fowler (1992, p. 23) observes that the leader in that situation must act as 'head of profession', retaining functional responsibility for staff's professional and career development, and holding regular meetings with them.

In relation to people, consideration must be given to the leader's own preferred style and characteristics. It is pointless to try to be 'authoritarian' if this runs quite counter to your personality and to others' fixed perceptions of the kind of person you are. This point has to be balanced against the preferred leadership style of the group and their own personal, occupational and professional characteristics, which may call strongly for one style rather than another. As was seen in the later stages of the Thatcher Government, quite intractable problems can occur when the style applied by the leader is increasingly unacceptable to the group, especially if that style is also clearly at odds with the tasks to be carried out by the whole team.

The matter of 'fit' is so important that it should be a critical factor at the selection stage. However, 'fit' must be seen in a wider context; adapting to the preferences and expectations of a group is not productive if the behaviour and performance is at odds with what is needed in the organization. In some situations a new leader may have to apply extreme measures if the current culture and performance of the training department is prejudicing the effectiveness and credibility of training in the organization.

EXERCISE

This exercise continues the experiences of the new Training Manager which were examined in Chapter 9 (see p. 186). As Training Manager, you report to the Personnel Director, and you have now been allocated one professional member of staff responsible to you. You can also call on the Personnel Department's administrative and secretarial support services.

The Personnel Director has told you that the young man who will be working with you is one of her ablest staff: IPM-qualified with three years' post-college experience in personnel work, all in this organization, although none in training.

One of the first tasks you have been asked to carry out is to recommend a training policy and strategy for the organization. The climate for this appears to be supportive, both in relation to your Director and to top management generally, who perceive that a planned approach to employee development is now essential if the organization is to achieve its goals in an unpredictable external environment. You do not yet know much about the general culture relating to employee development at other levels of the organization.

On this information only, how will you decide how best to organize and manage this young professional, and what ideas have you at this point about how to train and develop him?

FEEDBACK NOTES

There are many different ways in which you could respond to this task. I am taking a particular approach, in order to reiterate some key learning points already covered in this and previous chapters.

1 **Reflection.** You will have to consider carefully how to make the best use of this officer. You will have to decide on his tasks and targets, while avoiding defining these too closely at first. In this way, as the training section's work develops in response to perceived needs, his and your own aptitudes and interests can creatively influence the allocation of work and duties. If, therefore, you do eventually draw up a formal job description and personnel specification (and these will be essential aids to future recruitment into the section, as well as to appraisal and training) you should actively involve him in that process.

You will also need to ensure that as he makes progress in the job, he also makes progress in terms of a general career development plan. Career guidance will be needed, and encouraging him to draw up a personal development plan at an early stage will help in this process.

You yourself will need a high level of professional expertise in order to perform effectively across the spectrum of training tasks you face. You will have to find out from initial discussions where the young man has strengths that can be used and developed, and where there are areas needing to be improved. You can then agree together how best to organize his work and develop his potential, while also complementing your own skills and expertise.

When deciding on the kind of tasks he will need to perform now, the Lead Body's Qualifications Framework will offer a useful initial checklist, because you can identify which of the tasks he will be performing are likely to build up workplace experience and competence for which, ultimately, he may be able to get accreditation towards a qualification. It is likely that his tasks at first will fall mainly into the Lead Body Level 3 Statement of Competence (see Appendix 3), although in some areas of competence he may need to be nearer levels shown under Level 4.

You will also need to consider those processes he will need to master that are not covered in the Standards – especially those relating to political sensitivity and the need to become fully familiar with the organizational (including political) contexts in which he will have to operate. In this context, remember the importance of Kolb's learning cycle, and try to ensure that he is able, in the normal course of his work, to practise the skills of observation and reflection, analysis, creativity, decision-making and problem-solving, and evaluation. These skills will be central to all of his work and development.

2 **Analysis.** You will have to decide what kind of leadership style to use, and how best to organize yourself and him as a team. You have the chance of a creative, pro-active role for the function. A task culture would be the most appropriate for one to aim for, both in your small training section, and in relation to other functions and departments with which it must interact throughout the organization.

However, your ability to develop such a culture will depend to a large extent on how far the culture of the wider organization supports or is likely to hinder this. Clearly you will need to move out of the office from the start and go around the organization, 'walking and talking the job' in order to identify the main needs to which you should and can respond and to build up collaborative relationships. You will need to ensure that the young officer has political sensitivity and good interpersonal skills if you decide to operate as a close-knit team in this respect rather than to use him only to carry out administrative and paperwork tasks in the office. The latter strategy would in any case be likely to demotivate and underutilize him, given his qualifications, ability and experience.

3 **Decision-making.** Having fully reflected on all this information, and analysed it carefully, you should now find it relatively easy to generate alternative ways of using the young officer, and to decide how best to organize your small training section.

4 **Monitoring and evaluation.** You will need to monitor progress and evaluate the results of your decisions and operations, in order to determine where changes are needed in the future.

Building up a closely integrated, high-performing team is very challenging and time-consuming, and requires particular skills. It is therefore important to consider how far such a strategy really is essential. Casey (1985) queries whether all groups ought to function as teams. He points out that if the work to be done in a department is routine and/or highly specialized, then allocating it out to the most appropriate individuals, and managing people on a one-to-one basis, may be a more appropriate approach. Leadership skills in that situation consist of recruiting and selecting the right kinds of individuals, allocating and monitoring their work and performance, and ensuring that they remain motivated and competent. Individuals will also need to be developed to meet new types of work coming in to the department, or any cultural and structural changes requiring new attitudes or new patterns of interaction.

The more complex or innovative the tasks become, however, and the more uncertain the general environment of the group, the more people will need to work closely together, whether in sub-groups or as a total team. The leader does then need to ensure that the characteristics of effective teamwork are developed – what Woodcock (1979) calls 'the building blocks':

- Clear **objectives** and agreed goals
- An ability to support both **openness** and **confrontation**, and make them productive processes
- **Support and trust** between members, and between the whole group and the leader
- An ability to sustain both **co-operation** and **conflict**, and ensure they are used productively
- Sound and relevant **procedures** governing work tasks and processes
- An appropriate **leadership** style and methods
- Regular **review** of how the team is performing, and how it is maintaining itself as a group
- Support and plans for **individual development**
- Effective **relations** with other sections and groups in the organization

Woodcock (1979) has produced a number of questionnaires and activities whereby a leader can examine the extent to which the group already has the nine characteristics listed above and where it seems to be in need of further development, together with a range of excellent practical suggestions for achieving that development. Outdoor development courses are a particularly effective way of reinforcing team skills, but they need to be very carefully planned and organized, and their learning needs to be skilfully transferred to the workplace if they are to justify their high costs.

EXERCISE

After reading the case study below, please answer the three questions set at the end. A variant on this would be to try a role-playing exercise instead, using the questions as the starting point for a meeting between the new Training Manager and his or her staff.

'Vitex' is a well-known engineering firm in South-east England. Ten years ago it had a workforce of 2,000, and was extremely successful, operating in many home and overseas markets. Its Training Department consisted of a Training Manager, three specialist Training Officers, two Instructors who were responsible for apprentice and commercial training, a Clerk and a Secretary. Training tasks tended to be predictable and repetitive, and members of the department operated mainly as individuals.

Training policy and the annual company training plan were established by the Training Manager working in partnership with the Personnel Director, and thereafter work was allocated to the appropriate people, with monitoring to ensure the training budget was not exceeded. There was little real evaluation of training, nor any in-depth diagnosis of needs. It was assumed that the future would be very like the past and present, and so training itself was mainly a matter of sending people on external courses, or doing some internal, job-related training if this seemed necessary. Training staff tended to work on an individualized basis, with the three Training Officers working within different business units.

Owing to very severe competition and changes in its market, Vitex is now a much smaller firm, with a workforce of around 800, working on three sites, all within five or so miles of each other. It makes maximum use of new technology and has established a reputation for innovation and high-quality products. As part of the general move towards 'slimming down' and rationalization, the size of the Training Department has been reduced to a Training Manager, a Training Officer and a Secretary/Administrative Assistant. There is no apprentice or YT programme, and the previous Training Manager was moved three months ago into production management (where he had earlier experience). The Training Officer, a man in his forties without any professional qualifications but a good record as an administrator and instructor in the function, is one of the original three Training Officers; his colleagues have been redeployed to other service departments. There is a new Secretary, a pleasant and efficient woman of 30 who was moved from the Sales Department to Training a year ago.

You have just been recruited as the new Training Manager, with a brief to make the function diagnostic rather than reactive, your role being a mix of Pettigrew's (1982) training manager and role in transition (moving from provider to change agent). Top management fully support training but have made it clear that from now on the function must provide tailor-made answers to real organizational needs that have been expertly diagnosed. External resources can still be used, but only where the expense can be justified by the results likely to be achieved. Each business unit now holds its own training and development budget, with managers responsible for deciding on training needs in their units. The

Training Department has only a small central budget to meet organization-wide needs and special contingencies (usually caused by changes in the law etc.).

1 How will you decide what kind of leadership style to use in your department?

2 Do you see individualized work or teamwork as relevant to your new department? (Give reasons for your.reply.)

3 What is the first action you will take in relation to establishing leadership and work processes in the department?

FEEDBACK NOTES

You would need to analyse the following five factors, in order to decide on the most appropriate kind of leadership style:

1 **Environment.** This means the environment or organizational setting of the leader, the group and the task. Here, the wider organization is organic, team-based, and operating in an uncertain, highly competitive environment. This should push the training department towards a flexible structure, with values which relate to helping to achieve Vitex's mission, and to provide expertise which will meet organizational needs. Effective teamwork, in Woodcock's sense of the word, will be essential, and the function must become business-led if it is to establish and maintain credibility and serve the needs of its 'clients' in the business units.

2 **Structure and culture.** Although the Training Department may have had a bureaucratic structure and culture in the past, these are no longer appropriate. Leadership which will help to develop a non-hierarchical, creative, 'change agent' department is clearly needed, and there must be a collaborative role *vis-à-vis* line managers.

3 **Goals, strategy and tasks.** At Vitex, the goal is for training to provide tailor-made services to meet key organizational needs, so training tasks may change rapidly, and are unlikely to be routine or highly specialized. This emphasizes the need for effective teamwork rather than an individualized pattern of organizing and managing people in the Training Department.

4 **Technology.** Given justification, it seems likely that the Training

Manager could use new technology, e.g. computer-based training and learning, open learning projects, etc., as well as more conventional media and methods, but the justification must be compelling. Since this is a medium-sized manufacturing firm, making use of new technology in all its processes and needing to keep up with a fast-changing market situation, it needs flexible training and learning systems that can deliver results quickly and efficiently. The Training Department will have to become knowledgeable about such innovative approaches, and may in time have to use external consultants to design and pilot certain learning systems. They too will have to be carefully selected, managed and monitored (see the Sales Training initiative in Harrison, 1992).

5 **People.** Your own preferred style and characteristics have to be considered, as do the preferred leadership style of the group, and their own personal and professional characteristics, which may make one style more obviously appropriate than any other. A problem may arise with the 40-year-old Training Officer, who has worked in a very different kind of training situation, with an emphasis on administration and reactive tasks rather than on creative and diagnostic work, and on individual, departmental or unit-based working rather than close-knit teamwork. He will clearly need sensitive handling, and particular attention must be paid to his training and development. The Secretary, too, has worked in that situation for a year, and her expectations and perceptions of the new situation need to be explored.

What conclusions can we draw from this analysis? All the evidence points to the need for you to build a cohesive, flexible team, whose members can contribute to the overall goal of the Training Department, pooling knowledge and skills instead of working on an individualized and specialized basis. In this context, the contribution of the Secretary, and the image she gives of the Department, is crucial. If she proves capable and willing, her role and type of work could itself change, and incorporate other types of responsibility. Many excellent personnel and training officers started off as secretaries, and here it is very important to consider routes of development like the IPM qualification and guided experience.

The Training Officer, too, has valuable experience and skills to offer: giving him an early assignment of collecting information from external sources on new learning systems that might be appropriate for certain groups in the company would, for example, give him the chance to work on something of real importance, and to expand his area of knowledge as well as his network of external contacts.

One of your first actions should be to set aside a morning or afternoon for a staff meeting. You can then explain your role, and the goal and tasks of the Department as you see them. The staff can be encouraged to give their perceptions and expectations, and all can discuss ways in which the Department can best relate to the wider organization in its various key tasks. The meeting can then move on to consider how to achieve the kind of teamwork that will be needed in future, with particular reference to the nine characteristic Woodcock outlines.

Preliminary consideration can be given to the kinds of procedures and processes that could be set up immediately to facilitate the department's work (keeping them to the essential minimum). The views of staff should be sought on the kind of appraisal and development systems they would see as most likely to meet departmental and individual needs.

In these discussions a delicate but firm balance needs to be struck between pursuing a collaborative approach with staff, and demonstrating leadership that has a clear vision for the Department and a policy and strategy to ensure that vision can be implemented at the practical level. The extent to which inputs from staff can or should influence the determination of organizational training and development policy and strategy is something that only you can determine.

Organizing Line Managers with Training and Development Responsibilities

Great care must be given to the selection and organization of line managers who have specific training and development roles to perform, and to achieving commitment and expertise in all line managers in the key task of developing those whom they manage. The same basic principles apply as we have already noted for specialist staff: the nature of their roles, and of the tasks, competences, personal skills, knowledge and attitudes that they require must be identified to establish necessary guidelines.

Developing managers as trainers and developers at ICI
(by permission of ICI, who wish to point out that the following describes the situation there in *1991*)

At ICI employee development is a key area of every manager's job, and managers are appraised and rewarded for their performance in this as in other areas of responsibility. Appraisal and rewards are essential, because busy managers will not perform a training and development role unless they are convinced that they must, and are helped, monitored, and encouraged to do so.

At ICI, as at Etewel (page 127), managers have proved to be excellent trainers, with hundreds becoming certified IM [Institute of Management] trainers. A very wide range of procedures, initiatives and formal programmes have been established in order to ensure that they take their training and development roles seriously and are equipped to perform them to a high standard. Some of the approaches used are:

- Appointing line managers in key functions or departments to oversee training and development
- Running workshops about current major business topics with line managers and encouraging advocates among them for the training and development implications of emerging plans
- Selecting influential middle managers and training them as certified trainers
- Encouraging committed managers to raise the profile of training and development as part of line management through the agenda of management meetings
- Encouraging a mentoring system
- Creating more flexible methods for delivering training and learning, such as distance learning technology
- Requiring that all managers have personal development plans, and that they ensure that their staff do too.

The Effective Training Manager

In the Vitex exercise (see pp. 225–6) we paid particular attention to processes and skills needed by the training manager. Let us now summarize what is needed for success in the role, whatever its level in the organization, and whether held by specialist or line manager.

1 **Objectivity.** The training manager must always strive for objectivity. To identify in a personal sense with a particular individual or group when diagnosing needs, formulating a training policy and plans, and designing and evaluating training, will inevitably result in distortion in those processes, and in suspicion if not alienation of other key parties. The best way to avoid subjectivity is to use procedures which reduce the possibility of its occurrence – although, of course, wherever human beings are involved, complete objectivity will never be possible.

2 **Self-assessment and self-development.** The training manager needs to direct his or her own learning, taking all the necessary initiatives to develop in ways that will improve expertise, credibility and professional growth.

3 **Interpersonal skills.** Technical knowledge and skills are of little use to training professionals if they lack the interpersonal skills to deal effectively with people of all kinds. Training and development tasks call for a sensitive handling of the people who hold crucial information, and on whose support and commitment the training manager is so dependent. It is important to remember, above all, that the training manager is a member of an organizational team, and in most situations will be moving in and out of smaller teams in order to carry out the various tasks required. The building blocks of effective teamwork should be borne in mind in any form of team activity, and the manager should try to assess and develop his or her level of effectiveness in each area.

4 **Credibility.** Too often in the past training staff have become isolated in every sense from the rest of the organization, often complacent, and lacking the professional and political expertise that could improve their credibility (Pettigrew et al., 1982; Coopers and Lybrand, 1985). One important goal should be to obtain the relevant professional qualifications through courses that have been designed to give the student a high level of knowledge about training and development together with a grounding of skills and competences which can be developed by on-the-job experience.

Above all, however, training staff must speak the language of their organization and serve its needs. To quote the IPM in its response to the MSC paper *Developing Trainers* (1987):

> Obviously, direct trainers and educators need initial and continuing education and training both in their specialized subject(s) and in the broad fields of learning and teaching. They are ideally placed to become excellent, continuous self-developers, too . . . [but] people whose predominant role is a training role need, above all, to understand and make it their business to demonstrate how training contributes to the success of effectiveness of the organizations they work for.

An effective and efficient function. Training managers must be efficient, in the sense of providing full value in all that is done by the function for which they are responsible. The ability continually to demonstrate that value to the organization is a crucial part of the need to speak the organization's language to which we have just referred: the language of efficiency, effectiveness and the skilful, productive management of resources. The training manager must always be able to explain the costs that their activities will involve, and argue persuasively in support of those costs, as well as being able, ultimately, to justify them. Just as the consultant who gets the cost-benefit equation wrong is rarely invited back a second time by the client, so the training manager who lacks expertise in this area becomes increasingly marginalized by their internal clients until finally – as has happened in many instances – their function and position disappear, often in the name of cost-cutting.

A proactive approach. Training managers should not only respond effectively to agreed needs at organizational, operational and individual level. They should also seek to influence events, to look ahead and search for signs that indicate changes needing to be made in which training and development should play a key part. For employee development to become a part of the real life of the organization, it must be a proactive as well as a reactive function. The ultimate aim should be to influence organizational policy and strategy at the stages of formulation, not just at implementation. We shall deal with this point more fully in the next chapter.

Exercises

1 Assume that you are the tutor in charge of IPM studies at XYZ College – and assume also that colleges can submit proposals for the new 'elective' Stage 2 subjects. Draft a summary of such a proposal, outlining the learning objectives, the syllabus content and the methods of study, for ONE of the following:

(a) Learning methods;
(b) The training of trainers;
(c) Open and distance learning. (November 1989)

2 In XYZ Ltd a top management decision has been taken to merge the Personnel Department and the Office Services Department. The

former, comprising 12 staff, is headed by a Personnel Manager and three middle managers (Employee Development, Employee Relations, and Personnel Administration); the latter is managed by one Office Services Manager, aided by supervisors in Telephone Services, Typing Services, Duplicating Services, Catering Services, Conference Services and Safety (Total staff in Office Services = 50).

Imagine you are the Personnel Manager who will be in charge of the newly merged unit. You are keen to establish a 'single team' and to promote some movement across traditional boundaries below management level, because you believe it will prove possible to reduce staff numbers by about ten in the integrated operation. How and what do you plan, to develop the staff in your new unit to serve these ends? (May 1989)

References

ARKIN A. 'Specialising in strategic HRD'. *Personnel Management*, December 1991. pp. 7-8

CASEY D. 'When is a team not a team'. *Personnel Management*, January 1985. pp. 26-9

COOPERS AND LYBRAND ASSOCIATES. *A Challenge to Complacency: Changing attitudes to training.* A report to the Manpower Services Commission and the National Economic Development Office. Sheffield, MSC. 1985

DAVIES J AND DEIGHAN Y. 'The managerial menopause'. *Personnel Management*, March 1986. pp. 28-32

FOWLER A. 'How to structure a personnel department'. *Personnel Management Plus*, January 1992. pp. 22-3

HARRISON R. 'Employee development at Barratt'. In *Case Studies in Personnel Management* (Woodall D and Winstanley D, eds). London, Institute of Personnel Management. 1992

INSTITUTE OF PERSONNEL MANAGEMENT. 'IPM disappointed at MSC plans for training trainers'. *IPM Digest*, May 1987. pp. 3-4

KENNEY J AND REID M. *Training Interventions.* London, Institute of Personnel Management, 1986; third edition, by Reid, Barrington and Kenney, 1992

LEICESTER C. 'The key role of the line manager in employee development'. *Personnel Management*, March 1989. pp. 53-7

MANPOWER SERVICES COMMISSION AND THE INSTITUTE OF TRAINING AND DEVELOPMENT. *Trainer Task Inventory.* Sheffield, MSC. 1984

MANPOWER SERVICES COMMISSION AND THE INSTITUTE OF TRAINING AND DEVELOPMENT. *Guide to Trainer Effectiveness.* Sheffield, MSC. 1984

MANPOWER SERVICES COMMISSION. *Developing Trainers: MSC support for training of trainers and staff development.* Sheffield, MSC. 1987

PETTIGREW A M, JONES G R AND REASON P W. *Training and Development Roles in Their Organizational Setting.* Sheffield, Manpower Services Commission. 1982

PICKARD J. 'IPM claims new training standards fail to address essential points'. *Personnel Management Plus*, February 1991. p. 3

TORRINGTON D, HALL L, HAYLOR I AND MYERS J. *Employee Resourcing* (Management Studies 2 Series). London, Institute of Personnel Management. 1991

TRAINING AND DEVELOPMENT LEAD BODY. 'Setting standards for training'. *News Brief*, Issue No. 2, Sheffield, Training Agency. July 1990

TRAINING AND DEVELOPMENT LEAD BODY. *National Standards for Training and Development.* Sheffield, The Department of Employment. January 1991

WILLIAMS R. 'What's new in career development'. *Personnel Management*, March 1984. pp. 32-3

WOODCOCK M. *Team Development Manual.* Aldershot, Gower. 1979

Further useful reading

BENNETT R AND LEDUCHOWICZ T. 'What makes for an effective trainer?' *Journal of European Industrial Training*, Vol. 7, No. 2. 1983

GREENAWAY R AND BILL C. 'Competences of development trainers'. In *Trainer Competences for the 1990s Series.* Sheffield, Training Agency. 1989

INSTITUTE OF PERSONNEL MANAGEMENT. *Training: Bibliography 21.* London, IPM (Information and Advisory Services). 1986

MUMFORD A. *The Manager and Training.* London, Times Management Library. 1971

NADLER L. 'The Variety of Training Roles'. *Industrial and Commercial Training*, Vol. 1, 1 November, 1969. pp. 33-7

PEPPER A D. *Managing the Training and Development Function.* Aldershot, Gower. 1985

PINTO P R AND WALKER J W. 'What do training and development professionals really do?'. *Training and Development Journal*, No. 32, 7 July 1978. pp. 58-64

ROBINSON K R. *A Handbook of Training Management.* 2nd ed. London, Kogan Page. 1985

TRAINING OF TRAINERS COMMITTEE. *First Report: Training of Trainers.* Sheffield, Manpower Services Commission. 1978

WALTHER R H. 'ASTD members – their perceptions and training goals'. *Training and Development Journal.* No. 25, 3 March 1971. pp. 32-7

WILLIAMSON B (ed.). *Directory of Trainer Support Services.* London, Kogan Page and Institute of Training and Development. 1985

WRIGHT P L AND TAYLOR D S. *Improving Leadership Performance: A practical new approach to leadership.* London, Prentice Hall. 1984. (Like WOODCOCK, a very useful book, because it is full of practical exercises, checklists, and diagnostic activities.)

Chapter 11

Achieving strategic, business-led employee development

Learning Objectives

After reading this chapter you will:

1 be able to identify the forces that trigger the need for a strategic approach to employee development in an organization;
2 be able to draw up a mission and strategy for employee development in your own organization;
3 know how to develop a strategic and business-led employee development function in an organization;
4 know how to analyse training and development needs at the organizational level, and how to approach the task of assessing outcomes at that level.

Developing a Strategic, Business-led Employee Development Function: an Overview

In Chapter 3 we noted a widespread failure in organizations to think strategically about skill needs (see pp. 58–60) and we traced the course over many years of failure at governmental level to develop a positive, meaningful mission and strategy to ensure adequately skilled and educated human resources. It is vital to make training and development serve the ends of the business as well as promoting the growth of individuals; and it is essential to think and act strategically instead of continually reacting in an *ad hoc* fashion to the most obviously pressing needs of the moment.

At this point it is worth repeating the definition of employee development given in Chapter 1.

> Employee development as part of the organization's overall human resource strategy means the skilful provision and organization of learning experiences in the workplace in order that

> performance can be improved, that work goals can be achieved and that, through enhancing the skills, knowledge, learning ability and enthusiasm of people at every level, there can be continuous organizational as well as individual growth. Employee development must, therefore, be part of a wider strategy for the business, aligned with the organization's corporate mission and goals.

The term 'business' in this context refers to any kind of employing organization, public or private sector, service, process or product-driven.

Business-led employee development is development that is responsive to the important needs of an organization and improves its ability to achieve its corporate goals. It also makes possible a widening choice of business actions as the real potential of people at various levels of the organization becomes evident. Business-led employee development must be a dynamic function, moving in line with the cycle of business change. (For a real-life case study illustrating this point, read the story of Halford, Britain's biggest retailer of car accessories and cycles, during a critical period of business change in the 1980s in Sparrow and Pettigrew, 1988.)

Strategic employee development is development that arises from a powerful vision about people's abilities and potential, has a clear mission related to that vision and has a relevant and feasible strategy to achieve that mission.

Strategic employee development means employee development that is used as a major lever to enable an organization to get 'from here to there'. To be strategic, employee development must operate effectively at three levels of the organization:

- At the corporate planning level, where employee development considerations should be taken fully into account when business strategy is formulated, and should also form part of a human resource plan within the wider business plan
- At the business unit/divisional level (i.e. at line management level), where there must be policies that will ensure that people are trained and developed in line with the needs of the business – employee development should, like the wider function of employee resourcing of which it forms a part, be an accepted business function at this level, well integrated with other key functions
- At the operational level, where employee development must be an integrated part of daily routine and procedures, helping people to achieve performance standards and behavioural objectives and

building up the kind of workforce needed in terms of productivity, quality and flexibility

How does the function become strategic in this threefold sense? It needs:

1 **A good 'fit' with the business.** As we saw in Chapter 9, it must be organized in such a way as best to fit the characteristics and meet the needs of the system in which it has to operate.

2 **Expert personnel.** There must be expertise in employee development at three levels:

- **Corporate level.** Here the qualities that are vital are political skills, broad business orientation, an understanding of wider employee resourcing issues, and a proactive stance. The pressures of business changes will tend to lead to an increasing awareness of the need for employee development, and providing that they are accompanied by sufficient internal commitment at the top of an organization they can trigger off a more strategic approach to the function and a willingness to increase the level of investment in it. However, this will only happen if there is a conviction that employee development will have a real payoff, and the role of the spokesperson for training and development (who at this level will probably be the Personnel Director or equivalent role) is to ensure that there is this conviction. He or she must be knowledgeable about the implications for employee resourcing and development of alternative proposed business strategies, giving a persuasive assessment of where the balance of advantage lies between those strategies.

  Unless they take fully into account employee resource issues, including those relating to employee development, business strategies may prove impossible or damagingly costly to implement. On the other hand, a valid understanding of employees' performance and potential could make possible a wider range of strategic options for the business. (This proved to be the case at Halford – see Sparrow and Pettigrew, 1988.)
- **Unit/divisional level.** At this level there is a need for training and development staff who have a general managerial orientation and background, and who can work closely and collaboratively with line managers to help in the production of employee development policies and plans that will boost the performance of units. We have already discussed some of the skills needed here in Chapters 9 and 10.

- **Operational level.** What is required here is interpersonal skills and technical expertise in the specific operations and tasks of training and development.

3 **Effective management of personnel.** It is essential that all those responsible for training and development, whether line managers or specialist staff, are effectively managed and motivated. We have discussed the importance of this point in Chapters 9 and 10.

4 **Linkage of the employee development function to the line organization.** This must be done by identifying needs involved at strategic, managerial and operational level, drawing up strategy and plans to meet those needs and ensuring outcomes that justify the investment in the function.

To summarize, there are four key questions to ask about the employee development function that seeks to make a strategic contribution to the organization:

1. Does the way the function is organized enhance its ability to accomplish its strategy?
2. Are the employee development staff expert in their roles and tasks, and effectively managed?
3. Is there a good 'fit' between the mission and strategy of the employee development function and the mission and strategy of the wider organization?
4. Do the outcomes of employee development meet important business needs?

Producing a Mission, Strategy and Plans for Employee Development in the Organization

Let us now look at how to develop a mission, strategy, policies and plans for employee development (see pages 5–6).

Vision and culture for employee development

There must be positive values about the importance of people to the organization, and a strong, clear vision about the contribution a trained and continuously developing workforce can make to the achievement of organizational goals. Vision and values, as we saw in Chapter 5, underpin the culture of the organization and directly affect crucial decisions relating to investment and the deployment of the organization's resources, including its people. Training and development can achieve as much as, but no more than, the organizational climate allows them to achieve.

Mission and policy for employee development

Moving from a generalized vision about the importance of developing people to expressing that vision in a mission and policy that clearly state the purpose of employee development in the organization is a vital stage. Vagueness of vision and confusion in mission will result in a fragmented approach to the development of people (Sadler and Barham, 1988), in which what is carried out is training rather than development, and it is done at whim, becomes a cost and a luxury, is rarely if ever evaluated and is not tied to business targets.

My biggest mistake
(With acknowledgements to J Garnett and *The Independent on Sunday*)

This point about the need for a convincing business-led policy for developing people was emphasized in a revealing article in *The Independent on Sunday* (8 March 1992) by John Garnett, Director of the Industrial Society from 1962 to 1986, who admitted, 'My biggest mistake was trying to sell ideas in relation to my own objectives, rather than the objectives of the people I was selling to.'

He described how his passionate vision about the value of developing people's abilities and potential blinded him during his time as Personnel Manager of the Plastics Division of ICI to the equally important need to relate what he did to the objectives of the business. It led to the loss of his job:

> My work, in the view of the board, was irrelevant and, more seriously, distracting. They were in the business of making profits in plastics, while I seemed to be in the business of developing people, which took their eyes off the main purpose.

It taught him an unforgettable lesson: unless employee development is seen to be business-led it will fail to convince top management of its value to the business. This can lead to the entire function's demise.

Typical attitudes which, while supporting employee development, do no service to the function, must be confronted at this stage. Let us look at a few examples:

- Some will see development of employees as a crucial task, and argue for a heavy investment in it while at the same time showing no real concern to put it in the context of specific business needs or to measure and evaluate its outcomes. Like John Garnett, they simply believe that developing potential is answering a central human need, and is of such innate value that it is bound to bring benefits to the organization.
- Others may argue that employee development *must* be worthwhile because 'the best companies do it'. Again, there will be no emphasis on clarity of purpose, responsiveness to specific needs and measurement of outcomes.
- Others may believe that investing in employee development is justified by a particular organization's general employment philosophy and that any developmental activities, providing that they are well designed and stimulate people's 'growth', are worthwhile.

If the 'mission' (whether expressed formally or implicitly) rests on these kinds of assumptions, then the outcome is predictable: training and development will be unsystematic, non-strategic and unconvincing to sceptical managers because it does not seem to relate to the ends of the business.

> Establishing a training and development mission (or policy, in the macro sense of that word) for the organization involves clarifying the purpose of the function in the organization and setting longer-term objectives for the development of the workforce that link directly to the overall business goals and strategy of the organization.

The mission should be elaborated in an overall policy for employee development in the organization. Strategic objectives need to be defined that will meet business needs and are consistent with and supported by wider human resource strategy. Once employee development objectives are clarified, then a strategy can be drawn up to meet them.

If, as initially at Barratt (Harrison, 1992a), there is no existing employee resource policy, then it will be essential that one is formulated and underpins and reinforces the specific policy and strategy of the employee development function.

Employee development strategy and plans for its implementation

If a company's annual report has to contain a section within the business plan completed by every business unit about its human resources and their performance and productivity levels, together with information about investment in employee development in the unit, then employee development strategy and plans will be officially recognized as crucial to the success of business plans.

Once a strategy for employee development has been formulated, explaining the route to be followed to ensure the achievement of the objectives of overall employee development policy, plans covering each main area of training and development activity can then be drawn up. Singer (1977) suggests that for each area, a plan should show:

- the content of training;
- the performance standards to be achieved;
- where and how training will be given;
- who is responsible for making arrangements and for the training;
- the timing and sequence, bearing in mind priorities;
- the method to be used in assessing results.

Plans will usually operate on a rolling basis and to ensure their effective implementation there must be a high level of line management involvement in discussing and agreeing on those plans. Direct and obvious indirect costs (such as lost opportunity time, lost production time, reduced quality and wastage during learning time) should be identified, as should those benefits that will justify and hopefully outweigh the costs involved.

Objectives for training and development, and plans to achieve them, should be set at business unit/divisional/departmental levels, and at individual operational levels. The aim should always be to produce clearly defined objectives, together with agreed methods of measuring the outcomes.

It is particularly important that plans at the individual level are seen by the individuals concerned to be relevant and rewarding. At this point there will often be tensions, perhaps because of disagreement between the manager and the individual as to what training and further development is needed, and why; or because certain objectives regarded by the manager as essential in relation to business needs will not, if achieved, bring meaningful rewards for the individual; or because the parties disagree on priorities. All these tensions have to be resolved if employee development is to respond to business needs while also having the commitment of individuals. We will return to this theme in Chapter 13.

Figure 8 summarizes the stages involved in establishing an employee development programme.

Figure 8

Five steps in producing business-led development of people

1 Relate investment in the development of people to the corporate mission and strategy.

2 Produce and analyse an employee resource policy, and establish objectives for employee development.

3 Formulate a strategy to meet those objectives.

4 Agree on realistic, specific, measurable and well-costed plans to implement the strategy.

5 Establish mechanisms for monitoring, feedback and further relevant action.

(Adapted from Harrison, 1992b)

Here is a case study which illustrates some of the key points made so far in this chapter, and shows how a new business-led mission and policy for employee development was formulated at Marks and Spencer.

Employee development at Marks and Spencer (1991)
(With acknowledgements to E Williams and IIR Ltd)

Strategic business issues

Marks and Spencer, a company which has always set an exceptionally high value on its workforce and the contribution they can make to the business, is facing key business issues during the 1990s: expansion into international markets; more demanding customers; more innovative competition; and the changing composition of the business.

There are also a range of external and internal challenges on the employee resourcing front:

- The economic climate and competitive environment
- New technologies and computerization, demanding new skills and attitudes
- Demographic trends
- The growing demands and increasing expectations of new and existing employees
- The continuous pace of change
- A drive to achieve more with less

Employee development mission

Analysis of various strategic options for the business involved an examination of existing training practice. It became clear that, regardless of the intention or wording of the company's training policy, the strategy for delivering it was full of inconsistencies when held against the template of issues that business strategy had to resolve:

- Training took place off the job and away from people's place of work.
- It catered for generalized rather than specific needs.
- It was the responsibility of the personnel function.
- It was remedial.
- It was neither focused nor targeted on business needs.

A new mission for employee development was drawn up. The vision on which it was based was that the most effective learning comes from experience; and that individuals and the company derived most benefit from a situation where people took responsibility for their own training and development, with the primary place for this being the work environment.

The mission is that training and development at Marks and Spencer will:

- occur at the right time;
- be accurately focused on the needs of the business;
- be driven by the individual and their line manager;
- deliver people who are effective and proficient in their job;
- increase the motivation of people to constantly improve their performance.

Employee development policy

The new training and development policy at Marks and Spencer is, in outline:

- Every individual should take responsibility for their own continuous training and development, since those processes are something that people can do themselves rather than have applied to them by 'experts'.
- Every manager must support the development of their staff; this is an integral part of their job on which they will be assessed.
- Learning and work should be integrated.
- Training and development should take place mainly on the job.
- The development of people must be a fundamental, not an additional, activity.
- Training and development must lead to visible changes at work.

Employee development strategy and plans

The strategy and plans for training and development must therefore relate to that overall policy and to its specific policy objectives. Those objectives are not included here, but one of them is to give a priority to management development, with the aim of developing managers who will be:

- quicker on their feet, more adaptable and flexible;
- willing to experiment and take risks;
- capable of building a vision for themselves and others;
- more inquisitive;
- learners from experience.

This policy objective has led to a strategy of focusing management training on technical skills and general management skills, and management development on the enhancement of job performance and the maximization of future potential. The strategy is related to five areas of need: those at junior management, middle management, senior management, executive, and director levels. Policies and plans have been drawn up for each of these levels, detailing learning objectives, the key features of the learning system involved and the people whose needs the plans are intended to meet.

Establishing Organizational Employee Development Needs and Plans

We now need to look in more detail at how to assess employee development needs at the organizational level. Analysis of individual needs, and the design of events for special groups and needs, will be discussed in later chapters. Here, we will focus on the analytical approaches that can be used to identify organizational needs. In a learning organization (see Chapter 7), of course, the analysis of employee training and development needs is part of the process of continuous development in that organization. However, there must still be checks to ensure that the key strategic needs of the business are being met by training and development, as by any other business function.

We are going to look at three kinds of analytical approach:

- The total, or comprehensive, approach
- The problem-centred approach
- The business strategy approach

The comprehensive and the problem-centred approaches

These two approaches are based on the same general principles, but in their detailed operation they cater for different kinds of situation.

The comprehensive approach involves a systematic, full-scale analysis of all the organization's training and development needs, identified by discussions with managers (and unions if appropriate), by analysis of the corporate business plan, and by examination of any other sources of likely change affecting people in the organization. Its product is an organization-wide training plan containing unit and individual plans for the forthcoming year (a year is the usual planning period for this kind of approach). It can be useful in organizations where the environment is relatively stable, and where longer-term training plans can feasibly be produced and pursued, although it is unlikely to be used unless there is a specialist personnel or training function. If you are following this approach you must ensure that you have the necessary time and other resources, and that it will justify their expenditure.

For organizations which have to operate in a highly unpredictable environment, which are facing severe pressures, or which (like many small to medium-sized firms) lack the resources or expertise for the 'total' strategy, something more selective and more immediate in its payback is needed. For them, the 'problem-centred' analytical approach may be more appropriate. It focuses on urgent problems facing the organization and requiring a training or development response. It places minimum reliance on paperwork; on the assumption that the planning of training must be ongoing and focused on immediate needs, with long-term strategy at a minimum, there may be no formalized training plan other than papers that from time to time have to be drawn up for budgetary or external purposes. Training must respond quickly to any urgent needs, and so flexibility in the function and its operations is essential. Both approaches are systematic; it is the timescale and scope of assessment and planning that are the major differentiating factors.

The comprehensive approach

Here is an eight-step approach to comprehensive analysis.

1 **Identify major needs.** The first step is to study the organization's business strategy and plan. Training/personnel staff should then discuss with every manager the training and development needs for their units. At this stage, they need to bring into the discussions the implications of any impending organizational changes, new technology initiatives, new plant and machinery and new staff coming into the organization. In establishing training needs they should be influenced by the manager's interpretation of events as well as by the areas of need identified in corporate strategy.

2 **Agree possible solutions.** During this phase of the discussion, the degree to which training can contribute to meeting departmental needs must be assessed. The department's performance targets and outputs must be examined, together with any other data that will give substance and objectivity to the discussions. Information about many training needs may come from the results of appraisal interviews. Where an appraisal system is not yet in operation, information will come from the managers' views, performance records, career plans, potential reviews, etc.

Problems which are perceived initially by managers to have a training and development solution may on analysis prove to need some other solution, and vice versa. It is therefore essential to be clear as to the real nature of a problem: if performance is poor, for example, it may be because of inadequate or non-existent training, but it could as easily be because of poor motivation, ineffective management or faulty equipment (see Harrison, 1992b).

Thus in this second step the person with responsibility for training, whom we shall call the Training Manager even though that might not be their formal title, has detailed talks with every manager to ensure that the departmental and individual needs they raise will be best and most cost-effectively tackled by some form of training or development; also that those needs are jointly defined and agreed, using a prioritization system that reflects the overall objectives established in the organization's training policy.

3 **Select training options.** At this point it is important to discuss options for training, with a view to the process being as cost-efficient as possible. Initially the possibility of on-the-job events to achieve the required learning should be discussed rather than looking at external courses as a priority. Such discussion has led in many organizations to a significant overall shift from a reliance on external courses to an emphasis on in-house training, much of it done by consultants with tailor-made events, as well as by the organization's own staff taking over more training (for example, in appraisal skills and team building) once they have acquired the necessary level of skill. Such a shift, however, must be accompanied by appropriate training and development for those who will take on these tasks within the organization and careful monitoring and control of any external consultants (see Harrison, 1992a).

4 **Create a training plan.** Next the Training Manager constructs the first draft of the annual training plan, which identifies each department's and each individual's training needs and the relevant courses of action which have been agreed with the managers of those departments and individuals.

5 **Prioritize learning events.** The budgeting process conducted by the Training Manager starts at this point, when, within the training plan, he or she classifies training needs and events on some kind of scale (which could simply be an A–E rating system, A being 'essential', E being 'desirable but not necessarily this year'), according to priorities established in the organization's overall training policy. This means that each training event is prioritized according to corporate business needs, so that in the end the entire plan is geared to making the optimum contribution to present and future business objectives as well as to individual needs.

6 **Apply budgetary constraints.** After training has been categorized, the Training Manager should then estimate the costs involved in the initial draft of the training plan, including the options which were

discussed with managers. Costing should be done using current costs (an inflationary factor can be added later), examining both direct and indirect costs as in chapter 9.

In an organization where managers are required to submit departmental budgets for the coming financial year in, say, late January, total budget figures need to be allocated before the beginning of the financial year to enable managers to allocate resources appropriately according to their budget allocation, based on their January submissions. Once the Training Manager receives his or her budget allocation, adjustments to the plan are quite straightforward if the plan itself has been built up on a pyramid of costs (i.e. all 'A' events costing £x, all 'B' events costing £y, etc.). A reappraisal of the options available may result, for example, in the use of more internal training, or in dropping some category E training. In the latter event, there needs to be a subsequent reassessment of the original need, to see whether or not training is still appropriate.

7 **Communicate results.** Once the training plan has been fully costed and agreed by top management, a copy of the relevant sections should be given to each manager as an *aide-mémoire* and plan for each department. This then becomes an essential tool of reference for the review meetings the training manager holds with managers throughout the year.

8 **Monitor and evaluate implementation.** A continuous appraisal of progress and budgetary control should be maintained by the Training Department, using information supplied by management and those who go on training and development programmes. The task is not a difficult one when the training plan has been costed in relation to specific learning events and departments, with clear categories covering course fees, travel and related expenses, and fees paid to external consultants and trainers. Monitoring is vital for two reasons:

- It enables a tight control to be exercised over ongoing training, so that if at any point cost estimates are exceeded, appropriate action can be taken, whereas if costs are below those estimated, then there is flexibility either to include some of the hitherto-deferred category E training (if any has been deferred), or to do additional training to meet some unexpected contingency.
- It enables the Training Manager to build up a 'value for money'

statement which can be included in the annual report on the training plan. This can include statements related to key parameters like: the outcomes of training, in relation to the key needs it was intended to serve (using quantifiable and also qualitative measures); expenditure overall on training, compared with the previous year; the number and cost of person days of training, compared with the previous year; and the number and cost of person days of training carried out externally and in-house, compared with the previous year.

The problem-centred approach

Here is how the eight steps can be applied using the problem-centred approach. Once again, reference is made throughout to the Training Manager but this should be taken to mean anyone who carries the responsibility for formulating training policy and a training plan for the organization.

1 **Identify major needs.** The Training Manager should identify with managers on a continuing basis the most urgent problems or challenges they face, for which it is felt that some form of training or development would be the best solution. The analysis itself is carried out in a similar way to that outlined in the comprehensive approach. At regular intervals (determined by the length of the business planning cycle), the Training Manager must check on any information available about business plans and likely future changes, to see if training is needed to feed into them.

2 **Agree possible solutions.** Here, as with the total approach, the Training Manager must analyse not only whether particular problems are relevant for training, but whether training would be the most cost-effective process.

> Within the limits of overall company policy, the Training Manager is free to consider whether changing the organization, the equipment, or the job itself, or changing the people concerned by selection, would ease the problem, before the expensive, uncertain process of training is embarked on. (Gane, 1972)

With the problem-centred approach, priorities are determined by the extent to which the resolution of one problem would make a greater impact on immediate business performance than another. Areas of weakness which are currently impeding the achievement of results crucial to the company's survival must therefore be tackled first. Longer-term issues such as succession planning must also be tackled on an ongoing basis in the light of their importance to ensuring the continuity and calibre of key people.

3 **Select training options.** Here, agreement must be reached on who is to be trained, how many of them there are, when and where they will need training, and how they will be trained. Training can be done in any cost-effective, feasible and agreed way, but must take place in or near the work environment wherever possible, both to reduce costs and to ensure immediate relevance and the transferability of learning. Events selected under the problem-centred approach must be mainly concerned to achieve results in the shortest possible time, and in the most efficient manner.

4 **Create a training plan.** Other than training to meet certain major needs, which will usually be planned and agreed some time in advance (e.g. health and safety training, or retraining to cope with redundancies or redeployment of workers, or training to enable key workers to operate new technology), the training plan will be informal rather than heavily documented. A record should, however, be kept of the number and names of learners, of the training objectives, of the type, location and timing of the training, and of its cost and outcomes related to objectives.

5 **Prioritize learning events.** Although training with the problem-centred approach is done on a rolling basis rather than according to an annual plan, attention must still be paid to prioritizing events. Planning no more, probably, than a few weeks or months ahead, the Training Manager must still ensure that the training effort is put into those problem areas across the company where there will be the most significant return in terms of impact on the business. So, as with the prioritization of departmental or divisional training needs, attention must be given first to those areas which have a critical impact on the firm's survival, and are crucial to its future stability and growth.

6 **Apply budgetary constraints.** The Training Manager may not have

a budget (or may only hold a small central budget for core training and development needs), but be paid from the budgets held by line managers. It is therefore particularly important that he or she has a clear idea of what the business overall, and particular departments within it, are likely to be able to afford for the training they are requesting. All training must be costed very carefully, and when line managers hold budgetary control particularly close attention needs to be given to 'hidden' costs like lost opportunity and production, replacement or other costs involved in covering for people away from their jobs for a period of time, and so on. The Training Manager must be able to convince management that training can offer the value needed to offset costs.

7 **Communicate results.** With the problem-centred approach, initial requests for training must be acted upon quickly, and information about training and development activities that will be going ahead must be communicated to the managers concerned as soon as possible.

In situations where the problem-centred approach is used, certainty can rarely be built into any stage of the cycle; even at the last minute, action plans may have to be cancelled or postponed because of some contingency. Communications at that point must work particularly well in order to ensure that everyone is informed about the reasons for the changes, and that wherever possible alternative ways of responding to the initial request can be agreed (assuming it is still valid).

8 **Monitor and evaluate implementation.** Evaluation is essential in order to ensure that scarce resources (including time) are being used effectively. The task of evaluation should be eased if the initial specification of the nature of the problem and the exact outcomes training is intended to produce is clear, and if there is agreement between the Training Manager and line managers about how those outcomes will be measured. Identifiable improvements in competences, and the effect of the training on the indicators chosen beforehand – for example, material wastage rates, levels of employee absenteeism, turnover, learning times, indices of customer satisfaction, speed and quality of service provided – should all be used in order to assess the extent to which training has had an impact on the problems it was intended to resolve or reduce.

Effective use of either a comprehensive or a problem-centred approach in the analysis of organizational needs should promote a higher level of credibility for training in the organization, since both approaches focus on training being:

- **A means to an end, not an end in itself.** Because of the collaborative and business-focused processes used, training will be seen as a means to an end which is identifiable and agreed between the Training Manager and all the interested parties.
- **Cost effective.** Both approaches require the Training Manager to identify and justify all expenditure on resources.
- **Essential.** The close, business-led collaboration required between the Training Manager and line managers throughout the various stages of both approaches should demonstrate that training is a key business function rather than an optional or peripheral activity.
- **Collaborative.** Collaborative processes lie at the heart of both approaches, and are crucial to their success.

Using either approach, the aim is that the Training Manager and line managers should be assured of knowing at all times:

- what has been done;
- what needs to be done;
- what can be done;
- at what cost.

That will help ensure that training makes its full contribution to the business – and that is the measure of a good training function.

The business strategy approach

There are, however, strong reservations about the use of our first two approaches. The danger with the problem-centred approach is that it will gradually lead to a failure to focus at all on *development*, or on long-term training issues, and will result instead in a preoccupation with only the most immediately obvious training needs.

As far as the comprehensive approach is concerned:

> If you ask most practitioners to produce a training plan, there would be a perfectly reasonable reaction for the personnel or training specialist to go on a tour round departmental heads and to

> collect training requirements. Unfortunately this only rarely produces any training need which in any way can be said to be fundamental to the business. More often it is viewed on a more personal basis – filling skills gaps in relation to current job demands.
>
> To link training with business drivers you have to stand back and take the overview, and . . . you need the input of the managing director and the senior team of directors.
>
> (Jennings, 1991)

The business strategy approach to the analysis of organizational needs is based on the belief that needs must be assessed, and the training plan must be produced, at board level as part of the overall employee resourcing plan for the company. The employee resourcing plan itself must be driven by:

- The strategy for the business
- Operational priorities
- Key changes in the environment or technical base

These are what Jennings calls the 'business drivers'. Other training and development needs to be taken into account at that stage will be those revealed by information from performance appraisals and succession planning.

So rather than the training plan being initiated by a process of collaboration between training personnel and line managers, and finally being sent up to the Board for approval, the reverse occurs. Decisions about training (and any development of people) that is to take place, whether or not expressed in a formal training plan, are made at board level at the stage of producing business strategy and plans. These decisions are communicated to managers in the organization who must then decide how best to achieve the objectives they have been given.

Of course, the information on manpower needed by the Board still has to be provided by whoever is responsible for employee resourcing in the organization; the initiative still therefore lies with training personnel to put forward information that will support a case for the training and development needs that they perceive to be important. However, the focus is now on needs dictated directly by business strategy – and that decision about needs will be made at board level. It is this shift, occurring now in many organizations, that makes the presence of a personnel or training professional at board level so important.

Unfortunately, research indicates that even though personnel practitioners do have such a presence, in about two-thirds of UK organizations they tend to exercise little influence on the formulation of strategy – only on the human resource plan for its implementation. (See Anderson and Harrison, 1993; also Allen, 1991; Arkin, 1991; and Brewster and Smith, 1990.) Furthermore it would appear that only four out of ten UK organizations have a written human resource strategy, and only seven out of ten have any kind of personnel strategy at all (Brewster and Smith, 1990). An approach that leaves the crucial responsibility for analysing organizational training needs to a top level of management which in 30 per cent of cases does not produce even an unwritten personnel strategy seems unlikely to prove effective, especially at the stage of making decisions about the kind of training to be done and communicating those decisions to the rest of the organization.

The business strategy approach is particularly relevant for small to medium-sized enterprises (i.e. those employing up to about 500 employees), although the term 'strategy' is perhaps rather grandiose as a description of what tends to occur. The evidence is that various, mainly short-term and individualized, pressures drive training and development in the SME sector (Hendry et al., 1991). Those related to external factors, such as

- Competition
- Type of local labour market and training infrastructure.

Those related to internal factors, such as

- The nature of, and demands on, the production or service processes
- The life cycle of the firm: if it is in a stage of fast growth, this can both act as a trigger to training and make it more difficult because the very speed of events militates against strategic vision and careful planning (Hendry et al., 1991, p. 69).
- The employees' expectations and desire for betterment – clearly major factors in small workforces.

But often it is the personal values and philosophy of the owner manager or equivalent above all that explain decisions about training and development in small and medium-sized enterprises, leading to major differences in approach and activity between organizations that may in other respects be quite similar.

At the SME level, the approach to employee development, while it is business-led, will often lack strategic vision and be short-term and unsystematic – although, as research (Hendry et al., 1991) shows, there are striking exceptions to this. In larger organizations where the business strategy approach is taken, one can usually point to five steps in the process:

- Defining strategic company objectives
- Identifying key skill needs in every function/sector of the organization in order to meet these objectives
- Setting standards for individual tasks related to those objectives
- Setting specific training objectives for every training event
- Reviewing training outcomes in relation to strategic objectives

The business strategy approach to analysing organizational training and development needs

Let us take a scenario typical of both the public and the private sector: an organization that has to become more customer-driven, efficient, and flexible in the face of unpredictable environmental changes. We will call it a company but this should be interpreted widely to encompass, for example, a hospital unit, a local authority or a school or college.

The mission for training and development

In this company the mission for training and development is that it will serve the needs of the business by improving individual and organizational performance in ways that will contribute to achieving business goals, and by contributing to increased productivity and the return on assets employed. It is company policy that all training and development initiatives must have line management sponsorship, ownership and support, and that the main role of personnel and training staff is to ensure that this occurs and to act as a resource for line managers.

Training needs related to business strategy

The company is analysing and identifying different kinds of customer needs in order to target its services and products accordingly. Responsiveness to individual customer needs is now crucial to business success; knowing how to be responsive, in different roles and jobs throughout the organization is therefore one major training need.

The company is reorganizing its operations into about twelve units in order to relate to the needs and interests of each client better and more cheaply. This means the introduction of very sophisticated technology – another area of major training need.

Finally, the company needs to change its culture to one stressing the need for high standards of individual and team performance, of customer care and of quality. Clearly training and development, as well as other employee resource processes and systems, have a major part to play in bringing about the change in culture required.

So customer orientation and service, the efficient and effective introduction of new technology, and the introduction and operation of a new culture, become the three major areas of training and development strategy. The training staff must ensure that when this has been communicated to line managers, they themselves act, effectively, as internal consultants to help as required in the identification of needs and the design and delivery of learning events.

In order to ensure that appropriate training and development is carried out, the following procedures must be followed in all functional areas of the company:

1 The skills required to meet business targets related to the three strategic objectives must be identified, and must be compared with skills that already exist. Where training is the relevant remedy to close gaps, it must be carried out.

2 All tasks done by individuals must clearly specify the kind of skills, knowledge and attitudes they require, the standard to which they must operate, both in terms of performance and behaviour, and the way in which those standards are to be measured.

3 These specifications must guide the setting of objectives for training, and the design and content of learning events, as well as the measuring of the outcomes of those events. All training must have objectives that will ensure that identified needs are met, and there must be agreement at that point about how the outcomes of training will be measured, when, and by whom.

4 All learning events must be reviewed to establish their impact on key skill, knowledge and attitude needs related, ultimately, to the overall strategic objectives contained in the training plan.

The business strategy approach transfers the initiative for assessing organizational training needs to board level, and puts the main responsibility for training with line mangers. This does not mean that training personnel have no role to play. They still need to act as a help and support to line managers and, as we have seen, they need to be proactive in order to influence strategic decision-making at board level. They thus have a balance of reactive and proactive responsibilities to fulfil if training and development is to serve the needs of the organization in a truly strategic way. What this particularly requires is that the Manager is alert to signals that indicate coming needs for change (see Sparrow and Pettigrew, 1988).

Recommendations to the Board (or equivalent) for a higher level of investment will not be convincing unless they rest on up-to-date, comprehensive data which has been obtained in collaboration with key parties in the organization, and which has been rigorously analysed. It will also be important to seek the active support of certain top-level managers who can influence their peers – this political activity will be crucial to success.

Tactics like being able to quote examples of other, similar companies who have a higher level of investment in training and whose business strategy is clearly successful will be another persuasive tactic. So too will obtaining external funding to support certain employee development initiatives: it will give greater internal credibility to the initiatives being proposed, and will also help to offset the immediate cost of those initiatives to the organization.

The key processes in all three approaches – comprehensive, problem-centred and business strategy – are shown in Figure 9.

Measuring the Contribution of Employee Development to the Business

In organizations with a culture and values that view people as a major and long-term resource for the business, it will be taken for granted that development is essential in order to produce maximum growth of that human asset – and this tends to be the culture prevailing across most of our competitor countries (see Chapter 4). The culture is typified by organizations like Bosch, the German industrial group. When its new £100 million car component plant was opened at Miskin, Wales, in 1991 Martin Wibberley, Director of Human Resources, could not put a figure on how much had been spent training and developing the workforce for the start of full production, but estimated it at millions of pounds. He was quoted in *The Independent on Sunday* (Shankelman, 1991) as saying:

Figure 9

Eight key processes in producing business-led development of people

1 Establish informed, proactive, collaborative relationships with the key parties in the organization, especially at corporate and business unit levels.

2 Ensure that there is an understanding of key issues and commitment to action at the top level.

3 Walk and talk the job, in order to identify employee development needs and establish a proactive employee development presence in the business.

4 Carry out data-gathering and planning on a collaborative basis with line management and other key parties.

5 Link employee development policy and plans to business strategy, through a wider employee resource strategy.

6 State desired outcomes and bottom-line contribution in clear, measurable terms, with actual costs and estimated benefits spelt out.

7 Collaborate with management to ensure ongoing monitoring and feedback of results and relevant action arising from that feedback.

8 Keep fully informed about the business, acting on any changes in either corporate or human resource strategy that have implications for the development of people.

(Adapted from Harrison, 1992b)

> Training is absolutely crucial . . . If you think of people as an asset then you invest in them, but UK companies don't seem to have that attitude . . . Those companies that have been asset-stripping their human resources will find they can't recruit new people with skills and can't hang on to the people they've got.

When such a culture does not exist in an organization, the task of 'assessing the payback' has to be undertaken. The more detailed the assessment is required to be, the more complex the task becomes, and many models have been suggested to aid the process. In the end, however, what is needed is a simple, easily operated approach that presents the right kind of information, at the right time, to those who need it most. With that in mind, all that is offered here are a few basic principles. They do not amount to a model, but they will help the practitioner who is anxious to find out what kind of contribution their employee development function is making, and hopefully to convince others of its contribution to goals that management holds essential to the business. They are:

1 The evaluation of employee development strategy and activities should be related to the specific objectives originally set for them.

2 Measurement *of itself* will not achieve credibility for employee development. It is measurement of a kind already agreed between the key parties that is essential.

3 Wherever possible, and especially in training events, aim for specific, quantifiable outcomes that will produce a measurable improvement in performance.

Detailed guidance on how to evaluate outcomes and relate training and development to business performance is given in Chapters 17 and 21; also in Jackson (1990); Hall (1984); and Harrison (1992b), Chapter 6 of which relates the story of Cummins Engine Co. Ltd. of Darlington, a case study that demonstrates all the main points made in this chapter.

Exercises

1 You are the Training Manager of Vitex Ltd, whom we first met in Chapter 10 (see pp. 225–6). You have to decide how you are going to tackle the task of formulating a new employee development mission and strategy for Vitex. Your Personnel Director has stressed the need for a 'new broom' approach and wants some proposals from you. What will your proposals be? (For a description of how just such an exercise was actually undertaken, over a period of about a year, by one manager, a secretary and some part-time assistance to design a computerized data system, please read the story of Barratt in Harrison, 1992a.)

2 To win a National Training Award, an organization 'needs to be using training imaginatively and dynamically to solve well-defined business problems'. Either:

(a) draft a summary of an NTA entry for your organization, in which you make the case for an award; or
(b) suggest what your organization might do in order to gain an award. (November 1989)

3 What are the main influences on an organization's policy or policies for employee development? Select any TWO of the following issues, and draft a proposed policy statement covering each for an organization that does not yet have a written employee development policy:

- Identification of training needs
- Work experience opportunities for non-employees
- Performance appraisal
- Paid leave/release for educational purposes
- Line management's training role (November 1988)

References

ALLEN K R. 'Personnel management on the line: How middle managers view the function'. *Personnel Management*, June 1991. pp. 40-3
ANDERSON G AND HARRISON R (eds.). *Strategic Human Resource Management* (provisional title). Maidenhead, Addison Wesley. 1993 (in press)
ARKIN A. 'Still looking for a strategic role'. *Personnel Management Plus*, June 1991. pp. 18-19
BREWSTER C AND SMITH C. 'Corporate strategy: A no-go area for personnel?'. *Personnel Management*, July 1990. pp. 36-40
GANE C. *Managing the Training Function*. London, Allen and Unwin. 1972
GARNETT J. 'My biggest mistake'. *The Independent on Sunday*, 8 March 1992
HALL D T. 'Human resource development and organizational effectiveness'. In *Strategic Human Resource Management* (Fombrun C, Tichy N M and Devanna M A, eds.). New York, Wiley. 1984
HARRISON R. 'Employee development at Barratt'. In *Case Studies in Personnel* (Woodall D and Winstanley D, eds.). London, Institute of Personnel Management. 1992a
HARRISON R. *Developing Human Resources for Productivity*. Geneva, International Labour Office. 1992b (in press)

HENDRY C, JONES A, ARTHUR M AND PETTIGREW A. *Human Resource Development in Small to Medium Sized Enterprises.* ED Research Paper No. 88. Sheffield, Department of Employment. 1991

JACKSON T. *Evaluation: Relating training to business performance.* London, Kogan Page. 1990

JENNINGS R. 'Contributing to business strategy and operating performance by ensuring that training and development is an essential investment not an expendable cost'. In *Proc. Institute for International Research in Association with Sundridge Park Management Centre: Third Annual Forum on Developing Effective Business-led Management Training, London, 28 February–March 1991.* London, IIR Ltd. 1991

PETTIGREW A, SWALLOW P AND HENDRY C. 'The forces that trigger training'. *Personnel Management,* December 1988. pp. 28-32

SADLER P AND BARHAM K. 'From Franks to the future: 25 years of management training prescriptions'. *Personnel Management,* May 1988. pp. 48-51

SHANKELMAN M. 'When people are an asset, spending is an investment'. *The Independent on Sunday,* 27 January 1991.

SINGER E. *Training in Industry and Commerce.* London, Institute of Personnel Management. 1977

SPARROW P AND PETTIGREW A. 'How Halfords put its HRM into top gear'. *Personnel Management,* June 1988. pp. 30-4

WILLIAMS E. 'Harnessing the training and development needs and career aspirations of the individual to fulfil the long-term business objectives of the organisation'. In *Proc. Institute of International Research in Association with Sundridge Park Management Centre: Third Annual Forum on Developing Effective Business-led Management Training, London, 28 February-1 March 1991.* London, IIR Ltd. 1991

Further useful reading

APPLEGARTH M. *How to Take a Training Audit.* London, Kogan Page. 1991.

BURGOYNE J. 'Management development for the individual *and* the organisation'. *Personnel Management,* June 1988. pp. 40-4

MOORBY E. *How to Succeed in Employee Development: Moving from visions to results.* London, McGraw-Hill. 1991

PERSONNEL MANAGEMENT. 'Courtaulds harmonisation aims to change culture'. *Personnel Management,* February 1990. p.13

PICKARD J. 'Awards for employees who go through the mill'. *Personnel Management,* February 1990. pp. 36-41

WEBSTER B. 'Beyond the mechanics of HRD'. *Personnel Management,* March 1990. pp. 44-7

WILLE E. 'Should management development just be for managers?' *Personnel Management,* August 1990. pp. 34-7

Part Three

Planning, Designing and Delivering Learning Events

Chapter 12

Analysing jobs

Learning Objectives

After reading this chapter you will:

1 be able to use an appropriate strategy when analysing jobs for training purposes;
2 know the main approaches and techniques used in job training analysis, and understand their applicability to different situations;
3 know how to produce a job training specification.

When designing learning events in relation to particular jobs or tasks, it is necessary to identify the type and level of skills, knowledge and (as relevant) attitudes needed for effective performance. This information can be obtained through a process called job training analysis.

> Job training analysis is the process of identifying the purpose of a job and its component parts, and specifying what must be learnt in order for there to be effective work performance.

A crucial part of the job training analysis process is to identify the performance standards and methods of measurement required in a job in order that relevant objectives for a learning event can be set and evaluation can subsequently be carried out. Analysis should also identify aspects of a job which make it difficult to learn, so that special attention can be given to them during the learning event.

The outcome of the job training analysis process is a job training specification.

> The job training specification describes in overall terms the job for which training is to be given, or the key problem areas in a job which training will enable learners to tackle; it then specifies the kinds and levels of knowledge, skill and, where relevant, attitudes needed for effective performance, together with the standards that

will operate in the job and the criteria for measuring the achievement of standards.

All jobs comprise three broad components:

1 **Skills.** These may be, for example, manual, diagnostic, interpersonal or decision-making skills. They include any component of the job that involves 'doing' something.

2 **Knowledge.** This may be, for example, technical or procedural knowledge, or it may be concerned with company organization, but it always relates to what must be 'known about' or 'understood' in a job.

3 **Attitudes.** It may be important in a job that certain attitudes are demonstrated at all times, e.g. courtesy and sensitivity in dealing with customers or clients; flexibility and co-operation when working in a close-knit team; or calmness and patience in coping with various critical pressures in a job. Although training in attitudes will not be necessary for every job, certain attitudes are so crucial to particular jobs that it is essential to keep that component in mind when analysing.

Each of these components has implications for learning design and methods. A programme that is basically to do with developing skills will be very different in its design and operation from a programme whose purpose is to promote certain attitudes, or cover areas of complex theory or concepts which the job holder may need to acquire. With the possibility of many different combinations of these components, it is essential to choose an appropriate analytical approach and use relevant analytical techniques.

In this chapter we will look briefly at three interrelated issues:

- A strategy for carrying out job training analysis
- Four main job training analysis approaches
- Nine main job training analysis techniques

A Strategy for Carrying Out Job Training Analysis

I am indebted to Kenney and Reid (1986) for much of the information in this section. Their excellent chapter on Job Training Analysis makes it very difficult to find anything new to say on the subject!

A strategy for carrying out job training analysis can be divided into six steps:

1 **Initial investigation**. As we saw in Chapter 11 requests for training should always be met first by investigatory questions like:

- **Is training really the answer?** For example, poor performance may be due to ineffective supervision, lack of financial or other incentives, or lack of innate ability. If any of these is the primary cause, then training is not going to improve performance and job training analysis is pointless.
- **Is training the most cost-beneficial answer?** There may be other ways in which knowledge, skills or attitudes may be developed without involving the expense of formal training. Would careful integration of work and learning be more cost-beneficial? Or would buying in the skills or some other non-training solution be more appropriate?
- **Are there sufficient incentives for individuals if training is given for this task?** Fairbairn (1991) points out that training itself will not be effective unless people want it; and they will only want it if they see that the skills, knowledge and attitudes it is promoting are important in their job, and recognized, encouraged and rewarded in their workplace. There must therefore be an analysis of how far the task or job is valued in the organization, and how far effective performance in it will be supported and rewarded in some way that is meaningful to the individual.

  This is particularly relevant when organizations are attempting to achieve multi-skilling. For example, at Cummins Engines Ltd., Darlington, employees were offered financial rewards for going through each of a series of modular skills training courses related to different areas of skill. That rebounded to some extent, because to some the message it conveyed was that training, rather than the skills resulting from it, was what was valued; training had become an end in itself. As a result, Cummins had to look at ways of shifting the emphasis from rewarding people for undergoing training to rewarding them for the extent to which training actually resulted in changes in skilled performance (see Harrison, 1992).
- **Is analysis really necessary?** Perhaps reliable and up-to-date information already exists about the job. Perhaps there is already a

job training specification, either internally produced or drawn up by some external body.

- **Is the job likely to change?** If so, a new analysis will be needed when the change takes place, and that consideration has a bearing on the analytical approach to be chosen now. If change is likely, why, how often, and over what period of time is it likely to occur? Or is it a routine and stable job, which will not alter much, and which therefore will repay detailed analysis now? Is it a job that many people do, or is it fairly unique?
- **Should the person be adapted to the job, or the job to the person?** With certain jobs, for example those at the top level of the organization, those that are very specialized, or those involving a high degree of innovative talent, it may be more appropriate for the person to dictate the nature of the job than for the job to dictate the nature of the person. The job holder's vision of how the role should be translated into reality, and the identity they give to the job, may matter far more than any predetermined specification. In such a situation selection, not training, becomes the critical process.

2 **Select the analyst.** In most organizations it is specialist staff, whether internal or external, who carry out job training analysis. However, it is the line manager and the person who actually does the job who know most about it, so whoever carries out the analysis must be acceptable to those parties. A related point is that much sensitive information can be uncovered during the process of job training analysis: motivation, discipline and supervision problems; misunderstandings caused by ill-defined responsibilities; or conflict and inefficiency arising from inappropriate organizational structures or cultures. The analyst, having identified these issues, must know how to draw them to the attention of those who can deal with them and must influence those parties to take action. Until that is done, training itself cannot be effective.

3 **Gain co-operation.** Before the job training analysis process starts, everyone involved in and likely to be significantly affected by the activity must be given a clear explanation of its purpose, how it will be carried out, by whom, over what period of time, and with what probable outcomes. Their willing co-operation in the whole process will be essential to its success.

4 **Select the analytical approach and techniques.** Information obtained

in steps 1–3 will enable the analyst to decide which approach and techniques to choose. These will be explained in the next section.

5 **Carry out the analysis.** Here, the analyst needs to consider two factors:

- **Sources of information.** Written sources are liable to be produced on differing bases, and may be out of date or not comprehensive. Care must therefore be taken when referring to technical manuals or to records of various kinds. Records will hopefully reveal essential information such as whether there have been many problems in performance of the job; whether the norm is that good standards of performance are achieved relatively easily; whether there are any trends in labour turnover, absenteeism, sickness or lateness that could relate to difficulties experienced in the job; and so on. Job descriptions will be particularly useful, but will need careful checking to ensure that they are up to date, accurate and comprehensive.

  Oral sources of information, such as the job holder, the job holder's manager and fellow workers, are all liable to be biased, and may sometimes contradict one another in their perception of both the content and characteristics of the job and – very important – of the priorities to be achieved within it. Such sources may be deliberately or unintentionally misleading, and will call for the exercise of considerable interpersonal and political skills.
- **Depth of analysis.** In job training analysis, no matter which analytical approach is chosen the important question to pose is how much detail is needed about a task and the skills, knowledge and attitudes required to do it. Annett (1979) suggests that every task in a job should continue to be broken down and described until the point is reached where the remainder of the task can be readily learnt without training and does not in any case require flawless performance. As we shall see when looking at the different approaches, this principle will not always apply.

  The analyst must also look for any problems in the workplace – either social or work-related – that could make it difficult for the trainee to apply learning acquired in a training programme. If the training given is to result in effective performance in the job, it must prepare trainees for the kind of job environment in which they will have to carry out that job.

6 **Produce the job training specification.** When the process of analysing the job is finished and the information has been carefully checked, the analyst must produce a job training specification, ensuring that it is agreed as accurate by the key parties.

Job Training Analysis Approaches

There are many approaches to job training analysis. I have selected four of the most common for study here:

- Comprehensive analysis
- Key task analysis
- Problem-centred analysis
- Competency-based analysis

Comprehensive analysis

Here, there is a very detailed examination of every aspect of the job until each task has been fully described in terms of its knowledge, skills and (if relevant) attitudes. Each task must also be described by reference to its objectives, its frequency of performance, its standards of performance, and ways of measuring that performance. Clearly it is an extremely time-consuming analytical approach, and requires much skill. The first question to ask is, therefore, in which circumstances would you recommend this approach?

Here are some criteria for the choice of the comprehensive job training analysis approach (with acknowledgements to Kenney and Reid, 1986):

1 **Tasks are unfamiliar to learners, difficult, all more or less equally important to perform well, and must be learnt quickly and to standard.** Clearly such a situation calls for a very thorough analytical approach that will cover the full scope of the job.

2 **Change is unlikely and new recruits are fairly frequent.** If these conditions apply, the expense involved in comprehensive analysis will soon be offset by the number of times training resulting from it can be carried out before it is necessary to do any fresh analysis. New recruits may be frequent because this is a category of job held by large numbers of people in the workplace, or for some other reason such as unavoidably high levels of turnover in the job.

3 **The job is closely prescribed.** If little or nothing in the job can be left to the initiative of the job holder, then it is essential that they learn the correct ways of performing virtually all tasks in the job.

4 **Resources are adequate.** There must be the resources available (e.g. time, skill, numbers of staff) to carry out this detailed, complex and time-consuming approach.

Two activities are involved in applying the approach:

1 **Produce a job description.** This is a broad statement of the purpose, scope, responsibilities and tasks which constitute a particular job. The job description should contain:

- The title of the job
- The overall purpose of the job, preferably expressed in a sentence which sums up why the job is there at all and what it is for as far as the organization is concerned
- The name of the department in which the job holder works
- The title or titles of the person or people to whom the job holder is responsible, both directly and ultimately
- Brief details of any other key relationships, for example with staff in another department or unit or with people or institutions outside the organization
- A brief description of any major resources for which the job holder is accountable: finance, physical resources or personnel
- An indication of whether the job holder works mainly on their own, or is part of a fixed team, or is expected to move through various teams according to task needs
- A list of major tasks only – simply to give a picture of the main elements of the job
- Brief details of any difficulties commonly experienced in the job which need attention in training

2 **Produce a job training specification.** For every task of the job, divided as necessary into sub-tasks or elements, the job training specification should show the skill, knowledge and (if relevant) attitudes required; the standards of performance to be reached; and how performance will be measured. The way the specification is laid out and the kind of information it contains will depend on the analytical

techniques used (see pp. 273–9). However, the specification is a guide to action (because it leads to the design of a training programme), and must therefore have a simple, easily understood format, and be very clearly expressed.

Key task analysis

This approach takes only the crucial tasks within a job – those tasks in which performance of a certain kind is absolutely essential to effectiveness in the job overall. While comprehensive analysis is used most commonly for jobs consisting of simple, usually manual, repetitive and unchanging tasks, jobs involving more complex skills such as observation and reflection, analysis, creativity, decision-making and problem-solving, and evaluation, need a clear overview of the job, followed by a focus on what is most essential for successful performance. For them, this approach is often the best to use.

Once again, therefore, a brief job description needs to be produced, exactly as in comprehensive analysis, but the job training specification this time must be selective, covering only those tasks crucial to effective job performance.

Key task analysis is appropriate for any type of job where the following conditions apply:

1 **Tasks are varied and not all are critical.** The job should consist of a large number of different tasks, not all of which are critical for effective performance; it is assumed that the job holder only requires training in those tasks which are crucial to effective performance in the job.

2 **Changes are likely.** If the job is changing in emphasis or in content, there will be a continuing need to establish priority tasks, standards of performance and the skills and knowledge required.
(Kenney and Reid, 1986, p. 160)

Appendix 5 contains an extract from a key task job training analysis. It is not intended to be a model example, but simply a lay person's attempt to apply the approach to a particular job.

Problem-centred analysis

This approach focuses on defining problems which require a training solution. The analysis needs to describe the nature and causes of each problem, and the skills, knowledge and attitudes (if relevant) needed to cope successfully with it. The analytical process actively involves job holders in considering what kind of training they would find most effective. Warr and Bird (1968) have done some major work on this approach with their 'training by exception' technique, developed when their attempts to use first comprehensive and then key task analysis to identify supervisory training needs failed because of the great diversity of tasks in each supervisor's job and the amount of time needed to analyse them compared to the usefulness of the information obtained.

The problem-centred approach is best used when:

1. training is urgent, but analytical resources limited;
2. the job holder's work is satisfactory except in one or two 'problem' areas;
3. the involvement of learners in analysis is important.

It is a good approach to use in conjunction with key task analysis when designing training for people about to be appointed, or recently appointed, to jobs for which they already have most of the skills and knowledge required, but where it is important to get to grips quickly with any areas causing or likely to cause problems; and also to ensure that the job holders have a clear understanding of key tasks.

With the problem-centred approach there is no one way of gathering and collating information, although whatever methods are used must, of course, ensure that the perspectives of job holders and their supervisors, managers and any other key parties are obtained. Nor is a job description or a job training specification produced. The end product is simply a description of the problems and how they can be tackled in training. Problem-centred analysis will reveal:

1. **Common training needs.** Needs will emerge that are common to all or most of the group. These needs can form the basis of a core training programme or other kind of learning event.
2. **Individualized training needs.** There will also be needs specific to individuals which will have to be met by individualized learning events.
3. **Suggested training/learning strategies.** These are the learning approaches and methods which the job holders feel would most help teach them how to overcome identified problems.

4 **Commitment of the learners.** Because of the nature of this analytical approach, it is likely to be highly successful in obtaining the commitment of those who will be the learner group in the subsequent training programme. They have to take a leading role in the diagnosis and analysis of their problems and needs and in suggesting training solutions. The objectives and relevance of the training programme therefore become obvious to them; they begin to 'own' the programme and so the wish to learn and to apply the learning is a natural outcome of the analytical process.

Again, a practical example will be useful, and one is given in Appendix 6.

Competency-based approach

We have already discussed competency-based analysis in Chapters 2, 3 and 6 (see especially pp. 133–7). The approach involves identifying what is needed to produce effective performance in a role, job or function. Like the problem-centred approach, it is both job- and person-related and tends to be used in an organization when:

1 **There is a need to develop clearly defined standards of performance relating to one or more occupational groups.** This is usually because, in that organization, lack of such standards is impeding attempts to measure and improve performance and to establish clear guidelines for selection, training, development, rewards and succession and career planning.

2 **There is a need to relate training within the organization to national vocational training standards and qualifications.** Competences identified in a particular organization as necessary to the performance of jobs at different levels can be related to lists of competences required at each of four or five levels in order to achieve NVQs across different occupations. Appropriate schemes of training, development and assessment in the workplace can then enable individuals to acquire experience and competence that can gain accreditation for NVQ purposes (see pp. 29–30).

3 **The main concern is to identify the core behavioural attributes needed in order to perform effectively across a job sector and the extent to which those attributes are possessed by all job holders in that sector.** This usually, but not necessarily always, applies to the management sector.

Woodruffe (1991) observes that there are two quite separate senses in which the word 'competency' is used. In the job-related sense, it refers to areas of work at which a person is competent. Here, he recommends use of an alternative term: *areas of competence.* In a person-related sense, it refers to dimensions of behaviour that lie behind competent performance. Here, he recommends use of the term *competency.*

Many organizations now base training and development programmes on definitions of competences relating to a particular group or sector in the organization. The Management Charter Initiative's use of a competency-based approach to define occupational standards for managers at all levels, and to use these as aids to effective management training and development programmes has attracted widespread attention (see Chapter 19).

Competency-based analysis results in the production of:

1 a statement of the role or purpose of the general category of job being studied (e.g. managerial jobs, or managerial jobs at a particular level) in the organization;

2 a breakdown of that role into its discrete areas of competence;

3 statements of the standards needed to perform satisfactorily in each of those areas;

4 criteria for measuring competency in each area.

Job Training Analysis Techniques

There are many techniques that can be used within the overall job training analysis approach chosen. Well-known ones that need no repetition here include:

- Activity analysis (Miller, 1962)
- Manual skills analysis (Seymour, 1954; 1966; and Gentles, 1969), a widely used and often essential technique which is, however, a very time-consuming and highly skilled method with the danger that one change in an operating method may well lead to the whole analytical process having to be repeated
- Critical incidents analysis (Flanagan, 1954)
- Faults analysis (Kenney and Reid, 1986)
- Stages and key points analysis (Ibid.)

There are three sets of techniques which may be less well known, but which are valuable especially in relation to more complex jobs:

- Role analysis
- Interpersonal and interactive skills analysis
- Techniques related to competency-based analysis

Role analysis

In managerial jobs especially, it is vital to be clear about the role, or roles, that the job holder must carry. Certainly training for anyone who had to move into a training manager's job would greatly benefit from being based on role analysis as well as the more immediately obvious analytical techniques, because of the frequency of role problems in training jobs (see Pettigrew et al., 1982, and pp. 133–4). It is a technique derived from the behavioural sciences, notably from the work of the industrial psychologist McGregor (1960), who emphasized how important it was, if a manager was to be effective, to build up a shared perception of the role between different members of the manager's role set.

French and Bell (1978) summarize the various procedures involved, which basically require the job holder, their manager and (usually) one or more other members of their role set (i.e. those people with whom the job holder regularly interacts) each to produce a list of the duties and behaviour that they perceive as necessary if the job holder is to be effective. A role description is then produced from a joint discussion of the different lists, showing most of the important features of the job.

Durham University Business School based their 'expectations' approach on role analysis. Machin (1981) shows how the technique highlights any disagreements amongst job holder and members of the role set about the role in question, and generates open discussion to the point where, hopefully, a full understanding of the role has been achieved, most of the disagreements have been resolved and a job description can be drawn up. If, however, there should still be conflicting perceptions and expectations then the analyst should bring this to the attention of management, since clearly such conflict will impede job performance, create organizational problems and produce situations for which training is not a remedy.

Inter-personal and interactive skills analysis

A wide range of jobs, especially those that are supervisory, managerial, professional and technical, make heavy demands on the job holder in terms of their requirements for skill in dealing with face-to-face situations and in achieving the effective interaction of people and tasks in a work cycle. Such skills are difficult to analyse, but there are now a number of useful techniques available. These include the techniques of Rackham et al. (1971) for analysing interactive skills; transactional analysis, described very fully by Carby and Thakur (1977); and the diagnostic techniques and instruments related to teamwork skills that have been developed by writers like Woodcock (1979). If you need further information, you should read the work of the above authors, together with Cuthbert (1984), Simpson (1984), Argyle (1970) and Sills (1973).

Techniques related to competency-based analysis

There are many techniques that can be used here, including behavioural event interviewing (Boyatsis, 1982), a complex technique for which special training is required. To give a flavour of what is involved in competency-based analysis, let us look at two case studies and do an exercise based on them.

BP: The competency-based approach to management development
(With acknowledgements to J Greatrex and P Phillips, and *Personnel Management*)

QUESTION
What strategy lies behind the use by BP and Manchester Airport of a competency-based approach to management development in 1989? What is the main difference between the particular approaches that they used?

In the late 1980s BP carried out a lot of work on management competences, in order to ensure effective management performance, and training and development to cope with the major changes that, since 1987, had been taking place in the company. Because of new directions in its business strategy, its culture had to become more market-oriented and client-centred, its managers had to be more entrepreneurial in their approach to the business and there had to be a less hierarchical management structure, devolved accountability, and a more open and flexible management style throughout the company.

They were concerned to avoid relying on any universal list of competences. Instead, analysis was organization-specific, identifying those competences needed in order to manage effectively in the particular BP environment.

By 1989 a rigorous process of analysis had produced a list of 11 core areas of competence, grouped into four clusters of behaviours that differentiated high performers from the rest. BP has always placed a high value on assessment centres as a way of diagnosing training and development needs and highlighting potential. It now incorporated competency assessment into its assessment boards, and individual managers were assessed and ranked in relation to the 11 competency areas, using a five-point behaviourally defined scale to identify the extent to which they possessed each individual attribute. From this process of analysis and diagnosis, development programmes for individuals were eventually drawn up.

The approach proved particularly valuable as an aid for training, personal and career development, and self-development of managers.

Manchester Airport plc. (1989)

(With acknowledgements to L Jackson and the IPM)

A competency-based approach to management development was used by Manchester Airport in the late 1980s in order to achieve a systematic approach to the selection, training and development of senior managers at a time of fast growth and major changes when the airport became a plc in 1986.

The first stage in the design of a programme was 'to develop a template for superior performance at Senior Management level'.

> Between June and October 1988 the Directors met to agree the attributes which would communicate the company's expectations for management at this level, based on 15 of the defined McBer managerial competences – attributes which have been found to predict success in managerial jobs generally. . . . This involved re-examining the role for this group, as it was clear that the competences required for superior performance over the next two years would be significantly different from those likely to be present in this group as a whole. (Jackson, 1989)

The profile that emerged identified clusters of behaviours associated with the three core competences needed by all senior managers at Manchester Airport plc, whatever their specific jobs:

- **Understanding what needs to be done.** Critical reasoning, strategic visioning, business know-how.
- **Getting the job done.** Achievement drive, a proactive approach, confidence, control, flexibility, concern for effectiveness, direction.
- **Taking people with you.** Motivation, interpersonal skills, concern for impact, persuasion, influence.

This profile was checked against job analysis information already in existence at the airport to ensure its validity. It was also agreed that:

> The new criteria established for the successful performance of the job would be used for subsequent selection and promotion decisions within this group . . . [and] performance review and reward decisions would be based on the criteria agreed as underpinning superior performance. (Ibid.)

All managers then had to go through a two-day assessment centre, and were assessed by the directors (who had received special training) and the consultants who had helped the personnel staff design the whole project. Each manager was rated against every attribute. Attributes associated with core competences were defined in behavioural terms at four levels, from low to outstanding. Thus for example:

Attribute involved in 'getting the job done': Direction.
Definition: Being able to tell others what they must do and confront performance problems; to plan, organize, schedule, delegate and follow up.

Low: unable to confront others about performance problems, to enforce rules, or to insist that subordinates comply with directives. No experience or is unwilling to delegate to subordinates the responsibility for doing anything other than less significant tasks.
Outstanding: confronts staff when they fail to meet standards. Has contingency plans for all objectives. Sets demanding objectives for staff. Demonstrates the ability to organize large numbers of people.

After the centre, individual profiles were drawn up, summarizing the assessed level for each competence. Written reports were produced, and each manager had feedback sessions with a consultant, the Personnel Director, and his/her own Director.

Personal improvement plans were produced by each individual and were incorporated in annual targets for the forthcoming year.

Jackson detailed the positive results of the project, and concluded that the model for superior performance was confirmed by the evidence.

FEEDBACK NOTES

In both examples the strategy is the same: to define the core competences needed by all managers in the specific organizational context in which they must operate (whether or not they break them down into different levels within the management sector, as was done at Manchester Airport); and to use those competences both as criteria for the assessment of individuals in order to define training and development needs and as aids to improving work performance.

The difference lies in the ways competences were identified: at BP, analysis of the actual performance of BP managers let to the identification of clusters of attributes associated with what then emerged as the core competences that underpinned effective work performance. Analysis thus started with examining prevailing patterns of behaviour and led ultimately to the identification of core competences needed by all BP managers.

We are not told what particular technique was used to identify core competences, but it could well have been behavioural event interviewing (Arkin, 1991). Here, a range of job holders currently working in the organization are chosen, usually by senior managers, although sometimes the views of peers and subordinates may also be used. The aim is to select a mix of people who are rated as excellent in their performance and people who are rated as adequate but no more.

The next stage is to interview the job holders, using interviewers who have been specially trained for this purpose and who have no knowledge of the job holders' performance ratings. Each individual is asked to describe a number of events in which they played a key part, and are then probed to establish exactly what they did in each event, why they did it, the thought processes that they went through and that shaped their behaviour at the time, and the outcome of the event.

There is then a complex and very lengthy process of analysing the data from these interviews, with a number of cross-checks to ensure uniformity of standards and techniques and objectivity of analysis. The analysis leads to the production of a competency profile of each individual which is then compared to the rankings of their job performance. In this way, the characteristics and behaviour patterns unique to those who are high achievers emerge, and core competences required for excellent performance can thus be identified and described in appropriate behavioural terms.

A similar process, but aimed at identifying the characteristics of effective (rather than, or as well as, excellent) performance, can be devised, by widening the sample group to include some who are generally agreed to be less than satisfactory in their job performance.

At Manchester, the BP process was reversed. Core competences were defined first, using a universal model (McBer's); they were then checked against definitions of management jobs in the company and felt to be valid; analysis was then carried out to define the clusters of attributes needed to reach a satisfactory standard in each of those core competences. Finally, individuals were assessed to find out how much or little of each attribute they possessed, and development plans were produced accordingly, after a process of discussing and agreeing with managers that these were indeed attributes they recognized as necessary for the effective performance of their jobs. Final checks were made to ensure that the universal model had been used in a way that fully met the particular needs of the Manchester Airport senior managers.

Performance analysis

Analysing a job holder's performance can be classed as a technique, in the sense that it should show any problems being experienced or likely to be experienced in reaching required performance standards, together with typical faults encountered in the work and how to deal with them, and much other valuable information.

Where performance analysis is not an intrinsic part of an analytical technique it should always be carried out in addition to that technique. More is said about how to treat information arising out of performance analysis in Chapters 13 and 14.

Exercises

1 Describe a situation in an organization of your choice where it would be particularly valuable to use a competency-based analytical approach in relation to defining training needs, and explain how you would tackle the task.

2 Critically examine the main ways in which jobs are analysed for training purposes in your organization. What would you recommend to improve your organization's job training analysis activity?

References

ANNETT J, DUNCAN K D, STAMMERS R B AND GRAY M J. *Task Analysis*. Department of Employment and Productivity Training Information Paper No. 6. London, HMSO, reprinted Sheffield, MSC. 1979

ARGYLE M. *The Psychology of Interpersonal Behaviour*. Harmondsworth, Penguin. 1970, reprinted 1983

ARKIN A. 'Turning managers into assessors'. *Personnel Management*, November 1991. pp. 49-51

BOYATSIS R E. *The Competent Manger: A model for effective performance*. Chichester, Wiley. 1982

CARBY K AND THAKUR M. *Transactional Analysis at Work*. Information Report No. 23. London, Institute of Personnel Management. 1977

CUTHBERT D. 'Why working together means training together'. *Personnel Management*, October 1984. pp. 47-9

FAIRBAIRN J. 'Plugging the gap in training needs analysis'. *Personnel Management*, February 1991. pp. 43-5

FLANAGAN J C. 'The critical incident technique'. *Psychological Bulletin*, Vol. 52. 1954

FRENCH W L AND BELL C H. *Organization Development: Behavioural science interventions for organization improvement*. 2nd ed, Hemel Hempstead, Prentice Hall. 1978

GENTLES E M. *Training the Operator*. London, Institute of Personnel Management. 1969

GREATREX J AND PHILLIPS P. 'Oiling the wheels of competence'. *Personnel Management*, August 1989. pp. 36-9

HARRISON R. *Developing Human Resources for Productivity*. Geneva, International Labour Office. 1992 (in press)

JACKSON L. 'Transforming managerial performance – a competency approach'. In *Proc. Institute of Personnel Management National Conference, Harrogate, October 1989*. London, IPM. 1989

KENNEY J AND REID M. *Training Interventions*. London, Institute of Personnel Management, 1986; third edition, by Reid, Barrington and Kenney, 1992

MACHIN J. 'Inter-manager communication: matching up to expectations?' *Personnel Management*, January 1981. pp. 26-9

McGREGOR D. *The Human Side of Enterprise*. Maidenhead, McGraw-Hill. 1960

MILLER R B. 'Task description and analysis'. In *Psychological Principles of System Development* (Gagné R M, ed.). Eastbourne, Holt, Rhinehart and Winston. 1962

RACKHAM N, HONEY P AND COLBERT M. *Developing Interactive Skills*, Northampton, Wellens Publishing. 1971

SEYMOUR W D. *Industrial Training for Manual Operatives*. London, Pitman. 1954

SEYMOUR W D. *Skills Analysis Training*. London, Pitman. 1966

SILLS P. *The Behavioural Sciences*. London, Institute of Personnel Management. 1973

SIMPSON B. 'T-groups, TA, NLP: what should we expect from human relations training?' *Personnel Management*, November 1984. pp. 38-41

WARR P B and BIRD M W. *Identifying Supervisory Training Needs.* Training Information Paper No. 2. London, HMSO. 1968

WOODCOCK M. *Team Development Manual.* Aldershot, Gower. 1979

WOODRUFFE C. 'Competent by any other name'. *Personnel Management*, September 1991. pp. 30-3

Further useful reading

BOYDELL T H. *A Guide to the Identification of Training Needs.* London, BACIE. 1990

COCKERILL T. 'The kind of competence for rapid change'. *Personnel Management*, September 1989. pp. 52-6

DULEWICZ V. 'Assessment centres as the route to competence'. *Personnel Management*, November 1989. pp. 56-9

DULEWICZ V. 'Improving assessment centres'. *Personnel Management*, June 1991. pp. 50-5

FURNHAM A. 'A question of competency'. *Personnel Management*, June 1990. p. 37

GLAZE T. 'Cadbury's dictionary of competence'. *Personnel Management*, July 1989. pp. 44-8

HORNBY D AND THOMAS R. 'Towards a better standard of management?' *Personnel Management*, January 1989. pp. 52-5

JACKSON L AND POWELL C. 'Achieving measurable performance improvement through competency-based management development programmes'. In *Proc. Institute of Personnel Management National Conference*, Harrogate, 1991. London, IPM. 1991

JACOBS R. 'Getting the measure of management competence'. *Personnel Management*, June 1989. pp. 32-7

LAIRD D. *Approaches to Training and Development.* Maidenhead, Addison Wesley. 1985

MANSFIELD B. 'Getting to the core of the job'. *Personnel Management*, August 1985. pp. 30-3

PERSONNEL MANAGEMENT. 'Institutes unite to broaden professional training'. *Personnel Management*, July 1989. p. 7

PERSONNEL MANAGEMENT. 'Henley's middle management study finds twelve "supra-competences" '. *Personnel Management*, Septermber 1989. p. 7

PERSONNEL MANAGEMENT. 'Management Charter Initiative issues competence standards'. *Personnel Management*, October 1990. p. 17

PETTIGREW A M, JONES G R AND REASON P W. *Training and Development Roles in Their Organisational Setting*. Sheffield, Manpower Services Commission. 1982

YOUNGMAN M B et al. *Analysing Jobs*. Aldershot, Gower. 1978

Chapter 13

Analysing learning needs related to individuals

Learning Objectives

After reading this chapter you will:

1 understand the main categories of training and development need applicable to individuals in an organization;
2 understand and be able to analyse the key factors underlying and explaining individual performance;
3 have identified four key areas of learning needs for individuals: induction and basic training, the improvement of performance, the requirements of business strategy and change in the workplace, and continuous development and career planning;
4 be able to produce a training proposal for planned learning related to a particular area of individual need.

Identifying Individual Training Needs

As we saw in Chapter 12 the end product of job training analysis is a job training specification which explains the nature of the job in question, and the types and levels of skill, knowledge and attitudes necessary for effective performance in that job. However, this information in itself is not enough for the training designer. He or she must also identify the learning needs and characteristics of the individuals who will be receiving training. Once the demands of the job and the needs of the person are put together, learning objectives relevant to both can be outlined, and a strategy formulated in order to close the gaps between existing and desired performance.

Needs can be defined as gaps between the present and some desired future state. The gaps may be caused by factors operating in the learners, in their managers, or in their work and organizational environment (Robinson and Robinson, 1989). Needs may be to do with performance deficiencies, with adjustments to performance required because of impending changes, or with the release and development of the individual's general potential.

At the individual level, needs should therefore be identified in relation to:

- Induction and basic training
- Improvement of current performance
- Responding to the demands of business strategy and of change in the workplace
- Ensuring effective continuous development and career planning

Induction and Basic Training

Induction

What is the purpose of induction? Is it simply to act as an introduction to the newcomer's job and workplace, to the main systems and procedures with which they need to be familiar, and to the nature of the organization's business and the general climate in which it operates? Or is it also to do with orientating the newcomer to the mission and culture of the organization, to its particular values, beliefs and 'ways of doing things'? In other words, is it to facilitate dialogic learning, which Gilley and Eggland (1989) define as the kind of learning whereby individuals are helped to 'interpret policies, procedures, goals, and objectives within the specific meaning framework of the organization and the people with whom one works'? Its value is that it increases people's understanding of the organizational world in which they have to live, and helps them to adjust successfully to it.

In Chapter 7 we noted two other kinds of learning that are essential to the enhancement of human performance and potential – instrumental and self-reflective learning – and the latter is of particular relevance when designing induction programmes. It is through the self-reflective process that individuals learn more about their own values and belief systems, achieve greater self-assurance and self-esteem, and are helped to function confidently in the organization they have joined. Induction should, ideally, offer opportunities for this kind of learning to occur.

Many organizations arrange induction programmes for groups of new recruits rather than on an individualized basis. The programmes offer not only an introduction to the organization and those aspects of its operations and systems that are of immediate concern to newcomers, but also a carefully planned range of activities and experiences through which dialogic and self-reflective learning can be promoted. Outdoor development courses are often used, offering a learning environment that stimulates and reinforces values, attitudes and styles of behaviour that are consistent with the mission and culture of the organization, and focuses on the development of skills relating to teamwork and team-building, problem-solving, decision-making and creativity, and self-directed learning.

One example of this kind of approach to induction is at Fujitsu, in County Durham, a manufacturer of electronic devices and part of Fujitsu Micro Electronics, the major international group. At the Durham plant new operators first meet the Japanese Managing Director and the British Personnel Director, who spend time explaining to them the mission and values of Fujitsu, the kind of culture that exists in the company (whose plant in County Durham started production in mid-1991, with a workforce of approximately 320 which is planned to expand over the next few years to around 1,500), and the practical implications of the concept of a Fujitsu 'family' of employees. The nature of Fujitsu's business and its customer and supplier requirements are explained, and the importance of teamwork and quality are emphasized. The first batch of new recruits went on a three-day outward bound course where all these messages are reinforced.

Induction programmes often place considerable emphasis on self-development, culminating in individuals being helped to produce personal development objectives and plans which will contribute both to effective work performance and to personal growth.

A mentor can be allocated to each newcomer, to act as a guide, counsellor and catalyst of learning during the induction process, and thereafter to facilitate the third important kind of learning – instrumental – whereby the individual learns how to improve in their performance once a satisfactory basic standard has been achieved.

> Induction should be concerned with essential work- and job-related knowledge and with the promotion of dialogic and self-reflective learning. It should lead into any basic training needed, and thence into an effective process of instrumental learning and continuous development.

When analysing people's induction needs in more detail there are some important sources of information.

- Exit interview records, or other data indicating ex-employees' reasons for leaving the organization early, to establish what needs these might highlight that the induction period should tackle
- The views of recent newcomers to the organization on what they got out of the induction programme (both positive and negative), and whether or not it should be changed in its aims, design, content or operation; and if they did not have any kind of planned induction, what they think should be offered to newcomers
- Information about induction programmes run by other organizations, especially those similar to your own
- Job descriptions and, if any, personnel specifications relating to new recruits – these will offer important information about their main areas of work, the organizational environment of new recruits and the culture that prevails and the kinds of personal profile different types of recruits are likely to have, and will also be important when planning basic training courses for new recruits

Gateshead College: Part 2

Please reread the case study about Gateshead College on pp. 40–1.

Let us assume that the College is recruiting 20 new lecturing staff (plus about ten part-time lecturers) and about 20 staff in other areas of work in the College, from a new Business Unit Manager (Staff Development) to one or two new administrative and clerical staff. Most of the lecturing staff will take up their posts at the same time – the start of the academic year, three months hence. The other staff will arrive at various times between one and six months hence.

What should be the strategy for the induction of these employees? List the main issues you need to consider here, and the general principles that will guide you in making a decision. You are free to make any proposals you wish, as the College is anxious to establish good practice, and to achieve high motivation and commitment in all its employees from their point of entry into the organization onwards.

FEEDBACK NOTES

Before determining a strategy, there has to be a mission, or overall purpose, for induction at the College. This could be along the lines suggested by Fowler (1990a):

> To enable new employees quickly to become fully integrated members of their working groups and to prevent a high incidence of early leavers, by helping them to adjust to their new jobs and organizational environments and quickly become fully integrated members of their working groups.

Fowler observes:

> The main issues to consider are the use of individual and group training, what information to impart over what timescales, the duration, content and training methods of formal courses, and the induction roles of line-managers and personnel staff.

In order to decide on a relevant induction strategy for Gateshead College, you will find useful guidelines in Fowler (1990a and b).

Basic training

> Basic training should be determined by two main considerations: training policy as it relates to new recruits of different kinds and at different levels in the organization, and the special needs of individual newcomers.

Let us look now at training for new recruits.

Launching a new learning culture on Tyneside (based on Arkin, 1992)
(With acknowledgements to A Arkin and *Personnel Management Plus*)

In 1990 Swan Hunter shipyard and the eight unions representing its workforce achieved an agreement on flexible working practices that involved a major cultural change for the company. Swan Hunter had been 'a bastion of the craft apprenticeship system' in the 1970s, but 'privatisation by management buyout in 1986 and a subsequent freeze on apprentice recruitment spelt the end of this system'. In 1990 the aim was to focus on training new and existing employees of all kinds and ages. 'We wanted something that was standards-based, cost-effective, and plugged into recognized qualifications at NVQ level 3,' said Steve Whitely, the Human Resources Director.

A working party with equal representation of management and unions was set up to develop a new training scheme for all employees in the company. The key area of production was the first to be tackled, and small sub-groups of managers and trade union representatives carried out a thorough examination of the production skills needed in the company. Jobs were profiled, and questionnaires were sent to production workers 'to establish what they actually did, what they thought they should be doing, and what activities they thought likely to increase or decline in the future'. This exercise achieved the involvement of workers on a wide scale, and led to the identification of five major types of production tasks which then became the basis of a three-stage training scheme once the working party's recommendations had been accepted by the company and the unions.

This scheme covers existing and new employees. Stage 1, consisting of four or five months' induction and basic training, will be carried out at a local college and cover basic skills, health and safety, and the company's functions and history. Trainees will also be introduced to specific area-based processes as part of a BTEC programme which they will continue to study part-time thereafter.

Stage 2, designed to develop core skills in one of the five main task areas will be company-based, with the choice of skill area determined by the needs of the business and individual's own aptitudes, while Stage 3 will build on these basic skills, focusing on area, process and system skills.

As technological processes change, additional modules will be added to the company's existing wide-ranging modular training programme. Trainees will be expected to take two modules, with the choice determined by business needs but with individual preferences also considered.

The working party has now become a training committee, with a continuing role of assessing and reviewing the progress of individual trainees as well as helping develop training programmes for technical and commercial staff. Although the new training strategy has received some funding from a local TEC, it still represents a considerable increase in the company's training investment. That is considered well worthwhile in order to attract and retain valued employees.

This case study makes several important points:

1 It shows the value of a strategic, business-led and collaborative approach to the development of company training policy, strategy and plans, as we saw in Chapter 11.

2 It shows the value of the audit approach in obtaining vital information, and in gaining the involvement of key parties who will themselves subsequently be going through training and development. This was our main theme in Chapter 8.

3 It demonstrates how a company can view heavy investment in training as justified not only by immediate outcomes in terms of skill acquisition, but as a fundamental strategy to attract, retain and develop valued employees. We noted this especially in Chapters 1 and 7.

4 It demonstrates in a striking way the value of planning induction and basic skills training as a collaborative, integrated and business-led activity that will achieve the rapid integration of new employees into the culture, social groups and work systems of the organization as well as ensuring that they have the skills, knowledge and developmental opportunities needed at each key stage of their career in the organization.

5 It shows how basic training in the workplace can help employees gain competences that can then be related to national vocational qualifications – a very important consideration in any basic training programme.

Objectives and programmes for basic training should, therefore, be set out in a company's employee development policy. However, if as at Swan Hunter that policy has only just been established, or if no such policy has yet been agreed, how can the basic training needs of potential learners be identified? The case study offers some important guidelines.

1 **Define the people for whom basic training will be given.** At Swan Hunter, it was all new and existing staff, regardless of age, type of work or background.

2 **Define the objectives of basic training.** At Swan Hunter these included attracting the kinds of skilled people the company needed, as well as developing people from within, retaining those employees, providing training that was standards-based and related to NVQ qualifications, establishing a cost-effective way of reinforcing company culture as well as ensuring good standards of job performance, and building a base for flexibility of skills.

3 **Audit existing learning and performance.** At Swan Hunter this was done by setting up a working party which then split into subgroups to learn at first hand what training was needed in key task areas throughout the company and the employees' views of tasks, how they were being performed, and what was needed to achieve high standards.

4 **Produce proposals and plans.** Draw up and achieve agreement on integrated plans for induction, basic training and education, and continuous development for all learners. Training and development proposals for submission to senior management and any other key parties whose approval to implement those proposals is essential should be as brief as possible (for an example, see Gilley and Eggland, 1989, pp. 211–12), expressed in language its audience can readily understand. A proposal should cover the following:

- The aim of the training and development action
- Why it is needed, what it will cost, the outcomes it should achieve, and their value to the organization
- The numbers and types and levels of jobs of the learners, and any other relevant information on them
- Its timescale, and how it will be monitored and evaluated
- A brief outline of the training or other form of development proposed, showing design, main content areas, learning strategy, and the key personnel who will be involved in its delivery
- Any training of those personnel that may be needed – for example, if any competency assessment for NVQ purposes is to be done it will require expertise for which training will be needed (Arkin, 1991)

Writing a training proposal

This will consolidate and extend what you have learnt in this chapter so far. Read the Barratt case study in Harrison (1992a), as it relates to the Sales Training Programme. Read Gilley and Eggland (1989), Chapter 6. Then draw up a training proposal for senior management (e.g. your Personnel Director) recommending a particular induction or basic skills training activity.

Special needs of individual newcomers

Consideration must also be given to the individual new recruit who, for whatever reason, needs some form of basic training in order to achieve the required standards of performance quickly. This may be a newcomer to the organization, someone who has been transferred or promoted to a different type of job, or someone who has been promoted to a different role in the same area of work. The training may be for one individual or several. How are individual needs to be analysed?

The first thing to establish is the purpose and nature of the job in question and the kind of performance overall of the typical new job holder. It will be helpful if there is an up-to-date and accurate job description and personnel specification, or a job training specification. If not, that kind of information will have to be collected.

At this point, some form of problem-centred analysis should be used (see pp. 270–2). The evidence for actual or anticipated problems must then be examined. What is their nature? Are the problems essentially those of:

- task performance, connected with difficulties in carrying out one or more specific tasks related to the job?
- task management, connected with difficulties in general planning, problem-solving and decision-making in the job?
- boundary management, connected with difficulties in operating confidently and effectively in the job because of the social and political environment in which the job holder must operate?
- motivation, connected typically with mistaken expectations about the job or its level and content, or with unsatisfactory training, support and rewards, or with poor supervision and feedback on performance?

Then, what are their causes? As noted earlier in this chapter (p. 282), there are three major causes of performance deficiencies:

- causes due to the learner, because of a lack of the right abilities, motivation, values or understanding
- causes due to the learner's manager, who needs to act as an effective role model, coach, stimulus and communicator
- causes due to the organization, where barriers to effective performance may lie in its structure, culture, work systems, human resource strategy and policies or communications with employees.

We shall look at the analysis of poor performance in the next section. At this point, let us simply note the importance of tackling such problems in new recruits very quickly. Providing it is clear that they have the ability to achieve good job performance (i.e. that there has not been a fundamental selection error), problems in the early stages of a job are not likely to endure. However, if they are not sorted out at once they can take root deeply. This emphasizes the need for regular monitoring of the behaviour and performance of new recruits. Many probationary periods are wasted because the aims of probation – giving the recruit the opportunity for guided learning and familiarization with the job and its environment, help to perform all tasks to the standards required, and effective induction into the culture of the workplace – are not backed up by any workable system to achieve those aims. Instead, newcomers are left on their own, learning is by trial and error and lacking any systematic guidance, monitoring or feedback, so that neither they nor the organization can judge their real capabilities. Little wonder that in many organizations turnover is highest in the early stages of job occupancy.

The critical aims with new job holders with performance problems are to ensure that the causes of difficulty have been correctly identified and are best tackled by some form of training or developmental response, and that the most effective and efficient form of learning is then provided. That will be determined by what has to be learnt, by finding a learning strategy that will most suit the learners and by matching that strategy to available resources, including time.

Options might include guided experience with mentors to provide support and guidance, short training events, special assignments or projects, coaching by managers or other relevant parties in the organization, some form of programmed learning package, a sequence of visits to other organizations or departments to acquire particular kinds of information and insights and educational courses to achieve a higher level of professional knowledge or a broadening of business awareness.

In order to reduce the likelihood of performance problems occurring with new recruits, certain simple steps are recommended:

- Good induction
- Basic training to help surmount any major difficulties that typify the particular job or area of work (problem-centred analysis, as explained in Chapter 11, will establish what these are likely to be); to ensure that required standards of performance are reached in key tasks which all job holders must be able to perform; and to familiarize the job holder with any special systems, work processes and procedures or equipment affecting their work
- Personal development plans formulated by the recruits at an early stage, with the active support of their managers or their mentors to pursue them

- Targets for performance that, however they may be expressed, are understood and agreed between the job holder and the manager and can act as the basis for regular discussion, feedback and planning of work

Basic training for the PA job

Please turn to Appendix 5 which shows an extract from the job training specification document for a Principal Assistant (PA) (Personnel and Training) at the then North Eastern Electricity Board. Then examine carefully the personnel specification for the job shown in Appendix 7. This shows the kind of person who will actually be recruited into the job, and who will be going through the basic training programme.

You are the Training Manager who has been asked to design a programme for the new recruit to the PA job. The appointment is due to be made in two months' time. Since this position is to be used as one of a number to develop graduate management trainees in the company, the average length of time spent in it is unlikely to exceed a year or 18 months. This training programme will therefore be used regularly if not frequently.

What further information should you seek, before being able to design the programme?

FEEDBACK NOTES

You have three important pieces of information: the job description at the start of the job training specification shows the overall purpose and the key parameters of the job; the rest of the job training specification shows the knowledge, skills and attitudes required for effective performance in the job; and the personnel specification indicates the kind of person who will be recruited into the job.

Before designing a training programme, information is needed on many points, and the list below is therefore not exhaustive – you may well have included other areas where data is required.

1 **Previous programmes.** Have we run a programme for this job before? If so, are there any evaluations of it, formal or informal?

2 **Job changes.** Have there been any changes in the job – its purpose, key tasks, etc. – since the job training specification and personnel specification were drawn up? If so, do those changes have training or development implications?

3 **Training standards to be attained.** Is the training programme expected to take the new recruit up to the 'desirable' level indicated in the personnel specification, or to ensure that tasks are performed to the 'essential' level only? If this is an internal appointment, then is it known how far the new recruit is likely not only to have the necessary task-related skills, but also to have the experience or potential to cope with the task management and boundary management demands of the job and role?

4 **Level of recruits.** Is it known at this stage whether recruits will be expected to have only the 'essential' requirements indicated in the personnel specification, or only the 'desirable' ones, in each of the five categories shown? If they will already possess all the 'desirable' requirements – which means that they will be capable of performing the job satisfactorily virtually at once – then the programme should focus on effective induction, appraisal and continuous development. On the other hand if the typical recruit is likely to have only the absolutely essential requirements, then that it is a strong indicator that basic skills training should be provided for.

5 **Sources of recruitment.** Will recruits come from within or outside the organization (i.e. will this be a first post for management trainees, or will they come to it after experience elsewhere in the company?) Will they be likely to have previous experience of training roles? The answer to these questions will indicate how far boundary management skills need to be developed in the training programme.

6 **Timing of the training programme.** How soon after entering the company will recruits move into this particular training programme? As you can see much of the information needed to enable a good training programme to be drawn up cannot be provided until details about the individual recruit are known. If management trainees are to come on to the programme almost immediately after joining the company there will be little if any time to meet them in advance and check on their actual as against their predicted needs. This will affect the learning strategy chosen, which will have to lean heavily on early assessment of individual needs, and will require a programme flexible enough to adapt, while still developing the skills, knowledge and attitudes which the personnel specification shows recruits are unlikely to have yet which are vital to the effective performance of the job.

If we were examining a range of jobs currently being performed in the company, and planning basic training for those jobs, then the kind of additional information gathered at Swan Hunter would be necessary: asking job holders and other key parties how they viewed the tasks to be done in particular areas of activity, and what kind of training they felt was needed in order to perform tasks to required standards.

If, again, there were no job description, personnel specification or other similar documentation, then the information they contain would have to be gathered and analysed. In this connection, note the ways in which, in our case study, information in the personnel specification helps the training designer:

- It shows those areas of work where the emphasis is on potential rather than on proven skills.
- It shows the type of training, experience and development needed to take someone from a merely adequate to a very good performance in certain areas (see under 'Qualifications' and 'Occupational Experience' in Appendix 7).
- It shows requirements in relation to knowledge, skill and attitudes (see especially under 'Motivation').
- Without specifically using these terms, it makes clear which areas of skills relate to task mastery, to task management and to boundary management (see, for example, in the 'Desirable' column under 'Occupational Experience' where boundary management skills are indicated and under 'Motivation', where many task management skills are outlined).

Improving Current Performance

Here we are referring to existing job holders being helped to improve their current performance by some kind of planned learning intervention.

We have already seen that deficiencies in performance can be caused by:

- Conditions to do with the learners
- Conditions to do with their managers
- Conditions to do with the organization

First, therefore, the nature and causes of performance gaps must be identified by analysing those conditions to see where the barriers lie, just as with new recruits who have performance problems. If there is any kind of formal appraisal system, this should help the analysis. Other important sources of information include performance records of various kinds, levels of absenteeism and turnover, and exit interview data. In examining all such data its likely validity must be rigorously probed, as must its scope, relevance and the extent to which it is up to date.

Understanding performance

More will be said about appraisal in Chapter 14, both as a source of information about training and development needs and as a starting point for action planning in those areas. At this point, however, let us consider how different factors related to the individual, their manager and the organizational environment impact upon behaviour and performance.

Performance can be explained as the final outcome of the interaction between a person's needs, their perception of the results required from them and the rewards being offered to them, and the amount of effort, energy and ability they have available or wish to apply to the task in hand. Handy (1985) calls this the 'motivation calculus', by which he means the complex process that ultimately determines how a person behaves and performs. He explains that performance can be understood by reference to four parameters, which revolve around the learner, their manager, and their workplace:

- The needs of the individual
- The results the individual is expected to achieve
- The rewards offered for their achievement
- E factors: the individual's effort, excitement, energy and expertise

Needs

How far, in their mind, does a person's job or task relate in any positive way to needs that they bring to work? What we should try to discover is not all their needs, but only those by which they are influenced at work. If a particular task or job relates to those needs only in a minor way, then clearly we cannot expect more than minimal performance from the job holder. They can see no reason for exerting much effort.

Results

How far does the person really appreciate what is wanted from them?

Do they fully understand what the job is, what results they are supposed to achieve, and within what context of opportunities, constraints and challenges they have to perform the job? Have they had any opportunity to set work targets jointly with their manager, rather than simply having these imposed on them? There is must evidence to show that the joint formulation of work plans and targets leads to manager and job holder sharing a common view of the job, and to increased motivation and commitment in the job holder. Do they know when they are achieving good results, and why? Does the manager help them by acting as a good role model, reinforcing effective performance and discouraging poor performance?

Rewards

Does the task or job offer rewards to the individual that they value, in relation to their needs? Rewards can take many different forms: not just money and position (which may have less impact than the manager believes, or may not be within the manager's power to offer) but status, praise and recognition. It is essential to talk and listen to staff about what they find rewarding, instead of simply acting on assumptions about this crucial factor.

E factors

How far does the job holder see it as worthwhile to expend effort, energy, excitement and expertise on the task, given the results that are required and the rewards it appears to offer them? And what level of those E factors do they actually possess? Are assessments about this accurate, or have incorrect assumptions been made, so that either less or more is expected of them than they are actually able to give?

Let us take an example and try applying our analytical model to the information it contains.

The reluctant worker

A member of staff is invited by his manager to work on a new project that has come into the department. The manager knows that she cannot force him to take it on, as he already has a heavy workload, and there are other staff who could cope with it satisfactorily. However, having observed him at work over the two years he has been a member of the group, the manager believes he is motivated strongly by ambition. Since the task is a crucial one, and the member of staff, so the manager believes, is likely to be highly effective in carrying it out, she tries to enlist his commitment by telling him that if he does it, and does it well, it will significantly advance his prospects of promotion. To her surprise, he turns the opportunity down. Using our four factors affecting performance, produce a list of possible reasons for his decision.

FEEDBACK NOTES

There are many reason why the member of staff may not be motivated to apply most effort to the task in question. Using our analytical model, the following come immediately to mind:

Needs

Even though he may be ambitious, promotion may not be the reward he really seeks. He may be driven by the need, not for the increased responsibilities or high level of skill that promotion would involve, but for some form of status in his profession. That need may be satisfied by doing well in his present work and achieving high status among his professional peers. Another possibility is that he may want status in the eyes of his colleagues at work, again by being regarded as highly effective in his present job. Taking on another task when he is already expending maximum effort on his existing workload could mean a reduction in his overall effectiveness, and the loss of such status. Or he may have a need for personal power which is already being satisfied by the influence he can exercise over members of his existing work group.

All of these possibilities mean that a generalized term like ambition cannot adequately explain or help us to predict behaviour. Such generalizations can lead to serious miscalculations in managers' decisions about how to motivate their staff, and lead to reduced rather than improved performance in individuals and teams.

Results

He may have misunderstood the results he is being asked to achieve, or believe that the task involves too much effort. It is essential that tasks are clearly defined and agreed between manager and job holder. This requires meaningful performance objectives to be set, and methods of measuring performance against those objectives to be agreed. In this process checks must be made to ensure that the objectives are tight, demanding and precise enough, and that their implications are fully understood in terms of the skill, knowledge, attitudes and experience they require, of the kind of resources and of support from other personnel they require, and of the value and rewards attached to them by the organization.

Rewards

As we saw under 'Needs', the reward being offered – an increased chance of promotion – may not be relevant to the needs he brings to the work situation. On the other hand, the idea of promotion may appeal to him but he may not believe that it would actually happen. This may be because his manager often tries to get people to take on extra work by making promises that subsequently she does not fulfil; or because in the past it has been proved that she lacks the power to carry out her promises.

E factors

He may feel unable to expend any more effort or energy on new tasks because of the workload he already carries. Or he may not know his manager's high opinion of him and may believe (accurately or not) that he does not have the necessary ability. In either event he will not be motivated to perform the new task.

Note in this case how it is the particular interaction that takes place between needs, results, rewards, and E factors that explains the performance of the individual. Over time, the performance records of such a member of staff may show high levels of absenteeism and sickness, and notes of continued refusals to take on new tasks. These records may cause very unfavourable judgements to be made about him, to the point where it may be felt that there is little point in offering him training or development: he is written off as too lazy, apathetic or uncommitted to the job. Yet with more insights into the factors that lie behind performance, a more searching analysis of the information, and a probing discussion with the person involved, quite a different picture may emerge. That picture, on analysis, may lead to an awareness that changes need to be made in the ways in which staff recruitment, work allocation, leadership functions or appraisal are carried out in that department.

Performance is therefore the outcome of a complex interaction between needs, results, rewards and E factors, as perceived by the job holder on the one hand and their manager on the other. When we are trying to understand people's performance at work we must try to find out the meanings that govern their actions instead of simply making assumptions about those meanings, or interpreting others' behaviour by reference to the meanings that govern our own.

Training managers should build up close informal as well as formal interactions with managers and other personnel in the organization, so that they can develop valid insights of their own about the issues that lie behind performance instead of being over-influenced by the views of others. They will then need to ask many probing questions to determine whether performance can best be tackled by training or development.

To summarize this section:

> To identify accurately the nature and causes of poor performance, it is necessary to know the individuals concerned, their managers, and the workplace environment, well enough to be able to understand the key influences on individual behaviour and performance.

Identifying areas for action and deciding on training and development strategies

Having established the reasons for poor performance, agreement must be reached on those areas of performance where it is essential, rather than simply desirable, to achieve improvements. This will enable priorities for action to be identified, and appropriate learning strategies to be determined.

Romiskowski (1981 p. 108, Figure 6.12) gives an analysis schema that is helpful here. He explains that it points to 'an interrelation of the many aspects that might contribute to any given performance problem' and he shows in clear, practical terms how to undertake a rigorous analysis of learners' needs and a diagnosis of whether those needs justify a training or development response; and if they do, then of what kind.

Responding to the Demands of Business Strategy and of Change in the Workplace

Whether as a planned response to the needs of business strategy (see

Chapter 11), or on a contingency basis, from time to time new training and development strategies and initiatives will have to be introduced across the whole organization or sections of it. Typical triggers for such change programmes would be a drive for customer care or total quality; new company policies or concerns relating to equality in the workplace; standards of health and safety at work; the impact of new legislation; preparation for redundancy or retirement; or the forthcoming introduction of new tasks or patterns of work organization, new technology, or changes in organizational culture and structure. We shall look in detail at how to respond to needs relating to special sectors, contingencies and strategic initiatives in Chapters 18 and 21. However, some general guidelines are relevant at this point.

To analyse learner needs, it is necessary first to establish clearly the kinds of knowledge, skills and attitudes required in learners, together with standards to be achieved and methods of measuring performance in relation to those standards (see Chapter 12).

Turning to the learning population that has been identified – which in some cases may be the entire workforce, in others a section or sector of it – a profile of that population has to be established. The kinds of questions on which information needs to be obtained include:

- How many learners are going to be involved, and what is the available timescale for training or other developmental initiatives to be designed and delivered?
- What are the current levels and kinds of knowledge, skill and attitudes that typify the learning population?
- What kind of programme or other strategy is most likely to bridge the gap between what is needed and the current state?
- Given the expertise and other resources available, what kind of programme will be most effective and cost-beneficial for the type of learners involved?
- What should be the design, structure and method of delivery of the learning events?
- Are there any training and development needs related to the managers and organizational environment of the learners, in order that new learning can be implemented effectively?
- What should be the priorities for action? Here, it will be essential to identify those needs most likely to benefit the organization and ensure that adequate recognition and rewards are attached to meeting those critical needs, in order to motivate potential learners. (Fairbairn, 1991)

What methods can be used in the analytical process? The Swan Hunter case study illustrates some very useful approaches to obtaining information. Gilley and Eggland (1989) observe that there are 20 or 30 different methods and they deal in detail with six of the most useful: interviews, questionnaires, tests, group problem-centred analysis techniques, performance records and reports, and performance appraisals. They also give criteria to determine which methods to use in particular situations.

The description of the Sales Training Programme at Barratt in Harrison (1992a) offers an example of how learning needs related to an area of work directly impacting on the achievement of business goals were analysed by reference to the type of work and to those who needed training and development; how an appropriate learning strategy was formulated to meet those needs; and how the Training Manager convinced the Board that a completely new approach to sales training should be undertaken.

Ensuring Effective Continuous Development and Career Planning

We covered the issues involved in ensuring effective continuous development of individuals in Chapter 8. Career development needs can be identified and analysed through a range of processes including appraisal, assessment centre methodology and personal development planning, and these will be discussed in detail in Chapter 20.

Exercises

1 How would you establish the initial training needs of a small group of experienced sales representatives, externally recruited following their being made redundant by a competitor? (November 1989)

2 Draft a statement to your top management team proposing the introduction of one of the following:

(a) tailor-made self-study material;
(b) an equal opportunities education campaign;
(c) a top management skills development programme. (November 1988)

3 Explain the process you would adopt when identifying training needs stemming from one of the following:

(a) ongoing maintenance of a newly installed plant;
(b) appointment of a new group of safety stewards;
(c) use of workplace assessment for qualification purposes (May 1988)

References

ARKIN A. 'Launching a new learning culture on Tyneside'. *Personnel Management Plus*, March 1992. pp. 20-1

FAIRBAIRN J. 'Plugging the gap in training needs analysis'. *Personnel Management*, February 1991. pp. 43-5

FOWLER A. 'How to plan an induction programme'. *Personnel Management Plus*, September 1990a. pp. 20-1

FOWLER A. *A Good Start.* London, Institute of Personnel Management. 1990b

GILLEY J W AND EGGLAND S A. *Principles of Human Resource Development.* Maidenhead, Addison Wesley. 1989

HANDY C B. *Understanding Organizations.* 3rd ed. Harmondsworth, Penguin. 1985

HARRISON R. 'Employee development at Barratt'. In *Case Studies in Personnel* (Winstanley D and Woodall J, eds.). London, Institute of Personnel Management. 1992a

HARRISON R. *Developing Human Resources for Productivity.* Geneva, International Labour Office. 1992b (in press)

ROBINSON D G AND ROBINSON J C. *Training for Impact.* London, Jossey-Bass. 1989.

ROMISKOWSKI A J. *Designing Instructional Systems.* New York, Kogan Page. 1981

Further useful reading

ADVISORY CONCILIATION AND ARBITRATION SERVICE. *Induction of New Employees.* ACAS. 1985. (Available from regional offices)

ARKIN A. 'Staffing a greenfield site – Fujitsu'. *Personnel Management Plus*, October 1990. pp. 26-7

BAIRD L S (ed.). *The Training and Development Sourcebook.* 3rd ed. Amherst, Massachusetts. HRD Press. 1985

FOWLER A. 'How to set performance objectives'. *Personnel Management Plus*. February 1991. pp. 20-1

MAGER R F AND PIPE P. *Analyzing Performance Problems.* Belmont, California, Pitman Learning Inc. 1984

NADLER L AND NADLER Z. *Developing Human Resources.* London, Jossey-Bass. 1989

Chapter 14

Using appraisal to identify training and development needs

Learning Objectives

After reading this chapter you will:

1 be able to identify what, if any, improvements are needed in your organization's appraisal system so that you can establish and analyse training and development needs effectively;
2 be able to plan a motivating and developmental appraisal interview related to training and development needs, and to produce an action plan related to the outcomes of such an interview;
3 understand the tensions involved in using appraisal for developmental purposes and their typical causes.

Successful Appraisal

Appraisal lies at the heart of training and development, as it does of so many other personnel processes. As we shall see throughout this chapter, if appraisal related to training and development is to succeed, there must be:

1 **A shared perception of purpose.** The appraiser and the appraisee must have a shared understanding of the purpose and value of the discussion, and a shared commitment to its objectives;

2 **Mutual learning and understanding.** In the course of the appraisal discussion both parties, not just the appraisee, should gain insights into themselves as well as learning about each other. Performance should be analysed in the context of the main constraints and opportunities affecting it in the workplace, so that there is an increased understanding on both sides about issues related to the appraisee's areas of strength and weakness.

3 **Objectivity.** The discussion should avoid any tendency to blame or

judge; it should be supportive, centre on work objectives, and focus on the future.

4 **Diagnosis, planning and action.** The outcomes of appraisal should be an accurate diagnosis of learning needs, an agreed plan to tackle areas of major importance related to those needs, and action which is monitored and reviewed over time.

Integration of Appraisal Within the Organization

The appraisal process cannot be viewed in isolation. It always takes place within a context, and that context has a crucial effect on its conduct and outcomes. We will look at four aspects of the context of appraisal for training and development:

- The appraiser/appraisee relationship
- The aims and nature of the appraisal scheme
- The overall employee resourcing policies and systems
- The organizational mission, culture and structure

The appraiser-appraisee relationship

The relationship between the parties, to which we drew attention in Chapters 12 and 13, is the single most powerful influence on the conduct and outcomes of an appraisal discussion, and constitutes one of the major areas of difficulty with it. The most common problems are:

1 **The manager is not convinced of the need for appraisal, and has no incentive to carry it out effectively.** Like the wider responsibility of employee development, appraisal has to be made into a valued and rewarded part of every manager's role (see p. 195).

2 **The manager does not have the skills to carry it out effectively.** Appraisal is a highly skilled activity. The manager must have the knowledge and ability to carry out the tasks involved. Where any form of rating or ranking is involved, those tasks are particularly difficult and at the human level almost impossible to achieve in a way that is perceived as fair by all the parties.

> In performance assessment the probability that the measurement process is inept and unfair is very high because the technical problems in designing rating scales and the observational problems

> involved in using them are considerable; this makes it virtually certain that the assessment process is seen as uncertain by the appraisees. Hence the many references to the need for accuracy in ratings, which abound in the appraisal literature. (Randell, 1989)

At the level of human interactive processes, the skills involved are many: they include those of analyst, diagnostician, coach, counsellor and guide. Randell (1989, pp. 163–5) explains that whereas American practice has been to emphasize systems and assessment techniques, in Britain the emphasis has moved towards interpersonal skills. He sees appraisal as requiring the same kind of skills as are needed for successful leadership, and observes that they form part of any effective interpersonal behaviour between managers and staff. Training managers in how to be effective appraisers is therefore also training them in 'the micro-skills of leadership' (Alban-Metcalfe, 1984), and is thus of double value.

While there is an extensive literature on how to plan and conduct effective appraisal discussions (see Torrington et al., 1991; Fowler, 1991), training in process as well as task skills is essential. Unfortunately, the evidence suggests that although appraisal skills training is widespread, its focus is far more on tasks than on processes. (Long, 1986)

Training also needs to focus strongly on attitudes and climate, because without a real belief in and commitment to appraisal managers will not carry out the process effectively no matter how good their technical and interpersonal skills. Training in appraisal, therefore, should encompass these attitudinal dimensions and should take in the whole population of appraisers in order to help to embed into the organization the culture needed. Training in some form should also cover some if not all appraisees; this will help to create a shared framework of understanding about, and commitment to, the whole process and what is involved in both appraising and being appraised.

3 **The basic relationship between appraiser and appraisee is so poor that it makes appraisal itself impossible to carry out effectively.** If the relationship is not open and supportive it is most unlikely that a formalized appraisal system can make it so, and this will mean that the whole process can fail, with potentially disastrous results for the morale and self-confidence of the appraisee, and sometimes of the appraiser. It is a dilemma in appraisal that the relationship that produces information about learning needs may be so

poor that the validity of that information becomes suspect, and any chance of effective development of the individual in the workplace thereafter may be stifled. We shall return to this problem towards the end of this chapter.

The aims and nature of the appraisal scheme

Using appraisal to identify and analyse training and development needs requires an atmosphere in which weaknesses and gaps in performance can be openly admitted and their causes fully explored. To ensure such outcomes, the appraisal scheme must have the following characteristics:

1 **The objectives of the scheme must be clear and shared.** They must be objectives to which line managers, not just specialist personnel and training staff, are committed. They must therefore relate directly to the business and growth needs of units and of the organization as a whole.

2 **Objectives must be limited in scope and number and must not be in mutual conflict.** The objectives of a scheme whose focus is appraisal of current work performance, work planning for the forthcoming period and diagnosis of learning needs should not be in conflict with one another. Tensions will occur, however, if to those objectives are added others related to pay and promotion. The latter necessarily involve some form of assessment and a ranking system, and are therefore stressful and potentially threatening to the appraisee; they are bound to lead to attempts to hide weaknesses and overemphasize achievements, rather than openly to discuss gaps in performance and to concede that improvements need to be made.

Of course, judgements relating to pay, promotion and discipline must be made somewhere within the appraisal and assessment system; what is to be avoided is including them within the particular scheme of appraisal that focuses on job and growth-related training and development. The point appears to have been taken in the UK because Long (1986), in her survey of appraisal in a large sample of British organizations in both the public and the private sector, notes an increasing tendency for British firms to restrict the number of objectives served by a single appraisal scheme, and to separate appraisal of performance which leads to work planning, training and development decisions from other kinds of appraisal, both in the design of those schemes and in the timing of appraisal discussions.

This problem of tension between aims to do with control and aims to do with development has been well documented (see, for example, Townley, 1989; Bevan and Thompson, 1991). The conclusion to be drawn is that the two sets of aims should be dealt with in two separate appraisals. This issue will be dealt with further later in the chapter.

3 **The mechanics of the scheme should accurately reflect its aims.** If the scheme's objectives are to aid work planning and performance and to diagnose training and development needs, then there is no need for complex forms to be filled in, or for ranking systems. Only the most basic information needs to be recorded, sufficient to ensure that work targets and ways of measuring performance are agreed and noted, that plans for training and development are passed to those who will need to approve and take action on them, and that there is evidence of non-descrimination in the way the scheme operates. Support for this kind of approach is given by Long (1986), who found that in some organizations the problems of rating and ranking schemes (bias, skewedness and unequal standards) had led to their being abandoned. Anderson (1987) goes further and suggests that appraisal could actually be carried out without forms at all, but feedback on such a system did indicate that to rely entirely on memory could result in the demise of the system!

Randell (1989) puts the crucial point clearly when he argues that ratings are very widely used in appraisal schemes, yet they are only relevant if the individual's ability has to be assessed in some way (and he offers ideas about how this can be done to minimize subjectivity and achieve a result that is felt to be fair by the parties concerned). If, on the other hand, the purpose is development, then 'the dangers in going through an assessment stage are not likely to be justifiable no matter how technically competent the measurement devices are' (Ibid., p. 161).

4 **Line managers must be involved in the design of the scheme and the planning of its implementation.** The principle here is an obvious one; the more that managers are able to share in the creation of a scheme that is going to directly affect their own development and that of their staff, the more committed to it will they become. Organizations quite often use an external consultant to help them instal or change an appraisal system. The consultant can become a catalyst and learning resource, helping managers understand appraisal and, in working as a team to produce an effective system,

to develop task-related and teamwork skills that will be essential to the successful operation of the final scheme. In this way, the whole exercise becomes a vehicle for the continuous development of managers as a team, and this in turn helps the organization to develop (see Scott, 1983).

5 **Top management must demonstrate a full commitment to the scheme.** This means that they must be prepared to provide all the resources needed to ensure its effective implementation, and also to ensure that managers are themselves appraised and rewarded for treating appraisal and development of their people as a key area of responsibility. It is important to realize that appraisal is a very expensive process. It takes time, expertise and commitment to design a scheme, to prepare people for it, in terms of attitudes as well as skills and knowledge, and above all to operate, monitor and carry out action plans resulting from it. This means that the existing tasks and workloads of appraisers will need to be examined and possibly reorganized to ensure that appraisal is a responsibility that they can take on and perform effectively; and it means that there must be a high degree of skill in helping the organization to aborb the appraisal process, and to integrate it with other human resource management systems in a positive and consistent way.

6 **Training in appraisal skills must be given.** This point follows on naturally from the one above, and we have already noted its importance.

7 **The appraisal scheme should be regularly monitored and amended as necessary.** Without this, even the best scheme will decline in effectiveness and relevance, as personnel and situations change and new demands are placed on the organization and its members. Long's research (1986) indicates that a thorough evaluation at least once every three years is needed to check on the continued effectiveness and relevance of a particular scheme.

Appraisal at Nuffield Hospitals Group (based on Wilson and Cole, 1990)

(With acknowledgements to J Wilson and G Cole and *Personnel Management*)

Identify the reasons why the Nuffield appraisal scheme for

developing people is likely to achieve sustained success.

At the Nuffield Hospitals Group, schemes for objective setting and performance assessment related to promotion were already well established in 1989–90. The concern was to produce a simple scheme with the clear objective of focusing on personal development. The aim of the scheme was that staff should:

- be clear about the scope and content of their jobs and the results they were expected to achieve;
- know how they were progressing and where they stood, and that achievement was recognized;
- be informed and consulted about their career prospects and personal development;
- be able to communicate with their immediate manager about personal progress and about work generally;
- assist corporate succession planning by providing information about their skills and their experience.

The starting point is to make personal development programmes available to everyone in the organization. This is done by means of a planned interview with each person's immediate manager once a year, leading to jointly agreed action plans relating to the individual's development over the forthcoming year.

Paperwork at the appraisal discussion is minimal, serving only the purpose of an *aide-mémoire*. It is not filed centrally, and can either be discarded after the meeting or kept for reference by the two parties.

Discussion focuses on areas of achievement and weakness, with a commitment to identify the causes of problems and agree on any appropriate developmental action related not only to peformance improvement but also to enhanced personal development.

Before introducing the scheme (about whose design all staff were consulted), training was given to all appraisers throughout the 32 hospitals in the Group. In a two-day residential course, the emphasis was first on convincing people of the need for and value of development-centred appraisal, and then on helping them to acquire the relevant appraisal techniques, together with mentoring and coaching skills. The training programmes took twelve months to complete, and training is now offered to all new appraisers. Refresher workshops are also organized.

Managers themselves are appraised on the extent to which they can produce evidence of effectively appraising and developing their staff, and are required to brief all their staff about the scheme and its aims before interviews take place. They therefore take their roles as appraisers seriously. Departmental briefings are organized by the Personnel Department after each round of interviews in order to learn by trial and success.

The system was accepted without problems, in spite of the fact that 1989-90 was a period of upheaval in the NHS. The article by Wilson and Cole (1990) is essential reading for anyone wanting to use appraisal to identify training and development needs and achieve a high commitment to the process throughout an organization. It reflects principles outlined in another important article by Anderson et al. (1987), and echoes an earlier, very similar and successful scheme introduced at Trent Regional Health Authority. (George, 1986)

FEEDBACK NOTES

The basic reason why the Nuffield scheme is likely to sustain its early success is because it has resolved the tensions between appraisals used for developmental and control purposes. It has all the characteristics of an effective developmental scheme:

- The objectives of the scheme are clear and shared.
- Objectives are limited in scope and number and are not in mutual conflict.
- The mechanics of the scheme accurately reflect its aims.
- Line managers are involved in the design of the scheme and the planning of its implementation.
- Top management demonstrates a full commitment to the scheme.
- Training in appraisal skills is given.
- The appraisal scheme is regularly monitored and amended as necessary, with departmental debriefings ensuring that its operation and outcomes are absorbed into mainstream management activity and produce information that can influence wider employee resourcing processes and strategy.

The overall employee resourcing and development policies and systems

The last point in the above Feedback Notes is crucial: we noted at the start of this chapter that appraisal is part of a wider process. We can reiterate the point now:

> Appraisal should always be planned and perceived to be not an end in itself, but part of wider employee resourcing and development strategy and policies.

The organizational mission, culture and structure

We saw in Chapters 5 and 6 how pervasive the influence of the whole system of the organization is on what happens in employee development. Of the major elements we examined there it is the structure and culture of the organization (or of that part of it within which the appraiser and appraisee work) that have some of the most significant effects on appraisal schemes and discussions. It is no accident, surely, that so many closed, rigid, paper-bound and mechanistic appraisal schemes are to be found in bureaucratic role cultures or that it is so often in task cultures that one hears about innovative and developmental appraisal schemes.

Here is a practical example, showing how a positive and carefully planned interaction between culture and structure, appraisal, and people in an organization can produce a system which ensures not only that development needs are identified and acted upon, but also that high levels of individual and organizational performance are continually reviewed and improved. It is an example taken from the kind of small organization where any kind of formalized appraisal is fairly rare and by no means easy to achieve, not least because of the interpersonal tensions common within small professional workforces. The case study demonstrates the successful adaptation of principles that apply equally well to appraisal in larger-scale organizations.

Appraisal at Newlands Preparatory School
(By permission of Newlands Preparatory School, Gosforth, Tyne and Wear)

Newlands, a day preparatory school for boys in Gosforth, on the outskirts of Newcastle upon Tyne, introduced formal appraisal into the school in 1987, with the objectives of aiding work planning and performance and diagnosing staff training and development needs. The scheme was evaluated three years later and continues to operate effectively, with important consequences for staff performance, employee resourcing and the general management of the school.

The culture and structure of the organization

Since 1977 when it was under threat of closure and a new Headmaster, Nicholas Barton, was appointed, the school (capacity:

235 boys, 4–13½ years old) has rapidly become one of the most highly regarded and successful in the North-East. Although it is committed to being non-selective in its recruitment, with a school population spanning a wide social, ethnic and economic spectrum, and fees lower than most competitor schools in the locality, it achieves consistently outstanding academic and sporting results, has a full waiting list, and attracts and retains talented, enthusiastic and flexible staff.

The school has a task structure. The Headmaster works closely with the governors, who are mainly local business people including some ex-Newlands parents, and are highly dedicated to the school's welfare. They work with him at several levels. The teaching staff function interactively in the wide range of work and activities in which they are involved, and the boys too have important team roles to play, especially the senior groups (aged 11 upwards), with the prefects and Head Boy having responsibilities that keep them in close everyday contact with the staff and the Head. Finally, parents are fully involved, not in any proceduralized way but through a range of initiatives which contribute much to the life of the school and to the enjoyment generated by belonging there, whether as staff, pupils or parents.

The culture of the school rests on values of the family and of enjoying all the opportunities that are offered by the pattern of school life at Newlands to discover and fulfil the pupils' potential. The school is a very happy one, and old boys are frequent visitors throughout the year.

The product

The effort, energy and ability involved in maintaining the success of this small but complex organization is considerable, especially in an increasingly uncertain and competitive environment. For over ten years now, however, the school has maintained a leading position, and has continued to achieve its mission of taking boys of all educational levels and from a wide variety of backgrounds and fully enhancing the development of every child.

The appraisal scheme

In 1987 the idea of introducing formal appraisal was discussed with the staff. Appraisal in the educational sector has always been, and remains, a controversial subject, and at that time it was unusual to encounter formal schemes in the private sector, still less at preparatory school level. However, at Newlands a scheme aimed at helping work planning, training and development was seen as something worth attempting, and one was introduced in 1987 with the support of staff and governors.

The underlying principles have remained unchanged since then, although the form used was amended after the 1990 evaluation to simplify it and make it focus more clearly on work targets and training and development needs. A scheme of bonus awards was introduced at the same time.

The emphasis is on a two-way process, based on self-appraisal, with a form to be filled in by both parties before the main annual discussion in order to clarify their thoughts about work performance, any changes in work roles and tasks, work planning for the next year, and training and development needs, in preparation for the appraisal session. (A sample of the kind of form that could be useful in this context is given in Appendix 8.) The self-appraisal means that the initiative in the appraisal discussion rests with the appraisee. Part of the joint analysis of work performance also includes the individual's assessment of the Headmaster's performance as it relates to his management of and working relationship with them. (His own performance is also appraised by the governors in the context of the report on progress that he presents termly to the full Governors' Board.)

Forms are distributed at the end of the spring term, and appraisals are carried out by the Headmaster during the summer term. Although this involves the Head in about 20 appraisals, lasting two hours each on average, he feels that this activity is essential, ensuring that at least once a year he sits down with every member of his team and spends time on a thorough and wide-ranging discussion of their work and developmental needs, agreeing on future work targets and developmental action, and listening to their views on changes that they feel could be made to the systems and management of the school as these affect their areas of work and concern.

After the annual appraisal discussion, a summary form is completed by the Headmaster and returned to the individual for any comment and final agreement. Both parties keep a copy for future reference, and for the Headmaster to carry out and monitor any action agreed.

Relationship between appraisal and financial rewards

Bonuses at the school (as distinct from allowances for special educational responsibilities) were introduced in 1990. They are felt by governors and the Head to be an important way of recognizing the high level of commitment, achievement and out of hours school-related activity of most of the staff, and they are therefore given in a spirit of recognizing valued staff rather than of trying to improve performance levels.

The difference is crucial – it marks the distinction between using appraisal as a form of control and as a form of development, a distinction to which we shall return later in this chapter. At Newlands, bonuses are awarded for an individual's contribution to the effective overall performance of the school, with the base criterion being the number of hours worked over and above the national norms for teachers. However, that is only a base line: there is a careful analysis of the value of those hours in terms of outcomes for the school.

Valued effort can be of many kinds, in recognition of the different but equally important contributions that can be made by staff. Bonus awards are determined just before the annual appraisal interview, not as a result of it, and can be discussed at that interview if the individual wishes. This method of relating financial rewards to appraisal has worked singularly well since its introduction in 1990, despite fears that, especially in such a small community, it could have divisive and counter-productive effects. Not all staff achieve bonuses, nor are bonuses of equal value. However, the system is accepted as fair, disagreements are both rare and dealt with promptly and openly, and staff appreciate the fact that the governors value the many different types of contribution they make to the school to the point where, very unusually in this sector of education, they will divert to staff some of the direct financial rewards that the school gains from those efforts. The same kind of recognition is evident in a generous pension scheme, which offers transferable benefits between private and public educational sectors.

Outcomes of the appraisal scheme

After the first round of appraisals in 1987 the Head commented: 'I never realized how much I could learn from this!' – a striking example of the learning that can be achieved by the appraiser when appraisal is carried out well. In that first year, appraisals led to significant timetabling and wider organizational changes. Three years later, the scheme was evaluated by asking staff to respond to a brief questionnaire on its perceived aims, design, and outcomes. Much detailed information was obtained from this survey, and while it was clear that the scheme was generally felt to make an important contribution to the effective management of the school, and to the staff's work planning and development, there were inevitable criticisms and suggestions. These led to various changes being made to the paperwork and the processes of appraisal.

The views of staff have continued to prove valuable spurs to organizational and management action, and the overall team culture which helped to produce such a scheme in the first place has clearly been reinforced by its operation (see also Harrison, 1988).

A scheme which focuses on self-appraisal, high standards of achievement, and training and development, and which gives people the opportunity to consider and make suggestions about wider management processes, is particularly important in an organization like Newlands School, for two reasons:

1 It reflects and reinforces the wider team-based culture of the organization (see also the British Airways appraisal scheme, p. 172).
2 It stresses the importance of training and development as a key contributor to excellence in the individual's work.

To summarize:

> In inception, design and operation, the appraisal system should reflect and reinforce the organizational culture and structure, and focus on the key parameters of effective work behaviour and performance.

Planning an Effective Appraisal Discussion

In order to achieve a valid diagnosis of learning needs and a plan of action for the appraisee, the appraiser should plan the discussion carefully. This is not the place for a detailed explanation of how to carry out an appraisal of performance. For a review of that process, see Torrington et al. (1991), Chapter 16, and Fowler (1991). Our interest in appraisal is the part it can play in reaching agreement on an individual's training and development needs. The manager will need to be well briefed beforehand on:

- The individual's performance, and potential for development
- Future department and organization goals and new work coming into the department
- The methods of measuring performance used or to be introduced in the department, and how these relate to the work of the individual
- The individual's career objectives
- The different sorts of developmental experiences that could be provided

During the discussion the manager will need to identify and agree with the individual:

- the work to be done in the forthcoming period and any difficulties already being experienced in such work, or likely to arise for various reasons, and from this analysis, identify important needs that training or some other form of organized learning should tackle;
- any changes that have taken place in the individual's role, tasks or workplace that require a training or development reponse;
- the kind of action that could be taken to progress the individual's long-term career development aspirations.

To obtain this information, the appraisee and the appraiser could, as at Newlands School, consider a number of questions relating to the appraisee before they meet for discussion. These can then form the structure of the discussion itself (see Wilson and Cole, 1990, p. 48). All these questions should focus on the future rather than leading to a sterile preoccupation with past performance.

The appraiser should always examine the needs for training and development related to current work performance and the work plan for the forthcoming period, and also plans for the longer-term, continuous development of the individual. Individuals should be helped to learn how to take control of their own careers, and to think through exactly what goals they seek to achieve. It is in this part of the discussion that counselling, guidance and coaching should take place, no matter how informally. (We shall be looking at the area of career development in detail in Chapter 20.)

There must be clarity about exactly what kinds and levels of knowledge, skills and attitudes need to be strengthened or developed, and how these can be measured to ensure subsequently that training or other forms of development have achieved their objectives. There must also be a commitment to helping the individual subsequently to prepare for the learning events and then at a later point to utilize the learning in the workplace.

Actions finally agreed should:

- achieve the learning objectives;
- meet organizational as well as individual needs;
- be suitable in depth and scope;
- suit the individual's style and skills of learning (see Chapter 7 and 8).

When the discussion is ended, any action agreed should be recorded by reference to:

- The kind of training or developmental experience recommended
- When and for what kind of period it should take place
- The resources needed to support the action (personnel, physical, financial)
- A distinction between job-related training and development, and activities to promote the longer-term continuous and career development of the individual

The appraiser and the appraisee must leave the discussion with a clear and shared understanding of, and a commitment to, the action plan. Subsequently the manager will need to discuss the action plan proposals with any others whose agreement or co-operation will be needed in carrying it out. He will then have to inform the appraisee about the action finally arranged, discuss any proposals which have had to be postponed or cannot be carried out, and ensure that the individual is briefed before specific learning activities take place, and helped on their completion to transfer learning back into the workplace.

Dealing with conflict in appraising for development

The process of reaching agreement on the training and development to be undertaken by the individual can be beset by the kind of problems typically encountered in any exercise involving analysis of performance (see Chapter 13). But there can also be difficulties that arise out of the particular nature of this exercise.

1 **Some appraisers and appraisees may be unable to agree on learning needs.** There could be many causes for this:

- Some appraisees may not admit to failings, and become hostile and defensive at any attempt to discuss them.
- Some may have too low an opinion of their performance and potential, and may lack self-confidence.
- Some may have too high an opinion of their performance and potential, and be over-confident and resentful, seeing no need for training or development.
- Some appraisers may not be skilled or confident enough to deal with these forms of behaviour.
- Some may not know enough about the detail of what the individual actually does in their job, or about technical aspects of it, to feel able to give an appraisal or to diagnose learning needs.

2 **Prioritizing needs may pose problems.** The manager, for example, may think that the appraisee has a major need for interpersonal skills development, whereas the job holder may think that this relates to only a very minor problem, and see other training or development as much more important.

3 **There may be claims of discriminatory treatment.** The appraisee may not be able to appreciate why they are being denied opportunities for development or training that a colleague enjoys. If the appraiser cannot give convincing reasons then clearly the job holder has a justifiable grievance, and in certain cases this could lead to a case for discrimination being taken to an industrial tribunal on the grounds of not being given training or development that would give access to certain job or career opportunities in the organization.

What can be done about such problems? Three major aids are:

1 **Training to tackle common problems and to build up those task and process skills essential for effective appraisal.** Special emphasis should be given to ensuring that all appraisers know how to avoid discrimination in the operation of an appraisal scheme, and appreciate especially the need to keep records to show the patterns of training and development across the workforce, the procedures used to identify needs and provide related learning opportunities, and the outcomes of such action.

2 **The availability of ongoing guidance and counselling to help appraisees try out their new skills and improve with practice.** Note the Nuffield Group's provision of refresher training for appraisers in Wilson and Cole (1990).

3 **The avoidance of a scheme that uses ratings or rankings.** These cause tensions and are not in any case relevant to the analysis of training and development needs except in the loosest sense of noting which needs are essential to be met, and which are less important. In any subsequent collation of recommended action plans, this information will be necessary in order to decide the number, kinds and scope of various learning activities to be offered in the forthcoming period.

It may also be advisable to establish some form of appeals procedure, although some organizations prefer not to do so because of the fear that this in itself gives an image of appraisal being a potentially divisive process instead of a vehicle for joint problem-solving, planning and learning.

The training and development problem

Stage 1

In Appendices 9 and 10 you will find a brief for a manager who is about to move into the analysis of training and development needs during an annual appraisal interview. Having read the brief carefully, imagine that you are the manager, and decide how you are going to run this part of the interview. Give a brief explanation, with special reference to what you think will be the objectives, expectations and attitude of the appraisee. Do not look at Appendix 11 until you have completed this stage.

Stage 2

When you have completed Stage 1, turn to Appendix 11 where you will find the appraisee's brief. It will tell you his expectations and attitudes related to the interview that you have just planned. Please read it carefully, and then look again at your plan.

FEEDBACK NOTES

The basic issues involved in this situation are:

- Mutual antagonism between appraiser and appraisee
- A manager who needs to convince the appraisee of the need for more development of the latter's staff
- A manager who does not initially understand the appraisee's reasons for tackling the appraisal and development of his staff in the way that he does.

The appraiser's main objective should be to help the Quality Assurance Manager to see another point of view, and to accept that he (the appraisee) may need to change his approach in order to get more fully developed people with opportunities to realize their potential.

In order to achieve this the antagonism on both sides must be overcome by a strategy of focusing on objective, job-related issues. You must also uncover the appraisee's reasons for tackling the appraisal and development of his staff as he does, and must be prepared to discuss those reasons constructively, not in a judgemental way. You must try to understand the logic of the appraisee's point of view, and build on that understanding. This means that you must be prepared to accept the possibility that your initial assumptions about the appraisee's feelings, attitudes and management of his staff were incorrect.

How far do you think that you would have been able to obtain the crucial information from the appraisee that is contained in his brief? Tactics to ensure mutual learning are essential in this case, where the perceptions of the two men about one another, and about the central issues, are so opposed.

A self-appraisal strategy that focuses on the individual's own perception and explanation of their performance would be the most appropriate. You will have to practise your listening skills, remembering the need to learn and understand, not to judge. As you are listening and reflecting, you must also analyse ways in which you could bring about some change in the appraisee's views on the development of his people.

Once immediate needs have been agreed, then there should be a flexible discussion as to where his career might go from here and the kind of developmental actions that might be possible in the forthcoming period. Finally, an action plan has to be agreed, and followed up.

The Implications of the Shift towards Peformance Management

Throughout this chapter we have discussed how to use appraisal to identify, analyse and agree training and development needs, together with actions to meet those needs. The discussion has been logical and, I hope, persuasive. However, for those who are interested to take their study of appraisal further, it is perhaps worth introducing some further considerations.

Why is it that, with rather depressing frequency, thorough and effective identification and analysis are not attempted or not achieved, or fail at the stage of implementation? In the new appraisal system introduced for the entire management sector in British Rail in 1988, for example, it seemed as if all the appropriate actions had been taken: simplification of the grading structure; performance-related appraisal and rewards; around five objectives for all managers, one of which must be staff development; annual appraisal with a mid-year review to ensure a check on work performance and on the implementation of agreed action plans; an opportunity then to discuss training and development needs at a stage when there could be open and probing analysis because pay awards were not determined until six months later; and a survey, after the installation and initial operation of the system, whose results were 'generally encouraging', with most managers clear about their jobs and objectives. (Crabb, 1990)

Yet the survey also revealed that 'there was room for improvement on agreeing training and development plans' and that 'many managers were going through the motions and not following through on the results of the reviews'. Why should this be?

One reason, although it is unlikely to be the only one, is that there may not have been any training for the scheme – none is mentioned in Crabb's article. However, a more fundamental reason is probably the evident tension within the scheme between aims to do with control and aims to do with development. This tension is becoming a familiar phenomenon in performance management schemes, especially those – and they are increasing (Bevan and Thompson, 1991) – that are tied to individual performance-related pay.

The aim of performance management is to control: to control the targets that are set for people, and the standards that they reach; and to control their performance by rewarding what is assessed as up to standard, while withholding rewards from what is judged below standard.

The control often extends to behaviour, and is evident in many appraisal schemes, not only those that are part of a performance management initiative. The need to relate appraisal to the culture of the organization has been emphasized, and in the Newlands School example we saw the attractive face of such a scheme. However, expressed in a rather different way, appraisal is, of course, a strategy to prescribe and enforce the values, attitudes and styles of behaviour that top management have decided are desirable in employees in order to ensure their conformity to corporate values and goals. Many reports now appear on schemes that measure behaviour as well as task performance (e.g. Mumford and Buley, 1988), and a major thrust of assessment centre methodology, increasingly widely used in organizations searching to acquire and maintain a competitive edge and a more efficient, 'committed' workforce, is to measure personality variables in relation to the kind of behavioural style sought by the organization (see Chapter 20).

Without perhaps meaning to do so in quite this sense. Fombrun et al. (1989) make this aspect of appraisal very clear in their chapter (Chapter 7) on executive appraisal, notably where, concerning appraisal of managers, they write:

> The ability of the organization to successfully select, develop, and reward depends to a significant extent on its ability to identify the

> proper characteristics or behaviours of managers, to evaluate performance based on these criteria . . . and finally to distribute its rewards based on performance differentials (Ibid., p. 106).

Allied to the effectiveness of appraisal as a mechanism to enforce control in these ways, it is also a formidable method of reinforcing the power of superiors over their staff. (For a full discussion of this, see Townley, 1989, pp. 98–108.) We have already noted that it is the appraiser-appraisee relationship that is crucial in determining the outcomes of appraisal. We discussed this in terms of attempting to improve that relationship. However, remembering that life in organizations, as elsewhere, is very much about politics and power, it has to be understood that appraisal is a powerful instrument that can be abused in the interests of personal power. Again, we read in Fombrun et al. comments which, although unlikely to have been made with these points in mind, none the less reinforce them:

> Much of the determination of where an employee's loyalty will be driven will rest with who controls their access to organizational rewards (Ibid., p. 108).

The authors follow this with another, particularly important, observation:

> Organizations should understand that they can move the organization on the centralized-decentralized continuum by redistributing the power to appraise the performance of key staff personnel (Ibid., p. 109).

Townley (1989) makes the same point. She observes the increasing trend towards decentralization, notably in the NHS and local authority systems and emphasizes the need for the top of the organization to ensure that the autonomy given to the decentralized units is being used in ways that conform to the organization's overall values, culture, mission and business strategy. Appraisal offers a vehicle for the maintenance of corporate power and control, most of all when it is tied to systems of performance management within which there is an emphasis on performance-related pay, and which focus on behavioural as well as task aspects of performance.

The kind of appraisal carried out for purposes of controlling a system is not, in principle or in practice, the kind most likely to achieve development. At most it will result in the identification of, and action related to, the most urgent job-related training needs. The concern of controlling managers will naturally be to achieve improvements in current performance (and indeed Long's 1986 research showed a marked shift in appraisal schemes towards that objective), to ensure that their units achieve short-term, usually six-monthly or annual, targets (especially where performance-related pay is involved), and to make their workforce measurably more productive and efficient (especially where there has been delayering of that workforce). For some of them, an equal or greater concern will be to use the system to reinforce their personal power over their subordinates.

There is convincing evidence to show that some of these concerns are in fact felt quite widely, and at the expense of any but the most short-term forms of training and development – a theme we pursued in detail in Chapter 3. Bevan and Thompson (1991), describing the most recent large-scale research undertaken into performance management, make the issues very clear. They are discussing attempts to achieve an integrated approach to performance management in an organization:

> We are able to discern two broad thrusts to this emerging integration process. These different approaches we categorize as 'reward-driven integration' and 'development-driven integration'. The former approach emphasizes the role of performance payment systems on changing organizational behaviour and tends to undervalue the part played by other human resource development activities. This would appear to be the dominant approach . . . The second approach – development-driven integration – stresses the importance of ensuring that appropriate HRD activities are in place to meet the long-term objectives of the organization and, furthermore, to ensure that business needs and HRD are co-ordinated . . .
>
> There is a strong possibility that the tension between the two integrating processes may cause both to malfunction and that the reward-driven strategy will dominate at the expense of the development-driven strategy (Ibid., p. 39).

Where does this leave us in our attempt to identify and analyse individual training and development needs through an appraisal scheme? Perhaps with a recognition that a scheme, and a system within which it operates, may appear to be well designed, with all the right incentives and allocation of managerial responsibilities to ensure success in identifying and meeting such needs; yet the end result may still seem to be unsatisfactory. The reasons for this will probably lie in the fundamental nature of the aims of that appraisal activity. Increasingly these are about the maintenance of corporate power over a decentralized structure or the exercise of control over the values, attitudes, behaviour and priorities of various sectors of the workforce, with a focus on shorter-rather than longer-term performance.

Finding an explanation may not mean that the problem will be solved, but it does at least reassure us that the cause of the problem is not always a lack of skill in appraisers, or the poor design of an appraisal scheme.

Exercises

1 What do you see as the key elements of a staff appraisal system which is aimed primarily at identifying training needs and improving work performance? What 'rules' would you print on an appropriate report form, and why? (May 1991)

2 (For students taking specialist modules where there is a focus on appraisal.) Discuss the tensions between appraisal for control and appraisal for development by reference to their causes, and to an appraisal system in your own organization or one with which you are familiar.

References

ALBAN-METCALFE B M. 'Micro-skills of leadership: a detailed analysis of the behaviour of managers in the appraisal interview'. In *Leaders and Managers: International perspectives on managerial behaviour* (Hunt J G, Hosking D, Schriesheim C A and Stewart T, eds.). New York, Pergamon. 1984. pp. 179-99

ANDERSON G, YOUNG E AND HULME D. 'Appraisal without form-filling'. *Personnel Management*, February 1987. pp. 44-7

BEVAN S AND THOMPSON M. 'Performance management at the cross-roads'. *Personnel Management*, November 1991. pp. 36-9

CRABB S. 'On the right track to high performance'. *Personnel Management Plus*, August 1990. pp. 14-15

FOMBRUN C, TICHY N AND DEVANNA M A. *Strategic Human Resource Management.* New York, Wiley. 1984

FOWLER A. 'How to conduct appraisals'. *Personnel Management Plus*, June 1991. pp. 22-3

GEORGE J. 'Appraisal in the public sector: dispensing with the big stick'. *Personnel Management*, May 1986. pp. 32-5

HARRISON R. 'Nick Barton, special agent of change'. *Personnel Management*, February 1988. pp. 46-50
LONG P. *Performance appraisal revisited.* London, Institute of Personnel Management. 1986
MUMFORD J AND BULEY T. 'Rewarding behavioural skills as part of performance'. *Personnel Management*, December 1988. pp. 33-7
RANDELL G. 'Employee appraisal'. In *Personnel Management in Britain*, (Sisson K, ed.). Oxford, Blackwell. 1989
SCOTT B. 'Evolution of an appraisal programme'. *Personnel Management*, August 1983. pp. 28-30
TORRINGTON D, HALL L, HAYLOR I AND MYERS J. *Employee Resourcing*. London, Institute of Personnel Management. 1991
TOWNLEY B. 'Selection and appraisal: Reconstituting "social relations"?'. In *New Perspectives on Human Resource Management*, (Storey J, ed.). London, Routledge. 1989
WILSON J AND COLE G. 'A healthy approach to performance appraisal'. *Personnel Management*, June 1990. pp. 46-9

Further useful reading

FLETCHER C. 'What's new in performance appraisal'. *Personnel Management*, February 1984. pp. 20-2
FLETCHER C AND WILLIAMS R. *Performance Appraisal and Career Development*, Hutchinson. 1985
LAUD R L. 'Performance appraisal and its link to strategic management development'. *Journal of Management Development*, Vol. 3, No. 4. 1985. pp. 3-11
MEYER H H. 'Self-appraisal of job performance'. *Personnel Psychology*, Vol. 33. 1980
RANDELL G A, PACKARD P M A AND SLATER A J. *Staff Appraisal: a first step to effective leadership.* 2nd ed. London, Institute of Personnel Management. 1984
ROBINSON K. *Effective Performance Review Interviews: A self-help guide.* London, Institute of Personnel Management. 1983. (A brief but excellent guide for practitioners, particularly helpful for its ideas about what to do during and after the development discussion)

Chapter 15

Selecting the mission and strategy for a learning event

Learning Objectives

After reading this chapter you will:

1 know the stages involved in the inception, design and delivery of planned learning events;
2 be able to draw up an overall purpose and behavioural objectives for a learning event;
3 know how to produce a profile of a learning population and relate this to the choice of learning strategies;
4 understand the practical issues affecting the choice of learning strategies.

Planned Learning Events

In Chapters 7 and 8, in our discussion of the organization as a natural learning system, we saw that it is not necessary to have formalized training or planned learning events for valuable learning to be achieved; using ongoing work as a vehicle for continuous learning can develop individuals, groups and the organization as a whole, both immediately and in the longer term. We saw how the organization can be managed in order to promote such work-based learning, and how attitudes and practice conducive to continuous development in the workplace can be generated.

However, in all organizations there will be a need for some planned learning events, and it is with the design of these that the next three chapters are concerned. In these chapters the term 'learning event' will be used to mean any learning activity which is formally planned and delivered in order to achieve specified learning objectives. It therefore covers training courses, educational programmes, coaching sessions and other situations in which planned learning is promoted.

Figure 10 shows the nine stages involved in the inception, design and delivery of a learning event. In Chapters 11–14 we covered the first stage; in this chapter we shall cover Stages 2–4; in Chapter 16 Stages 5–7; and in Chapter 17 Stages 8 and 9.

Figure 10

Stages in the inception, design and delivery of planned learning events

1 Confirm needs.

2 Agree on the overall purpose and objectives for the learning event.

3 Identify the profile of intended learning population.

4 Select the strategy, and agree on the direction and management of the learning event.

5 Select learners and produce detailed specification for the learning event.

6 Confirm the strategy and design the event.

7 Deliver the event.

8 Monitor and evaluate the event.

9 Assess organizational payback.

As we saw in Chapters 11–14, needs can be identified in a number of ways, relating to both a current situation and future contingencies. Once needs have been agreed and prioritized, there must be confirmation that some form of learning event is required to meet those needs. The next stage is to clarify the purpose and overall objectives of learning.

The Purpose and Overall Objectives of Learning

The overall purpose is another way of expressing the mission of the whole learning event, while its overall objectives explain the outcomes which it has to achieve. It is essential to define purpose and objectives clearly, since these provide the context of the learning event. If there are errors at this stage, then expensive resources are going to be wasted in carrying out irrelevant activities.

> The overall purpose of a learning event answers the question *why* the event is taking place, whereas its objectives define *what* attitudinal, behavioural or performance outcomes are to be achieved by that event.

Ideally, the designer of the learning event should have been involved in formulating its learning objectives, in line with an overall purpose which has already been agreed with a 'client' in the organization. In reality the designer may have to work to objectives that have already been established by someone else. This can pose many problems if, even when it seems clear that objectives should be changed or modified in some way, such change seems impossible. Here is a case study whose content is based on fact. It represents a situation which will be familiar to many students and lecturers.

X College and the course review

X College was concerned at its consistently poor level of examination success in a three-year part-time professional course. An internal review produced the following information:

1 The national professional body in question had become preoccupied in the previous four or five years with producing 'competent practitioners' rather than, as in the past, knowledgeable and informed students who would develop skills from that knowledge base once they moved out into their first professional 'apprentice' posts.

2 With this changed overall purpose, the learning objectives for the national professional examinations had also become very skills-orientated. However, the final method of assessment remained what it had always been: a series of formal examinations. The questions in these examinations required students to show not only what they knew, but also to explain what they would do, in relation to specific situations. The format of each examination, however, remained a conventional three-hour, closed-book paper, with a choice of four out of ten or twelve questions.

3 Students who did well in the examinations tended to be those

with proven academic abilities, whether or not accompanied by professional competence, rather than those who had been found to be competent in a variety of practical activities and assignments on the course and in their workplace roles.

4 The skills-orientated objectives called for classroom, material and staffing resources which the course tutor, struggling with the large classes that the college's financial situation required him to recruit, and with inadequate staffing ratios, could rarely obtain. Access to film, closed-circuit television, video or computer equipment was difficult, because of the scarcity of those resources compared to the demands made on them; technical support was also patchy and unreliable.

5 New students were very heterogeneous in their existing skills and knowledge in relation to the course content, as was to be expected in such a large part-time course. They also had widely varying levels and types of learning skills and styles. Several had no ongoing experience at all of one or more of the key subject areas, so that practical activities during class time provided the only medium through which they could be helped to acquire such experience. Visits to organizations were usually out of the question, because of the large numbers of students, and because of timetabling problems. Good outside speakers were highly valued but little used because of their cost: staff tended to rely largely on voluntary speakers, whose performance was variable.

The review concluded that the examination failure rate was understandable in the circumstances, and was likely to continue until such time as the professional body concerned could be persuaded to reconsider the overall purpose of its examinations, or the learning objectives, or the type of assessment system which was used, and until the college put more resources into the course.

In time the professional body, while confirming the purpose and most of the overall objectives of the course, did alter the structure and methods of assessment. A new emphasis was placed on developing competences and assessing them through continuous assignments and various skills-based assessed activities. The final assessment of students was expanded to include a major work-related project. Resourcing, however, remained a problem, as for so many colleges.

In this case study, note the influence exercised by the overall purpose and the learning objectives of the professional course in question. Discrepancies there started off a chain of difficulties which led, in the end, to unsatisfactory outcomes for the whole complex learning event. If the tutor and staff had looked more critically at purpose and objectives before designing the college's course, they could at the least have alerted the college to the likely problems they faced. Given sufficiently powerful arguments there might then have been some reallocation of resources, or the beginning of a dialogue with the professional body concerned that might have led more quickly to the eventual review of the purpose, objectives and methods of assessment.

We can conclude our examination of this case study by stating that:

> The designer of the learning event should always challenge its purpose or overall objectives if they seem inappropriate in some important way.

Levels of objectives

Except in very simple learning situations, it is helpful to formulate learning objectives at two levels: final and intermediate.

1 **Final behavioural objectives.** Sometimes known as ultimate, or criterion or overall objectives, these explain the kind of outcomes which the learner should have achieved once the learning event is completed.

2 **Intermediate behavioural objectives.** Sometimes known as interim or specific objectives, these explain the kind of outcomes which the learner should have achieved at key stages of the learning process.

You may have noted the use of the phrase 'behavioural objectives' in the above definitions; also the reference to 'outcomes'. This is because the clearest guide to design can be obtained, not so much by stating what the learning event aims to do in general terms, but by closely specifying what the learner should be capable of by the end of parts or whole of the event.

To illustrate this point, consider the difference between two ways of defining one of the objectives of this chapter:

- One of the aims of this chapter is to explain the term 'learning objectives'.
- After reading this chapter and completing the various activities it contains, you should be able to understand what is meant by

'learning objectives' in order to be able to draw up objectives for a learning event.

From the reader's point of view, the first definition says what the chapter aims to do, but only in a very generalized way, with no explanation of intended outcomes. On the other hand, the second gives concise information on the outcomes. It should therefore act as a stimulus, by explaining what they will be able to do by the end of the chapter (providing, of course, that the learning outcome is something they want to achieve).

From my own point of view, if I had simply been given the brief set out in the first example, it would be hard to decide what to put into the chapter. However, with the second it is clear that a simple explanation of 'learning objectives' will not be enough. I know that I must help the reader to understand the meaning of the term 'learning objectives', and then to make practical use of the concept. So I will have to build in a variety of practical illustrations (like this one) and exercises as well as theory.

So expressing objectives in behavioural terms clearly identifies not only what the learning event aims to do, but what sort of skills, knowledge or attitudes it will help the learner to acquire and the kind of content and methods of learning that will be relevant.

> Behavioural objectives give a clear focus to the learning event and to its design by explaining the outcomes it will help the learners to achieve.

Objectives should indicate the conditions under which the learners will ultimately carry out the learning, and the standards they will need to reach. We can therefore say:

> The most helpful behavioural objectives are those which describe not only the kinds of behaviour to be achieved at the end of the learning event but also the conditions under which that behaviour is expected to occur and the standards to be reached in that behaviour.

Identifying the Profile of the Intended Learning Population

Once the needs, general purpose and overall objectives of the learning event have been agreed, the type of learners to be involved should be identified. At this stage little may be known about individual participants – selection for the learning event will probably come at a later stage. What will be known is the sort of numbers likely to be involved, the levels of the organization from which they will be drawn, and the kinds of learning strategies likely to be most relevant for them.

Information should at this stage be sought on four aspects of the learning population; subsequently, when participants have been selected, this information will need to be expanded and the design of the event adjusted as necessary:

- Numbers and location
- Jobs and competences
- Learning styles and skills
- Attitudes and motivation

Numbers and location of learners

Small numbers should facilitate relatively individualized learning. However, the location of the learners will be important here: a small number spread over different, and widely dispersed, locations could indicate a need for some form of distance learning, with occasional workshops to bring the group together (see, for example, the Sales Training Programme proposed by Hugman in Harrison, 1992a). On the other hand if it is important that, although widely dispersed in a physical sense, these learners form a cohesive group and establish a strong team identity through the vehicle of the learning event, then it would be better to have a course, or modular courses, or some form of learning that is delivered through a series of meetings where they all come together. If it is a small group from a single workplace, the best strategy may be to arrange the event around their work location, or in proximity to it. On the other hand, it may be desirable to take them away from the work environment and focus their attention on wider issues – which may argue for one or more external, residential events.

> The numbers and location of the learners must, therefore, be viewed in the context of the purpose and objectives of the learning event in order to help decide on an appropriate learning strategy.

Jobs and competences of the learners

At this early stage, it is important to acquire as much information as possible on the kinds of jobs held by the learners and their general level of competence in those jobs. Once individual learners have been selected, a more detailed analysis will need to be carried out.

Learning styles and skills

We looked at learning styles in Chapter 8. We noted Honey and Mumford's (1986) four-fold categorization system, but it should be remembered that people can usually develop learning skills in more than one mode, and that some learners can move easily between the four modes, able to learn equally well in any of them.

While little may be known at this stage about specific individuals, none the less the types of jobs held by the proposed learning population, together with their overall age and ability range, their length and type of experience, and other similar information will give useful insights into the types of learning styles and skills they are likely to have. This information will indicate those situations and methods most likely to promote stimulating and effective learning for them.

In selecting a learning strategy – and later in designing the detail of learning events – it is important to consider not only how the event can build on the learners' primary learning styles and learning skills, but also to what extent the event should itself seek to change those styles and skills. Honey and Mumford's work (1986), for example, has indicated that trainers as a profession tend to be activists rather than reflectors or theorists. If this is the case (and getting a particular learning group to complete the Learning Styles Inventory and send it to the designer some time before the learning event begins should give some helpful indicators), then any event seeking to train trainers should aim to redress that imbalance by involving learning experiences that will promote styles and skills in all four modes, rather than simply encouraging continued dependence on and preference for only the activist approach to learning.

When a learning event calls for learning styles and skills of a fairly high order, and the type of learner who will be involved is unlikely to have reached the required level, then a study skills input can serve a very useful purpose before the main event begins, or even a full foundation course which introduces the main topics but at a lower level, thus developing the skills over a longer period of time and in a different way.

Attitudes and motivation

Even at this early stage, enough will probably be known about key behavioural aspects of the intended learning population (rates of absenteeism and turnover, performance levels, reactions to earlier learning events and any conflict patterns) to assess their likely motivation. Little useful learning can occur if the individual does not want to learn, so it is important to assess the probable needs and expectations learners will bring to the learning event, and to take these into account when choosing an overall learning strategy.

Motivation can be considered under two headings (Gagne, 1965): social motivation, and motivation related to task mastery.

Social motivation

This relates to the social situation in which the learners are placed: their social needs, characteristics, problems and types of relationship with each other and with the training staff. All these factors will affect their motivation during the learning event. For example, designing a course in a new and difficult area of skills for a group of employees, whether from the same or from different organizational departments or levels, calls for skilful use of social factors.

If the learners are brought together into a cohesive group from the start, sharing expectations and concerns, it will help to build up an atmosphere of social supportiveness which will stand them in good stead as they try to master the various learning tasks. Many organizations, including colleges and universities, hold outdoor development periods towards the start of training or educational programmes. The aim is to bring participants together and bind them into a cohesive social group, motivated to tackle a long-term learning experience as a team rather than as a heterogeneous collection of individuals, and to develop appropriate learning styles and skills. Outdoor development periods can also be used at key points during a long learning event, as a way of consolidating and progressing learning in key areas (see Arkin, 1991a and c; and *Personnel Management Plus*, 1991).

Another approach, often used in conjunction with outdoor development work, is to help individuals to develop personal learning goals and plans that relate to the learning event as well as to outcomes that they value at a personal level. Skilfully done, such an exercise should result in greater motivation because the learning event's direct relevance to their needs is clearly established (see Chapter 20).

Motivation related to task master

This raises the issue of what drives different learners to succeed. Some may seem to be spurred on by a need to 'win', and achieve most in a competitive learning situation; others may be stimulated by any opportunity to learn something new – a 'curiosity' motive. While classifying learners in such ways may prove to have considerable practical value in some design situations*, generalized assumptions must be avoided. As we saw in Chapter 13 (pp. 295–9), performance is the final outcome of a complex interaction between a person's needs in a particular situation, their perception of the results they want from it and the rewards they perceive that will obtain by achieving those results, and their effort, energy and ability in that situation. The design of any learning event must pay careful attention to those four factors in relation to the specific learner group.

In Chapter 16, where we look at motivation at the more individualized level, there is a practical checklist to help the designer and trainer in the task of achieving and sustaining learner motivation, and of stimulating them to master their learning tasks.

When selecting an overall learning strategy, the following points about motivation should be considered. Depending on the extent to which they are likely to be present in a particular learning population, considerable flexibility may have to be built into the learning system selected, so that adjustments to the planned content, delivery and focus of certain components can be made just before, or even during, the event.

1 **Unpredictability.** Motivation will vary, often significantly from one group of learners to the next, even with types of learning events that have often been run before.
2 **Individual differences.** There can be significant individual differences in motivation and expectations within a group of learners.
3 **Dynamism.** Motivation is dynamic, often changing during the course of the learning event.

* See Otto C P and Glaser R O *The Management of Training*. London, Addison-Wesley. 1972 for a detailed classification system of this kind.

The strategy chosen must allow time for careful monitoring of learning events. Time must be spent before, at the start of, during, and at the end of key events in diagnosing the needs and expectations of the learners, and in responding to them. This requires close collaboration between designer and trainer (if the two processes are carried out by different people) from the outset and during monitoring stages, so that any motivational problems that do arise can be carefully analysed, and the style, pace or content of the learning event adjusted accordingly.

Let us end this section by tackling a real-life consultancy assignment (although minor details have been changed to ensure the anonymity of the client organization). The main purpose of this exercise is to reinforce the learning we have covered in this section. However, because the assignment itself is about appraisal, you should reread Chapter 14 before starting the exercise and refer to it to help you with it.

The retail store's appraisal project: part 1

You are a management consultant, and you have just been invited to visit the big local branch of a national retail store in order to discuss the possibility of carrying out training in appraisal skills for about 15 managers and supervisors. The work is to be done in the next two months.

You arrive at 9.00 a.m., and are met by the Personnel Officer, an IPM-qualified woman of about 55, well-liked by employees, and a long-serving member of the staff. She tells you that the Managing Director (MD), with whom you are both going to spend the morning, is new to the job, having been appointed six months ago from a senior management position in another chain of stores. He is 38, a high flier, with an impressive record of success behind him. He is already establishing himself as a man of action, open, committed to increasing the store's turnover, and full of ideas about how that can be done. Once he makes a decision he puts it into practice at once. He wants to make a major impact on the store, with results coming through in 18 months at the most.

Throughout the subsequent discussion the Personnel Officer says very little, since the aim of that discussion is for the MD and yourself to talk about the proposed assignment, and arrive at some conclusions about it.

You start off by asking the MD to explain what the assignment is about. He replies that he wants you to 'train all the managers and supervisors in appraisal so that I can find out what their performance really is, get a few standardized disciplinary procedures sorted out, diagnose training and development needs, assess potential, and get the managers working together as a team'. He wants the training done within the next two months.

He explains that the store, a long-established one, is profitable but that its turnover has declined in the last five years, and competition is increasingly severe. It has had a paternalistic role culture for some years, and this has stifled the drive and initiative of its managers and supervisors, most of them long-serving employees in their forties and fifties. A few have become complacent, because profits are still good (owing to price increases and customer loyalty).

When the new MD arrived, there were some redundancies at all levels of the store, approved though not initiated by him, and a makeshift appraisal scheme was used to determine who should go. This caused quite a lot of trouble and has led to a belief in some quarters that the MD himself is a hatchet man, with a list of those he intends to get rid of in the next year or so. This is, in fact, a mistaken belief: the MD is genuinely determined to build up a high-calibre, committed and enthusiastic team of people who will regain the store's hold on the market. He has already reduced the management hierarchy from five to three levels, and having given early retirement on advantageous terms to three directors, has reorganized their jobs and brought in two new directors in their early thirties, who work closely with him, and are fully committed to his way of doing things. His style is open and positive. He sets high standards and rewards those who achieve them, while seeking to understand the reasons for poor performance before passing any judgements. His views on appraisal can be summed up in the sentence, 'I may not know much about the detail of appraisal, but I know what I want it to achieve for me.'

He says that he wants to start off with closed appraisals, because he thinks anything else at this stage would be 'too threatening'. By closed appraisals he means that each appraiser should produce a written report on their staff; that report may or may not be followed up by an appraisal discussion with the staff concerned, but in any event, staff will not be able to see the reports. The reports will then 'be pushed through the system', to enable him to see what sort of skills and potential exist in his workforce, and what kind of performance is being achieved, as well as examining needs for training and development. The MD adds that he does not want a complicated ranking system on the reports, just something simple and understandable.

He wants to be involved in the training. He himself is appraised by the Chief Executive of the chain of stores, and appraises his two directors. He intends the appraisal system to stop at supervisory level, with supervisors being appraised but not, at this stage, appraising levels below them.

You have broken off the discussion for lunch, and are due to resume in a couple of hours. What issues will you then raise with the MD, and what will you try to achieve during your discussion with him, in order to reach agreement on the task that you will help the organization to carry out?

FEEDBACK NOTES

The initial discussion between the consultant (myself), the MD and, later on, the Personnel Officer in reality took almost a day. However, at the end of that time the crucial issues had been straightened out, leaving the way clear for agreed action. Obviously you will have all sorts of ideas about how to tackle the discussion, and all I can usefully do, therefore, is to tell you the major issues that any similar discussion needs to confront, and how they were actually dealt with in this case.

The overall purpose of the learning

The first issue to clarify is the true reasons for the consultancy assignment. At present there is no clear overall purpose, and there is also an inconsistency in objectives, so that many questions relating to the initial need for training must be asked. There is also a confusion in terms: the MD refers at one point to 'appraisal' and at another to 'assessment', as if they are the same activity, whereas to the consultant they are quite different activities, the former related to examining current work performance, the latter to diagnosis of potential. Terms must be defined at the outset and a common language developed if any lasting agreement is to be reached between the parties.

What is the MD really after? He mentions the need to find out about people's abilities and performance, but also a need to develop fair disciplinary procedures. He refers to a need to discover people's potential, but also a need to find out their training and development requirements. He talks about a major need for teamwork, but then refers to closed appraisals. These are mutually contradictory needs. Too many of the results he wants from appraisal would appear as threatening to his managers and supervisors and would result almost certainly in their opposition to appraisal and to any training related to it.

A discussion of this issue did, in fact, lead to agreement that what he most wanted was to introduce appraisal as an aid to reviewing work performance, helping work planning, and diagnosing training and developing needs. If this could be achieved as a first step, then establishing effective disciplinary procedures, sorting out how to perform assessments of potential and so on could be tackled at a later date, when confidence had built up in the least threatening process, that of appraisal related to current work and to training and development, and when an appraisal scheme was working well. This part of the discussion also looked at what was meant by the terms 'appraisal' and 'assessment'. The MD realized he had been using the terms indiscriminately, and once the distinction between us had been clarified and agreed, many other things became clearer, and a shared frame of reference and language began to develop between us.

The learning objectives

The next issue is the behavioural learning objectives. The MD has referred to 'appraisal skills training', but what, specifically, are to be the outcomes of any training that takes place? Initially, his one answer, that his managers should be able to operate a closed system of appraisal, presupposes three things: that there is an appraisal scheme already in existence, to which training can be related; that it has the support of his managers and supervisors, so that they will welcome training; and that closed appraisal is consistent with his overall purpose of using appraisal as an aid to reviewing work performance, helping work planning, and diagnosing training and development needs.

Discussion of this issue took a long time, but in the end significant progress was made. It emerged that:

- There was no appraisal scheme worthy of note – the one used for selection for redundancies was agreed to be unsuitable from every point of view.
- Therefore before skills training could take place, an appraisal scheme would have to be designed.
- Closed appraisal, especially coming at this particular time, would be viewed with great suspicion. It would be far better to involve the managers and supervisors in the design of an appraisal scheme, opening up the entire design as well as the operational process from the start. Such an approach would also be consistent with the MD's other major need, to bind his managers and supervisors together into a close-knit managerial working team. The design task could start to build up that relationship.
- If the objectives of the appraisal scheme were simply to do with work review and planning and the diagnosis of training and development needs, then no rating or ranking system related to performance was needed. Furthermore dispensing with it would further reduce the fears of the managers and supervisors that there was some ulterior motive behind the exercise.

Profile of the learning population

The third issue is the learners. What are their characteristics and situations in relation to the consultancy assignment? It is vital to get as much information about them at this early stage as possible, in order that the whole of the learning task facing the consultant is clearly understood.

Discussions on this issue confirmed that the managers and supervisors were mainly in the 40–50 age range, and that most had been with the store since youth. In terms of learning styles and skills, they had no management training or education, although they had whatever technical and professional qualifications were needed, and they would tend to be activists in the learning situation, distrustful of theories and simulated situations unless these were very clearly relevant to their work situation.

As to motivation, over the last ten years with a rather old-fashioned, complacent and authoritarian leadership right at the top, some managers had become disillusioned and pessimistic about their futures. Others felt that they had received little support from the top in their attempts to perform efficiently and effectively, and this bred a lack of confidence as well as confusion and some stagnation. Overall, energy and excitement were at a low ebb, and although the MD had a high opinion of their real levels of ability and potential, it was essential to restore their original enthusiasm and excitement. Also, one or two seemed to see no need to work harder or differently from the way in which they worked at present. What therefore would be the incentive for them either to design an appraisal scheme, or to undergo skills training for it – or indeed to do any of the things desired by the MD?

The MD believed that the motivation would come as they began to realize all the possibilities that lay before them: a market which they could start to win back and develop; the opportunity to become a small, cohesive, high-calibre and high-achieving professional team, with rewards for those who proved their worth in meeting challenging standards. It was also evident as he spoke that he was quite determined that appraisal would be introduced; he was totally committed to both the concept and the reality. Furthermore, his two directors would be positive in their support for the initiative, and this would do much to convert any apathy, suspicion or apprehension into a willingness to experiment, and a commitment to try to make appraisal work, once there was a belief that this was not just one more 'flavour of the month' technique but a strategy offering real benefits.

In terms of relevant skills and knowledge, few of the managers (including, said the MD, himself) knew anything much about appraisal.

The agreement reached with the MD

The final issue was to establish, after all this discussion, what the learning strategy should actually be and how it should be implemented. The following agreement was reached:

1 The consultancy assignment would proceed in stages, with both consultant and client able to withdraw at the end of any stage if that seemed necessary or desirable.

2 Stage 1 would consist of initial information-gathering by the consultant, to determine whether the kind of diagnoses made in this initial discussion were valid, or whether other needs and problems existed which called for a review of the tentative conclusions reached at this stage.

3 If the diagnoses did prove to be valid, then the consultant would run a workshop for all 15 managers and supervisors, with the aim of working with them to design a simple appraisal scheme for the store. Initially it would be a pilot scheme, covering only managers and supervisors. If subsequent evaluation proved positive, it would then be extended to the rest of the store. Recommendations for a scheme would be presented to the MD at the conclusion of the workshop, in order that he could present a report on them to the Board of Directors.

4 Stage 2 would consist of appraisal skills training, to develop those skills needed to introduce and operate the pilot scheme. The details of that stage (which again would fall into the two components of initial information-gathering and a workshop) would be determined once a decision has been made on whether or not the consultant was to go ahead and carry out that stage.

5 Stage 3 would take place once a pilot scheme had been introduced and was under way. It would consist of a review day in which consultant, management team (which included those titled 'supervisors') MD and Personnel Officer would come together to review the scheme's operation and agree on any further action needed.

Thus agreement between consultant (myself) and client (the MD) was reached by a process of jointly identifying the real learning needs and agreeing on:

- The overall purpose and objectives of learning
- The profile of the learning population
- A learning strategy

Note how important it was for me to do what was advised early on in this chapter: to challenge learning objectives if they seem inappropriate in some important way.

Selecting a Strategy, and Agreeing on the Direction and Management of the Learning Event

As we saw in our discussion of NVET (Chapters 2 and 3), strategy is the route to be followed in order to achieve the mission. In the case of a learning event, 'mission' means the overall purpose and general objectives. Learning strategy therefore involves looking at alternative ways in which the purpose and objectives of learning can best be achieved and then choosing the kind of events and delivery pattern which seems most likely to achieve them.

In the case study the learning strategy agreed on was one of helping the learners to design their own appraisal scheme, using the consultant as a facilitator; and then of providing skills training to enable appraisers and appraisees to operate the scheme effectively. In order to enhance teamwork and develop the learners as managers, the strategy included taking the whole management group away on two residential workshops, rather than organizing learning events for some or all of them within the workplace itself.

Strategy must take practical considerations into account. These relate to resources, the management of the learning events, and the organizational climate in the workplace.

Resources

We have already dealt with learning resources in Chapter 10. They involve internal and external training resources, the time available for the learning event, and the natural learning opportunities that exist in the workplace.

Alternative learning strategies must be analysed in relation to their likely cost, the time they will involve, and the extent to which they will utilize and relate to learning in the workplace.

Direction and management

Different strategies will make different demands on expertise, so there must also be an analysis of how a particular strategy will need to be managed: how many people will be needed to carry out the work involved in design, direction and control, administration, delivery, and evaluation, and who they should be. We dealt in detail with many aspects of the management of learning in Chapters 9 and 10, but we should note here that if the learning strategy to be pursued is one of training courses, then internal or external specialists will have to provide them, and will need careful briefing and management throughout. If the strategy includes an educational programme using day or block release, then there will have to be effective liaison with the educational institution concerned. Any requirement to assess workplace competences and then use them for accreditation purposes will need extensive preparation, including the training of workplace assessors (see Arkin,

1991b). If there are to be elements of work-related learning, or a strategy of continuous development, then relevant experiences and the best way to organize them must be agreed with the managers concerned, and it will probably be advisable to establish mentor roles.

> What matters most is that design and content are agreed between the key parties as being fully relevant to the pupose and objectives of the programme, and to the type of learners concerned; that they are feasible and cost-efficient; and that ways of transferring learning to the workplace are agreed and put in place before the programme begins. (Harrison, 1992b)

Agreement must also be reached on how, at what stages and by whom monitoring and evaluation of the learning event will be carried out (see Chapter 17).

The culture of the organization

Finally, what is the climate of the organization, and especially of that part of it from which learners will be drawn, in relation to different strategic possibilities? As we have seen, there has to be a particular organizational culture, as well as policies, procedures, roles and skills, if continuous development through the integration of learning and ongoing work is to be an effective strategy. An organization planning to move into the delivery of learning through computerized systems and distance learning packages will have not only to set up the administrative machinery to make that strategy possible, but also to prepare people – both learners and their managers – who have only thought of learning in terms of conventional training or educational programmes, to see the benefit of these approaches. It will also have to decide how they can best be organized and the learning from them be effectively transferred to the workplace.

The culture of the workplace, too, needs to be one that will support learners who come away from a learning event with new knowledge, new skills, perhaps changed attitudes. Cultures are slow to change, and those who have 'been away' on a learning event may find invisible and possibly impenetrable barriers awaiting them on their return. New learning must be fertilized if it is to take root, and too often that process does not occur because no one in the organization has seen the need to preprepare the ground beforehand (see, for example, Webster, 1990).

An example of the importance of all these practical issues in designing a learning event can be shown by looking further at the case study on which the previous exercise was based.

The retail store's appraisal project: part 2

Once the overall purpose and learning objectives had been agreed in outline, the MD, the Personnel Officer and I spent considerable time together deciding how to carry out Stage 1 of the project. The discussion revolved around resources, and the following points emerged:

Direction and management of the project

The management of the project was agreed without difficulty: the MD would approve the overall parameters of each stage, leaving the Personnel Officer and me to work on the detail relating to staffing, materials and physical accommodation.

I would determine the detailed behavioural objectives, both final and intermediate, of each workshop, and would be entirely responsible for its design and running. I would return six or so months later to carry out a one-day review (Stage 3 of the project) with the workshop members, and the Personnel Officer would arrange pre-workshop and post-workshop briefing and debriefing sessions for all workshop members and their managers, with special reference to following up action agreed in the workshop. The Personnel Officer would also organize longer-term evaluation, a year after the whole project had ended.

Staffing posed some problems. It needed more than one person to run the workshops, both at Stage 1 (designing an appraisal scheme) and at Stage 2 (developing appraisal skills). The Stage 1 workshop required one other tutor, and the one at Stage 2, if it was carried out, would require four tutors in all. It was eventually decided that the Personnel Officer would act as co-tutor on the first workshop. It was agreed to leave the matter of staffing of Stage 2 until a decision had been made about whether or not that stage would, in fact, go ahead.

Another resourcing problem was that for the Stage 1 workshop, there would have to be either one event for all the course members, with the Personnel Officer and me there throughout the two or three days, or two events, with half the membership attending one and half attending the other, staffed by the Personnel Officer and me throughout on both occasions.

The direct cost of running the first option was less than the cost of running the second (because it would only involve one lot of fees for me, and only one sustained period of absence for the Personnel Officer instead of two); but the difficulty of releasing all 15 store staff at the same time, together with the obvious indirect costs incurred with these key people all away from their departments for three days during a week, might make the second option necessary. On checking the dates when the course members and I would all be available at one time, it became clear that the first option could not take place within the two-month period initially desired by the MD.

On the other hand, the second option would take longer to carry out than the first, and this again brought us up against the time factor. It would also split up the learning group, when an important objective was to keep them together in order to build them up as a work team. And if the workshop could be carried out over a long weekend, then the problems of all the managers being away from the store together would not arise.

Physical resources

The materials and equipment needed for the workshops were available, and they constituted a relatively cheap part of the programme. Accommodation proved more difficult; the store had conference accommodation, although of limited size, and at first the MD felt that, for obvious cost reasons, all workshops should be held there. We then discussed the psychological advantages of taking the whole management and supervisory team of 15 away from the store to a local hotel for the duration of the workshops. The relationship between myself and the course members, which it was so important to cement quickly, given the demanding task they jointly faced, would benefit greatly from such a location. The social, as well as task mastery, motivation of the course members would also receive a strong and continued boost. Equally important, managers and supervisors would be together as a team for a sustained period, away from their usual work situation, and this would be a very positive way of starting to develop the managerial team identity that the MD saw as so crucially important. This strategy was subsequently agreed by the MD.

Finance

A maximum budget for the entire three-stage consultancy project, was agreed, based on tentative costings I produced. The budget was tight but not absolutely inflexible; it did, for example, allow for the possibility of some increase in initial costings over the period of the three stages. However, financial considerations did pose certain problems related to staffing the workshops, as I explained above.

Organizational climate

After discussion, it was agreed that it would be sensible to proceed more slowly than orginally hoped in order to give time for a positive climate about appraisal to be developed in the store. The MD also decided that the objective of building up a strong managerial team from the start was more important than his wish for the whole project to be concluded quickly. It was therefore decided that there should be just the one workshop, involving all 15 people, spread over a long weekend, as outlined above, with a relaxation of his initial timescale, so that Stages 1 and 2 would be spread over a five-month instead of a two-month period. This timescale would have the final and important advantage of allowing time for a considered decision to be reached after the end of Stage 1 on whether or not to proceed to Stage 2, rather than rushing it and possibly getting it wrong.

I hope that this case study has helped to demonstrate how important practical issues – resources, management and organizational climate – should, in conjunction with an analysis of learning purpose and objectives and of the profile of the learning population, help to decide the choice of an overall learning strategy in a particular situation.

Exercises

1 Draft a handout for distribution to either

(a) established trainers attending a course on distance learning methods; or
(b) line managers attending a course on 'on-the-job coaching'.

The handout should summarize the main learning outcomes of the course, and offer a source of reference for those who wish to apply their new learning within their own organizations. (May 1991)

2 Draft a statement in which you outline the significance of assignments in the IPM Professional Education Scheme, and the learning methods involved. Incorporate suggestions whereby this element in the scheme might become more useful for both future students and your organization. (May 1989)

3 For what purposes would you expect a manufacturing organization to patronize 'outdoor education' courses such as those run by the Outward Bound, Brathay Hall and Leadership Trusts? How would you suggest people attending such courses should be briefed before, and debriefed after, attending a course of this kind? (November, 1988)

References

ARKIN A. 'Great outdoors'. *Personnel Management*, August 1991a. pp. 49-51

ARKIN A. 'Turning managers into assessors'. *Personnel Management*, November 1991b. pp. 49-51

ARKIN A. 'The course of strategic HRD'. *Personnel Management*, December 1991c. pp. 47-8

GAGNE R M. *Conditions of Learning*. Eastbourne, Holt Rinehart and Winston. 1965

HARRISON R. 'Employee development at Barratt'. In *Case Studies in Personnel* (Woodall D and Winstanley D, eds.). London, Institute of Personnel Management. 1992a

HARRISON R. *Developing Human Resources for Productivity*. Geneva, International Labour Office. 1992b (in press)

HONEY P AND MUMFORD A. *The Manual of Learning Styles*. 2nd ed. Maidenhead, Peter Honey. 1986

OTTO C P AND GLASER R O. *The Management of Training*. London, Addison Wesley. 1972

PERSONNEL MANAGEMENT PLUS. 'Outdoor training'. *Personnel Management Plus*, March 1991. p. 25

WEBSTER B. 'Beyond the mechanics of HRD'. *Personnel Management*, March 1990. pp. 44-7

Further useful reading

BASS B M AND VAUGHAN J A. *Training in Industry: The management of learning*. London, Tavistock Publications (Behavioural Science in Industry series). 1967

BLOOM B S. ed. *Taxonomy of Educational Objectives: Cognitive domain*. Harlow, Longmans. 1956

GILLEY J W AND EGGLAND S A. *Principles of Human Resource Development*. Maidenhead, Addison Wesley. 1989

KENNY J, DONNELLY E AND REID M. *Manpower Training and Development*. 2nd ed. London, Institute of Personnel Management. 1979

KENNEY J AND REID M. *Training Interventions*. London, Institute of Personnel Management. 1986; third edition, by Reid, Barrington and Kenney, 1992

KRATHWOHL D R, BLOOM B S AND MASIA B B. *Taxonomy of Educational Objectives: Affective domain.* Harlow, Longmans. 1964

NADLER L AND NADLER Z. *Developing Human Resources.* London, Jossey-Bass. 1989

ROBINSON D G AND ROBINSON J C. *Training for Impact.* London, Jossey-Bass. 1989

ROMISKOWSKI A J. *Designing Instructional Systems.* New York, Kogan Page. 1981

SIMPSON E G. *Taxonomy of Educational Objectives: Psychomotor domain.* Champaign, University of Illinois. 1966

TAYLOR B AND LIPPITT G. *Management Development and Training Handbook.* London, McGraw-Hill, 1983

Chapter 16

Designing and delivering the learning event

Learning Objectives

After reading this chapter you will:

1 understand the issues involved in the selection of learners;
2 be able to define specific learning objectives for a learning event;
3 be able to apply practical guidelines related to the principles of learning to the design and delivery of the learning event;
4 know how to design a learning event.

In this chapter we continue our analysis of the nine stages involved in the design of learning events shown in Figure 10 (p. 327) by looking at Stages 5, 6 and 7.

Selecting Learners and Producing a Detailed Specification for the Learning Event

Selecting the learners

Often the choice of learners will be out of the hands of the person planning and designing the learning event. However, if selection or criteria for selection are within their control, then they should focus attention on the overall purpose and objectives of the event, identifying those for whom the learning outcomes will clearly be of most benefit and whose existing competences, attitudes and learner characteristics indicate that they will be able to cope well with the level and kind of learning involved.

A training course intended to update the skills of experienced computer operators will not suit new recruits with deficiencies at the basic levels of competence; an MBA intended for high-flying executives about to enter the ranks of senior management is not likely to meet the needs of those with only one or two years in a specialized job, or of established middle managers looking for a course offering a range of useful managerial techniques and skills whereby they can improve current job performance.

Mistakes in selection for a learning event are often made. The danger is probably greatest with externally provided courses, because when places are hard to fill the temptation is strong for the provider to accept nominees or applicants whose needs or abilities do not match the course profile. The menu-driven approach to the provision of learning events will always tend to result in insufficiently discriminating selection procedures and experience has taught many organizations to be more critical not only of external providers but also of many internal training functions whose stance is one of selling 'off-the-shelf' products rather than demonstrating a wish and an ability to meet the needs of a clearly defined group of learners.

A major source of information about the extent to which potential learners are in fact 'trainable' and how their potential not only for training but for development thereafter can be assessed is a trainability test.

Trainability tests for manual workers were pioneered by Sylvia Downs at the Industrial Training Research Unit at Cambridge.

> The trainability test comprises the detailed instruction of a job applicant in a piece of work which is part of the job being applied for. The applicant then has to perform the task without any further assistance while under scrutiny from the instructor. He or she is rated according to the number and type of errors made while performing the operation. (Kilcourse, 1978)

Trainability tests have the following special features:

- They are designed to include parts of the training which trainees find difficult, as well as elements of the job itself.
- They involve a structured learning period.
- They include the use of detailed error checklists written in behavioural terms.

(Downs, 1984)

Thus the focus is on how the individual learns the task. 'They weed out those who are untrainable or who will take too long to train to acceptable standards.' (Kilcourse, 1978)

There are four factors that need to be considered before a decision is made to use trainability tests. All involve weighing costs against the need for a high degree of discrimination in selecting learners. The main concern should always be the individual's suitability not so much for the event itself, as for the position, responsibilities or situation for which that event is a preparation. It is the match between the individual and that ultimate situation that is the crucial issue. The four factors are:

1 **Cost.** A trainability test is a specialized instrument. Each job has to have its own test, so the expense can be high.

2 **Design and validation.** Tests need to be carefully designed and validated, so those who administer them must be fully trained – another high cost element.

3 **Time.** Trainability testing is very time-consuming and therefore, again, expensive.

4 **Insurance.** Special attention must be given to insurance against accidents for non-employees who take the tests.

In spite of these provisos, there is no doubt that trainability tests have proved to be a major aid to selection and training in a wide range of manual jobs, especially in the clothing industry. A very positive evaluation exercise involving tests in the mining industry has been carried out by Cowling and Gripton (1986).

As for non-manual jobs, work is being done in developing trainability tests for supervisory and managerial positions, and in this connection task observation, while not amounting to full trainability testing, can provide useful information about existing levels of ability in certain key tasks. The individual is asked to perform a typical activity which is an important part of the total job (for example, an applicant for a managerial position may be put through an in-tray exercise, or asked to present a brief report on a particular topic to a board of directors) and their existing level of competence is then assessed. Work sampling of this kind, taken to its logical conclusion, leads to the comprehensive and structured methodology of assessment and development centres, which will be briefly described in Chapter 19, and which can provide another useful, if expensive, method of selecting for entry to learning events.

Specifying the learning required

This takes us back to Chapters 12 and 13. The knowledge, skills and attitudes required in the job, and needed by the particular group of learners, must be identified and analysed so that a clear specification is produced of the gaps that the learning event needs to fill. The nature of those gaps, and fuller information about the type of learners than was initially available, will enable a final decision to be made about the learning strategy to be used, and learning objectives can be clearly defined for each discrete stage of the learning event.

Here is an example of the planning and design of a complex and lengthy learning event, to demonstrate some of the key points made in the previous chapter and in this one so far.

Planning and designing a management development programme for clinical directors
(By permission of the Northern Regional Health Authority and Durham University Business School)

Figure 11 demonstrates the pattern of activity that led to the successful design and operation of a complex management development programme run collaboratively by the Northern Regional Health Authority (NRHA) and Durham University Business School (DUBS) for clinical directors in the region during 1991–3. (Initial information on this programme was given in Chapter 8 – see p. 178.) It also shows the main components of the programme. The programme was nationally funded, so decisions about learning strategy and the general structure of the programme had to be made at the stage when funding was being applied for – in the event, a year before the programme itself actually began. Detailed planning and design were, however, only undertaken once selection for programme members was underway.

Purpose

The purpose of the programme, which was run on a pilot basis and evaluated by two external bodies as well as by the NRHA and DUBS, was to help to prepare senior consultants, some already in a clinical director role, others shortly to move into it, to fulfil the managerial demands of that role to the benefit of their departments and units, and ultimately of patient care. There were 24 participants, split into three intakes of eight in order to ensure a very individualized learning system, fully responsive to their needs.

Figure 11

Northern Regional Health Authority – Durham University Business School Consultants' Management Development Programme

Processes and components of Programme 1

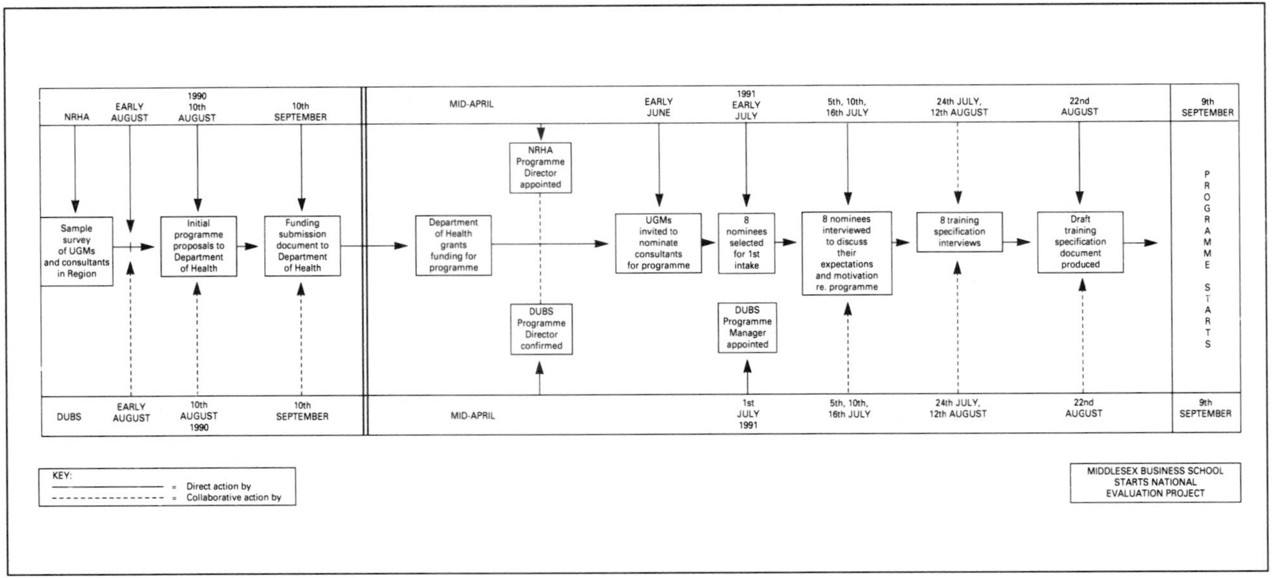

Figure 11 *continued*

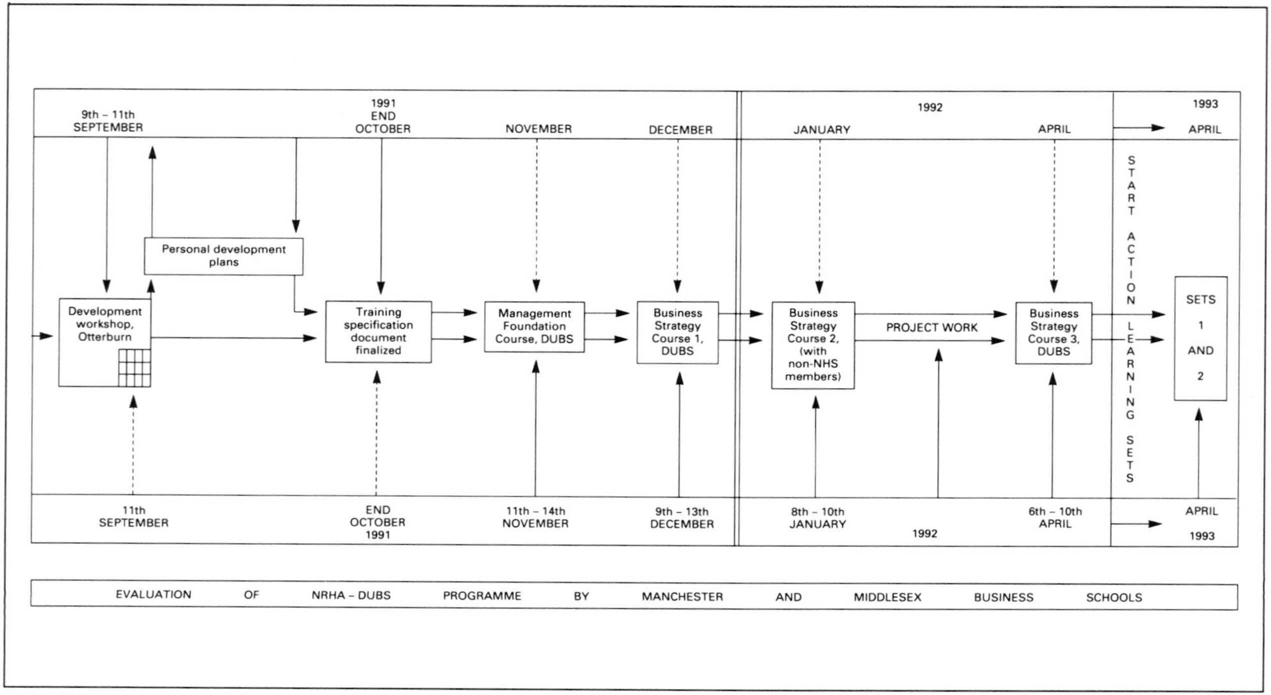

Analysis of the learning needs of the job and the participants

In order to design the programme effectively, a training specification was produced by NRHA and DUBS programme planners, using a wide range of information both about the new role of clinical director and about the first eight consultants selected to come on to the programme. Producing the specification was a difficult task, since the clinical director role, a new one within the radically changed NHS structure introduced in April 1991, had little official documentation at any level, and proved to be different in its interpretation and operation across virtually every organization where it existed. The first eight participants, too, were extremely heterogeneous in their professional, managerial and personal characteristics. Lengthy interviews were held by NRHA and DUBS staff with each of them and with their managers, to identify the needs and expectations of these key parties in relation to the programme. This exercise was repeated with each intake, and adjustments to the ongoing programme were made accordingly.

Flexibility in relation to content and to methods of delivery was a major key to the ultimate success of the programme. The training specification was kept in draft form until just before the first Business School component in order to include in it final items of information about the strength and prioritization of individual needs that were obtained during a three-day diagnostic workshop organized by NRHA staff. The workshop incorporated team-building work done through an outdoor development period, analysis of a previously completed computerized assessment questionnaire about each consultant's managerial competences and needs as identified by themselves and a sample of their managers, subordinates and peers, and work on personal learning goals and plans.

The training specification made it clear that the first formal learning event at DUBS, the Management Foundation Course, must ensure that the consultants developed a common understanding about 'management' and basic knowledge and skills related to organizations as systems, the management of change, and the management of self and others. This shared understanding encompassed also a common language about management which underpinned the more advanced work they had subsequently to do on business strategy and planning. Project work reinforced and extended the three subsequent and interlocking Business Strategy modules of the programme, one of which took the form of a skills workshop where the course membership was expanded to include eight senior executives from non-NHS organizations, and where the focus was on a range of interpersonal, negotiating and influencing skills.

At the conclusion of the formal components, the programme moved for a 6–8-month period into action learning groups (see Chapter 20; Mumford, 1991; Revans, 1971) where major workplace projects were chosen as the learning vehicles, and sets of four consultants, each with a trained set adviser, utilized learning from the programme, experience from the workplace, and the knowledge, skills and support of their set colleagues to develop their ability to plan, implement and progress those projects effectively.

Every major learning event in the programme – the diagnostic workshop, the Management Foundation Course, the three Business Strategy courses and the action learning period – had its own stated purpose and three or four clearly defined learning objectives. Within each component, objectives were also established for each main element. These objectives, both of parts and of the component as a whole, became the criteria against which the learners were asked by the programme planners to evaluate the component.

In this case study, the focus was on the overall purpose, objectives, learner population and learning strategy chosen for a complex learning event. Little has been said about the resources, timescale and organizational climate which affected the choice of strategy and the organization of the programme, although each of those had a major impact, and continued to do so throughout the programme. Little has been said, either, about the detailed design of the various parts of the programme. This brings us to the sixth of our nine stages in designing and delivering learning events.

Confirming Strategy and Designing the Learning Event

Confirming strategy

By this stage enough information will be available to confirm or change the learning strategy initially proposed. Although in most cases confirmation will be all that is required, from time to time it may be that the more detailed information gained when analysing jobs and examining the needs of the learners selected to come on the learning event indicate that the strategy originally proposed is not appropriate. Occasionally the information may even indicate that changes need to be made to the original objectives or purpose of the learning event. Such indicators should never be ignored, or the whole viability and effectiveness of the proposed learning event may be at risk.

Designing the learning event

As has just been seen in the case study, designing the learning event requires first that each component of the event needs to have clear behavioural objectives which, when achieved, will mean the achievement of the overall purpose and final objectives of the event as a whole.

There are then many factors that influence design. We will now examine how to choose the content, media and methods of learning events, and how to apply general principles of learning to their design.

Choosing content, media and methods

The learning content will be determined by the training specification (or its equivalent) and the learning objectives for each component of the event. This information should make clear the level and kind of knowledge, skills and attitudes to be achieved in each component, and the standards against which learners will be measured. The media and methods of transmitting content to the learners then have to be selected.

We can make the following distinction between media and methods:

- The media of learning are the routes, or channels, through which learning is transmitted to the learner.
- The methods of learning are the ways in which that learning is transmitted.

Learning media and methods – often called learning technology – can often leave much to be desired. For example, in the 1987 ITD media awards the standard of entries proved to be too low to justify gold awards in any but one category. Announcing the winners at the presentation ceremony, the ITD treasurer Ken Gardner said that lack of adequate support material, unsuitable choice or use of the medium and an inadequate statement of objectives, of the target audience, and of methods of use were the main weaknesses. He added that in several cases expensive well-produced programmes, made by commercial companies, were aimed at such broad audiences that they were probably ineffective within any sector. This is a telling indictment, which indicates that lack of skill in crucial areas of training is far more widespread than many would suppose, and extends to a considerable number of external professionals whose services would be a significant cost to any organization employing them. The more training staff working within organizations develop expertise, interpersonal skills, credibility and cost-effective approaches to the design of learning events, the less likely it will be that their organizations will have to bear the consequences of such expensive mistakes.

The opposite danger, perhaps, is to become so immersed in the pursuit of new training technology that the fundamentals which make for a successful learning event are forgotten. In the first of *Personnel Management*'s new section on training and technology, Nick Rushby, head of the Training Technologies Unit at Sundridge Park Management Centre, wrote:

> I have an uneasy feeling that training technologists become too concerned for the glamorous technology – to the detriment of the training, and of the necessary process of innovation which involves much more than providing alternative ways of training. (Rushby, 1988)

Let us now look at some of the most widely used media and methods. Figure 12 shows some major media together with examples of the kinds of methods most frequently associated with them. Obviously a learning event can use several media and a great variety of methods. For example, an external management course would be, by definition, using the off-the-job medium. However, like the NRHA-DUBS Clinical Directors' Programme it might include a significant element of work-related project work, to be completed when the manager goes back to the workplace, so there it would also be using the on-the-job medium. Furthermore, it might rely heavily on the oral medium, and also make significant use of the medium of printed texts.

On the other hand, virtually the entire programme might be off the job, but reliant on a mixture of radio, television, and printed texts, as with the Open University's Effective Manager Unit. So:

> One learning event may use several media as well as a number of different methods.

Figure 12
Some media and methods of learning

MEDIA	METHODS
Oral (spoken word)	Talk, lecture, discussion, seminar
Printed (written word)	Handouts, books, distance learning texts
Radio, TV, computers	Wide variety of methods
On the job	Learning from a supervisor or fellow worker; picking up learning by trial and error; using a training manual or a self-administered training package; coaching; job rotation
Off the job	Any learning event organized away from the place where the learner does their everyday work
Vestibule	Simulated work situation, in a training room or centre or other premises near the workplace

For a full discussion of media and methods, Torrington (1983) has a most informative chapter, and Kenney and colleagues are, as usual, very helpful (1979; 1986). There are also many articles in personnel and training journals, a few of which are listed in the References section in order to demonstrate the topics which are at present of particular interest to designers of learning events. One of the clearest and most practical discussions I have read is in Gagne's book (1965), and again in what follows I have been influenced by his ideas.

It is important to be clear that there is no one best medium or method, whether in relation to a particular kind of learning objective, or of learner, or of learning event. Certain media and methods may enjoy current popularity. For example, computer-assisted learning methods are in vogue because of their increasing availability and cheapness, the stimulating interaction they offer between the learner and the learning material, and the fact that they are adaptable to the learner's needs in terms of time, place, pace and feedback. Open learning can be described as a generalized medium, to which maximum publicity was given in the 1980s by the wide variety of MSC sponsored Open Tech projects and by the Open College initiative. Within the open learning medium, distance learning is a widely popular method, which may be used through the media of television, radio, cassettes, printed texts and computerized instruction courses. In this connection it is interesting to note that part of the Open College scheme involves a national Distance Learning Centre, to which all learners will have access through a great many local and regional access points.

However, no matter how popular a medium or method may be at a particular time, there is no evidence to suggest that any one medium or method is generally superior, so other criteria for choice must be found. A simple three-point checklist will act as an adequate guide to the designer. We will illustrate its use in an exercise.

Designing a one-day workshop on time management

It has been decided to hold a workshop on time management for up to 20 members. It is to be held off the job in the company's training centre. The learning objective is that course members should, by the end of the day, know and be able to use about six methods of time management in the organization of their daily workload. How should it be designed?

FEEDBACK NOTES

Consider the purpose and objectives of the learning event and the characteristics of the learners.

Clear learning objectives will tell you about the sort of situations to which the learner will have to respond after completing the learning event, and the specific behavioural outcomes that the event must help the learner to achieve. These situations and outcomes must be built into the learning event in some way, and this will give you ideas about appropriate media and methods. There will by now be more information available about the learners than at the earlier stage when all the designer knew about was a generalized profile. It will therefore be possible to identify the characteristics of the learners fairly closely, and select those media and methods most likely to succeed with them.

Learning styles and skills will have a major influence on how well the learners can organize and control themselves in relation to the learning event, and on how effectively and efficiently they are able to bring their attention to bear on the learning process and make progress in learning. Learning styles and skills are usually formed at quite an early age, and this leaves little possibility that they can be rapidly altered to suit the needs of a particular learning event. Initially, therefore, the design of a learning event should build on existing styles and skills. For example, many learners may find distance learning hard to cope with, but can learn quite effectively in a face-to-face learning medium; those who do not learn well when lectures predominate may respond much better to more active forms of learning like group and practical work of various kinds supplemented by work-based projects; those who cannot review their own learning processes can be helped to do so by using a learning styles inventory, and by regular discussion with a trainer or 'mentor' about how they are coping with the learning situation, which learning processes they most or least enjoy, and why.

The spoken word could be used as a primary medium, with methods ranging from lectures to one-to-one tuition and guidance, and including large or small group work with or without tutors at particular points in the learning process. Alternatively the oral medium could use methods like audio cassettes or a video to transmit information, depending on how effective these are likely to be given the particular group of learners concerned. Case study work based on learners' real-life situations will be useful learning vehicles, but in-tray exercises are likely to be even more effective, since they offer exact simulations of everyday reality.

Consider the principles of learning and their practical application

Here we should recall the importance of four factors in achieving effective learning: drive, stimulus, response and reinforcement (see pp. 153–6). For a workshop like this, which media and methods would ensure the most effective learning system?

Perhaps orally guided instruction would achieve better stimulation and reinforcement of learning, whereas printed instructions alone may not be clear enough for some of the learners. Or perhaps a printed list could act as a back-up to the oral medium? If the learning has to be done quickly, but the results applied immediately in the work situation, then undoubtedly the learners will need some form of written record, and to ensure accuracy, a *short* printed list given out by the tutor will probably be of real value to all of them.

When thinking about whether to use case studies or an in-tray exercise, prior discussion with some of the learners may well reveal that they would prefer the in-tray exercise, and would find case studies too artificial (no matter how carefully designed) and time-consuming. The in-tray exercise may take just as long, but will offer highly transferable learning, stimulate the learners, and help them achieve and reinforce correct responses.

So at this second stage we have narrowed the field of choice by selecting those media and methods that look as though they will best incorporate the main principles of learning.

Consider practical issues

We must look at what is most feasible by reference to our total budget and to the learning environment. Remember here the importance of the culture and structure of the organization, which may favour some media and methods, while rejecting others. For example, some senior managers may not support external courses as a way of developing their subordinate managers, while other may see such courses as an essential part of the developmental process. We must also obtain data on the past effectiveness of certain media and methods, and on their current effectiveness in other organizations which use them for similar learning situations – and so on.

At this point we may discover that one of the best methods of starting off our day on time management, given previous experience with similar groups, is to give the learners about an hour around the table to take it in turns to explain briefly what they hope the day will achieve, and particular problems they have encountered in time management. Focused group discussion of this kind is an extremely cheap as well as an obviously effective learning method. In the same way all the other media and methods are checked out against this third criterion, and final choices are made.

To summarize, when selecting media and methods of learning the designer should consider:

- The purpose and objectives of the learning event and the profile of the learners
- The principles of learning
- Practical issues

Most learning events need a combination of different media and methods, and must be flexible enough to enable changes to be made if learning problems develop.

Applying principles of learning to the design and delivery of learning events

We have already mentioned the importance of considering the basic principles of learning when choosing media and methods. Let us now look more closely at this very important issue. There are eight important points that can act as guides in relating principles of learning to a practical situation. In discussing them I am drawing significantly on Gagne's (1965) ideas; his book not only offers a scholarly and clear discussion of the psychology of learning, but also excellent practical advice about the design of learning events. The eight points are shown in Figure 13.

Figure 13

An eight-point checklist for applying the principles of learning to the design and delivery of learning events

1 Design an appropriate structure and culture for the learning event

2 Stimulate the learners

3 Help understanding

4 Include appropriate learning activities

5 Build on existing learning

6 Guide the learners

7 Ensure that learning is retained

8 Ensure that learning is transferred

Preparing a talk

There are a number of practical points to be observed in designing a learning event in such a way as to incorporate the four main principles of learning. If you are preparing a talk, what general guidelines should you follow in order to ensure that it really helps them to learn? One might be to stimulate the learners to make the talk interesting enough to gain and keep the attention of the audience throughout.

Now try to produce six or seven more.

FEEDBACK NOTES

Using the eight-point checklist, we can prepare in the following way.

Design an appropriate structure and culture for the talk

We have already discussed the concept of structure and culture in relation to the wider learning strategy. In this context, 'structure' means the framework of the talk: the way it is shaped and the type of interactions planned to occur within it.

Structure also refers to how tightly or loosely controlled by the tutor this learning event should be. For example, where active participation is particularly desirable in a training programme, how structured or unstructured should that programme be? Should the learners actually decide for themselves (given certain learning objectives, resources, and a timescale) what the design, content and learning media and methods should be, virtually running the event themselves, and using the tutor as a resource and final reference point? Or, at the other end of the scale, should there be close control over participation, so that where, for example, group work is used, it is tightly organized, and feedback is engineered by the tutor to lead to the conclusions that the tutor wants to achieve?

Culture is about the ways in which tutors or managers of the learning situation and the learners themselves are expected to behave in relation to one another and to the learning event; it is also about the values they share in relation to the learning.

Stimulate the learners

To stimulate the learners initially, you should help them to relate to the overall purpose and the learning objectives of the event; if they cannot identify with those, then the basic drive to learn will be missing. To ensure continued stimulation, consider choosing from a variety of methods like films, slides, discussions or practical activities of other kinds. Think also about how to emphasize the most important parts of the talk so that they stand out. This is what is called giving perceptual distinctiveness to key parts of the learning event.

Remember the three particular issues related to motivation that we discussed in Chapter 5:

- Unpredictability
- Individual differences
- Dynamism

Even in giving a short talk we should allow for continuous adjustments to keep the audience interested. Remember that it is the first and last few moments of a talk that make most impact – so make sure you get the essence of your message across at the start, and repeat it at the end!

Help understanding

Choose your content so that it strikes a chord with the audience. Meeting on common ground will mean that they will more easily understand what you are trying to get across to them. Again learners can be helped to understand what is being taught by seeing from the start how it relates to them and their interests or preoccupations. Thus clear objectives should be given at the start, together with a brief outline of the content, before going into the talk in detail. Thereafter, try to illustrate your main points in ways that will help the learners to relate them to their own needs and experiences and so ease the task of learning. A brief summary at the end will round the talk off and, hopefully, fix its essentials in their memory.

Include appropriate learning activities

Well-chosen activities are important to stimulate people, to aid understanding, and to give opportunities for practice. Even in a short talk, small activities can be built in that will help people to grasp and remember the key points: pausing to invite questions from the audience; showing an overhead slide containing key points for discussion; distributing information before the talk, and asking for it to be read and questions prepared on it.

Build on existing learning

Try wherever possible not to contradict or fight against the existing skills, knowledge and attitudes of the learners. There is almost always *some* area of ability or experience which they can apply in the learning situation, or some attitude that will positively help them in dealing with it. A simple question like, 'Does anyone know anything at all about this, just to give us a lead in to the discussion?' can elicit quite a variety of responses, providing that it is phrased in such a way as to reduce fears of being singled out for any kind of rigorous questioning.

Guide the learners

It is essential that the learners should have feedback and guidance available as they move through any learning event, from a talk to continuous development in the workplace. This is for four main reasons:

- To **reinforce** key learning points or stages
- To help **overcome difficulties** with the learning
- To give learners regular **checks** on their learning progress
- To maintain **motivation**

With long events such as modular courses or educational programmes, the need for this kind of help and support will be proportionately greater. The tutor will not only have to be technically competent in instructional functions, but also skilled at the interpersonal level in order to build up and maintain a supportive relationship with the learners. Once this has been achieved, the whole learning task becomes a joint effort rather than a didactic experience, and the tutor becomes an enabler and resource.

Ensure that learning is retained

There are two major issues to consider here:

1 **Practice.** Practice reinforces learning until the point is reached when the new behaviour patterns become habitual. But how much practice? The concept of learning curves is useful here, even in the context of a short talk. A learning curve means the average amount of time it takes a particular type of learner fully to master knowledge or skill, or to demonstrate changed attitudes. Learning curves vary greatly from task to task and person to person, being related to the difficulty of the task, the characteristics of the learner and the duration and spacing of practice.

   Learner characteristics do not just refer to the skills and knowledge of the learners, but also to their attitudes, their learning styles and skills, and their motivation. All of these will have considerable effects on the rates at which they are likely to master particular kinds of learning, and therefore on the amount and spacing of practice or repetition of information they will need.

   We can rarely give the ideal amount and spacing of practice in relation to *every* piece of learning that must be acquired. We must choose the areas of learning which are most important or most difficult, and give priority to those. Thus, for example, in this chapter I have not built exercises and examples of various kinds around every learning point, only those which are either the most important, or can be expected to be the most difficult for the average reader to understand. The activities and examples are also spaced out in order to give variety and interest to what would otherwise be a mass of material that most readers would find less and less interesting and easy to absorb as the chapter went on.

   With these considerations in mind, you should build up a store of information about learning curves in relation to the sort of learning events in which you will be involved. Past performance and reactions of different sorts of learners in relation to learning events should give acceptably valid indicators of the sort of practice periods to build into the learning event, and the way in which those periods should be spaced. Where such information does not yet exist, then careful examination of the three key factors should produce valid conclusions:

- The difficulty of the task
- Learner characteristics
- Practice periods

However, careful monitoring of the learning process will always be necessary, with a flexible enough event to allow for changes to the duration or sequencing of practice periods if this should become necessary. One audience may absorb most of your talk in minutes, while another has problems which require you to expand, illustrate and interact for very much longer!

2 **Reward or punishment?** A response can be reinforced positively by a reward or an attempt may be made to 'punish' an incorrect response. Quite simple rewards for the learners, such as a smile, a word of praise, a pat on the back, may be enough to reinforce correct performance or behaviour in the learning situation. However, it is also important to explain why they have been successful, in case they have only achieved the correct response by chance.

The punishment of incorrect responses, on the other hand, is less predictable in its consequences. A critical comment, a harsh word or more obvious types of punishment may frighten or shame the learner into renewed efforts to succeed, but equally they may cause negative reactions which inhibit further learning. In the extreme case the learner may simply give up. Usually, failure is in itself punishment enough. To correct it, slow demonstration by the trainer, followed by repeated practice by the learner, may be effective, or a repetition of the initial instruction session, using slightly different methods, or a joint discussion of precisely what the learner has found to be an obstacle, and how they may be helped to overcome it. There are a great many ways in which initial failures can be overcome, and confidence and motivation sustained, providing always that the basic ability is there.

Where the ability is lacking, or there is no drive to learn, there has probably been a selection error which may prove impossible to deal with in any way except by the removal of the learner from the programme. There should, therefore, always be provision for the counselling and guidance of learners in any except very short learning events, and exit points and procedures must be designed for longer programmes. In your short talk, you will need to give the audience points at which they can actively participate, in order to ventilate any problems or complete misunderstandings and deal with them at the time rather than let them gather momentum throughout the whole period.

Ensure transfer of learning

Even with a short talk, the aim should be for the audience to take away something that can be of use in relation to their workplace situation. In a broader context, transfer of learning from a previous job or experience into the new learning situation will be positive if that previous job or experience provides skill, knowledge and attitudes that can be used in the new situation. It will, however, be negative if previous knowledge, skills and attitudes cannot be used, or are actually counter-productive. Thus a manager who has previously managed people successfully in a unit or small-batch production firm may find it difficult to see why he needs to learn how to manage people in a mass production system. Yet Woodward (1980) makes it clear that the differences between those two types of technology are so significant that they present many learning needs to such a manager. However, his attitudes and previous experience may put such barriers in the way of learning new attitudes, knowledge and skills that there is only a negative transfer of learning.

At the end of the learning event (where learning has not been continuously integrated with work, but has been separately organized) learning must be transferred to the learner's real-life situation, and this too can be difficult. To a significant extent, successful transfer will depend on ensuring:

1 **Appropriateness of the purpose and objectives of the learning event.** If the event is one of questionable relevance to the learner's needs, or beyond their capabilities to master, or has not been agreed with their manager, then transfer is unlikely to occur.

2 **Relevance of learning throughout the learning event.** This can be done by reference to the guidelines explained above.

3 **How far learning outcomes are achieved.** Learning cannot be effectively transferred if it has not been fully mastered, so checks, tests and discussions, are some of the many ways to measure achievement.

4 **How far learning is used after the learning event.** To prepare the learner for the event, there should be a pre-event briefing with their manager, establishing what the purpose and objectives of the event are, how they relate to the learner's needs, how the learning will be used in the work situation once the learner has finished, and agreeing on any preparation needed before the event begins. A post-event discussion can check on what has been learnt, discover the learner's views on the event, and agree on how the new learning can be applied in the workplace. Where learners are not in employment, or are pursuing learning (e.g. in a distance learning course) on their own initiative, careful thought needs to be given as to how transfer can best be achieved.

Delivering the Event

If an appropriate overall strategy has been chosen, learners have been well selected and properly prepared, and the event has been well designed and is being effectively managed, then the delivery should proceed relatively smoothly. The processes that lead up to the learning event can be time-consuming and, especially where it is a collaboratively managed event, will require significant interpersonal as well as professional skills in order to ensure a good end result.

In the case of the Clinical Directors' Programme (see pp. 352–6), the lead time for the programme itself was a year, involving intense activity and some inevitable tensions in its design and management. Continuous effort was needed in order to move successfully from the point when the overall strategy and general structure of the programme was agreed, through the many stages of negotiation, fact finding, the production of a meaningful and agreed training specification, modifications to design, and the selection of learners and tutors, to final delivery. Similar processes continued throughout the programme, ensuring that adjustments were made to planned events whenever ongoing evaluations by the programme members and the design team indicated these to be necessary. It was subsequently agreed that these processes had been vital to the success of such an individualized programme, time-consuming and expensive though they proved to be. Costs, in particular, had needed very careful consideration from the start, in order to take adequately into account the complexities and the level of expertise needed not only in those who delivered the programme itself, but in those who planned, designed, organized and monitored it.

> In designing and delivering a learning event, the interpersonal and managerial processes leading up to the event will be as critical as technical expertise in ensuring ultimate success.

For a full discussion of the planning, design, management and delivery of learning events, see Gilley and Eggland (1989, pp. 213–40).

Exercises

1 Choose either:

(a) an aspect of managerial behaviour which you would like to eradicate; or

(b) an aspect of managerial behaviour which you would like to promote.

Draft a suitable training programme to that end, outlining and justifying the learning methods proposed. (May 1989)

2 You have been asked to speak for 30 minutes at a future meeting of your organization's top management team, the subject being 'The use of audio-visual aids in formal presentations'. Summarize your plan for your presentation. (May 1989)

References

COWLING A AND GRIPTON J. 'Evaluating selection tests'. *Training Officer*, August 1986. pp. 239-40, 242

DOWNS S. 'Trainability testing'. *Personnel Management*, October 1984. p. 79

GAGNE R M. *Conditions of Learning*. Eastbourne, Holt, Rhinehart and Winston. 1965

GILLEY J W AND EGGLAND S A. *Principles of Human Resource Development*. Maidenhead, Addison Wesley. 1989

KENNEY J, DONNELLY E AND REID M. *Manpower Training and Development*. 2nd ed. London, Institute of Personnel Management. 1979

KENNEY J AND REID M. *Training Interventions*. London, Institute of Personnel Management. 1986; third edition, by Reid, Barrington and Kenney. 1992

KILCOURSE R. 'Trainability testing as an aid to selection'. *Personnel Management*, May 1978. pp. 33-5, 43

MUMFORD A. 'Learning in action'. *Personnel Management*, July 1991. pp. 34-7

REVANS R W. *Developing Effective Managers*. Harlow, Longmans. 1971

RUSHBY N. 'How many psychotherapists are needed to change a light bulb?' In *Training and Technology, Personnel Management*, January 1988. p. 57

TORRINGTON D AND CHAPMAN J. *Personnel Management*. 2nd ed. London, Prentice Hall. 1983

WOODWARD J. *Industrial Organization: Theory and practice*. Oxford, Oxford University Press. 1965, reprinted 1980

Further useful reading

BASS B M AND VAUGHAN J A. *Training in Industry: The management of learning*. London, Tavistock Publications (Behavioural Science in Industry Series). 1967

COOPER C L (ed). *Improving Interpersonal Relations: Some approaches to social skill training*. Aldershot, Gower. 1979

CROFTS P. 'Distance learning's broader horizons'. *Personnel Management*, March 1985. pp. 22-5

DOWNS S AND PERRY P. 'Can trainers learn to take a back seat?' *Personnel Management*, March 1986. pp. 42-5

DUNCAN K D AND KELLEY C J. *Task Analysis: Learning and the nature of transfer*. Sheffield, Manpower Services Commission. 1983

FOWLER A. 'How to use visual aids'. *Personnel Management Plus*, September 1991. pp. 20-1

GRANT D. 'A better way of learning from Nellie'. *Personnel Management*, December 1984. pp. 31-3

HILDGARD E R AND BOWER G H. *Theories of Learning*, 3rd ed. London, Appleton-Century-Crofts. 1966

HOLDING D H. *Principles of Training: Research in applied learning*. Oxford, Pergamon Press. 1965

INSTITUTE OF PERSONNEL MANAGEMENT. *Training, Bibliography 21*. London, IPM (Information and Advisory Services). 1986

INTERNATIONAL YEARBOOK OF EDUCATIONAL AND TRAINING TECHNOLOGY. London, Kogan Page. 1992

JAMES R. 'The use of learning curves'. *Journal of European Industrial Training*, Vol. 8, No. 7. 1984

OTTO C P AND GLASER R O. *The Management of Training*, London, Addison Wesley. 1970

PATRICK J. 'What's new in training'. *Personnel Management*. September 1984. pp. 44-7

PATRICK J AND STAMMERS R B. 'Computer assisted learning and occupational training'. *British Journal of Educational Technology*, Vol. 3, No. 8. 1977. pp. 253-67

PISCIOTTO M, ROBERTSON I AND COLLEY R. *Interactivity: Designing and using interactive video*. London, Kogan Page. 1989

ROBERTS K. 'The slide to video'. *Personnel Management*, April 1984. pp. 30-4

ROBINSON K R. *A Handbook of Training Management*. 2nd ed. London, Kogan Page. 1985

RYNN B. 'Taking stock of computer based training'. *Personnel Management*, June 1984. pp. 44-8

SKINNER B F. *Science and Human Behaviour*. New York, Free Press. 1965

STAMMERS R AND PATRICK H. *Psychology of Training*. London, Methuen (Essential Psychology Series). 1975

TRAINING DIRECTORY. London, Kogan Page and BACIE. 1992

WELFORD A T. 'On changes in performance with age'. *Lancet*, Part 1. 1962

WRIGHT D. 'Keeping up with computer based training'. *Personnel Management*, October 1981. pp. 60-3

Chapter 17

Evaluating the event and assessing the payback for the organization

Learning Objectives

After reading this chapter you will:

1 understand the key issues involved in monitoring and evaluating a learning event;
2 be able to choose an appropriate evaluation strategy for a learning event;
3 be familiar with a range of evaluation methods, and know how to choose those relevant for a given evaluation strategy;
4 be able to plan an evaluation exercise;
5 understand how, in general terms, assessment of the organizational payback of learning events can be achieved.

In this chapter we look at the last two of our nine stages in designing and delivering learning events (see Figure 10, p. 327): monitoring and evaluating, and assessing the extent to which they make a real contribution to corporate needs.

Monitoring and Evaluation of the Learning Event

Monitoring and evaluation are essential to the success of any learning event. They ensure control of the event during its delivery, validation of its outcomes by comparing actual against intended results and analysis of information vital to future planning.

With a lengthy programme, regular monitoring will be needed, with a final evaluation carried out by some neutral party against its original purpose and objectives. With a short learning event, the methods and timing of monitoring progress and results can be established according to need and to resources available.

> The main principle is to achieve a sensible balance between the need to check on what is happening at various stages of a learning event, and the feasibility of such checks given the resources and expertise available to carry out monitoring and evaluation.

It is not the purpose of this chapter to review the literature about evaluation or to assess the merits of the various approaches that can be encountered there. For that kind of discussion, see Kenney and Reid (1986) and Hall (1984); and for a detailed account of the two models on which I have mainly based my approach in this chapter, see Hamblin (1974), and Warr et al. (1970). I will also not cover evaluation techniques in any detail, as I am concerned rather with the criteria that should govern the selection of techniques. Relevant references are, however, given in the Further Useful Reading section.

The aims here are to help you to develop a simple, practical approach to the key issues underlying the evaluation task, and to suggest ways in which you can convince management of the impact of employee development activities on business performance and growth.

Evaluation must be concerned with validating learning – that is with checking whether learning objectives have been achieved. But it must go wider than that and question whether all that has been done is worthwhile, given the overall purpose of the event and the investment made in it.

> Evaluation looks at the total value of a learning event, not just at whether and how far it has achieved its learning objectives. It therefore puts the event in its wider context and provides information that is essential to future planning.

Six general points need to be made about evaluation:

1 The more the learning event is concerned with 'soft' (i.e. behavioural) skills and issues rather than 'hard' (i.e. quantifiable and simple) ones, the less easy it is to measure.

2 The higher up the organization the learning event, the less easy it is to measure its impact, because of the complexity of jobs and of the factors affecting behaviour and performance in them.

3 The longer the delay in measuring the learning event, the less easy it is to do – again because of the effects of a multiplicity of intervening variables.

4 In order to achieve any meaningful measurement, there should be an analysis of the 'before/after' situation. Measurement of changes achieved once the learning event is over should be done at more than one time in order to measure retention of learning in the work situation.

5 Measurement must be apt, systematic, objective and feasible. It must focus, not on *all* outcomes, but only on those agreed to be the most important.

6 Measurement must be a collaborative process, with strategy, focus and methods approved at the highest level. Providing that the parties concerned agree on what is to be measured, how, and to what purpose, there should be no insurmountable problems in agreeing on the outcomes and value of the learning event – unless, of course, there are wider organizational problems which the learning event cannot resolve, yet which impact directly on the function and on its initiatives.

Faced with an evaluation task, the first step is to answer five crucial questions:

- Why is evaluation to be done?
- What will be evaluated?
- How will evaluation be done?
- Who will do the evaluation?
- When is it to be done?

Let us look now at these questions in detail.

Why evaluate?

A Challenge to Complacency (Coopers and Lybrand, 1985) emphasized the importance of evaluation as a means of changing attitudes to training by showing in measurable ways the value of investing in it. It also reported a generally low level of skill in either cost-benefit analysis or evaluation as a total activity, notably among personnel practitioners. So as a generalization, evaluation of training is a major need in most organizations today, if training is to become a mainline business function.

There are many reasons why evaluation may be required in a

specific situation: perhaps to justify the cost of a particular learning event, or to establish its effects on the learners, or to measure the impact of the event on job performance, or on the profitability, performance, flexibility or survival of the organization as a whole. In every case, evaluation must be concerned with the future more than with the past: with assessing the kinds of learning event that can promote future performance and growth, and with how they can best be carried out. Evaluation is a vital aid to planning.

Each kind of aim may involve the evaluator in a different set of activities, and will provide the frame of reference for all the remaining questions. The answer to this first question, '*Why?*' will therefore also lead on to answering the questions '*What, how, who and when?*'

What to evaluate

A fourfold framework is helpful here, drawn from models provided by Warr et al. (1970) and Hamblin (1974), whose texts are essential reading especially for the practical guidance they give on evaluation techniques and procedures. Another fundamental text is Jackson (1990).

The four factors to be evaluated are:

1 C. The **context** within which the learning event has taken place: how accurately needs were initially diagnosed, why this particular kind of learning event was decided on as a solution, and whether the right kind of learning objectives were set. Examination of the organizational culture and structure is an important part of context evaluation.

2 I. The **inputs** to the learning event: the resources used to meet the learning needs (time, money, staff, physical accommodation, materials, natural learning resources in the organization); the chosen learning culture and structure developed for the event, the content and the methods used; and how far selection choices for entry to the event were valid, given its purpose and objectives. The costs of all these inputs need to be identified, so that their effectiveness and efficiency can be assessed.

3 R. The **reactions** to the learning event. What are the learners' reactions to the event? (These will influence future participants, as

well as being important in their own right.) What are the reactions of the other parties involved in or affected by the learning event, compared to the reactions it was hoped the event would provoke? For example, in the British Airways 'Putting People First' and 'Managing People First' programmes (see p. 172), it was felt to be important to make membership of the courses optional. However, the hope was that the first groups of people to go through the programmes would be so enthusiastic that this would influence their peers to opt for the training. This hope was more than fulfilled, and virtually the entire workforce in the sectors concerned finally wanted to be trained.

4O. The **outcomes** of the learning event: the effects of that event by reference to the objectives set for it and the outcomes it has actually achieved.

How to evaluate

This will depend on what is being evaluated. Using the CIRO framework outlined above, evaluation can be carried out as follows:

1 **Evaluate the context of the learning event.** Look at how and by whom the information that gave rise to the diagnosis of the need for the learning event was collected. Then examine how that information was analysed and learning needs identified from it. This evaluation will be concerned with material covered in Chapters 11–14.

Then examine how learning objectives were set; how well they related to the overall purpose of the event and the needs it was intended to serve; how far they took into account the organizational context within which the learning would have to take place; what standards were established, and how achievement of standards was to be measured; and what kinds of skills, knowledge and attitudes were to be acquired.

2 **Evaluate the inputs to the learning event.** Here, the evaluator should consider the resources used, the learning culture and structure, the content and methods chosen, and the kind of learners selected for the event, in the light of the factors we discussed in Chapters 15 and 16:

- The purpose and objectives of the learning event; and the learning group
- The principles of learning
- Practical issues

The concern here is with how well-chosen the inputs were, and how cost-efficient, cost-effective and feasible; and with how well, and at what costs, the learning event was planned, managed, designed and delivered.

3 **Evaluate reactions to the learning event.** The kind of reactions sought will depend on the aims of the evaluation exercise. If the main concern is with learning that has been achieved, then the reactions sought should be about how far participants feel they have learnt what was identified in the objectives for the learning event. If, on the other hand, there is a particular concern with whether content, methods and delivery were effective, then learners should be asked for their views on those.

It may be important to test reactions after every session of an event, or after every key element, or – in a modular programme – at the end of every module. In the Clinical Directors' Programme (see p. 352), which because of its strategic importance was subjected to evaluation by many parties, the Business School staff gave out daily reactions sheets for the Management Foundation Course, testing views on how far the stated objectives were being achieved and on content and delivery. Subsequently, however, they only distributed questionnaires at the end of each course, testing reactions to each main component of that course. This elicited essential information while avoiding what otherwise could have been an excess of questioning in view of evaluation exercises also being conducted at regional and national level.

The evaluation of reactions, then, must suit the needs of the exercise. Hamblin (1974) reinforces this view, recommending, for example, the use of session assessments on training courses, to look at each session in terms of any aspects in which the evaluator is interested – enjoyment, length of time given to discussion, level of presentation, informational content, relevance, length of the session; or to monitor the progress of a practical activity, perhaps with a view to establishing typical learning curves of different types of learners. Assessments can be done at the end of a session, or at the end of the whole programme, or at periods after the completion of the programme.

4 **Evaluation of outcomes.** Outcomes can be measured at any or all of the following levels, depending again on the object of the evaluation exercise:

- **Outcomes for the learners:** the reactions of the learners to the learning event (as described above), and changes in their knowledge, skills and attitudes measured at the completion of the training – for example by tests – compared with the level and type of knowledge, skills and attitudes at the start of that programme (as established by techniques such as appraisal, tests, repertory grid, etc.)
- **Outcomes for the workplace:** changes that subsequently take place in the learner's job behaviour, as measured by appraisal, observation, discussion with their superiors, colleagues and staff, performance records, the views of the learners themselves and how far these are in line with the views of others about that performance (research quoted by Warr et al., 1970, indicates that there is usually quite a close correlation between the two sets of views)
- **Outcomes for the team/department/unit:** changes that take place in part or all of a department as a result of a learning event, using the kind of techniques described above
- **Outcomes for the organization:** changes that take place in the organization as a whole after the completion of the training programme

These last two kinds of outcomes are the most difficult to evaluate. Yet with careful thought, reasonable evaluation even here should be possible, providing that clear objectives have been set before training begins, and ways of measuring the achievement of those objectives have been agreed. The sort of changes that could be involved include changes in departmental output, costs, scrap rates, absenteeism, turnover, accident frequency, productivity rates, or the effectiveness in some other way of the total organization. Or at a wider organizational level, it could involve evidence of a change in the culture of the organization (as at British Airways), more flexibility and reduced levels of conflict in relation to the introduction of change (as at Cummins Engines Ltd – see Harrison, 1992b), and an enhanced ability to attract and retain valued workers (as at Etewel, see pp. 127–8). More will be said about organizational outcomes and their value later in this chapter.

Who should evaluate?

Choosing the evaluator is a key task in the evaluation process. Trainers, line managers, personnel staff, top management and external consultant will all bring their own viewpoints and aims to the task, so that none can be relied upon to be free of bias. If no one in the organization really understands the process the organization is then very vulnerable to manipulation.

Evaluation is also a sensitive and technically difficult process, whose outcomes can only be as reliable and valid as the process that has produced them ; for a formidable critique, for example, of the customary end-of-course evaluation run by trainers, see Easterby-Smith and Tanton (1985).

Evaluators must therefore be carefully chosen. A practical five-point checklist that can be applied to potential candidates is as follows:

1 **Objectivity.** How objective are they likely to be, in relation to the learning event? What, if any, connection have they had with its design, running and outcomes? Are they likely to cover up any weaknesses or strengths in the event – or to exaggerate them?

2 **Expertise.** How skilled are they likely to be? Have they done any evaluation before? For whom? With what results? Can anyone give you an assessment of their abilities in the field? Does their explanation of how they will approach the task convince you of their knowledge, skill and professionalism?

3 **Interpersonal skills.** Are they likely to obtain accurate and comprehensive information? What sort of relationship do they have, or can they be expected to form, with those whose views they need to obtain? How will people react to them? Can they expect to receive full trust and co-operation? What sort of relationship have they established with you, and what does that tell you about their interpersonal skills?

4 **Credibility.** How credible are they likely to be with people in the organization? This will largely depend on the factors already examined above: their perceived objectivity, expertise and interpersonal skills. However, it will also, and crucially, depend on how quickly and well they establish an understanding of the organization: its tasks, structure and culture, technology, people, and environment. It is not necessary for an evaluator to have previous knowledge of the organization itself, but certainly previous knowledge of a similar organization, and the ability to demonstrate an awareness of its business, and of its social, political, system, are very important. Careful questioning and the requirement that potential evaluators should explain in detail how they would approach and handle their task will help to assess their likely credibility.

5 **Cost.** What will be the cost of using them? If, for example, you are considering using a consultant, will the fee be worth the end result? Could anyone else do the job more cheaply, and to an acceptable standard? If you were to use your own staff, how long would the task take them? Could they be spared for that amount of time? Would they have the expertise to do the task? If you use a consultant, what will happen when they leave? Will they have trained your staff to take over from them, especially in implementing any further stages of a lengthy project? Robinson (1985) observes that staff should be trained to give effect to consultants' recommendations, adding:

> Incurring the cost of a resident consultant to carry out the implementation stage of the project is unnecessary, although it is advisable that the contract should allow for access to a consultant for advice (Ibid., p. 69).

When to evaluate

There are several choices possible here. Evaluation should always be carried out before and after the learning event. It may also be needed:

- During the event
- Some time after it
- In the longer-term – say a year afterwards

The decision on when to evaluate should be made by reference to the purpose of the evaluation activity, and to what is to be evaluated.

If the purpose is to find out how valid the learning event was in helping the learners to reach identified standards by the end of it, then monitoring standards reached before and at the end of the learning event may be sufficient, although it would be advisable to evaluate at least once again, at a later date, in order to assess how far learning has been retained.

If the cost-efficiency of the inputs is to be evaluated, then evaluation using the reactions of the learners during and at the end of the event, and pre- and post-tests of the learning they have acquired in relation to the objectives of the learning event would probably prove sufficient.

However, if the cost-effectiveness of a programme needs to be evaluated in order to decide whether the organization should invest again in such a programme, then it may prove necessary to evaluate by reference to job performance in the short term, and to its longer-term impact on both job performance and overall organizational trends in, perhaps, profitability, morale and flexibility.

What is ideal in theory is rarely feasible in practice, so the timing of evaluation must also take practical considerations into account. To evaluate in depth, using sophisticated methods, at five different points in time, for example, would require a high expenditure of resources, and this may not be possible or justifiable given the benefits likely to accrue from the exercise. On the other hand, a simple form of monitoring carried out at fairly regular intervals will be cheap and, given all the advantages of information, control and good planning that it offers, will usually repay the effort.

> The decision on when to evaluate depends on the purpose of the evaluation, on what is to be evaluated, and on practical considerations.

It is always important to ensure that learners focus their thoughts before the learning event takes place on its objectives and its relevance to their needs, and that learning is transferred to the workplace once the event is over. It is also important to involve the managers of participants at various stages, as this will help to ensure the managers' commitment to the event (Easterby-Smith and Tanton, 1985), and to achieve effective integration of what is learnt with ongoing work. These considerations show the value of carrying out some form of evaluation, no matter how simple and informal, before, during and after most learning events:

1 **Before the event.** In order to assess the individual against desired levels of competence or attitudes use can be made of techniques such as repertory grid, personal constructs, or some simpler method. Evaluation of another kind – to check on what the individual feels about the forthcoming learning event, and to discover their expectations and needs – can be done by discussion (involving the individual's mentor or manager wherever possible), or by a simple questionnaire to be returned before the event takes place.

2 **During the event.** Tests, questionnaires, review sessions, discussions with managers and mentors are all ways of checking on progress and the relevance of learning at various points during a learning event.

3 **Shortly after the event finishes.** The same kind of techniques used before the event can also be used at this stage, to measure the extent of learning and change.

4 **In the longer term.** Information should be collected that can be used to assess the impact of learning on the job, the department or the organization – ranging from opinion surveys and discussions with peers, superiors and subordinates, to climate surveys across the organization. The emphasis should be on finding evidence for opinions, so that people are asked to give specific examples in order to substantiate their views.

Choosing an evaluation strategy

Having identified the main issues relating to the five questions – why, what, how, who and when to evaluate – we must now turn to the matter of choosing a strategy for tackling a given evaluation task.

Looking at practice across organizations, five different kinds of evaluation strategy are apparent:

- The value for money strategy
- The investment value strategy
- The objective-centred strategy

- The auditing strategy
- The business-led strategy

The value for money strategy

This strategy (see Hall, 1984) is relevant to use when top management's view of training is that if it cannot prove its financial worth, then it should not be done, although if this is the *only* form of evaluation that is carried out, it may lead to a situation where so-called employee development is reduced to a very limited package of short-term, job-related, quantifiable skills-based training initiatives. On the other hand, as we saw in Chapter 9, training and development resources and activities should be costed and managed in such a way that full value is obtained for available money, and that where at first sight priority needs cannot be met within current budgets, a sound case can be put forward for obtaining more money, or the needs can be met using alternative approaches. So a balance needs to be struck. There should be a continuing effort to present employee development as a necessary function, given the high asset value of people to the organization, but on the other hand, training practitioners must be able to speak convincingly about the costs and benefits of what they do, and show that money, time and expertise is being well spent on valuable learning processes and events.

The 'value for money' approach was covered in detail in Chapter 9 where the following guidelines were given ('training' in this context means any measurable learning event):

1 **Measure identifiable costs (outflows) of training, direct and indirect.** This means identifying the basic annual cost of running the training function, and the costs of running particular training activities.

2 **Measure identifiable benefits (inflows) to the firm in financial terms (or those that can easily be equated with money).** Performance measures can be categorized, starting with the most directly quantifiable and going on to more qualitative indicators (see Fowler, 1991). If, for example, a group of people for whom training programmes are being established do work where good performance is a matter of carrying out quantifiable tasks in an efficient manner to reach clearly defined standards of performance then measuring the

results of training is a straightforward matter. Achievement of objectives will probably include tests and other activities during and at the end of training, followed, in the workplace, by monitoring of performance to standards for as long a period of time as is needed after training to ensure that full transfer of learning to performance on the job has been achieved. Robinson and Robinson (1989, p. 263, Figure 2) give a range of useful indicators.

3 **Compare costs and benefits to give a cost-benefit ratio or rate of return for capital employed.**

4 **Assess whether other types of learning event, or other media or methods of learning, are likely to be more cost-beneficial than those currently in use.**

The investment value strategy

This goes a step further than the value for money approach. The emphasis is on assessing not only the immediate cost-benefit of learning events but also wider, less tangible outcomes, and also on deciding whether the end results have been of real value to the organization or whether it would have been better to invest money, time and effort in some other way.

Thus a training course may be highly cost-beneficial: it recovers its direct and indirect costs, contributes to annual running costs, and achieves its stated objectives to the satisfaction of the parties. But the investment value approach would ask whether those objectives were really necessary or relevant. Or could something else entirely have been done, which would have been of more value to the organization in relation to the kind of overall purpose that had to be achieved, for example focusing on recruiting new people instead of training or retraining existing employees; or introducing a system of performance management and/or performance-related pay in order to increase motivation and boost performance levels; or reorganizing tasks or roles; or introducing new equipment, technology, methods or procedures (see Hall, 1984).

The objective-centred strategy

This approach can also be used in conjunction with others. The focus is on the 'client' and the Training Manager (or equivalent) working together on setting objectives for the learning event, agreeing together on what kind of outcomes to measure and how to measure them once the event has taken place, and an undertaking on the 'client's' part to accept a final evaluation that may have to be imprecise in some areas.

Reddin (1989) gives a 'job effectiveness description' showing how the job of the Training Manager can itself be expressed in terms of objectives and outcomes to be achieved. The presumption is that if those outcomes *are* achieved, then it is accepted by the organization that the job holder has performed in a way that makes the most appropriate and effective possible contribution to the organization.

> What matters most is that the parties concerned agree on the one hand how to express the kind of targets to be achieved, and on the other how to measure performance in relation to those targets.

The key parties must agree and be committed to the way or ways in which people will be developed to meet the objectives, and there must be a joint assessment of the costs and likely results of a variety of approaches. Options should be analysed not only for their direct cost-benefit, but also for their suitability to the types of learners concerned and their needs, their feasibility in view of the organization's culture and resources, and the extent to which they are likely to achieve the learning objectives.

At Book Club Associates (Armstrong, 1987, pp. 33–4), all training and development programmes had the purpose of improving output and minimizing costs, and were designed to support productivity drives. The specific objectives of such programmes are easy to define because the company has performance management programmes that include the specification of very clear standards against which, through a formal review procedure, people's performance is appraised.

The auditing strategy

This approach to evaluation has already been described (see pp. 167–70). An excellent practical illustration is given on pages 286–7 showing how it can be used to assess an event or events and then to provide invaluable information that can be fed directly into the planning process for future training and development activities.

The business-led strategy

This evaluation strategy is in some ways a logical extension of the objective-centred approach, but the objectives are squarely those of the business, at corporate, strategic level. It involves a process that starts at the point where corporate strategy and its resultant objectives are determined (see Chapter 11, pp. 256–8).

The crucial questions with this evaluation strategy relate to where the organization is going; to the kind of workforce it must have if it is to get there; to the role this requires employee training and development to play if there is to be the human capability to achieve those organizational goals; and, finally, to the kind of ED strategies and activities which will best ensure the role is fulfilled (see p. 145, paragraph 3). The story of Venture Pressings (pp. 158–60) shows how a high level of investment in employee development, expressed in a coherent, wide-ranging series of initiatives, well-integrated with wider human resource strategy, and implemented consistently through time, was judged from the outset by an organization in the forefront of new technology to be absolutely necessary if its workforce was to reach and sustain the level of flexibility and efficiency needed to achieve corporate business goals.

Hendry et al. comment (1991, p. 67) that, whilst overall business performance does not of itself provide a source of evaluation for training, it does throw into sharp relief – most notably in small and medium-sized enterprises – the costs of *not* developing and/or training people. Research (e.g. Prais, 1990) has shown how productivity can be dramatically reduced, for example, when intermediate skilled staff have not been adequately trained and educated in their executive and administrative responsibilities and higher-grade personnel have then to spend much longer on basic chores, to the detriment of business development, strategic decision-making and related tasks. Furthermore, lack of adequately skilled people on production lines leads to increased downtime whilst maintenance people are called in to deal with machine breakdowns.

This kind of evaluation, essential for the organization whose position depends through time on a high-quality flexible, committed workforce (as the example of ICI on pages 192–5 demonstrates), does not ask 'Do we train or develop our people?' but rather 'How do we train and develop our people?' It is tellingly illustrated by the case study on pages 396–8, summarized on page 468.

Selection of evaluation techniques

The choice of which techniques to use is again largely determined by the answers to our five basic questions: why, what, how, who and when.

Where there is a lack of objective, detailed information, a short time available in which to carry out evaluation, and a need for a relatively cheap exercise, the most obvious techniques to use are informal discussions with key parties; questionnaires of sample groups (preferably samples of those who have been through a learning event and of those who have not, in order to establish some kind of control group); and follow-up interviews on a selective basis. Where there is much more information available – for example, evaluation forms of various kinds, documentation about training needs and objectives, costings of activities, and identification of resources – then more sophisticated techniques can be employed. However, a simple approach, acceptable to the parties and therefore likely to generate reasonably comprehensive and valid information, is always to be recommended.

> The choice of evaluation techniques should be determined by the purpose of the evaluation, what is to be evaluated and how, who is to evaluate and the time available for the exercise. Techniques must be cost-effective and acceptable to those involved in the exercise.

Planning the evaluation of a management development programme

You are a training manager, planning a six-month management development programme involving a mix of off-the-job formal modules and work-related projects for the managers concerned. From what has been learnt so far in this chapter, what are the five or six activities that must be carried out in order to achieve effective evaluation of the programme?

FEEDBACK NOTES

From all that has been said so far, the following practical guidelines can be given in relation to setting up this, or any other, evaluation exercise:

1 **Decide on the aims of the exercise and on the choice of evaluators (why and who).** The timescale, resources available, and arrangements for managing the exercise must be identified at this point.

2 **Establish the key outcomes the learning event has to achieve, and whether the evaluation will aim to examine all or only some of those outcomes (what).** The objectives and standards to be achieved must be identified. These outcomes will become the criteria against which the effectiveness of the learning event is to be evaluated.

3 **Establish how the achievement of those outcomes is to be measured (how).** Thus, for example, if an objective of a management course is that managers should be able to motivate their teams effectively, then ways will have to be found for measuring 'effective motivation of teams'. Two questions have therefore to be answered:

- What does each objective mean in terms of measurable behaviour?
- How can a direct relationship between learning in the learning event itself, and subsequent behaviour and performance be established to the satisfaction of those needing to assess how far the training has been sucessful?

4 **Monitor and measure the development of required knowledge, skills, attitudes and behaviour from before the learning event to some point subsequent to its completion (when).** Methods that could be used could include one or more of the following:

- **Pre-course, interim, and post-course assessment.** Put the participants through some form of assessment process before the learning event in order to establish their present standards of performance and types of attitudes and behaviour. (Personal development plans can be an aid to this process, and to helping to assess the final impact of a learning event.) Put them through a similar process during and after the programme in order to measure changes.
- **Pre-course, interim and post-course opinions (semi-structured or unstructured) about performance.** Obtain general views about their behaviour and performance from their managers both before the learning event, and when they are back in the workplace. A checklist of questions can be used in order to ensure that the process is reliable, and it should include checks on participants' and their managers' views on how far the programme, as it progresses, is felt to be helping behaviour and performance.
- **Pre-course and post-course ratings of performance.** Obtain the views of peers and colleagues in deciding how far training has achieved its objectives with the managers concerned, using

behavioural rating scales and other structured evidence of specific behaviour and performance.

- **Pre- and post-course appraisal.** Where there is a system of regular appraisal incorporating, perhaps, self-appraisal, behavioural rating scales and evidence of specific achievement, it may be possible to use this to obtain ratings on participants before and after the programme.

5 **Involve the learners' managers in monitoring and evaluating the programme.** Ensure that managers are involved from the start in discussing the objectives of the programme, its relevance for the learning needs of their staff and how far, as it progresses, the programme appears to be meeting those needs. The more they are involved, the more, ultimately, they will help to ensure a good transfer of learning both during the programme (project work and other kinds of work-related assignments) and once it is over.

6 **Ensure feedback of results to the key parties in ways that will ensure that they influence the planning of future events.** With a lengthy evaluation exercise there may have to be interim reports. For example, with the Clinical Directors' Programme (see pp. 352–6), there were regular meetings between the various evaluating groups to discuss their findings with the NRHA-DUBS team, and between DUBS and NRHA staff to discuss continuing progress of the programme. There may also need to be provision for adjustments to the learning event should these be shown to be desirable.

Assessing the Payback for the Organization

In Chapter 11 we discussed general principles to be followed in measuring the impact of learning events on the business (see pp. 256–8). Elaborating on the three points made there, the following checklist shows how the value of a learning event to the organization's business goals can be established in a manner likely to convince management.

1 Draw up objectives for training that will meet needs agreed with the 'client', and are feasible in view of wider employee resource strategy. They must be meaningful to the organization, and must be challenging enough to make a real impact on areas of value to it, whether at the overall level, or at the levels of the business unit, the group or the individual.

2 Identify the costs of training. These should be both direct and obvious, and indirect but critical costs.

3 Identify the likely benefits that will be obtained by realizing the objectives, both direct and less tangible, in the short and the longer term.

4 Agree on who is to measure and assess the results of the programme, when, and how.

5 Assess the value of those outcomes of the programme which it has been agreed are vital, at whatever levels are agreed to be most important, and use initially agreed methods of measuring achievements. Line managers, in particular, must be able to state how and why things have or have not changed, and be specific in their evidence.

6 Ensure that feedback on results is timely, goes to the interested parties, and influences the next stage of planning.

For an excellent example of how to convince management of the value of a programme to the business, see the study of BOC in Chapter 18 (pp. 396–8), and note the ongoing monitoring and evaluation that achieved that conviction. See also the study of the Sales Training Programme at Barratt in Harrison (1992a), and the way in which the value of training and development to the business was established at Cummins Engines, Darlington, in Chapter 6 of Harrison (1992b). As cases throughout this book have shown, where employee development initiatives are carefully thought through, related to the needs of the business as well as of departments and individuals, and produce results which relate positively to the aims agreed for them originally, the function as a whole has every likelihood of increasing in strength and credibility.

> There is no one best way of measuring the outcomes of training. However, providing that learning objectives are clearly agreed between the key parties and relate well to the overall purpose of the development programme, what really matters then is to get the agreement of the key parties that they have found meaningful methods of measuring performance against those objectives, and that they are fully committed to using those methods.

Exercises

1 Before starting to evaluate a learning event it is necessary to ask and answer a number of questions. What do you suggest these questions might be, and how would you set about determining appropriate answers? (May 1989)

2 'The trouble with textbooks and journal articles on the subject of "evaluating training" is that they always take a theoretical, scientific and logical approach which ignores mainstream operational aims.' Comment on this statement, and suggest practical evaluation measures within your organization which can overcome the implied criticism. (November 1988)

References

APPLEGARTH M. *How to Take a Training Audit.* London, Kogan Page. 1991

ARMSTRONG M. 'Human resource management: a case of the emperor's new clothes?' *Personnel Management*, August 1987. pp. 30-5

COOPERS AND LYBRAND ASSOCIATES. *A Challenge to Complacency: Changing attitudes to training.* Report to the Manpower Services Commission and the National Economic Development Office. Sheffield, MSC. 1985

EASTERBY-SMITH M AND TANTON M. 'Turning course evaluation from an end to a means'. *Personnel Management*, April 1985. pp. 25-7

FOWLER A. 'How to set performance objectives'. *Personnel Management Plus*, February 1991. pp. 20-1

GILLEY J W AND EGGLAND S A. *Principles of Human Resource Development.* Maidenhead, Addison Wesley. 1989.

GLAZE T. 'Cadbury's dictionary of competence'. *Personnel Management*, July 1989. pp. 44-8

HALL D T. 'Human resource development and organizational effectiveness'. In *Strategic Human Resource Management* (Fombrun D, Tichy N M and Devanna M A, eds.). New York, Wiley. 1984

HAMBLIN A C. *Evaluation and Control of Training.* Maidenhead, McGraw-Hill. 1974

HARRISON R. 'Employee development at Barratt'. In *Case Studies in Personnel.* (Winstanley D and Woodall D, eds.). London, Institute of Personnel Management. 1992a

HARRISON R. *Developing Human Resources for Productivity.* Geneva, International Labour Office. 1992b

HENDRY C, JONES A, ARTHUR M AND PETTIGREW A. *Human Resource Development in Small to Medium Sized Enterprises.* ED Research Paper No. 88. Sheffield, Department of Employment. 1991

JACKSON T. *Evaluation: Relating training to business performance*. London, Kogan Page. 1990 (Recommended by *Personnel Management*'s reviewer: 'For any training department fighting for recognition or survival, this is the book to read.')

KENNEY J AND REID M. *Training Interventions*. London, Institute of Personnel Management. 1986; third edition, by Reid, Barrington and Kenney, 1992

MURPHY M P AND SWANSON R A. 'Auditing training and development'. *Journal of European Industrial Training*, Vol. 12, No. 2. 1988. pp. 13-16

PRAIS S J AND NIESR RESEARCH TEAM. 'Productivity, Education and Training: Britain and Other Countries Compared'. *National Economic Review*. London, National Institute of Economic and Social Research. 1990

REDDIN B. *The Output Oriented Organisation*. Aldershot, Gower. 1989

ROBINSON D G AND ROBINSON J C. *Training for Impact*. London, Jossey-Bass. 1989

WARR P B, BIRD M AND RACKHAM N. *Evaluation of Management Training*. Aldershot, Gower. 1970

Further useful reading

CONFEDERATION OF BRITISH INDUSTRY. *Evaluating your Training: Matching outcomes to needs*. London, CBI. 1989

DEMING B S. *Evaluating Job-related Training*. Washington DC, American Society for Training and Development, and Englewood Cliffs, New Jersey, Prentice Hall. 1982

GREATREX J AND PHILLIPS P. 'Oiling the wheels of competence'. *Personnel Management*, August 1989. pp. 36-9

INSTITUTE OF PERSONNEL MANAGEMENT. *Attitude Surveys in Industry*. Information Report No. 3. London, IPM. 1970

INSTITUTE OF PERSONNEL MANAGEMENT. *Evaluation of Training. Bibliography 103*. London, IPM (Information and Advisory Services). 1986

KENRICK P. *Costing, Budgeting and Evaluating Training*. Luton, Local Government Training Board (Open Learning Pack). 1984

NEAGLE J J. 'Practical methods of evaluating and validating training, Parts 1 and 2'. *Training and Development*, Vol. 2, Nos. 5 and 6. September and October, 1983

SMITH M. 'Using repertory grids to evaluate training'. *Personnel Management*, February 1978. pp. 36-7, 43

SWANSON R A. 'Training technology system: A method for identifying and solving training problems in industry and business. *Journal of Industrial Teacher Education*. 1987

SWANSON R A AND SLEEZER C M. 'Training effectiveness evaluation'. *Journal of European Industrial Training*. Vol. 11, No. 4, 1987

TRACEY W R. 'Training evaluation – another perspective'. *Personnel Management*, March 1977. pp. 38-41

Part Four

Promoting Individual and Organizational Growth

Chapter 18

Responding to the needs of special groups and contingencies

Learning Objectives

After reading this chapter you will:

1 understand why the basic steps involved in the inception, design, and delivery of training and development for special groups and contingencies are the same as those for any learning event or programme;
2 have achieved an increased understanding of widely encountered areas of special need through analysis of practical examples, and be able to generalize from that analysis;
3 be able to use a checklist of practical questions as an initial guide to planning training and development for special groups and contingencies.

This chapter covers training and development for special groups and contingencies in an organization, but the main principles to be observed are the same for each case and take us back to the basic theory about the inception, design and delivery of learning events, and to the nine stages outlined in Figure 10 (see p. 327):

1 Confirm needs.

2 Agree on the overall purpose and objectives.

3 Identify the learning population profile.

4 Select the learning strategy, and agree on direction and management.

5 Select the learners, and specify the learning.

6 Confirm the strategy and design the event.

7 Ensure delivery.

8 Monitor and evaluate.

9 Assess organizational payback.

I have selected some areas of special need which are commonly encountered: supervisory development, training and development related to equality, and health and safety training. I have then analysed some examples of good practice in order to show the general principles of planning and design to which they conform.

Supervisory Training and Development

Supervisors as first-line managers are critical to organizational success. They have a major responsibility for organizing and managing people in teams, for ensuring the high quality and profitability of products or services, for improving safety, for cost control and for other functions which require them to possess a considerable knowledge of the commercial, economic and customer care aspects of a business. They also need many interpersonal skills in order effectively to manage the individuals and teams for whom they have responsibility.

Research has made it clear that while many supervisors may hold these kinds of general responsibilities in common, beyond that their roles and tasks, and the competences and attitudes needed to perform well in them, are specific to the particular organizational context (Warr and Bird, 1968). Like all areas of training and development need, this too is one requiring careful analysis in order to ensure that the most appropriate strategies and methods of learning are selected to suit individual circumstances.

Developing supervisors at BOC Distribution Services (based on Kane and Wallace, 1991)
(With acknowledgements to J Kane and T Wallace and *Personnel Management*)

QUESTION
How far can you see the nine stages set out above being followed in this case study? And what other important lessons

emerge about how to achieve successful employee development?

At Transhield, part of BOC Distribution Services, and the provider of a dedicated food distribution service to a major high-quality high-street retail chain, the need for a special focus on supervisory training and development was clearly identified in 1988 by reference to changes in business strategy. Challenges facing the company called for greater operational efficiency, with particular emphasis on:

- Reducing costs
- Maintaining a high-quality, efficient and flexible business
- Improving productivity
- Improving receptiveness to change at all levels

Supervisors had key roles to play in these changes, and therefore went through a special on- and off-the-job development programme, with their managers being trained first in mentoring in order to play their full part.

The purpose of the programme was to ensure that supervisors could quickly learn how to implement, maintain and take ownership of the many changes in working practices and methods soon to be introduced at shop-floor level. Learning objectives were to do with improving the quality and profitability of operations, improving safety, achieving a high level of interpersonal skills and generally enabling them to tackle a varied range of practical projects and problems confidently and effectively.

A careful analysis of the kind and number of supervisors involved, and of their profile and needs in relation to the purpose and objectives of the programme, led to a decision to deliver a series of 2½-day workshops with up to ten participants and two tutors in each, working on projects based on workplace issues identified and set by senior depot managers. Preliminary work had to be done, and at the workshop projects were tackled on a group basis. The methods of learning used required the supervisors to practise teamwork and interpersonal skills as well as task-related skills, and assessment covered both technical task learning and behavioural processes. Project findings were presented to senior depot management with a view to adoption, thus ensuring a high degree of transfer of learning.

The programme was extremely successful, and led to a National Training Award for the company.

The evaluation of this initial programme, incorporating the views of the learners and their managers, led to the identification of further needs, including many related to financial management. Using the same successful strategy of 'learning by doing', further programmes were designed, with off-the-job workshops in which supervisors were helped to take more ownership of their own learning by carefully structured self-assessments. Again, managers were trained to help supervisors in their development both before and after the workshops occurred.

As a result of all these learning events, many more learning needs of supervisors have been identified in the company, relating to induction, basic skills training, and continuous development widening into preparation for promotion. Certain competences have also emerged as crucial to supervisory effectiveness:

- Preparing, planning and organizing work
- Leading and briefing groups
- Effective one-to-one interviews and conversation
- Decision-making

Now the company has an induction and basic skills period in which an open learning unit provides the medium for supervisors, helped by their mentor managers, to obtain basic knowledge and the basis for further training. There is a learning strategy of ongoing development which is dependent on management mentoring and the active involvement of the supervisors, linking in with off-the-job workshops focusing on real problems and assignments.

Finally, and as an extra incentive and reward for supervisors going through the programme, it is tied to the National Examining Board for Supervisory Management's qualifications. Supervisors can, at the end of the workshop programme, undergo a competence-based assessment paper leading to an Introductory Award. Further studies, successfully completed, lead to the full Certificate in Supervisory Management. This process also enables the company to identify those supervisors with the potential and motivation to succeed.

By July 1991 four certificate courses were under way in the company, with a high level of interest from supervisors.

The supervisory training and development initiatives are thus planned to extend from recruitment to the company through basic skills training and continuous development, and then to link in to long-term career planning and development. This policy for developing supervisors is part of an overall company training strategy which was formulated during the period of the programme by a training strategy group, charged by the company with developing a three-year training plan for all levels of employee. Supervisors constitute one of seven key priority areas.

Meanwhile the learning methods used in the supervisory programme – learning by doing, in-line mentoring and individual ownership of development – have been extended to all levels of management, thus helping to ensure consistency of learning strategy throughout the company, as well as reinforcing the strategic approach to human resource development.

FEEDBACK NOTES

An analysis of this case study reveals some important points:

1 **Planning, design and evaluation of learning events should be done on a continuous basis.** While it is easy to see how the nine stages involved in planning, designing and delivering a learning event were followed in the case of Transhield, the way evaluation was carried out led to a continuous planning cycle. Information about the impact of the various learning events immediately led not only to improvements and innovations in those events next time around, but also to the design and delivery of further initiatives as other learning needs became apparent.

2 **The identification of the key competences of the learning group involved is crucial in determining what they need to learn.** In this case, identification of core competences only emerged as training and development took place, although the key areas of knowledge and skills had, of course, been identified and analysed before the programme was designed. In theory, as we saw in Chapter 12, identification of core competences should be a starting point in the design process, enabling a clear focus to be established and standards of performance and behaviour to be put in place. However, the case study shows how, even when reality does not conform strictly to theory, good design and careful evaluation can still achieve the desired result in the end!

3 **Business strategy is a major trigger to training and development.** In this case, changes in business strategy clearly signalled a need for supervisory training and development, and this alignment of employee development with business goals gave the necessary commitment at all levels to that learning process, and was crucial to its success.

4 **Well-planned and effective learning events can have an ever-widening impact on employee development mission and strategy in the organization.** In this case, while the relationship of training and development to wider business strategy was clear from the start, it was not possible initially to link it to wider training strategy, since none existed. However, with the success of the programme and the insights achieved by continuous monitoring and evaluation, the need for such a strategy became evident, and led quite quickly to the formulation of a company training plan covering all employees. The proven success of the job-related, continuous development learning strategy used in the supervisory programme also led to the extension of that strategy to managers, and so the company began to formulate

an integrated and strategic approach to the development of all its managers and supervisors.

Thus even when, initially, there is no formal training plan in existence, probing evaluation and the feeding through of information to senior management about the wider implications of a successful training and development programme can lead to one being established.

5 **External factors can trigger off a more strategic approach to employee development throughout an organization.** In this case, the initial triggers were to do with a more competitive environment and consequent changes in business strategy. However, at a later stage achieving a National Training Award led to a series of initiatives whose outcomes included a more strategic approach to employee development in the company. Such awards give a degree of status and recognition to training that can do much to boost its internal credibility and perceived importance as a function. Investors in People status (see Appendix 1) is aimed at producing the same results across a wide range of organizations as gaining a National Training Award achieved at BOC. The Training Manager (or whoever holds those responsibilities) should take advantage of such external sources of support, which can act to the advantage of the function within the organization.

6 **Companies are coming increasingly to realize the importance of linking internal training and career development to external occupational qualifications.** We have already seen this in earlier chapters. Such linkages help to motivate and reward employees for training, and, when training and qualifications together are linked to promotion, then the message that 'training counts' becomes very clear to individuals, encouraging them to invest in training since it brings benefits to them as well as to the company (see pp. 56–7).

Development Related to Achieving Equality in the Workplace

Equality at work is a major area of concern today. Inequality occurs when one person or group is unjustifiably treated less favourably than another is, or would be, treated in the same sort of situation. It is essential to ensure that every effort has been made to prevent discrimination occurring in the organization and to achieve full equality of treatment and opportunity for all employees.

At present the law offers protection against discrimination on the grounds of sex, marriage, race, colour, nationality and ethnic or national origin and, in part, of disability. However, other forms of discrimination can operate in the workplace, related to age, religion (it is only in Northern Ireland that discrimination on grounds of religion is forbidden by law) or sexual orientation. Discrimination on the grounds of age and disability is particularly widespread yet ageism, in particular, is counter-productive in a country which, in the grip of demographic change, has a significantly ageing workforce. In relation to disability, firms like Remploy show the great release of potential that effective training and employment practices can achieve in disabled people (Barnes, 1981). It is important, therefore, to strive to achieve equality for all, not only for those protected by the law.

As an increasing number of organizations are becoming preoccupied with achieving effective human resource management in order to gain a competitive edge, increase their efficiency, or generally add value to employees (see, for example, Storey, 1992), it should become easier to make them aware of the importance of ensuring equality of opportunity in the workplace by emphasizing the costs of failure to do so. Whereas the only real push for equality has in the past tended to come from external sources – the law, and codes of practice to which an organization and those within it might merely pay lip service – now equality can be seen to make sound business sense: maximizing expensive and scarce human resources holds a payoff for the bottom line, whether that bottom line is expressed in the language of pounds profit, or of services offered to the community.

So what are the implications of all this for employee development mission, strategy and activities? Basically, the aim is to ensure that the employer operates within the law, and then to maintain the kind of good practice that will help the organization to attract, retain and develop a fully effective workforce. The following points summarize the kind of goals to which employee development policy should make a contribution (Commission for Racial Equality, 1983):

- To ensure that there is no unlawful discrimination in the establishments
- To develop good employment practices for all employees equally
- To identify groups which are under-represented in certain jobs and to take any necessary action to remedy this
- By effective monitoring, to have a defence against complaints of racial discrimination
- To eliminate both overt discrimination and employment practices which are discriminating in the ways in which they operate

- To provide special training for those employees who would otherwise be unable to enjoy the full benefits of an equal opportunity policy

This means considering training and development in relation to three specific areas.

General knowledge and practice in the organization

Training and guidance should be available for everyone who decides policies and procedures, administers or is in any way actively involved in the key employee resourcing processes in the workplace, in order to ensure that all practical steps are taken to avoid discrimination. Such personnel include supervisory and managerial staff, employee resourcing specialists and receptionist staff. The key processes are those to do with:

- Employee resource planning
- Recruitment and selection
- Basic pay, terms and conditions of work
- Appraisal, training and development
- Career development, promotion and transfers
- Benefits and rewards
- Health, safety and welfare
- Termination of employment

Relevant training and guidance is particularly important for those concerned with the recruitment and selection, appraisal, training and development, promotion or transfer of personnel. They must understand what direct and indirect discrimination means, and know how to identify any discriminatory attitudes that may affect decision-making. They must be made aware of the need to record ways in which applications for positions, training and rewards are handled, as well as the decisions made in those cases. Without such records, showing that all reasonable practical steps have been taken to avoid discrimination, they will find it difficult to disprove any claims of unlawful discriminatory treatment.

There must also be a knowledge of the law on providing access to opportunities for training and to promotion or other forms of reward or development. For example, if it is a condition of a management development programme that all participants must spend six months on a course in another area or region and there is no real justification for this (because there is a good course run locally, or the learning could be achieved by distance learning or in some other way), then the condition could be held to be unlawful because it discriminates against those caring for children, who would always find such a condition more difficult to comply with than other employees.

Problems of communication and understanding often cause or increase discriminatory attitudes and behaviour at work. Training, especially to raise awareness of how these problems can arise and of the special needs of minority groups in the workplace, can make a vital contribution to reducing these problems.

If there is an equal opportunity policy, then guidance must be given so that it is fully understood at every level, and that responsibilities under it are clear and are carried out competently.

Avoiding unlawful discrimination in employee development

Information about training and development opportunities and how to apply for them must be made known to all eligible employees, and must not be communicated in such a way as to exclude or disproportionately reduce the numbers of applicants from a particular racial group or sex.

There must be no direct or indirect discrimination in selecting people for training and development, and checks must be made regularly to see whether people from a particular racial group or from one or other sex do not apply for employment or promotion, are not recruited or promoted at all or are appointed but in significantly lower proportions than their rate of application. If any of these problems are occurring then the Training Manager must find out whether a major cause lies in a lack of the appropriate training or qualifications of these individuals. If it does, and if the reason is that training or other forms of development were not as accessible to them as to other employees, or that the design or 'language' of the learning methods involved posed particular problems for them, then changes must be made.

Positive action in training

Where, in the previous 12-month period, there have been no or proportionately few employees of a particular sex or racial group in certain jobs, areas or levels of work, then:

- Employers may provide access to training facilities which will help to fit them for such work or responsibilities.

- Employers may encourage them to apply for training or education, whether it is provided internally or externally.
- The Training Manager may design training schemes for school leavers, designed to reach members of such groups and may arrange training for promotion or skills training for those who lack particular expertise but show potential. (Supervisory training may include language training.)

It is also lawful to give access to relevant training when minority groups have special needs in respect of education or training. For example, if the workforce includes employees whose English is limited, then the Training Manager should ensure that communications are helped by training in English and communication skills, by training for managers and supervisors in the background and culture of racial minority groups, and even by providing, where possible, interpretation and translation facilities for grievance and other procedures and terms of employment.

> Discrimination in employment will not be solved by one or two major actions . . .Solutions will be found by avoiding complacency and paying attention to the several areas where discrimination can manifest itself or where the needs of ethnic minority employees require sensitive examination . . . Good human resource management involves making the best use of all available talent; it requires effective, i.e. bias free, systems of selection, training and motivation. (Roots, 1982)

Women's management training regularly attracts interest as more evidence is uncovered of a continuing bias against women striving for promotion in a male-dominated sector. However, women in non-managerial jobs have career development needs too, and Arkin (1991a) describes an award-winning personal and career development programme for such women, Springboard, pioneered at the BBC.

Personal and career development for women in non-managerial positions (based on Arkin, 1991a)
(With acknowledgements to A Arkin and *Personnel Management*)

What does the case study emphasize in terms of the planning, design and delivery of programmes catering for special groups and needs?

Springboard is a women's development programme that evolved from the women's development programme launched by the BBC in 1989, which won the Lady Platt Award for the best equal opportunities training initiative.

The programme arose out of a perceived need that, whilst the BBC had done much to open up opportunities for women managers, it was essential to widen these initiatives, extending personal and career development opportunities to the women (between 8,000 and 9,000) employed in non-managerial positions at the BBC. Better utilization and motivation of such a huge organizational resource was clearly in the interests of the business as well as to the benefit of individuals.

A consideration of the kinds of learning media and methods that should be used indicated at first sight that distance learning would be the most appropriate medium, given the extremely large size of the learning population. However, an analysis of the profile of that population highlighted the importance to the learners of support and encouragement from other women, and this led to the decision to design a programme which involved much face-to-face learning:

- Three one-day workshops held over three months
- A 250-page workbook involving about three hours' work a week for participants, and involving a range of self-assessment and personal learning plan activities
- The formation of formal and informal networks
- A mentoring system in the workplace
- The involvement of senior women in the organization

The programme, designed by the BBC's Management Training Unit working with Biographic Management consultancy, has become so highly regarded that it has been renamed Springboard and tailored for the use of other organizations including Grand Metropolitan Foods, Europe, who have integrated it into a much larger employee development initiative called the Learning Edge, designed to create a learning environment in which all employees can develop their full potential.

FEEDBACK NOTES

While an analysis of the study shows how carefully it was tailored to needs which were clearly of major importance to the organization as well as of the individuals concerned, the particular points to note here are:

1 **The learning medium and methods must be appropriate, efficient and flexible, given the needs and situation of the learners.** Choice was determined by an analysis of the purpose and objectives of the programme and of the profile of the learning population involved, of the need to encourage, motivate and stimulate the learners, and of the practicalities of the situation, resulting in a programme that met the needs of the very large group involved by offering a well-integrated variety of media and methods that were clearly both relatively cheap and highly effective. The costs of designing and reproducing the workbook would very quickly have been offset by the numbers of people using it, and it offered an ideal way of helping the learners to prepare for practical sessions, reflect on learning and transfer it continuously to their own individual situations. Thus choice of media and methods echoes those principles discussed in Chapter 16 (see p. 364).

2 **External recognition of the programme, and publicizing its continued success, led to its extension to similar groups in other organizations.** As with the BOC example, we can see the value that external recognition (the Lady Platt Award) can bring to a programme. The extension of Springboard to other organizations has been of great significance to many more women than the original BBC group for whom it was first intended.

3 **Particular initiatives in employee development need to be integrated into wider training and development strategy and plans.** This is the significance of Grand Metropolitan's reaction – that a programme designed to meet the needs of a special group must also become an integrated part of overall employee development strategy in the organization. Without such integration, any special initiatives can quickly lose their impact and die once the needs of a particular set of individuals have received a specific training response.

Still in the field of equal opportunities, but moving also into the wider area of the retention and development of valued employees, let us now look at another initiative.

Retainer and Re-entry scheme, Leicester City Council
(By permission of Leicester City Council)

What points does this case study make about training and development for special needs? And what are likely to be the benefits of the scheme described as far as the organization is concerned?

Leicester City Council employs approximately 4,400 people, and in 1975 it adopted an equal opportunities policy. In 1981 it decided to adopt a higher profile in this area, and by 1983 research into the position of women within the Council had led to the identification of areas for immediate action. Part of the research had involved circulating a questionnaire to all employees who had left the Council over the past two years on maternity leave. Only 5 per cent subsequently returned to work at the Council although 95 per cent, according to questionnaire responses, intended to take up employment again in the future and about 10 per cent had already done so, although not with the Council.

Clearly such a loss of valuable human resources could not be ignored. The loss applied to ethnic minorities as much, if not more, than to other groups, and it seemed likely that any scheme involving attempts to retain those who had taken maternity leave, and to ease problems of re-entry into the Council, would be taken up as much by those from ethnic minority groups as from others. The 'retainer and re-entry' initiative introduced in 1986 offered positive action on a range of barriers to equal opportunities in the workplace. It was applicable to anyone who left for domestic reasons, and therefore extended, for example, to those (including men) who had had to leave work temporarily to care for a dependent relative.

The scheme is a striking application of the Council's overall policy on equal opportunity in employment, whereby all employees and applicants for employment are to be given equal opportunities in recruitment, in training and in promotion to more senior jobs, irrespective of their racial origins, sex, disability, marital status, religious beliefs, social background, or sexual orientation.

The scheme, which involves a medical examination as a condition of re-entry, consists of an integrated package of activities:

1 **Undertaking ten days' work experience during each year of absence,** not necessarily in a two-week full-time block. This enables employees to acquire new skills and knowledge and prevent current skills from becoming obsolescent.

2 **Attending an annual refresher training course of 2½ days during each year of absence.** This enables the analysis of training needs, and establishing what work areas should best be included in the annual work experience period.

3 **A re-entry induction training programme during the six-week period prior to return.** This involves work on personal effectiveness, dealing with stress, assertiveness, time management, career planning and matters related to the particular jobs of the individuals concerned. Individual reinduction may

extend over the first two or three weeks of return, and involve guided reading, visits to new locations, introductions to relevant employees within and outside their section, etc.

4 **A six-month probationary period with formal reviews and counselling at three-, six- and 12-month intervals for every returner.** The 12-month review provides a further opportunity for manager and employee to come together to discuss personal development planning following re-entry.

5 The appointment, if returners wish, of a mentor to smooth the re-entry process.

6 Payment of one set of professional fees during the first year of return.

In its first year of operation (1988) take-up was small, as had been expected given the problems involved in targeting potential applicants, but in 1989 it had risen to from 3 to 14 out of 100 potential returners, all women, four being Asian and ten white. Their salary levels varied from £7,600 p.a. to £14,700 p.a. and previous jobs ranged widely from clerical to professional. Only manual staff were under-represented, and this is an area which received particular attention.

The scheme is seen as important to the Council's goal of improving equality of opportunity, and other initiatives to achieve that goal include planning for child care provision and job sharing.

FEEDBACK NOTES

We see in this case study an example of a training and development programme which is being used to retain valued staff who otherwise would leave the organization permanently. A particularly interesting feature is the use of the auditing method. It established the exact nature of the need initially identified, and in this case led to valuable data being gathered that both reinforced and extended an understanding of the needs involved, the benefit, to the organization as well as to individuals, of responding to them, and ways in which they might most effectively be tackled.

The use of an audit of some kind is invaluable when tackling the analysis and planning of training and development related to special needs and contingencies.

The benefits anticipated from the scheme were established at the start as being centrally related to business needs. This was essential in order to get the full backing of the Council. They included:

- Improved returns on the training of staff, and the retention of skills and talents of some of the Council's employees which might otherwise be lost (the audit showed how many people, once skilled employees of the Council, left after maternity leave and took up work elsewhere, and how many more intended to do so – a great waste of expensively trained resources)
- A pool of trained, committed ex-employees who could be available to cover peaks in workload, holidays, long-term absence and maternity leave
- Savings in recruitment and relocation costs

The design of the scheme was tailored to the particular needs of the learning population concerned, both during their period of absence from the organization, and during their re-entry to it. It smooths the path of re-entry for all types of applicant, and ensures a learning support system that extends through and after their period of probation.

Health and Safety

Health and safety is an area of major concern in training, both because of the need to comply with the law, and because of the many ways in which neglect in these areas can directly damage an organization's personnel, products and image. In the field of catering, training in food hygiene is an urgent priority, especially given the public's increased awareness and concern.

The Food Safety Act (1991) requires catering organizations to provide hygiene training for all food handlers, and if this requirement is ignored the Government, after consultation, can impose training itself.

Sutcliffe Catering's approach to food hygiene training (based on Arkin, 1991b)
(With acknowledgements to A Arkin and *Personnel Management*)

Sutcliffe Catering Group is one of the largest industrial catering companies in the UK, with a very dispersed workforce and the high turnover of staff typical of this kind of business.

Training in food hygiene was essential for many reasons, including the possibility of enforced training by government regulation and the need to maintain Sutcliffe's reputation for providing high quality and reliability of service.

> We introduced the programme to reassure our clients and also to give our staff the confidence of knowing they are acting in a very professional and safe way. (Peter Dixon, Sutcliffe's Director of Training and Development, quoted in Arkin, 1991b)

Given the number of learners, and the geographical spread of the 1,700 establishments in which they were employed, distance learning was clearly an essential medium, and the company worked with the Royal Society of Health to produce a programmed learning package comprising five units of competence in food hygiene.

Having completed the package, employees must then pass an externally administered and assessed examination leading to the Royal Society of Health's Certificate in Essential Food Hygiene. This gives credibility to the exercise and, being a nationally recognized qualification, helps to motivate and reward successful employees, especially those with no previous qualifications.

By early 1991 3,500 employees had sat the examination, with predictions of 100 per cent success. Furthermore workers in the company were already showing a greater awareness of the importance of hygiene, and an interest in further training.

This 'Quality Through Hygiene' programme is part of an overall training strategy that won Sutcliffe a National Training Award in 1989.

> A flexible, modular approach is used at all levels, and efforts are made to integrate learning into people's jobs. Six members of staff who recently completed a Diploma of Management Studies programme, for instance, gained most of their credits through the accreditation of prior learning [in the workplace]. (Arkin, 1991b).

Arkin reports that the company is seeking to become a 'learning organization', with training acting as a major way of retaining valued and expensive employees.

The case study reinforces important learning points made earlier in this chapter:

1 Well-planned and effective learning events to meet special needs can have an ever-widening impact on employee development mission and strategy in the organization, and can themselves lead to the identification of other important learning needs within the organization.

2 Where business strategy and its related needs can be shown to be the major trigger for a particular learning event or events, this will do much to secure management's commitment to that event and to its outcomes.

3 The aim should always be to locate particular employee development initiatives clearly within the framework of wider employee development and resourcing strategy and plans.

4 The use of an audit of some kind is an invaluable tool when tackling the analysis and planning of training and development for special needs and contingencies.

5 Planning, design and evaluation of all learning events should be done on a continuous basis, with information from evaluation influencing the next stage in the planning cycle.

6 The identification of the key competences needed is often the most effective method of determining the focus and content of the learning event.

7 The learning media and methods must be appropriate, efficient and flexible, given the needs of the particular learning initiative.

8 Wherever possible training should be tied to external vocational qualifications, as this is an important way of attracting staff, as well as of motivating and benefiting the individuals involved in the learning event.

9 External recognition of particular training and development initiatives often provide the trigger for such initiatives being extended both within and outside the organization.

Principles and Practical Guidelines for Training and Development for Special Groups and Contingencies

The main principles to be observed in the inception, planning, design and delivery of such learning events are the same from one case to the next, and go back to the basic theory about the inception, design and delivery of learning events as outlined in Figure 10 (see p. 327). However, some initial practical questions to ask in the planning and design processes are:

1 **At which levels and across which sectors in the organization do the needs exist?** Needs may be at one or all of the following levels: corporate, business unit and operational (see p. 235). They may be specific to one sector (for example supervisors) or may relate to many or all employees (for example, initiatives to do with equal opportunities, health and safety, total quality or customer care).

2 **At what stages of the employment cycle should the learning events related to these needs be provided in relation to:**

- Induction and basic training (therefore aimed at newcomers or those newly promoted)?
- Improving current performance (therefore aimed at existing job holders with knowledge, skills or attitudinal deficiencies)?
- Continuous development and career planning (therefore aimed at potential and new recruits and those who are established in their present positions)?

(See pp. 283–5)

3 **How should the needs be analysed?** A wide range of approaches and techniques have been outlined in Chapters 12–14. However, with a special contingency, as the case studies in this chapter have shown, the audit is an invaluable method. It establishes the nature and extent of the need as perceived by the key parties, it will reveal the kind of outcomes required in relation to tackling the need, and it will yield vital information about the most appropriate design, content and methods for learning (see, for example, Ashton et. al., 1980; Murphy and Swanson, 1988; Applegarth, 1991).

4 **Are knowledge, skills, attitudes needed in relation to:**

- Task performance?
- Task management?
- Boundary management?
- Motivation?

(see pp. 289–90)

5 **What kind of learning should be involved:**

- Instrumental?
- Dialogic?
- Self-reflective?

(See pp. 161–2)

6 **Could the learning events lead to NVQs?**

Exercises

1 To win a National Training Award (NTA) an organization 'needs to be using training imaginatively and dynamically to solve well-defined business problems'. Either draft a summary of an NTA entry from your organization, in which you make the case for an award; or suggest what your organization might do in order to gain an award. (November 1989)

2 Department X is staffed by a manager, a supervisor and 20 experienced employees. A 12-month developmental plan has just been agreed between the manager and his or her superiors; the plan includes provisions whereby:

(a) a new computerized statistical system will be introduced, requiring all members of the team to enter operational data into computer terminals, and to interpret feedback data; and
(b) those below supervisory level will be reduced by four members (who will be transferred to another department) without any reduction in work.

The manager has asked for your advice. Draft a 'first thoughts' set of training plans to deal with the change. (November 1989)

References

APPLEGARTH M. *How to Take a Training Audit.* London, Kogan Page. 1991
ARKIN A. 'A springboard to equal opportunities'. *Personnel Management*, February 1991a. pp. 57-8

ARKIN A. 'Keeping it clean'. *Personnel Management*, March 1991b. pp. 55-7

ASHTON D, BRAIDEN E AND EASTERBY-SMITH M. *Auditing Management Development*. Aldershot, Gower. 1980

BARNES D. 'What's so different about training disabled people?' *Personnel Management*, September 1981. pp. 45-7

COMMISSION FOR RACIAL EQUALITY. *Equal Opportunity in Employment: A guide for employers*. London, CRE. 1983

KANE J AND WALLACE T. 'Developing supervision'. *Personnel Management*, October 1991. pp. 46-7

MURPHY B A AND SWANSON R A. 'Auditing training and development'. *Journal of European International Training*, Vol. 12, no. 2, 1988. pp. 13-16

ROOTS P. 'Special provision for ethnic minorities'. *Personnel Management*, November 1982. pp. 24-7

STOREY J. 'HRM in action: the truth is out at last'. *Personnel Management*, April 1992. pp. 28-31

WARR P B AND BIRD M W. *Identifying Supervisory Needs: Training Information Paper No. 2*. London, HMSO. 1968

Further useful reading

BELBIN R M. *Training the Adult Worker*. London, HMSO. 1964

CUTHBERT D. 'Why working together means training together'. *Personnel Management*, October 1984. pp. 47-9

DONNELLY E AND BARRETT B. 'Safety training since the Act'. *Personnel Management*, June 1981. pp. 43-6

FOWLER A. 'How to build teams'. *Personnel Management Plus*, March 1992. pp. 25-6

GLUCKLICH P. 'Women's management training in a ghetto?'. *Personnel Management*, September 1985. pp. 39-43

INSTITUTE OF PERSONNEL MANAGEMENT. *Age and Employment: IPM statement*. London, IPM. 1991 (An important reference for everyone concerned with decision-making about people at work)

JENNINGS C, McCARTHY W E J AND UNDY R. *Managers and Industrial Relations: The identification of training needs*. Sheffield, Manpower Services Commission. 1983

LEWIS J AND McLAVERTY C. 'Facing up to the needs of the older manager'. *Personnel Management*, January 1991. pp. 32-5

MARSHALL J. *Women Managers: Travellers in a male world*. Chichester, Wiley. 1984

MUNYARD T. 'Homophobia at work and how to manage it'. *Personnel Management*, June 1988. pp. 46-50

NAYLOR P. 'In praise of older workers'. *Personnel Management*, November 1987. pp. 44-8

PARKYN A. 'Operating equal opportunities in the Health Service'. *Personnel Management*, August 1991. pp. 29-33

PERSONNEL MANAGEMENT. 'Supervisor training: factsheet 6'. Supplement to *Personnel Management*, June 1988

PERSONNEL MANAGEMENT. 'Outdoor training: factsheet 9'. Supplement to *Personnel Management*, September 1988

PERSONNEL MANAGEMENT. 'Training Extra' section. *Personnel Management*, monthly. (This section contains important practical examples of training and development related to a wide range of special groups and needs in organizations, and as such constitutes an essential learning resource.)

WAINWRIGHT D. *Learning from Uncle Sam: Equal opportunity programmes.* London, Runnymede Trust. 1980

Chapter 19

Developing managers for the organization

Learning Objectives

After reading this chapter you will:

1 understand what management development involves and how it should relate to the employee development and resourcing functions;
2 understand the importance of linking management development to organizational goals and strategy;
3 know the basic components of a management development system and what will make the system effective;
4 understand the main issues involved in the debate about management competences and the aims and work of the Management Charter Initiative, and be able to relate them to the needs of management development in a particular organization.

Introduction

Management development can be defined as the planned process of ensuring through an appropriate learning environment and experiences the continuous supply and retention of effective managers at all levels to meet the requirements of an organization and enhance its strategic capability.

The function of management development comprises three essential activities:

- Analysis of present and future management needs
- Assessment of existing and potential skills and effectiveness of managers against those needs
- Production of policy, strategy and plans to meet those needs.

Management development can focus on one or both of two issues:

- **Manager development** – building on the performance and potential of individual managers and providing a continuous supply of trained and competent managers to fill future vacancies
- **Management development** – building a shared culture across the whole management group and enhancing management capability throughout the organization in order to improve the organization's capability to survive and prosper

Management development in this latter sense forms part of the overall development of the organization. (Burgoyne, 1988) 'Organisational performance and managerial effectiveness are inevitably intertwined . . . Managerial effectiveness can only be considered in its organisational context.' (Brodie and Bennett, 1979)

Management development must be centrally concerned with organizational values and with attitudinal change. On the first point, Lippitt (1983) warns:

> If study reveals that an organization's value system is the result of dogmatic, authoritarian attitudes . . . the inability of its present management to keep pace with a changing world may render useless whatever management development takes place in the individual employee (Ibid., p. 37).

On the second, he writes:

> The most meaningful aspect of personal change resulting from a management development process is the examination and alteration of attitudes within the organisation. Reinforcement will need to be related to meaningful renewal systems (Ibid., p. 38).

This means that management development must focus on opportunities for self-reflective as well as instrumental and dialogic learning (see pp. 161–2), and this highlights the importance of focusing on methods involving project work, case studies, role-playing, sensitivity training, action learning and self-development. For a detailed discussion of these and other methods, see Sadler (1989, pp. 230–7) and Mumford (1989).

Let us look first at the wider context of management development, and then at its practice in organizations.

National Concern About Management Development

Major reports, 1969-87

Management development came under much scrutiny during the 1980s, with a series of reports pointing to the urgent need for improvements in the UK (Deloitte, Haskins and Sells, 1989). However, long before that there had been evidence of major deficiencies.

1 **The Mant Report (Mant, 1969)** showed that only 7–8 per cent of British managers attended courses lasting a week or more, and most of these were high fliers. The report highlighted the dangerous and growing attitudinal gap between such uneducated but experienced managers and many new recruits with business or management qualifications. It also emphasized the scepticism with which senior managers often viewed classroom learning.

2 **The Owen Report (Council for Industry of Management Education 1970)** looked at a sample of companies in the manufacturing industry and their attitudes – in the main very unfavourable – towards products of the rapidly expanding undergraduate and postgraduate courses in business studies. The report concluded that courses should focus more on the competences typifying successful managers, and aim for a working knowledge of the various functions of management. The report was critical of business schools, of their quality of provision and of the credibility and expertise of their staff in relation to the real world of management.

3 ***Competence and Competition*** **(Institute of Manpower Studies, 1984)** focused on vocational education and training in the UK, comparing it very unfavourably with key competitors West Germany, the USA and Japan. The link between education and training on the one hand and the ability to achieve and sustain a competitive edge on the other was made clear, and the inadequacy of the link in Britain was powerfully expressed.

4 ***A Challenge to Complacency*** **(Coopers and Lybrand, 1985)** reiterated and expanded on the message of *Competence and Competition*, showing in particular a disturbing mixture of ignorance and apathy among British senior managers about the development of their

human resources. Attitudes emerged as a vital focus in any attempts to improve the development of managers and their staff.

5 **The Mangham and Silver Report (1986)** was a major survey of management training in the UK which showed that over half of British companies made no training provision for managers, with one fifth of even the larger companies (with over 1,000 employees) falling into this category. 'Of those that did, the medium expenditure per annum was only £6.00 per manager – and senior managers were apportioned even less' (Sadler, 1989, p. 228).

6 ***Developing Directors*** **(Mumford et al., 1987)** was based on research involving over 140 directors of 45 organizations during 1985 and 1986. It concluded that whereas some companies did have systematic developmental schemes, and a few could see links between the outcomes of the schemes and the performance of the company, most of the directors themselves did not attribute their success to any formal processes of development.

7 ***The Making of Managers*** **(Handy Report, 1987)** compared management development in the USA, West Germany, France, Japan and the UK. The message was that, no matter which country was examined, and how different were the routes to and through management in each country, the UK suffered badly in all comparisons.

Handy (1987) made some key international comparisons in management development practice:

- In America the route to a managerial career in a large corporation is the MBA. In Britain at that time there were only 1,200 MBA graduates being produced every year, whereas the USA produced 70,000. Although the USA is four times as big as Britain, figures of those with degrees in business, whether undergraduate or postgraduate, were 40 times bigger. 85 per cent of top managers in the USA and Japan had degrees, compared with about 25 per cent of top managers in Britain.
- In Germany, 54 per cent of the directors on management boards of the 100 largest companies had doctorates in engineering, science or law. On the other hand, there were only 4,000 qualified accountants in Germany, and in Japan 7,000, while British business was, and has remained, dominated by that profession, with over

120,000 qualified accountants in 1987 – one immediately obvious explanation of the obsession of British business with short-term bottom-line payoff, to the detriment of investments needing a longer-term perspective, notably research and development and human resource development (see Chapter 3).

- Most well-educated Germans do not join a large company until about 27 years of age, because most follow an apprenticeship after school and then pursue a degree and often a higher degree in subjects such as engineering, law or economics. In Japan and in Britain, the average age for joining such a company is 22, but in Japan, unlike Britain, the potential manager will study law or engineering at a top university and, after entry to a large firm, will go through a 'rigorous process of job rotation, private study and classroom learning which can last for up to 15 years' before being promoted to the first level of management. (Handy, 1987)
- In France the route to management in a larger organization is either through a *grande école* in business or engineering, or through some other educational pathway leading to the same kind of functional qualifications as in Japan and Germany. In France, too, the law requires all firms to spend 1·4 per cent of their wage bill on continuing education and training, and corporations over about 2,000 employees spend three times that amount, with about one third going on management training. As we have seen in Chapter 4, such investment is common across most of mainland Europe and the USA, on a scale unknown in the UK.

Clearly, management education, training and continuous development have a very high priority in countries which are our main competitors. In the Handy Report, the development of managers, as of the rest of the UK workforce, emerged as haphazard, lacking the commitment of top management, and dominated by short-termism and chronic under-investment. Surveys such as that quoted by Handy (1987, p. 10) indicating that 36 per cent of middle managers had received no management training since starting work gave vivid meaning to his conclusion that 'management training in Britain is too little, too late, for too few' (Ibid., p. 11).

8 ***The Making of British Managers* (Constable and McCormick, 1987)** argued that in the UK it was lack of opportunity that was now proving to be the main deterrent to effective management education,

training and development, with the average UK manager receiving only about one day's formal training each year and the majority having none. All development should be tied closely to organizational needs.

One very powerful message coming from all these reports is that those who are uneducated, untrained and undeveloped themselves are not likely to be committed to the education, training and development of others – so that the widespread apathy and ignorance of British management about training and development, to which *A Challenge to Complacency* (Coopers and Lybrand, 1985) drew attention, are unsurprising and likely to continue. The same is true of the ignorance displayed about how best to organize learning and the lack of importance and expertise attached to its systematic planning and evaluation, also highlighted in that report. This ignorance has been displayed with particularly damaging effects in relation to Youth Training, as Keep (1989) strikingly shows. However, recent research indicates that attitudes are now changing, and that new techniques in management development are being tried by many organizations, albeit in a fragmented and *ad hoc* way. (Storey, 1991)

The debate about qualifications and competences

The Management Charter Initiative

The immediate outcome of the Handy and Constable and McCormick Reports and the publicity they received was the Management Charter Initiative (MCI) supported by the CBI, the BIM and the Foundation of Management Education. A Council for Management Education and Development (CMED) was established, headed by Bob Reid, Chairman of Shell UK, with the brief of providing a forum for many management development issues. In 1988 the CMED, broadened in scope, became the National Forum for Management Education and Development (NFMED), a policy-making, standard-setting and accrediting body.

The MCI, run by and for employers, is the operating and marketing arm of the NFMED. In 1988 the MCI launched a ten-point Code of Practice and by 1990 over 530 organizations representing about seven million people in both the public and private sectors had joined the Initiative.

The NFMED is the Lead Industry Body for developing management and supervisory standards. It has established, though the MCI, a network of local employers and providers of educational support, working closely with TECs and LECs at local levels. These MCI forums seek to involve all those interested in promoting good management in an area or sector, building on existing local activities and strengths. They also aim to bring to local employers MCI products and services which are being developed centrally and to take a central role in promoting the MCI's Code of Practice, so that gradually 'the MCI as a mass movement will become a ''bottom up'' rather than ''top down'' organization'. (Blake, 1990)

The ladder of management qualifications

The MCI has promoted the establishment of national professional management qualifications at three levels: certificate, diploma and degree/masters' level, with existing qualification courses such as DMS and MBA being integrated into a national hierarchical structure. This ladder of qualifications is envisaged as complementing the continuous development of managers in the workplace. In November 1990, national standards of competence, applied to first level and middle management and developed by the MCI after a widespread consultative process, were launched (*Personnel Management*, 1990). The intention is to extend them to supervisory and senior management levels. Subsequently the Council for National Academic Awards has pioneered a set of pilot certificate courses to test the concept of and market for a national certificate in management.

The concept of the Chartered Manager

The concept of the Chartered Manager who gains 'professional' status having climbed the qualification ladder and having acquired appropriate competences and experience, was one that the MCI initially tried hard to promote. However, the aim of achieving some kind of chartered professional status for the huge and amorphous body of 'managers' is generally perceived to be unrealistic, and has given way to a wider concern with ensuring national standards of competence tied in some feasible way to a flexible structure of management qualifications. Exponents of the system argue that there does need to be:

> . . . an architecture of qualifications easily understood by individuals so that they can identify what they should be studying once they have made the initial step. In this way the whole revolution of self-development will be taken a stage further. (Bob Reid, in Syrett, 1988b)

The competences framework

The approach used to derive management competences was functional analysis, and fears have already been expressed that this will lead to a skills training approach in management education and development. However, the competences are proving popular with many companies who, like Safeway, the first to receive MCI endorsement for a management training scheme, see the value of national standards as measuring tools in staff recruitment and appraisal as well as in training and development. There is also the attraction for trainees of being able to get a national certificate qualification after completing a first-level management training scheme.

In May 1991 *Personnel Management* reported that there appeared to be a widespread lack of interest in the MCI by employers, according to a survey by BDO Consulting, which was sent to 2,000 companies in process industries, with a response from 141. 71 per cent of respondents said they did not intend to make use of the MCI national standards of management competence, and the impression was that employers thought the initiative 'was too general and did not take account of organisations' culture and needs'.

However, the survey did show that in 80 per cent of respondent companies investment in management training and development had increased in the past three years, with between half and three quarters expecting to invest in various forms of training more heavily in the forthcoming three years.

Criticisms of the management competences approach

Opponents of the use of competences to determine the training and development needs of managers, and as the basis for attempting to assess their performance, argue that the complexity and diversity of managerial work makes the concept of a 'profession' and measurable units of competence leading to national qualifications both suspect and dangerous. (Syrett, 1988a; Dixon, 1988; Sadler, 1989) There is much research evidence to support these views, as the following summaries indicate:

1 **The tasks of managers are hard to define at any but the most generalized level.** Schools of thought from Taylor (1911) and Scientific Management through Human Relations and early Organizational Psychology to Systems theories have emphasized the rational, controlling nature of the work that managers do. The concept has been one of clear-cut roles performed according to a hierarchy of defined activities, 'where the manager is seen as a rational actor who is in charge and who can control the organization' (Partridge, 1989, p. 204). It is this concept that dominates the functional analysis approach taken by the Lead Body for Management Development.

However, research into what managers actually do consistently shows a different picture:

> Managerial work across all levels from chief executive to foreman is characterized by pace, brevity, variety and fragmentation . . . It is hectic and fragmented requiring the ability to shift continuously from relationship to relationship, from topic to topic, from problem to problem (Partridge, 1989, p. 205).

Mintzberg (1973) lists ten key management activities or roles, in three general categories – interpersonal, informational and decisional. While his model is widely respected, it enhances our understanding rather than acting as a practical guide to developing and assessing management competences. This is because, as he also shows, managerial roles are highly variable and involve pursuing a variety of objectives, often in parallel, in changing ways according to the decision of the individual manager in the particular situation. This explains why managers are usually allowed a very wide span of discretion; it enables the individual to choose how best to operate, what tasks to tackle, and how, at any point. 'Competence' is therefore a matter of wide-ranging, ever-changing and fragmented activity across many organizational, job, task, time and resource boundaries, not of the orderly execution of discrete units of activity in unchanging ways through time.

There is also the point that the 'competence' of managers depends on others' efforts and behaviour as well as their own. While managers 'may well be responsible for the performance of their units . . . it is almost impossible to determine the individual contribution of the manager' (Partridge, 1989, p. 207).

2 **Management is a political and pressurized activity.** Research also

shows that management is not an objective and consistently rational activity. Instead, it involves constantly trying to find 'a way through contradictory demands in a world of uncertainty'. (Edwards, 1990) The manager is confronted daily with a multiplicity of unique pressures that are usually unpredictable in their frequency, type or strength. Political skills and creative ability play a leading part in enabling them to cut their way through these complexities in order to control the processes and produce the results for which they are responsible.

3 **Managers' roles and jobs are changing, often rapidly.** Research carried out by Ashridge Management College (Barham et al., 1988) indicates that management's role is moving 'from an old order based on efficiency, production, optimisation, conformity and authority, to a new order emphasising enterprise, marketing, management of change, initiative and leadership' (Sadler and Barham, 1988, p. 51). Sadler (1989) points out that by the turn of the century typical managers will be in charge of service not production activities, and economic activity will be knowledge-intensive rather than labour- or capital-intensive, with the skills they need being those:

> . . . of leadership, motivation and managing change, with particular emphasis on managing an educated and articulate workforce; understanding of, and ability to use, information technology; the development of innovative, creative and entrepreneurial ability; sensitivity to environmental trends; and the development of the individual's ability to adapt to change personally (Ibid., 243).

What conclusion can we draw from the points raised in the debate about competences and qualifications? First perhaps, in relation to competences, while in the short term, and in the more stable organizations, a competence-based approach to management development can produce excellent results (see Chapter 12), competences should be analysed in the context of the particular organization and agreed as meaningful and relevant by the key parties involved in and affected by the management development programme. Secondly, even in changing conditions a competency-based approach can be used, providing that there is a high degree of certainty and agreement of the kind of qualities and skills needed by those who will have to cope effectively with those conditions. And thirdly, where it is clear that tomorrow's competences will be radically different from today's, with no certainty as to their exact nature and interrelationship, some alternative approach to management development will be needed.

As to qualifications, Chambers (1990) made a telling point when she contended that most of the national reports and surveys, while promoting a healthy debate on management education, have led to a preoccupation with the provision of more management qualifications instead of with finding the answer to the fundamental question: do qualifications produce more effective managers?

Mumford (1987), examining how senior managers developed themselves, concluded that the possession of a management qualification was of little relevance: what promoted the most effective learning was experience and role models. The majority of them have learned deliberately but incidentally from their experience and from contact with wise experienced managers. It is for this reason that the Association for Management Education and Development (AMED) promotes the idea of user-driven management development, with an emphasis on self-development which helps managers cope with and learn from the challenges of working in a greatly diversified range of roles over a wide variety of organizational settings.

These points are in line with Japanese practice which, however, is a highly integrated and carefully planned mix of activities and processes. The focus is on recruiting people with a high standard of all-round education and then giving them a rigorous, coherent, continuing discipline of experience, supplemented by on- and off-the-job training when relevant, and with a major focus on self-development. These processeses usually continue for ten or more years before promotion to management becomes a possibility. The Japanese produce only about 60 MBAs a year (Handy, 1987), and the Germans none, yet their strategies of management development are, judging by business performance standards, highly effective. However, it should not be forgotten that in both cases the recruits have a very high standard of education before they enter employment – not a characteristic of the average British manager. The case for the educated employee therefore seems clear, but the case for the management-educated manager much less so.

Making Management Development a Business-led Activity

> By and large in most organizations . . . MTD (Management Training and Development) is bolted on and not actually integrated into the business strategy. It raises all sorts of difficulties because it means people have to think things through, have a pretty clear view of what the strategy is, what the implications are and how it all hangs together (Brown et al., 1989, p. 75).

At this point, let us look at a case study that makes important points about management development, some of which have been raised already, while others will follow.

Management development at British Rail (based on Collof and Goodge, 1990)
The views that follow are those of the two authors and should not be taken to represent an official statement by BR about its management development strategy and programme, both of which have in any case changed subsequently.

How was management development made into a business-related activity at British Rail?

Changed managerial roles, tasks and competences

BR is one of those organizations, increasingly common in both the public and private sectors today, whose structure has had to change completely in line with the demands of product diversification or the need to provide local services more efficiently and effectively. During the 1980s and early 1990s it became a decentralized business, with 125,000 employees working across the country in what are effectively separate businesses, further subdivided into profit-accountable units. Managerial jobs in the new structure are radically different. They are also bigger, requiring highly able business managers.

> Managers are no longer expected to run smooth, problem-free operations and nothing more; and meeting traditional targets is not enough. Managers are expected to develop their businesses, to build revenues, reduce costs, seek and penetrate new markets. In short, managers are expected to be entrepreneurs as well as efficient operators.
> . . . Commercial judgement, financial competence, strategic planning, marketing, customer-orientation and the ability to sell ideas persuasively are topics which now matter just as much as the traditional focuses of leadership, motivation, of staff, problem-solving and time management (Colloff and Goodge, 1990, p. 50).

Succession planning for an unpredictable future

By the late eighties BR faced the additional problem of a gap in supply – there were not enough managers of the kind now needed. Succession planning in the past had been of the conventional long-term kind, developing graduates over a 20-year time-span, with courses and assessment processes geared to identifying those who could fill particular posts in the next five or ten years. Now, the time-scale was much shorter, and the nature of the business – and therefore of the kinds of managers needed to run it – was subject to such a fast rate of change that the competences needed for the effective manager today or tomorrow might change dramatically over a longer period, and be impossible to predict in terms of even five years, let alone longer.

A business-led management development system

The system has several components, including a systematic performance and development review programme for the top managers, involving two reviews a year and time for improvement between reviews. This process leads to identification of high-fliers and their needs in the context of business objectives. A data bank has been established, with high fliers attending a special MBA programme run with three business schools.

A development planning centre lies at the heart of the system, and consists of three days of intensive management assessment and development planning, focusing on the needs created by smaller business units, rising expectations of customers, and market changes. The centre is 'exceptionally clear [in its] purpose, an elitist centre, a business-oriented centre, and a centre committed to concerted action through line management'. (Ibid.)

Its aim is 'to get able entrepreneurs into senior management quickly. It openly communicates this aim to all participants:

> The centre's objectives are to set concerted and appropriate development programmes for high-potential individuals and to improve personal career decisions, succession planning and senior appointments through the provision of better information on people (Ibid., p. 51).

Selection is stringent, involving the assessment of seven competences agreed by the centre, relevant line managers and nominees as crucial to success for business unit managers, and the completion of an enterprise project which must be about taking a new business opportunity, costed, with projected figures and showing a likely profit. Selection does not depend on management level, experience, qualifications or age. 'The centre is elitist but it is not closed' (Ibid., p. 52).

Key competences are at present mainly about getting business units going, and are therefore entrepreneurial in their bias; however, they will be redefined as and when the units reach maturity and need more of the kinds of skills of running a mature business efficiently.

> Every participant leaves the centre with a development programme which specifies present competency levels, appropriate developmental priorities, learning targets, and a timetable of training and development methods. Most development programmes involve six months of intensive work, often using in-company experience, projects and guidance, plus some training courses pitched at an appropriate senior level. (Ibid.)

Participants' managers are fully involved in the planning process, and in the implementation of the programme arising from it.

Monitoring and evaluating the outcomes of management development

Evaluation by reference to the reactions of the learners and their managers has revealed a very high level of perceived value attached to the management development system and its outcomes. Evaluation by reference to outcomes in the job and departmental situation show that most development programmes have been fully carried out, and none have been ignored.

Evaluation of outcomes for the business is ongoing, but the centre has so far identified senior management potential in about 80 per cent of its participants, and has uncovered much previously unknown management potential. In addition, 'reports and plans created by the centre are being fed into BR's new process for auditing and managing talent' (Ibid.) and details of the abilities of participants are being made known to business units with further information for appointment or succession planning purposes available on request.

Costs

Although there are high setting-up costs, the ongoing management development programme is 'low cost, with no direct expenditure involved, and contributes to the participant's current job performance' (Ibid., p. 53).

FEEDBACK NOTES

The key points about management development indicated by the case study include the following:

- The aims of management development were clearly defined and directly aligned to business strategy.

- The management development system was designed carefully, with the full commitment of top management, to achieve those aims.
- Its objectives were clearly communicated.
- Personal development programmes ensured that individuals were developed systematically and relevantly, with their own commitment and that of their managers.
- Succession planning in the light of an unpredictable future was tackled, focusing on: general areas of competence rather than rigidly defined units of competence; reviewing those competences for their relevance through time; actively involving business units in the nomination and development of high fliers; and operating an assessment centre which, while elitist, was also open to anyone with the required indicators of potential.
- There was careful monitoring and evaluation of outcomes.
- Costs were minimal, as learning was based mainly on guided learning from experience.

Designing a business-led management development programme

When designing management development programmes particular attention must be paid not only to the purpose and objectives of that programme and the needs and types of learners, but also to the practicalities of how to manage, deliver and evaluate the programme. We shall deal with those practicalities in the next section. In the meantime, here is another exercise to test your creative skills!

Using management development to improve business performance

You are the Management Development Manager of one of the country's leading companies supplying a diverse range of electronic, analytical and computational products and services. It has always been characterized by high innovation and quality, and for its positive values related to managing its people.

By the mid-eighties a combination of external pressures meant that the company managers had to become more strategic in their culture and abilities, capable of responding to the macro issues the company was facing, both as individuals and as members of a company-wide management community. The managers come mainly from a technical background, and fewer than 40 per cent have any formal business education. Most have worked for years in an extremely successful company where costs received little emphasis. They are also used to the autonomy and local cultures of the company's functional matrix management system. With key markets on the decline, new technology needing heavy investment, major competition from small companies and low-cost foreign companies, and costs rising rapidly within the company, these managers must now quickly learn new attitudes and become much more entrepreneurial in their abilities and outlook.

Working with a national business school whose reputation for high-quality, effective business programmes is excellent, you now have to design a company-wide management development programme aimed at senior middle managers, aged 30-40, with ten years or more of service in the company, a technical background and education, and responsible for 20-50 people. Promotion prospects are decreasing, so it is important that this programme is not seen as a promotion ticket, but as a way of improving managerial competence in current roles. Key criteria for the programme are:

1 It must be business-focused, cost-efficient, have the involvement of senior management, and reflect corporate issues.

2 It must have a national focus.

3 It must be capable of being delivered by each of the company's regional training teams, and within their resources.

4 It must emphasize managers' responsibility for self-development, and stimulate them to a real commitment in this respect.

5 Teamwork must be a key feature, so that participants learn from and support each other in the learning processes.

6 The programme must focus on making the target population more effective in their current role.

Outline the kind of programme that you think will be appropriate, and its rationale.

FEEDBACK NOTES

Clearly the possibilities are many, but the following are the principles followed in one programme designed to meet this kind of case.

1 **The programme must focus on the strategic business issues that the company faces.** These will need to be defined by senior management, and one measure of the success of the programme will be how far it has helped managers to make a real impact on those issues.

2 **Methods must involve learning from and through experience, in order to increase competence and test it on real issues.** The best methods will involve project work, practical assignments, etc. These methods can help to achieve organizational change as well as focusing on particular strategic issues. The knowledge and techniques needed to tackle the issues can be provided in part by theoretical inputs, in part by help from skilled senior managers, and in part by external educationalists. Teamwork can be achieved by group-based projects supported by informal networking systems extending beyond the programme back into the various workplaces of the participants.

3 **There must be active involvement of regional training staff during the programme.** This can be achieved through a rotation of such staff in the delivery of the programme, as well as their involvement in programme design.

4 **The business school must work collaboratively with the company, and not impose ivory-tower attitudes or content on the programme.** Faculty members will therefore need to form part of the core planning team (say two, together with the Management Development Manager and a rotating regional training manager). They can then partner senior managers on the programme and respond to participants' need for 'a blend of internal knowledge and external wisdom which participants can exploit, particularly in developing their projects'. (Carter and Lumsdon, 1988)

Such a programme was in fact organized at Hewlett Packard, although it operated in the wider context of developing the company's European managers. Carter and Lumsdon's (1988) article describes the programme in detail, and presents a fascinating account of the challenges, problems and successes involved in an approach to management development in the company that produced major results for Hewlett Packard while also gaining the commitment of top management and the European middle managers who were programme members. The whole programme centred on groups of managers carrying out project work related to the ten most important strategic issues facing Hewlett Packard Europe. Top management took a leading role in identifying and explaining the issues, agreeing the projects, evaluating them, and being committed to their implementation. Relationships with the business schools involved proved very effective because of the many ways in which they responded positively to the perspectives and needs of the managers.

The task at Hewlett Packard was to change the attitudes and improve the current effectiveness of their middle managers. This was done through a programme that not only helped to provide the necessary training in skills, but also broadened the knowledge and began to influence the culture of the management group concerned; in other words it focused on both manager and management development and took account of attitudinal factors and organizational values. (Lippitt, 1983)

It also made the vital link between management development and strategic advantage. Developing managers, and especially senior managers, to improve their abilities in strategic decision-making, choice and implementation has a direct impact on the strategic capability of the organization. Fonda (1989) shows how to make the links between today's management development and tomorrow's business performance by building a management development system whose outcomes, as at Hewlett Packard and at British Rail, will give the organization an enhanced ability to survive, be profitable and grow.

In many companies, such aims are overlaid by a long-term need: to provide a continuing supply of high-calibre managers who are in key respects different from those who have dominated the system in the past, and from whose ranks will emerge in due course the ultimate leaders of the organization.

Succession planning and management development

The British Rail case study pointed to the central role of succession planning in management development – an issue dealt with in detail by Gratton and Syrett (Gratton, 1990; Gratton and Syrett, 1990) in their survey of different approaches to succession planning in a range of UK organizations. They emphasize the point made by Colloff and Goodge (1990) that systems for succession planning should vary according to the needs of business strategy in the organization, and should take account of rapidly changing organizational structures. They also emphasize the importance of building the needs of the individual into succession programmes if key personnel are to be retained and used to their maximum advantage.

> Senior jobs, particularly in smaller fluid organizations, tend to be built around the individual's needs and attributes. Yet many companies still base succession on career structures that are imposed on participants rather than developed with them (Gratton and Syrett, 1990, p. 38).

The conventional model

Conventionally, succession planning has been based on a model of identifying needs related to the business plan, identifying high fliers at an early stage and grooming them over an extended time-scale for positions at the top of the organization. Development in this model has usually been based on initial formal training followed by specialization until a very late stage, when those still left in the race have been rotated through various different functions in order to become generalists. Assessments, often using incomplete, unreliable and subjective information, result in a decreasing number of the original cohort continuing to climb steadily up the ladder, with others falling from it at various points into permanent positions in the structure. Wastage, in this model, can come arbitrarily, and may mean that some of the most valued people leave the organization unpredictably, with consequent gaps occurring at stages where they may prove difficult or impossible to fill.

This model assumes that there is a long-term business plan, that it is accessible to those responsible for human resource development, that it is sufficiently detailed for succession planning needs to be identified from it, and that the longer-term future of the organization is predictable. The model also presupposes a stable, hierarchical structure of positions through which people are developed and progress along specified career pathways that remain in place through time. Finally, it assumes the exercise of centralized rather than localized control over the whole process, and ownership of career development by the centre rather than by individuals.

While such models may still typify some large organizations, they are not relevant for the many whose shape, type of business and market, and rate and pattern of growth or decline is unpredictable beyond, say, the next three or four years – perhaps even less. Furthermore decentralization, as we saw in the British Rail case, leads to major changes in the kind of managers and competences needed at every level, and requires above all people who have a wide-ranging knowledge of the business, and who have the flexibility and innovative, entrepreneurial skills that can only come from multi-functional experience and a constant requirement to adjust to rapidly changing situations. In such an organization, a management development policy based on competences defined by reference to the present roles and tasks of those in senior positions in the organization cannot be a valid approach to succession planning.

Royal Insurance Holdings' approach to succession planning and management development (based on McKay, 1991)
(With acknowledgements to A McKay and IIR Ltd)

Royal Insurance Holdings is a company facing a constantly changing pattern of external demand, challenges and opportunities, with the same kind of unpredictable future that so many organizations now confront. Their response to the need to plan for management succession in a dynamic situation is to:

1 **Analyse future needs of the business by reference to the business strategy and plans.** The business needs to be assured of a continuous supply of high-quality managers through to the top of the organization, but the nature of their roles, tasks and priorities in any reasonably long-term scenario cannot be predicted except at the generalized level of saying that in future they will require people who are flexible in their approach to a wide variety of problems.

2 **Identify the critical success factors needed to achieve that flexibility.** At Royal Insurance there are two factors: wide-ranging experience which will enable people to learn by doing and gain an intimate knowledge of the business; and learning ability, which will enable individuals to apply previous experiences relevantly to current problems.

3 **Select appropriate training and development strategies to ensure the provision of wide-ranging experience and the development of individual learning ability.** At Royal Insurance the chosen strategy involves:

- Challenging assignments relating to the jobs that people do, which can be agreed with the manager during a personal development planning discussion
- Training courses that are shown to provide very powerful developmental experiences for participants
- Effective personal development planning, i.e. development planning that in many ways drives job content, by methods such as development related to the demands and opportunities of the job itself; special assignments; appraisal by subordinates, peer group and superior; coaching and counselling; self-development; and training courses that relate positively to needs identified in the personal development planning process
- Ownership of personal development, i.e. the active involvement of the individual in self-development, through the use of personal learning objectives, the availability of a variety of

distance learning approaches, and helping individuals to see their own development as part of a bigger picture, related to their current job and to potential future jobs

4 **Monitoring the process carefully.** The whole developmental process is monitored by the central Personnel Department, to ensure consistency across personnel systems and regular reviews of the individual's progress.

5 **Maintain flexibility.** At Royal Insurance this is done by organizing objective and regular assessments throughout people's careers. The approach is to have assessment centres at various levels within the organization. There is also annual reappraisal of potential for every member of management identified as a high flier in order that those whose potential has changed are either added to or taken off the fast track list. 'In this way we allow people the opportunity to step off the "fast track" for periods and maximize our search for potential by allowing people to step on at any point.'

The dangers in such a system of management succession include the possibility that it will focus on short-term rather than longer-term needs, and that, having loosened up on the exercise of central controls, the new system depends significantly on local identification of needs and co-operation of individuals and their managers in order to ensure that the whole process really works. However, the potential advantages appear to more than offset these dangers, especially when the alternative traditional approach to succession planning and management development has itself so many vulnerable areas. The role of the central personnel group in monitoring action, reviewing outcomes and feeding this information into the ongoing planning system is crucial to the success of the whole strategy in a case like this.

Who Manages the Management Development System?

Two points are important here. First, the development of managers, one of the most powerful sectors in any organization, is a very political process, needing effective collaboration between the key parties if it is to succeed. Secondly, it is essential to ensure the integration of management development with wider employee planning and resourcing systems in order to achieve consistency across the key processes of employee resource planning, recruitment, selection, appraisal, rewards and development. The aim should also be consistency of the system over the years, in order to allow longer-term outcomes to be achieved. (Storey, 1991)

Management development and succession systems, to be successful, must link positively with the organization's recruitment, selection, appraisal and reward systems. Development here, as for all employees, must form part of an integrated, strategic approach to employee resourcing if it is to make a lasting impact. This argues for the employee resourcing function to play a key role in managing the management development system. However, as we have already seen in a range of studies, that system must also have the full commitment of management at every level – its management must therefore not be dominated by specialists.

Further considerations arise when the organization is decentralized. The Hewlett Packard study shows the importance of actively involving the units as well as the centre in planning, operating and evaluating the system, and Royal Insurance has shown the need on the one hand to ensure that management development is 'owned' by units yet on the other hand is well integrated as a system and set of processes across the whole organization.

The danger of loosening central control is that divisions or units will take too much power into their own hands, and end by doing things their own way according to their own cultures. The danger of putting central control into the hands of a personnel function is that it may hold insufficient power, and be seen as 'outside' the real management system.

Managing management development at United Biscuits
(With acknowledgements to M Doyle, E Norman and IIR Ltd)

What lessons can be learnt from this study about how to manage systems of management development?

United Biscuits has moved rapidly from a small centralized organization to a large, divisionalized organization where managing directors have a very high level of autonomy.

The central personnel group carried out a review of the perceptions of management development across the company, and from this it was clear that there was widespread agreement on the need for management succession to be achieved through a continued strategy of cross-divisional or cross-functional moves. The group therefore decided to involve the divisional managing directors actively in responsibility for management development.

A Management Development Executive was set up, consisting of the Managing Directors and the Personnel Director and Management Development Director. This Executive produced a mission for employee development (including management development). They also agreed on a strategy concerned with ensuring that the best people were available, and that high individual performance must be achieved. Mission and strategy were by definition business-led, supporting business objectives. The mission was to generate and drive training and development activities that enabled all individuals to achieve the standards of performance demanded by the business. The strategy was that all employees must receive the necessary levels of training specific to the needs of their job and as appropriate development to prepare them for their next role. Management development would be achieved through a development programme with three components: management essentials, experienced manager development and high potential managers' development.

The respective roles of the centre and the divisions in management development were then identified. Members of the Executive negotiated and agreed with Personnel what would be done collectively and what would remain divisional. As a result, the centre has responsibility for all management development policy and practice, and must agree all senior appointments. Divisions have to implement company-wide practices.

Components of the management development system

Management essentials targets direct-entry graduates, other external recruits, and managers promoted from within (typically aged under 30). The aim is to give them job knowledge and skills, ensure that they are knowledgeable about all the key business functions of the company and that they achieve required standards of performance, and equip them with the skills and knowledge for managing people. This component lasts about two years, and ends with a diagnostic career development workshop leading to identification of ongoing development needs, and planning for their subsequent career.

Experienced manager development is aimed at all other established managers and focuses on needs tightly related to the individual's job performance, and on self-development activities that must be recorded by the individual Self Development Journal and are reviewed with their manager. All managers are responsible for the training and development of their people at United Biscuits, and so they themselves are thoroughly trained and developed in how to appraise, identify training needs, coach and develop, and use work-related experiences to help people learn.

High potential manager development is managed through appraisal audit and divisional reviews, co-ordinated and driven on a groupwide basis by the Management Development Executive. All individuals are evaluated annually with the aid of a dossier of their learning and development activities, and must attend the only three centrally organized programmes at the company, covering business management, managing change and strategy.

Results, two years later

After some initial tensions caused by the apparent loss of autonomy by personnel directors working in the divisions, the relationship between them and the new Executive became highly effective, and the Executive itself, meeting every two months, had in two years demonstrated a strong and active commitment to the management development system. It had introduced a new and more business-led appraisal scheme, achieved a changed remuneration system and reviewed the current strengths and weaknesses, and the future needs, of functions in the business. Human resource planning and succession planning is reviewed annually, with assessments and career development movements of individuals carefully considered at every point, and divisional priorities and plans for management development are agreed at Executive level.

Working to a common mission, with collective responsibility for auditing on a shared basis, and agreed areas of standardized training and development practice for all operating and service divisions, has produced a system whose management is carried out by a strong team of divisional management development and training managers contracted to work in the best interests of the group and their own divisions.

FEEDBACK NOTES

Some of the important lessons of this case study are:

1 **The management development system and its processes and practices must be owned by management.** Managers and personnel practitioners should work as a partnership, clear as to their respective roles and responsibilities.

2 **Both parties need to be skilled in their respective roles.** Line managers need to be trained in the key processes involved in training and developing others, and must have a shared commitment to, and responsibility for, the system across the organization. Personnel staff will need a thorough knowledge of the business, its goals and strategy in order to advise on an appropriate design, and how best to manage, implement and evaluate the operation of the system.

3 **The management development system must have a mission and strategy that clearly relate to the interests of line managers involved in its control.** This means that the system must be led by the needs of the business, as well as being responsive to individual needs and continuously identifying, assessing and developing the potential of people throughout the organization. It also means that mission, strategy and plans must all be tightly negotiated and agreed between management and any personnel specialists involved in the system.

Key Features of an Effective Management Development System

Going through the material in this chapter, and reading as many as possible of the articles and extracts to which it refers, identify up to 12 requirements that any management development system should meet. To start you on this activity, here is one of the key requirements: that management development must be a strategic business activity, meeting key business needs.

FEEDBACK NOTES

Here is a 12-point checklist.

1 Management development must be a strategic business activity, meeting key business needs and enhancing the strategic capability of the organization.

2 It must produce managers who are effective in their current positions.

3 It must develop managers to meet future needs.

4 It must have a clear mission and strategy, and feasible plans for implementation that have the agreement and commitment of managers throughout the organization.

5 It must encompass appropriate levels of the organization.

6 It must focus on key processes as well as activities, notably personal development planning, self-development, performance reviews and appraisals.

7 It must be capable of changing or reinforcing attitudes as well as knowledge and skills.

8 It must lead to the achievement of organizational as well as individual growth, and achieve the commitment of the individual in that process.

9 In planning management development, there must be careful analysis of the nature of the culture and structure of the organization, and of the prevailing value system.

10 Development of managers needs to be reinforced by and well integrated with employee resource planning and management systems.

11 It must be carefully monitored and evaluated, and its outcomes must be capable of some form of meaningful measurement.

12 Results of monitoring and evaluation must be fed through into the planning cycle, with particular attention being paid to the perceptions of the key parties of the actual, as distinct from the intended, aims, progress and outcomes of the development system. (See especially Ashton et al., 1980; Brodie and Bennett, 1979)

Broadening the Base of Management Development

There is one final point. Consideration of the uncertainties of the future may well result in an organization's management development system needing to embrace the total employee population rather than being restricted to those who are currently in management positions or have been identified at an early stage in their careers as having the potential to move into such roles. Going a step further, an argument can be made for management development to be a fully integrated function in the business of the organization, with all actions by every employee becoming part of a total process of learning, improving and change (see Wille, 1990).

Exercises

1 What do you see as the basic components of a management development system? When introducing such a system into an organization for the first time, what management training would you advise to ensure that the system can work effectively? (November 1989)

2 Formulate a management development policy for your own organization, and outline a related strategy and plans for its implementation.

3 Produce a draft report outlining how succession planning and related management development could be effectively tackled in an organization of your choice.

References

ASHTON D, BRAIDEN E AND EASTERBY-SMITH M. *Auditing Management Development.* Aldershot, Gower. 1980

BARHAM A K, FRASER J AND HEATH I. *Management for the Future.* Berkhamstead, Ashridge Management College and Foundation for Management Education. 1988

BLAKE N. 'Local Levels'. *Times Higher Education Supplement*, 6 April 1990

BRODIE M AND BENNETT R. 'Effective management and the audit of performance'. *Journal of General Management*, Vol. 4, Spring 1979

BROWN H, PECCEI R, SANDBERG S AND WELCHMAN R. 'Management training and development: in search of an integrated approach'. *Journal of General Management*, Vol. 15, No. 1, Autumn 1989. pp. 69-82

BURGOYNE J. 'Management development for the individual *and* for the organisation'. *Personnel Management*, June 1988. pp. 40-4

CARTER P AND LUMSDON C. 'How management development can improve business performance'. *Personnel Management*, October 1988. pp. 49-52

CHAMBERS C. 'Self reliant'. *Times Higher Education Supplement*, 6 April 1990

COLLOFF S AND GOODGE P. 'The open track to elite status'. *Personnel Management*, November 1990. pp. 50-3

CONSTABLE J AND McCORMICK R. *The Making of British Managers.* A report for the British Institute of Management and Confederation of British Industry into Management Training, Education and Development. London, British Institute of Management. 1987

COOPERS AND LYBRAND ASSOCIATES. *A Challenge to Complacency: Changing attitudes to training.* A report to the Manpower Services Commission and the National Economic Development Office. Sheffield, MSC. 1985

COUNCIL FOR INDUSTRY OF MANAGEMENT EDUCATION. *Business School Programmes: The requirement of British manufacturing industry* (Owen Report). London, British Institute of Management. 1970

DELOITTE, HASKINS AND SELLS. *Management Challenge for the 1990s: The current education, training and development debate.* Sheffield, Training Agency. 1989

DIXON M. 'How best to find out what managers need'. *Financial Times*, 6 April 1988

DOYLE M AND NORMAN E. 'Ensuring continuing commitment to management training and development by winning senior management support'. In *Proc. Institute of International Research in Association with Sundridge Park Management Centre: Third Annual Forum on Developing Effective Business-led Management Training, London, 28 February–March 1991.* London, IIR Ltd. 1991

EDWARDS P. 'Uncertain worlds'. *Times Higher Education Supplement*, 6 April 1990

FONDA N. 'Management development: the missing link in sustained business performance'. *Personnel Management*, December 1989. pp. 50-3

GRATTON L. *Heirs Apparent: Succession strategies for the 1990s.* Oxford, Blackwell. 1990

GRATTON L AND SYRETT M. 'Heirs apparent: succession strategies for the future'. *Personnel Management*, January 1990. pp. 34-8

HANDY C. 'Management training: perk or perquisite?' *Personnel Management*, May 1987. pp. 28-31

HANDY REPORT. *The Making of Managers.* A report for the National Economic Development Council, the Manpower Services Commission, and the British Institute of Management on management education, training and development in the USA, West Germany, France, Japan and the UK. London, NEDO. 1987

INSTITUTE OF MANPOWER STUDIES. *Competence and Competition: Training and education in the Federal Republic of Germany, the United States and Japan.* London, Manpower Services Commission/National Economic Development Office. 1984

KEEP E. 'A Training Scandal?' In *Personnel Management in Britain* (Sisson K, ed.). Oxford, Blackwell. 1989

LIPPITT G. 'Management development as the key to organisational renewal'. *Journal of Management Development*, Vol. 1, No. 2, 1983. pp. 36-9

MANGHAM I L AND SILVER M S. *Management Training: Context and practice*. London, Economic and Social Research Council and Department of Trade and Industry. 1986

MANT A. *The Experienced Manager: A major resource*. London, British Institute of Management. 1969.

McKAY A. 'Keeping the business strategy in sight when integrating succession planning with management and career development'. In *Proc. Institute for International Research in Association with Sundridge Park Management Centre: Third Annual Forum on Developing Effective Business-led Management Training, London, 28 February-1 March 1991*. London, IIR Ltd. 1991

MILLER P. 'A strategic look at management development'. *Personnel Management*, August 1991. pp. 45-7

MINTZBERG H. *The Nature of Managerial Work*. New York, Harper and Row. 1973

MUMFORD A. *Management Development: Strategies for action*. London, Institute of Personnel Management. 1989

MUMFORD A, ROBINSON G AND STRADLING D. *Developing Directors: The learning processes*. Sheffield, Manpower Services Commission. 1987

PARTRIDGE B. 'The problem of supervision'. In *Personnel Management in Britain* (Sisson K, ed.). Oxford, Blackwell. 1989

PERSONNEL MANAGEMENT. 'MCI launches standards for first two levels'. *Personnel Management*, November 1990. p. 13

PERSONNEL MANAGEMENT. 'Survey finds "lack of interest" in the Management Charter Initiative'. *Personnel Management*, May 1991. p. 3

SADLER P. 'Management development'. In *Personnel Management in Britain* (Sisson K, ed.). Oxford, Blackwell. 1989

SADLER P AND BARHAM K. 'From Franks to the future: 25 years of management training prescriptions'. *Personnel Management*, May 1988. pp. 48-51

STOREY J. 'Do the Japanese make better managers?' *Personnel Management*, August 1991. pp. 24-8

SYRETT M. 'Taking licence with the future of management'. *Sunday Times*, 10 April 1988a

SYRETT M. 'Enterprise era sets new goals'. *Sunday Times*, 24 April 1988b

TAYLOR F W. *The Principles of Scientific Management*. New York, Harper and Row. 1911

WILLE E. 'Should management development be just for managers?' *Personnel Management*, August 1990. pp. 34-7

Further useful reading

CHAMBERS C, COOPEY J AND McLEAN A. *Develop your Management Potential: A self-help guide*. London, Kogan Page. 1990

DRUCKER P F. *The New Realities*. London, Heinemann. 1989

GUNZ H. *Careers and Corporate Cultures: Managerial mobility in large corporations*. Oxford, Blackwell. 1989

KOLB D, LUBLIN S, SPOTH J AND BAKER R. 'Strategic management development: experiential learning and management competencies'. In *Creative Management* (Henry J, ed.), London, Sage and Open University. 1991

MINTZBERG H. *Mintzberg on Management: Inside our strange world of organizations.* London, Macmillan Free Press. 1989

MORGAN G. *Riding the Waves of Change: Developing managerial competencies for a turbulent world.* San Francisco, Jossey-Bass. 1988

MUMFORD A. 'Learning in action'. *Personnel Management*, July 1991. pp. 34-7

RASHID S. 'An activity analysis of unit general managers'. MA dissertation, Nuffield Centre for Health Studies, University of Leeds. 1986

REED M I. *The Sociology of Management.* Hemel Hempstead, Harvester Wheatsheaf. 1989

SAYLES L R. *Managerial Behaviour.* New York, McGraw-Hill. 1964

STEPHENSON T E. *Management: A political activity.* London, Macmillan. 1985

STEWART R. 'The nature of management? A problem for management education'. *Journal of Management Studies*, Vol. 21, No. 3, 1984. pp. 323-30

STEWART R. *Managers and Their Jobs.* London, Macmillan. 1967

STOREY J, AKASAKI-WARD L, SISSON K, EDWARDS P AND GOW I. *Managers and Management Development in Britain and Japan.* Oxford, Blackwell. 1992

TAYLOR B AND LIPPITT G. *Management Development and Training Handbook.* Maidenhead, McGraw-Hill. 1983

WILLMOTT H. 'Images and ideals of managerial work'. *Journal of Management Studies*, Vol. 21, No. 3, 1984. pp. 349-68

Chapter 20

Career development: achieving individual and organizational growth

Learning Objectives

After reading this chapter you will:

1 understand the importance of a strategic approach to career development in the organization, the benefits it can bring, and the typical triggers for the function;
2 be able to identify the levels at which career development planning should be carried out in the organization, and the key roles and responsibilities at each level;
3 know about some of the major methods of assessing the needs and potential of individuals in relation to career development;
4 be able to draw up career development objectives and a personal development plan.

Triggers to a Planned Approach to Career Development

What is career development? Gilley and Eggland (1989) define it as 'an organized, planned effort comprised of structured activities or processes that result in a mutual career plotting effort between employees and the organization, (p. 48).

Factors triggering a concern for career development planning in an organization include:

1 **A policy of internal promotion and growth** which will help to attract and retain the kind of employees the organization needs, and ensure continuity of supply. This, of course, is widespread in the larger Japanese companies (see pp. 87–8), and the rigours and organizational benefits of the strategy of recruiting high-calibre employees and then investing heavily in their internal development and promotion

are well described in Wickens (1987) and White and Trevor (1983). Such a policy requires a planned approach to career development, and the Etewel case study (pp. 127–8) offers a good example of this. Such a policy also stimulates employees to seek development themselves.

2 **A commitment to long-term security of employment** for people who have been with the organization for more than a specified number of years. This, again, inevitably leads to planned career structures.

3 **Affirmative action programmes**, such as the Civil Service's and National Health Service's in relation to female employees. Their implications mean that long-term career progression patterns have to be identified and career paths clearly established in the organization.

4 **A desire or need to improve levels of motivation and job satisfaction, commitment to the organization, and productivity.**

> In addition to reducing performance problems, the career development process can also promote more efficient allocation of human resources and greater loyalty among employees. (Gilley and Eggland, 1989, p. 48).

Career development is to the mutual advantage of the organization and the individual, and should be a joint effort, with the individual taking the initiative in developing a career plan, setting objectives and working out how these could be achieved, and the organization taking responsibility for the management of careers, treating career development as a strategic process which has to be pursued at corporate, unit and operational levels of the organization. (Hall, 1989)

The Organizational Contribution

The management of careers in the organization

When considering the management of careers, Hall (1989, p. 175) points out that development should be planned across the lifecycle of employees. This means that managers should ensure that, when planning the running of their units, the organization of work and workers, the design and allocation of jobs, and general human resource policies, they provide a structure for the career development of employees that encompasses four stages:

1 **Entry to the organization.** At this point individuals need information about themselves and their career opportunities. They should be involved in self-assessment activities, in drawing up personal development plans to initiate a long-term process of self-directed career planning, and have opportunities for a variety of developmental experiences. We discussed this important stage in Chapter 13 under the heading of induction and basic training.

2 **Progress within particular areas of work.** Established employees who are steadily progressing in particular jobs or areas of work need interesting, challenging tasks, and supervision that gives autonomy and support while making clear its high expectations of what the individual can achieve. There needs to be skilled career coaching, counselling and planning, mentoring, job design and appraisal in order to manage employees' career paths effectively at this stage. Training in such skills will therefore need to be provided at unit level, together with the kinds of monitoring, incentives and rewards that will help to develop positive attitudes in managers at this level. We shall see shortly how individual career plans can be linked to work objectives, and this linking process is another essential factor that will ensure that managers perceive the direct relevance of career development for the business.

3 **Mid-career.** This is probably the most difficult stage to manage (see Lewis and McLaverty, 1991). It is essential not only to facilitate the continued development of the high fliers, but, perhaps even more important, to help those unable to move up, on or out to see that they still have careers in the sense of meaningful work, challenges and opportunities for stimulation and achievement. The menopausal manager is a particular problem here, and one which has been well researched (Davies and Deighan, 1986; Hunt, 1982; Sofer, 1970). Hall (1989) lists some of the ways in which the careers and growth of those who have reached their ceiling can be enhanced: job rotation, cross-functional moves, job redesign, recognition and rewards for job performance, and temporary assignments outside the company, including consultancy opportunities. It is also important to keep more mobile employees informed about corporate career

opportunities and high-level technical or professional positions available elsewhere in the company, since these openings are often not adequately publicized.

4 **Later career.** As employees move towards the end of their careers with the company, either as a natural process or because of redundancy or other reason, their careers still need careful management. It is particularly important that the effects of low morale, disenchantment, anxiety and stress caused by a preoccupation with the forthcoming termination of employment do not spread through the workforce. Imaginative planning is needed to minimize such disruptions and help the employees concerned to achieve a positive phased transition from their jobs. Helpful methods include flexible part-time work, job sharing, pre-retirement planning (which needs to start about five years before the date of retirement), and secondments to other organizations where their skills will be valuable and where there will be opportunities for enlarging their network of contacts.

As much attention should be paid to induction for retirement at the end of the employee's career with the organization as to induction for life in the organization at its start. The benefits to the individual are obvious, but there are also benefits to the organization, especially when it is trying to develop close and proactive links with the wider local community and a good image in the recruitment market. Organizations like Lever Brothers show their awareness of this in their imaginative approach to pre-retirement training. (Barry, 1989)

Career development as a strategic function

Hall (1984, pp. 176–81) points out that, to be strategic, career development must be part of business planning and strategy at corporate level, where it must be the direct responsibility of senior management, not of personnel specialists. It is essential to be able to ensure full commitment not only to developing objectives and policy for career development throughout the organization, but to ensuring that policy is implemented effectively – and only top management can do that.

Strategic career development at BP
(By permission of BP)

When Robert Horton became Chairman of BP in 1990 he sent the following statement about BP's mission to all employees:

> **BP Vision, Values and Themes**
> BP is a family of businesses principally in oil and gas exploration and production, refining and marketing, chemicals and nutrition. In everything we do we are committed to creating wealth, always with integrity, to reward the stakeholders in BP – our shareholders, our employees, our customers and suppliers and the community.
>
> We believe in continually developing a style and climate which liberates the talents, enthusiasm and commitment of all our people. We can then respond positively to the increasing pace of change in a rapid and flexible way to achieve real competitive advantage. With our bold, innovative strategic agenda BP will be the world's most successful oil company in the 1990s and beyond.

Horton then outlined the principles and values to which the group is committed and which will underpin BP's vision. They are reflected in its responsibilities to all its stakeholders: customers, employees, suppliers, the community and, at the centre, the shareholders.

The statement of values relating to employees reads:

> For every employee our values mean a trusting, equal opportunity, non-discriminatory working environment. Our company offers challenging and exciting work. We will vigorously promote career development and we will aim to offer all employees a challenging career. We will seek to recognise both individual contribution and collective teamwork. We will encourage our employees to strike a balance between their responsibilities to BP and to their home life.

The issue of Horton's statement was part of the process of developing a new culture and structure at BP. Project 1990 had just been unveiled; it announced the radical restructuring of the group, with delayering and decentralization of authority. There was a reduction from 11 to five levels of management, and job cutbacks were followed swiftly by programmes right across the group aimed directly at changing attitudes and behaviour. (Butler, 1990)

Although Horton has now departed the company, the crucial importance of human resource management and development at BP remains.

Career development at unit levels

At this level managers must be stimulated to take responsibility for managing the career development of their people. This responsibility needs to be made into a key result area, on which they are appraised, trained, and rewarded. The skills they need to acquire are those related to job design, career coaching and counselling, mentoring, succession planning, the giving of feedback, and the assessment of potential. They or specialist staff should arrange job movements, including inter-unit co-operative arrangements such as transfers, secondments, special projects and other assignments.

Career development at corporate and unit levels at ICI
(By permission of ICI)

At ICI, most career development is planned and organized by the individuals and their business units (e.g. ICI Paints and ICI Pharmaceuticals) or functions (e.g. ICI Engineering), as they are seen to be best placed to analyse individual and organizational needs. However, in 1990 a group-wide training and development initiative was also introduced, which defined standards of knowledge and skill in four effectiveness areas (personal, business, management and professional) for all new entrants into professional and managerial jobs. This core development programme was a systematic approach to personal and career development, initiated at corporate level but implemented at local level by individuals and their line managers. Its perceived benefits included:

- A shared sense of purpose, values and understanding among managers and professionals
- Comparable standards of knowledge and skill across the group
- A better supply of managers and professionals capable of ensuring that the group meets customers' needs in the 1990s and beyond better than its competitors
- Better planned and implemented personal and professional growth and development
- Individually agreed personal learning and development plans
- An aid in attracting and retaining the best people globally

Career development at operational levels

Here, there should be a variety of resources and facilities to which employees can have access to promote self-development plans, processes whereby assessment of potential can be carried out, and specific programmes to implement organization-wide development policies and practices.

Resources might include personal and career development workshops and seminars to encourage individuals to take responsibility for their careers, and resource centres such as those at Rover and Fujitsu, where there is access to a variety of opportunities for self-directed and self-paced learning, often, as at Fujitsu, at the company's expense although in the employee's time. Such centres could usefully contain occupational guides, educational references, computerized self-assessment questionnaires or other diagnostic instruments to help people consider their career interests, values and competence, and a range of computerized educational and training programmes. The company might also have special access to the career and counselling services of local colleges and universities, and to the vocational and non-vocational courses they provide.

Arkin (1991b) describes the imaginative programme to help BBC staff manage their careers at a time of major organizational change, and to raise their level of performance. The programme includes career development workshops and a resource centre.

Assessment of potential can be carried out through assessment centres, through self-assessment, or by other means, as will be seen later in this chapter.

As you can see, managing careers in organizations means focusing on needs and systems at corporate, unit and operational levels, and on integrating career planning with wider employee resource planning. It is particularly important to ensure that career development policy and plans take fully into account structural and cultural factors and the opportunities, but also any constraints, that they offer. In this connection, Mayo (1992), while observing that career management is made more difficult when an organization has to operate in rapidly changing and unpredictable situations, and in situations where there are structural trends such as flatter organizations, decentralized profit centres and the elimination of central overheads, none the less offers excellent practical guidelines. Hall (1989, pp. 178–80) gives an important account of how career development, carefully planned and managed, can meet the needs of the organizational as well as the individual lifecycle, and can influence, as well as needing to be influenced by, the structure of the organization.

Roles of the Organization and the Individual

The individual should be seen and treated not as the 'servant' of the organization but as someone with the power to either expend or withdraw effort, energy and ability, and therefore someone whose willing commitment must be obtained if lasting development and change is to occur. This leads to the concept of the individual and the organization as bound together not only by a legal contract that specifies duties, terms and conditions, and material rewards, but also by a 'psychological' contract consisting of felt and perceived expectations, needs and rights that form the framework of an ongoing relationship. Career development is a major part of that contract, and as Robert Horton perceived at BP, if managed effectively it offers a unique opportunity to achieve organizational as well as individual growth.

However, the process of career development will only secure the full commitment of the organization if it is seen by line managers as well as top management as being a business-led activity. It must, therefore, be a jointly managed process. Burgoyne and Germaine (1984) worked on a successful project at Esso Chemicals whereby career development was negotiated in this way between organization and individual, centring on the three processes of organizational planning, individual planning, and joint career planning. This kind of model has subsequently become widely used.

1 **Organizational planning.** This involves the organization in producing short- and long-term business plans from which decisions are made about the work that is to be done, the structure required for the organization, the roles needed within the structure and, ultimately, the work and targets of the individual. At BP, a commitment to career development meant that structure, culture, roles and tasks were all looked at very carefully to see what alternatives were available in order both to satisfy the needs of the business and to promote the maximum development of employees.

2 **Individual planning.** This involves the individual in thinking through their overall life goals, what part their work should play in relation to those goals, and therefore the kind of career plans that would be appropriate and that they would like to follow. This process is helped by a workbook with a diagnostic self-assessment questionnaire.

Gilley and Eggland (1989, p. 72) list four questions on which each individual should continuously seek information:

- Who am I (in terms of abilities and potential)?
- How am I viewed by others?
- What are my career options?
- How can I achieve my career goals?

3 **Joint career planning.** This involves the individual and the manager (or some other person or body responsible for career development in the organization) in exchanging information from the previous two processes and then in negotiating ways in which the individual's career can be progressed in the forthcoming period in order to satisfy both their own needs and their work requirements.

Career development to achieve organizational and individual growth at IBM
(By permission of IBM; the information below relates to the situation of the company in 1990)

At IBM, a company which places a major emphasis on career development for all the reasons listed at the start of this chapter, and one which, of course, is committed to internalized careers and to long-term security of employment, there is a joint approach to the process. A number of guiding principles and policies underpin this:

- Selection methods should be objective and visible.
- All suitably qualified candidates should have equal opportunities to be considered.
- Career progression should be planned and should reflect individual performance.
- Promotion should be on merit.
- Each employee should have the opportunity to participate fully in the appraisal and counselling programme.

The appraisal and counselling programme brings individual and manager together to carry out development planning on an individual basis. The process is explained in a company booklet:

> The process starts with the employee development plan form which notes the employee's preferred job type or area of the company, the time available for transfer, and geographic mobility.

> Employee development plan forms are a planning tool within the wider context of manpower plans developed by line management and personnel staff. A manpower review group with representation from all major areas of the company monitors the overall situation to assess supply against demand.
>
> Second line managers review development plans for equity across departments. Career review boards help to ensure that selection procedures are carried out consistently across larger groupings of departments . . . Personnel staff carry out a monitoring role . . . to ensure that equal opportunity guidelines are followed and that promotion candidates meet the skill and experience requirements laid down for the jobs.

IBM explain the reasons for their career development policy and practices, and the benefits accruing from it, as follows:

> In recent years, especially, the business environment has continued to change as a result of the dramatic growth in competition and an ever-quickening pace of technological advance. These developments have changed the face of IBM's business . . .
>
> There have been other changes too. For example, attrition rates, formerly as high as 10 per cent and more, have stabilised at much lower levels. Fewer employees feel prepared to move family and home to take up a job at a different location. The company's changing age profile has led to a different mix of attitudes towards career goals. The combination of employee and business changes has resulted in changing patterns of motivation.
>
> IBM has responded to these changing motivation patterns in a number of ways. The need for relocation is minimised, wherever possible. Opportunities to increase job satisfaction through job development are explored. Emphasis is placed on training and retraining – to help employees acquire new skills for new careers – and on the part that career counselling can play in matching employee expectations with the changing level and nature of opportunities.
>
> Above all, through the employee development process, IBM tries to ensure not only that it has the flexibility to adjust to business change but that it can match changing career expectations with employee motivation.

Notice in the case study how career development arises out of, and in turn is dependent on:

- A long-term commitment to employees in the organization, and the perceived value of developing them in ways that meet their own as well as the organization's needs

- Changing patterns and demands in the external environment
- Human resource planning at corporate and unit levels of the company
- Jointly negotiated action plans for career development.

Assessment of Needs and Potential in Career Development

Clearly at the heart of any career development planning there must be a process of assessment in order to establish the needs and indicate the potential of individuals.

Such assessment can be done in a variety of ways, either through systems established by the organization, or by processes initiated by the individual. In the former category, appraisal systems have an important role to play in identifying career development objectives and the proposed plans of the individual, and in offering a vehicle whereby, as already described, manager and individual can agree on appropriate action. This was discussed in Chapter 14.

However, that kind of process is not adequate, nor is it an appropriate occasion, for a full-scale assessment of potential. Of the processes that are relevant we are going to look at only one: assessment centres. However, that process is of growing importance in a wide range of organizations in the public and private sectors (particularly in the National Health Service, where the methodology has become very popular for selection, development and promotion purposes especially at management levels), and in smaller as well as larger organizations.

Assessment and development centre methodology

In an informative article Stevens (1985, p. 28) writes:

> An assessment centre is a systematic approach to identifying precisely what is required for success in a particular job and then labelling these requirements in terms of a short list of tightly defined criteria. Leadership, integrity, tenacity and team-building skill are typical criteria which might be included for a management position.
>
> The assessment centre combines a series of job-related exercises which are designed to enable the applicant to demonstrate whether he or she has the skills required. The exercises are observed by a (trained) team of company managers who later

> pool their information and reach an agreed objective assessment of the candidate. *The approach not only ensures that sound decisions are made on which candidate has the closest 'fit'; it also provides a list of each candidate's training and development needs which can be used as the basis for that individual's development plans.* (Italics mine)

Stevens names a number of companies, including Woolworth, who have benefited greatly from the assessment centre approach, and Shepherd (1980) describes the success enjoyed by Ford in their use of assessment centres to aid the selection and training of first line supervisors.

Dulewicz (1991), however, strikes a warning note about the many things that can go wrong using this methodology – poor design, lack of expert assessors, lack of commitment of managers in the organization to ensuring transfer of learning, lack of long-term monitoring. He recommends the appointment of a mentor for each participant as a method of proven value in many organizations, and says that at the end of the day the critical factor is the commitment of the individual, and how much the participant does to develop him or herself.

All these accounts, while demonstrating some of the difficulties and dangers involved in the introduction of assessment centres or assessment centre technology, give striking evidence of their advantages, particularly the following:

- **Improved decision-making.** Decisions relating to the selection, transfer, promotion, and training needs of staff are based on substantially more 'facts' than in the past.
- **Improved feedback.** Assessment centre methodology offers an increased opportunity for meaningful feedback on performance and potential, and this is especially valuable in relation to career and other counselling services.

You may have noticed that, although the heading for this section referred to development centre methodology, we have so far only discussed assessment centres. What, if any, is the difference between the two approaches? To many writers there *is* no difference, and Stevens (1985) makes it clear that he, for instance, sees assessment centres as a way of not only assessing potential, but also helping to diagnose people's training and development needs related to current performance. However, increasing use of the term 'development centres' makes it worthwhile briefly defining it here.

In an article describing the use of development centres at British Telecom, the difference between assessment and development centres was explained as follows:

> In both cases groups of participants gather to take part in a variety of job simulations, tests and exercises with assessor observers, who assess against a number of pre-determined, job-related dimensions. If the collected data is used to diagnose individual training needs, facilitate self-development or provide part of an audit for OD [Organisational Development], then a 'development centre' would seem the more appropriate, less ambiguous term. (Rodger and Mabey, 1987)

Rodger and Mabey emphasize that development centres are entirely about assessing individual strengths and weaknesses in order to diagnose individual and organizational development needs, and therefore that this objective should be fully understood and agreed by those assessing and being assessed from the outset.

In a case study by Bower (1991) there is a very instructive account of how Rover's experience of assessment centres used primarily for selection purposes during the 1980s was only of mixed success, and how their decision to shift from assessment to development centres proved very successful. They used competence-based criteria, and this 'gives greater visibility and credibility to the process and offers spin-off benefits in performance appraisal, training objectives and for succession and development planning purposes' (Ibid., p. 53).

The following points emerge as vital to the success of any assessment programme aimed at highlighting learning needs:

1 **Context.** The use of assessment and development centres must be placed firmly in the context of major training and development programmes, so that they are seen to be a positive aid to all who go through them, rather than a threat.

2 **Involvement of management.** Line management must be involved from the start in the development and operation of assessment and development centre methodology.

3 **Expertise.** There must be a high level of skill in the design, operation and assessment of individuals, and in the handling of feedback to them. Dulewicz (1991) shows the damage that can be caused if this factor is not taken adequately into account.

4 **Confidentiality.** It must be clear who will have access to the information produced by the assessment processes. Without this, the trust and commitment of those being assessed cannot be gained.

5 **Action.** Assessment must lead to action although, as Rodger and Mabey (1987) observe, 'for a whole host of reasons development activities may not happen immediately'.

6 **Evaluation.** There must be a full evaluation of the results achieved by the use of such methodology, including an analysis of the effects its introduction has had on personnel at various levels in the organization.

Self-assessment and self-development

The learning needs at the individual level can also be assessed by the individual alone, using self-assessment in order to determine their strengths and weaknesses, formulate appropriate ways of meeting the needs that are thereby revealed, and plan for the ongoing monitoring and evaluation of their performance.

Pedler et al. (1978) have done much to popularize self-assessment for managers. They recommend four stages in the process:

1 **Self-assessment.** This must be preceded by a careful analysis by the individual of their work and life situation.

2 **Diagnosis.** Analysis must lead to the identification of the individual's learning needs, and to their prioritization.

3 **Action planning.** This involves identifying objectives, aids and hindrances to action, the resources (including people) needed to carry out the action plan, and a time-scale.

4 **Monitoring and review.** Monitoring and review procedures must be established, and a time-scale determined for those processes to take place.

Self-assessment involves individuals in rating themselves in each area of skill in their job, or in each area of occupational competence. Pedler et al. (1978) have therefore drawn up a detailed questionnaire to help a manager to carry out that and the other three processes. Such questionnaires can be completed in two ways:

- **By the individual alone.** He or she goes through the questionnaire, considering each area of skill in turn and rating themselves as best they can.
- **By the individual working with someone else.** Each can then interview the other, in an attempt to make the partner think through their levels of competence in each skill area as fully and objectively as possible. Particularly interesting discussions always take place in the area of interpersonal skills where, left to themselves, individuals often arrive at facile self-assessments (usually favourable!), but where, probed by someone else, a much deeper, different, and more critical self-assessment almost invariably emerges.

This way of tackling self-assessment also has the advantage of developing diagnostic and even counselling skills in the partner who, in the process of questioning, also has to practise and learn more about those skills of observation, listening, discussion and appraisal that Singer (1979) highlights as vital to the good coach. The more productive the skills are found to be, the more mutual learning emerges from the whole exercise.

The individual can also, of course, carry out self-assessment with the aid of a colleague, perhaps someone who is also involved in a self-development programme, or just someone interested in the process and willing to help. A friend or partner can often be just as effective in the role as someone at work.

Appendix 12 contains a self-assessment questionnaire produced by the IPM. It can be used as part of a wider and ongoing analytical and self-developmental process. The notes that precede it emphasize the importance to development planning of identifying the organizational barriers and aids to learning and development, while the range of possible developmental methods reminds us that development can take place not only at work, but also away from work, and not only through formalized activities, but also in a wide range of informal ways. For example, belonging to clubs, committees or other activity or interest groups outside work can offer developmental opportunities, and can help to develop skills, knowledge and attitudes highly relevant to longer-term career aspirations.

A Planned Approach to Career Development

Finally, here is a case study illustrating a planned approach to career development that summarizes most of the key points we have made in this chapter.

Career development at Volvo Car UK Limited (1990)
(By permission of Volvo Car UK Limited)

Volvo Concessionaires, in Buckinghamshire, is a company with a high investment in human resource development. Career development spans a number of activities, which in chronological order included in 1990:

1 **Employee appraisal.** A system was introduced based on agreed activity plans (MBO), which acted as a major determinant of basic pay increments each year. The same system has also been used to initiate a discussion around training and development needs both for current jobs and to aid career development. Self-assessment plays a key role in this system which, however, is now being reviewed to relate appraisal of process and behavioural skills more clearly to a competency model, and appraisal of task achievement to activity plans. There is also a concern to find ways of generating more thorough training and development discussions.

2 **Generic competency models.** Generic competency models were researched and introduced for the three main levels of management. Around these have been designed three management development centres to provide for better-quality data regarding readiness for promotion, lateral transfer, individual training or development plans to support career development, and significantly enhanced self-awareness to generate ownership of these development plans.

3 **Core training programmes.** The data from these centres has also supported the identification and design of various core training programmes for supervisors and managers, and of key training and development interventions, as well as providing indicators of preferred styles of team membership and leadership in the company.

4 **Extension of the scope of career development.** The principle of individual appraisal has been extended to unionized blue collar employees, although without links to individual determination of pay.

5 **A manager/employee feedback system.** This aims to enhance managers' self-awareness and to incorporate employee feedback into their managers' development plans. It is intended to improve managers' process understanding and skills, stressing the role of managers as coaches, appraisers, developers and leaders.

Exercises

1 What are the likely effects of the proposed reductions in school leaver numbers between now and 1999? (November 1988)

2 What would you recommend within your organization as an appropriate future 'preparation for retirement' system? (November 1988)

3 What are the main training needs of the newly engaged management trainee? What training do you expect such employees to receive prior to their first full management appointment? (NB: Training should be interpreted as including all planned educational and developmental activity.) (May 1989)

References

ARKIN A. 'Turning managers into assessors'. *Personnel Management*, November 1991a. pp. 49-52

ARKIN A. 'The BBC's career planning programme'. *Personnel Management Plus*, December 1991b. pp. 16-17

BARRY A. 'A phased approach to retirement training'. *Personnel Management*, February 1989. pp. 52-7

BURGOYNE J AND GERMAINE C. 'Self-development and career planning: an exercise in mutual benefit'. *Personnel Management*, April 1984. pp. 21-3

BOWER D. 'Case Study: Rover'. In 'Improving Assessment Centres' (Dulewicz V). *Personnel Management*, June 1991. pp. 52-3

BUTLER S. 'Cutting down and reshaping the core'. *Financial Times*, 20 March 1990.

DAVIES J AND DEIGHAN Y. 'The managerial menopause'. *Personnel Management*, March 1986. pp. 28-32

DULEWICZ V. 'Improving assessment centres'. *Personnel Management*, June 1991. pp. 50-5

EVANS P. 'New directions in career management'. *Personnel Management*,

December 1986. pp. 26-9

GILLEY J W AND EGGLAND S A. *Principles of Human Resource Development.* Maidenhead, Addison Wesley. 1989

HALL D. 'Human resource development and organizational effectiveness'. In *Strategic Human Resource Management* (Fombrun C J, Tichy N M and Devanna A, eds.). New York, Wiley. 1989

HUNT J W. 'Developing middle managers in shrinking organisations'. *Journal of Management Development*, February 1982.

LEWIS J AND McLAVERTY C. 'Facing up to the needs of the older manager'. *Personnel Management*, January 1991. pp. 32-5

MAYO A. 'A framework for career management'. *Personnel Management*, February 1992. pp. 36-9

PEDLER M, BURGOYNE J AND BOYDELL T. *Manager's Guide to Self-development.* Maidenhead, McGraw-Hill. 1978

RODGER D AND MABEY C. 'BT's leap forward from assessment centres'. *Personnel Management*, July 1987. pp. 32-5

SHEPHERD R. 'Off the line into management: an exercise in selection and training'. *Personnel Management*, December 1980. pp. 20-4

SINGER E J. *Effective Management Coaching.* London, Institute of Personnel Management. 1979

SOFER C. *Men in Mid-career: A study of British managers and technical specialists.* Cambridge, Cambridge University Press. 1970

STEVENS C. 'Assessment centres: the British experience'. *Personnel Management*, July 1985. pp. 28-31

WHITE M AND TREVOR M. *Under Japanese Management.* London, Heinemann. 1983

WICKENS P. *The Road to Nissan.* London, Macmillan. 1987

Further useful reading

CLUTTERBUCK D. *Everyone Needs a Mentor.* London, Institute of Personnel Management. 1991

DULEWICZ V. 'The application of assessment centres'. *Personnel Management*, September 1982. pp. 32-5

DULEWICZ V. 'Assessment centres as the route to competence'. *Personnel Management.* November 1989. pp. 56-9

HIRSH W. *Women, career breaks and re-entry.* London, Institute of Manpower Studies. 1985

INSTITUTE OF MANPOWER STUDIES. *You and your Graduates: The first few years.* IMS Report 191. London, IMS. 1990

MABEY W. 'The majority of large companies use occupational tests'. *Guidance and Assessment Review*, Vol. 5, No. 3, 1989. pp. 1-4

MAYO A. *Managing Careers: Strategies for organizations.* London, Institute of Personnel Management. 1991

MEGRANAHAN M. *Counselling: A practical guide for employers.* London, Institute of Personnel Management. 1989

ROBERTSON I T, SMITH M AND COOPER D. *Motivation: Strategy, theory and practice*. 2nd ed. London, Institute of Personnel Management. 1992

WILLIAMS R. 'What's new in career development'. *Personnel Management*, March 1984. pp. 32-3

WOODRUFFE C. *Assessment Centres: Identifying and developing competences*. London, Institute of Personnel Management. 1990

Chapter 21

Building a flexible, committed, high-quality workforce for the organization

Learning Objectives

After reading this chapter you will:

1 appreciate the need for employee development to be a carefully planned mixture of experience and activities, fuelled by continuous and self-development processes;
2 understand the ways in which it should relate to wider employee planning and resourcing strategies and policy, and how employee resourcing should itself be integrated with other business functions, serving the overriding goals and mission of the organization;
3 understand the strategies and processes whereby organizations can attract, retain and develop high-performing, flexible people who will enhance organizational performance and growth.

Triggers to a Concern with Human Resource Management in Organizations

An increasing preoccupation with human resource management in organizations is explained by a widespread need to build a flexible and committed workforce in order to respond successfully to a variety of pressures and opportunities that characterize the environment of many organizations (Hendry et al., 1988). These include uncertainties in the market, technological advance, demographic trends which threaten their traditional sources of labour, the implications not only of membership of the single European market but, in many instances, of the need to operate competitively in a global market, and a need to provide high-quality products and services and become more customer-sensitive.

Few organizations today are exempt from such external forces. For example the public sector in every area – the NHS, education, social and community care and a widening range of local authority departments – is under pressure to perform more efficiently and effectively, to recognize and act on the concepts of customer service and care, total quality and the achievement of specific targets, and to decentralize and devolve much greater autonomy to middle levels of management in order to increase the speed of responsiveness and decision-making. These issues were explained in some detail in Chapter 19, where we looked at their implications for the development of managers in such organizations.

The need to invest in the development of all employees does seem, according to the latest evidence (Storey, 1991), to be quite widely accepted, yet at the same time much of the old complacency and ignorance about what is being done and what ought to be done about development still remains. In this final chapter we are not going to focus on development, at least not in a narrow sense. Instead we are going to examine what it is that appears to make workforces flexible, committed and able to acquire new skills, attitudes, competences and knowledge quickly.

Keys to Achieving High-quality, Productive, Flexible and Committed Workforces: Lessons from Germany and Japan

Considerable structured, in-depth research has now been carried out on highly productive organizations, particularly in Germany, Japan and Britain. The findings have important implications for employee resourcing and development practices.

Integration of factors leading to high productivity

Research comparing productivity levels in German and Japanese parent companies and their subsidiaries in Britain indicated an interlocking spectrum of factors accounting for high-producing firms:

- Superior product design
- High-quality and well-planned production systems
- Continuous improvement of methods by employees at all levels
- Flexible labour, achieved particularly by skills-related pay systems
- Tight manning levels and technically expert line managers

- Good communications and labour relations
- Ongoing preventative maintenance, with the main responsibility with operators
- Target-based performance with speedy and constructive feedback
- Careful selection and high-quality recruits

(Sawers, 1986, p. 19)

German and Japanese firms are not managed in ways fundamentally different from those used in British firms, but the managers are much better educated, especially at the technical level, and have a thorough knowledge of company operations, markets, competitors and new technology. They pay meticulous attention to detail, and have the will continuously to improve in all that they do (Ibid.).

A pragmatic approach to employment practices and to work systems

Research is showing that Japanese employment practices are changing (Gleave and Oliver, 1990), and that only about 30 per cent of Japanese workers are being offered lifetime employment with major companies, a steadily decreasing figure (Briggs, 1991, p. 36). So the stereotype of long-term security of employment, pay linked to length of service, and internalized careers must be treated with caution. Mistaken, too, is the belief that there is a package of employment practices that are specifically 'Japanese'. This is not the case. Most, if not all, practices in Japan are also found in other countries (see, for example, Ackroyd et al., 1988), and many techniques were taken from elsewhere and implanted in Japanese companies.

What is clear, however, is that the Japanese, especially when locating abroad, are pragmatic, willing to adapt to situations by choosing the most appropriate systems and strategies. (Storey 1991)

> If there is one lesson to be learnt from Japan's success it is how ideas which have originated in one context can be learnt, adapted and effectively applied to another (Gleave and Oliver, 1990, p. 68).

Gleave and Oliver go on to point out that human resource management systems in subsidiary companies have been 'a compromise between local ideas and corporate preferences'. (Ibid.) None of this is to imply an *ad hoc* approach: once systems are chosen, they are installed for the long term, regarded as an essential investment in order to attract, develop and retain high-quality workers. It does, however, demonstrate that the overriding concern is with business goals rather than with employment practices or systems of a particular kind: adaptation and adoption are more than justified by the results they bring.

Strategic capability of managers at all levels

This emphasis on the overall focus, the end result, leads to another crucial determinant of organizational capability: the superior strategic ability of managers. Because of their educational level and the integrated mix of continuous training, experience and development that they receive from joining their organizations, German and Japanese managers usually have a significantly higher level of strategic ability than British managers. (Sawers, 1986; Storey, 1991) A lack of competence in strategic thinking, decision-making and implementation at the managerial level ultimately means a loss of strategic capability for the organization (Miller, 1991), and building up that competence therefore becomes a vital activity for any organization needing to gain or maintain a competitive edge. The Hewlett Packard exercise (see pp. 430–2) illustrates this, and further illustrative material is found in Fonda (1989) and Chambers (1990), who describe the major programme launched at Thorn EMI in 1987 to improve the strategic capability of general managers by learning based on real strategic business issues, in order to make a powerful impact on Thorn's overall business strategy and performance. Such articles, however, are to do with what might be termed emergency measures. The real answer is, again, the long-term one – start with rigorous recruitment and selection, and then provide the kind of learning organization that will give the ongoing mix of carefully planned experience, training, continuous development and self-development opportunities that will identify and 'grow' business people and strategic thinkers throughout the organization (see the British Rail case study (pp. 427–30) for an example of this philosophy; also Wille, 1990).

Integration of all business strategies in pursuit of a common mission

Strategic capability itself, however, is not enough. Another feature of Japanese management is its tight and pragmatic integration of all business strategies, including human resource management, marketing and manufacturing, and a subordination of all to a single overriding strategic goal. (Reitsperger, 1986; Miller, 1991; Storey, 1991) Within human resource strategy, there is an integration of the key systems and processes, so that consistency and coherence is achieved between human resource planning, recruitment, selection, training, appraisal, development, reward systems and organization and deployment of personnel (Ackroyd et al., 1988; Storey, 1991). It is this integration and strategic approach to human resource management that is rare still in Britain (Storey, 1992) despite clear signs of a widening take-up of many specific initiatives to do with increasing the investment in people and in experimenting quite adventurously with a range of techniques to improve flexibility and commitment (Storey, 1991; 1992).

Consistency, coherence and integration of human resource management and development policies and systems

One of the reasons why there is still little integration of, and consistency between, employee resourcing processes and systems is because in Britain short-termism is still widely prevalent. By this I mean not just the attitude that has led in the past to such inadequate investment in the training and development of people (see Chapter 3), and that springs from a variety of ecomomic, governmental, social and cultural causes, as well as being perpetuated by the dominance of the accountancy function at top levels of so many British organizations (see Chapter 19). I also mean short-term vision: a failure to take a long-term perspective, leading to systems – and particularly employee development and resourcing systems – being put in as 'quick fixes', without proper planning and preparation across the organization, and often without giving them time to prove their value.

Attempts to improve job performance through quality circles, team briefings and other similar approaches do fail when they are not consistent with the general culture, or with the structure and control systems, of the organization. One example of this is given in Develin and Partners' 1989 report on quality improvement programmes in British business. They identify middle management as the main obstacle to quality improvement in British industry, with shop-floor problems occurring in only 15 per cent of the 3,000 UK companies surveyed. They concluded that it was essential to involve middle management from the start in quality improvement initiatives, and to ensure that tangible benefits would be achieved by programmes at an early stage in order to prevent disillusionment. Ron Collard (1989) shows a similar need to make total quality programmes an integrated part of the organization's culture and systems, and to plan their introduction carefully.

In Japan, by contrast, systems are installed for the long term (Storey, 1991), with particular techniques or approaches such as 'just in time' and 'total quality' being embedded in the structure and culture of the organization rather than grafted on with a sticking plaster of training and pay awards.

Integration and coherence underpin the Japanese and German approaches to employee development: it is not the particular techniques used so much as the coherent, well-planned mix of off- and on-the-job training, continuous development, learning from experience and a strong philosophy of self-development that characterize the approaches. Such characteristics are still rare in British employee development systems.

Ownership of employee development by managers and individuals

One of the most striking points made in Storey's (1991) account of the three-year research, funded by the Economic and Social Research Council and undertaken by Warwick University, into a comparative study of managers and their development in Britain and Japan is about Japanese perceptions of who is responsible for management development. Comparing four major Japanese firms with four British organizations reckoned to be very progressive in the area of employee development, the Japanese consistently rated heads of department and each individual extremely highly (anywhere between 67 and 93 per cent), and the Japanese ratings were always significantly higher than British – sometimes to an extreme degree, and particularly in relation to the responsibility of the individual (Storey, 1991, p. 26).

As we saw especially in Chapters 9-11, this identification of core responsibility for employee development as lying with line managers and with individuals is something which is now being seen as crucial to the success of employee development by a growing number of organizations. However, acceptance of that responsibility is still hindered by the deep-rooted attitudes in Britain which see human resources as costs, not assets, and therefore constantly seek a bottom-line, highly quantifiable payback for development. In our main competitor countries (see Chapter 4) human resources are regarded as assets, and therefore the need to make the most of them and add to their value by continuous training and development is generally taken for granted. In Britain, on the other hand, the continuous querying of the value of development often reduces it to the level of an activity instead of an ongoing process. This, in turn, generates a variety of negative perceptions:

- That development consists of things that are 'provided' or 'done to' some people by others
- That development therefore needs 'specialists to do it' rather than being a natural process under the control of managers and individuals
- That training and development are often threats or punishments, to do with remedying deficiencies, rather than welcome opportunities to which every employee has a right, and which lead to enhancement of abilities, growth and potential

Primacy of self-development and continuous development

Because of the 'taken for granted' value of employee development in Japanese and German companies (and in those of other key competitor countries), and because of the attention to continuous improvement, continuous development and self-development are fundamental processes, facilitated and complemented by relevant and timely training and a variety of self-developmental learning opportunities and facilities. We saw in Chapter 20 how some British companies are seeking to achieve the same kind of culture and behaviours, as they try to attract, retain and ensure high-quality and committed employees.

Attempts in Britain to Achieve Enhanced Organizational Performance and Growth by Focusing on Human Resource Management

In recent years there has been much uncertainty as to the real, compared to the rumoured, extent of take-up in Britain of something that could distinctively be labelled human resource management (HRM), concerned with policies and systems aimed at developing high-quality, committed and flexible workforces and so helping to ensure high-performing organizations (see especially Sisson, 1989). Recent research has, however, given convincing evidence that a very significant number of widely varying types of organizations are experimenting with a wide range of human resource management practices. Typical are the following:

- Flexible manpower strategies, focused on a core of firm-specific jobs, and an outer ring of non-specific jobs for peripheral workers (e.g. those on short-term or part-time contracts, self-employed people or employees of sub concontractors). Such strategies centre not on the old divisions between blue- and white-collar workers, but on new divisions between core and peripheral workers (Atkinson, 1984, p. 29).
- Long-term security of employment for core workers, together with a continuous development and harmonization of pay and terms and conditions of service. Thus, for example, Rover in April 1992 achieved acceptance (by a narrow majority) by their workforce of 'Japanese-style work practices' (Gribben, 1992), with a programme that is probably the closest that any traditional British car manufacturer has so far come to a cradle-to-grave career structure. It features long-term security of employment, all employees paid in the same way, a single company council to negotiate terms and conditions, team working, and assembly operations mixed in with maintenance jobs – reforms all aimed to narrow the productivity gap with Japanese manufacturers and improve profits and efficiency.
- Selective recruitment and rigorous selection. We have seen in various case studies (notably in Chapters 11 and 20) the use many organizations are making of focused recruitment and more objective and testing selection methods.
- Intensive induction and training, focused on business needs
- The introduction of performance management systems, including objective-centred appraisal, focusing on behaviour as well as on task achievement
- Single-table bargaining/individually negotiated contracts
- Comprehensive consultation and communication procedures
- Single-status conditions and a simplified grading structure

However, the research also reveals that there is little or no attempt to take an integrative approach to the application of such practices, still less to combine them in a way that will produce strategic human resource management in the organization. Experimentation remains patchy and sometimes short-term, so that the parts rarely cohere within a strong and overarching policy. This in turn means that there is still a generally poor or non-existent fit between HRM practice and corporate strategy, even though HRM as a function seems now to be emerging with a distinct identity, dominated by line managers rather than by personnel specialists, and is clearly becoming more business-led.

In *Personnel Management*, June 1990, Stephen Crabb tells the story of how BICC in Helsby, Cheshire, 'met the challenge of cultural change and turned the concept of the "vision" into something which has begun to have real meaning for its workforce'. (Crabb, 1990) Helsby is the headquarters of the communications and electronics division of BICC Cables, and is the manufacturing site for the datacoms cables business. The story is of a company which, fighting in an increasingly difficult market, and having already reduced its workforce and rationalized its products, turned to many of the HRM practices described above to achieve a change in culture, and a more flexible, committed, efficient workforce.

The BICC story does show evidence of a coherent and integrated approach to HRM. The grading system has been restructured. A clear vision and mission have been formulated, and training and development have been carefully planned to change attitudes and culture and to build up teamwork in the company, with senior management playing a leading part in the design of training and of learning material. Careful attention has been given to effective selection, induction and basic training, with assessment centres, and all new supervisors undergo a six-month probationary and training period during which they must acquire core team leader skills and successfully complete a business project, and are allocated a mentor. Company training strategy has also been revised, and now includes a comprehensive training needs analysis for the manufacturing cells that has already revealed important skills shortfalls, and targeted training for all new recruits, covering basic factory knowledge, operational processes, and final on-the-job training. Negotiation with unions has ensured that the changes in working practices are recognized and opened the way for further progress towards flexibility (Crabb, 1990).

Two years on, the company could point to important outcomes including reduced production and lead times, increased output and productivity, marked increases in openness, problem-sharing and joint problem-solving, together with effective teamwork (Ibid.).

Similar strategies have been developed at Cummins Engines, Darlington. (Harrison, 1992) There, while the approach has been pragmatic, searching for what can best be achieved in particular circumstances in order to minimize conflict and raise trust and commitment, the vision, values and mission for employee resourcing and development have been very clearly defined, are tightly aligned to business strategy, and are underpinned by a long-term perspective, summarized as 'We're in it for the long haul', that means that systems and processes are given time to work and are evaluated, and lessons are learnt from failures in order to build on already impressive successes.

Let us finish with a case study which describes, not perfection, but another example of the painstaking, pragmatic yet coherent and intergrative approach to employee resourcing and development that is essential if the aim of building up and retaining a flexible, committed and high-performing workforce is finally to be achieved. It is a real-life example, but at the request of the company it has not been identified.

Malin Manufacturing Services

Malin Manufacturing Services (MMS) is one of the manufacturing centres of Malin Pharmaceuticals, a highly successful company, whether judged by profitability, market share or research and development record. Malin focuses on ethical pharmaceuticals (sold only on prescription), and on major therapeutic areas where compounds are needed by millions, not hundreds, of people. It therefore has to develop blockbuster products, and discover new compounds while also continuously developing mature products. A vital part of its corporate mission is to produce, to the most exacting standards, better and safer medicines to the highest quality and benefit to society. This requires the most advanced machinery and equipment, together with a highly skilled, dedicated staff who can adapt to new demands in a fast-changing technical and market environment.

It is therefore not surprising that Malin invests hugely in its people – it has the resources to do so, and the nature of its business is such that, although labour costs are relatively low, people at every level are crucial to its success. In its manufacturing centres, employees must ensure high quality and excellence in every aspect of task performance, and be highly flexible and committed.

There is therefore a need for a strategic and integrated approach in employee resourcing and development if that high-quality, committed and flexible workforce is to be guaranteed for the organization.

Human Resource Management at MMS

The MMS site is responsible for manufacturing medicines for supply around the world. In late 1990, when major changes were made in Malin worldwide, with manufacturing services being split off from marketing and sales functions in order to ensure a clear vision between those two key areas of the business, that site, like all other manufacturing centres, had to undergo radical structural and cultural changes. It became a highly autonomous business unit with only three levels of authority between the Centre Manager and the shop floor. The hitherto traditional personnel function had to develop a new human resource management role, and was itself reorganized to carry out its now business-led functions more effectively. The challenges of employee resourcing involved personnel staff:

- developing from being administrators to being facilitators;
- understanding their new HRM role;
- adapting to changing circumstances;
- developing a philosophy of adding value to all that they did;
- focusing on attracting, retaining and rewarding the best people in the right jobs with the strongest motivation.

The process proved painful, needing many changes, especially of attitudes. Predictably there were many who found the adjustment difficult or impossible, especially those who did not agree with an approach which required personnel management to become a hard bottom-line function. Furthermore many new directors were entering the company at MMS in 1990, determined to do things their way and driven by a perceived need to add value and a concern to apply task analysis to HRM activities and measure the outcomes of the function in business terms.

In time, however, a closely integrated, high-performing and committed team was built up at the MMS factory, sharing a common culture based on core values and a shared mission.

Results of changes in human resource management

What have been the key policies and activities of the human resource management function that have contributed to this success?

1 **Helping MMS's senior management, in 1989, to work out the centre's role in the Malin Group, and produce a mission, aims and values.** These relate to the unique importance of people, to which all agreed, and which have been communicated throughout the company.

Business success is dependent upon the commitment and motivation of every member of staff. At MMS everyone has the opportunity to be involved. Across the site there are teams of staff at all levels working towards shared objectives.

2 **Introducing assessment centres to improve the higherto rather subjective selection and development processes.** Existing managers and senior executives as well as candidates for selection were put through the centres. All were assessed in relation to 12 key competences, clustering around three core areas. The assessment process was rigorous, and not everyone proved suited to their new roles and tasks. Some left, on very generous terms; others were put through lengthy development programmes geared to achieving the required competences. The result has been to build up, at executive level, a much more integrated team with a clear and shared culture.

Team leaders, in the reorganized company, have crucial positions, involving considerable autonomy and financial responsibility. These key new roles were filled, in 1990, by requiring all candidates to go through assessment workshops and, on appointment, to pursue a two-year development programme. Those who were unsuccessful in the workshops were moved into other jobs that better suited their abilities. This process was not unfamiliar, since Malin has a culture of assessing people, with all its employees being put through psychometric and occupational skills tests at the selection stage.

3 **Introducing performance management for managers to upskill and reward creativity, innovation and flexibility.** All managers must agree with their superiors key result areas in their jobs, with objectives related to these, some of which are 'learning' objectives. Training and development is provided to close gaps in competences and help people to reach their objectives, and there are quarterly appraisals of performance, held on a joint basis. Throughout the year the focus is on development and on steady improvement in performance through guided learning. Pay is only discussed once, at the end of the year, when the individual is assessed against objectives. Increases in pay are related to performance against objectives and to market forces.

Performance-related pay is thus used as a mechanism for developing the skills and abilities of people, not as a simple or crude mechanism for calculating achievement of targets.

The system is very carefully monitored. Objectives must be achievable by the individual, with checks carried out by the HR function by auditing a random sample of objectives. Constant monitoring ensures consistency in the kind and level of objectives set across the board, and in assessments made. This continuous process of monitoring and maintenance is essential to the success and credibility of the system.

4 **Training and developing employees for high performance and flexibility.** MMS is still very dependent on manual operations, and a high-quality workforce is therefore essential. It operates flexible manning practices, with a group of about 300 core employees, all of whom receive training and development, and an outer ring of peripheral employees, who do not (see Atkinson, 1984).

There are four production lines, each manned by teams operating in shift. Malin involved employees in the design and layout of the lines in 1990, giving them ownership of the new regime. The use of teams (with training in teamwork also provided by the company) has also created a strong sense of identity. Team members are rotated around tasks at intervals in order to maintain interest and flexibility of skills.

New recruits are fully trained in each task they will be required to perform before going on to the line. All team members have to enter a skills block matrix on appointment, and must learn three major sets of skills, receiving pay awards as they acquire each new component. Thereafter they can move through as many of the four skill blocks – people, scientific, engineering and business control – as they wish, with further pay awards attached to the acquisition of each new set of skills. Any core employee may pursue further education, beginning with day release for BTEC etc., and leading up to degree level should that prove within their capabilities. They can thus broaden out their learning into major occupational development by pursuing a mix of training, experience and educational opportunities. For some, this will ultimately lead to promotion.

The whole developmental scheme, apart from the basic three boxes, is voluntary, with some employees being able, because of existing skills and qualifications, to start at a higher level than others. About 40 per cent of operators aim to progress to the top, which can open up the opportunity to enrol for degree-level courses. The career advancement made possible by the scheme has therefore already achieved widespread motivation, as well as building up a reservoir of skills and knowledge in the company.

5 **Designing and delivering, with the help of outside consultants, major organizational development and behavioural change programmes in the company.** These have clear objectives and well-defined anticipated outcomes.

6 **Establishing and implementing a coherent employee development policy.** This involves continuously and systematically developing business-led training and development plans, working them through from shop floor to managers, and taking a proactive stance in relation to the anticipated as well as current needs of the company.

7 **Establishing clearly defined aims and outcomes to be achieved by the human resource function.** These aims and outcomes are communicated throughout the company, and the function 'lives' the values that the company itself espouses in its mission:

- Seeking continuous improvement in all that is done
- Achieving genuine two-way communications
- Realizing the full abilities of all employees
- Looking ahead and maintaining the vision

Measures for success are established for every initiative the HRM function introduces, and milestones are installed along the way so that they can be monitored regularly, not simply measured at the end. As an example, there are company-wide standards in quality, service, health and production, and those form the broad categories within which performance is measured in the performance management system that is co-ordinated by the HRM function.

8 **Giving wide responsibility for day-to-day personnel management to line managers.** They will also be helped in key areas such as communications, where they are shortly to have their own computerized record system for staff which they, not the HRM function, will control.

The HRM function itself has become more business-led and more strategic. The process has not been easy; many of the original personnel staff have left, and new people with skills and attitudes more appropriate to the new culture and roles have been recruited. The function does, however, have widespread credibility, working closely with line managers in a business partnership, focusing on targets to be achieved and the resourcing and developmental systems and processes needed to succeed.

It would be easy to be cynical about the MMS story. A company whose major problem is how to spend wealth in a way that produces value for shareholders can easily afford to cast some of it on the waters of employee development. The cynicism would be misplaced. What the case study illustrates is not profligate expenditure, but a continuous attempt to produce a strategic, business-led approach to employee resourcing and development in order to secure a high-quality, flexible, committed and high-performing workforce. It does not illustrate the whole range of best practice, but a two-year effort by a team of managers and human resource practitioners to find and apply ways of developing a company of people with shared mission, values and aspirations. It does not illustrate a soft approach to people – the rate of management attrition, in particular, over those three years has been significant, with an estimated £5-6 million saved by radically reducing levels and numbers of management – but a carefully planned, coherent set of processes and activities to build up a core of skilled and efficient workers. At MMS medicines are manufactured that ultimately reach millions of people across the world. Any slip at any point in the production process, by any member of each small production team, could result in a worsening of illness, or in death. So human resources, while cheap in terms of payroll, are absolutely critical to the company's continued success and high reputation.

Above all the case study illustrates, like many throughout this book, that employee development does have a central role to play in attracting, retaining and continuously ensuring the provision of those kinds of people needed in order to enhance organizational capability, survival, profitability and growth. However, that role can only be performed effectively if it is reinforced by and integrated with relevant and effective employee resourcing strategies and systems; and if these operate within a structure, culture and set of values about people that in turn reinforce them; and, finally, if employee resourcing is linked both reactively and proactively to business strategy at the operational, unit and corporate levels of the organization. On the evidence so far, this is rarely the case, but it must be the urgent goal, if employee development is to make any real impact on organizational as well as individual performance and growth.

References

ACKROYD S, BURRELL G, HUGHES M AND WHITAKER A. 'The Japanisation of British industry?' *Industrial Relations Journal*, Vol. 19, No. 1, Spring 1988. pp. 11-23

ATKINSON J. 'Manpower strategies for flexible organisations'. *Personnel Management*, August 1984. pp. 28-31

BRIGGS P. 'Organisational commitment: they key to Japanese success?' In *International Comparisons in Human Resource Management* (Brewster C and Tyson S, eds.). London, Pitman. 1991

CHAMBERS C. 'Taking a pro-active approach to the challenge of culture change through management development'. In *Proc. Institute for International Research Conference on Improving Performance Through Business-led Management Training and Development, London, 10 April and 1 May 1990.* London, IIR Ltd. 1990

COLLARD R. *Total Quality: Success through people.* London, Institute of Personnel Management. 1989

CRABB S. 'The way to cable change'. *Personnel Management*, June 1990. pp. 50-3

DEVELIN AND PARTNERS. *The Effectiveness of Quality Improvement Programmes in British Business.* London, Develin and Partners. 1989

FONDA N. 'Management development: the missing link in sustained business performance'. *Personnel Management*, December 1989. pp. 50-3

GLEAVE S AND OLIVER N. 'Human resources management in Japanese manufacturing companies in the UK: 5 case studies'. *Journal of General Management*, Vol. 16, No. 1, Autumn 1990. pp. 54-68

GRIBBEN R. 'Rover men agree to ''Japanese'' work deal'. *Daily Telegraph*, 14 April 1992

HARRISON R. *Developing Human Resources for Productivity.* Geneva, International Labour Office. 1992 (in press)

HENDRY C, PETTIGREW A M AND SPARROW P. 'Changing patterns of human resource management'. *Personnel Management*, November 1988. pp. 37-41

MILLER P. 'A strategic look at management development'. *Personnel Management*, August 1991. pp. 45-7

SAWERS D. 'The experience of German and Japanese subsidiaries in Britain'. *Journal of General Management*, Vol. 12, No. 1, Autumn 1986. pp. 5-21

SISSON K. 'Personnel management in transition?' In *Personnel Management in Britain* (Sisson K, ed.), Oxford, Blackwell. 1989

REITSPERGER W D. 'Japanese management – coping with British industrial relations'. *Journal of Management Studies*, Vol. 23, 1 January 1986

STOREY J. 'Do the Japanese make better managers?' *Personnel Management*, August 1991. pp. 24-7

STOREY J. 'HRM in action: the truth is out at last'. *Personnel Management*, April 1992. pp. 28-31

WILLE E. 'Should management development be just for managers?' *Personnel Management*, August 1990. pp. 34-7

Further useful reading

CONNOCK S. *HR Vision: Managing a quality workforce.* London, Institute of Personnel Management. 1991

HERRIOT P AND PINDER R. 'Personnel strategy in a changing world'. *Personnel Management*, August 1992. pp. 36-9

MARTIN P AND NICHOLLS J. *Creating a Committed Workforce*. London, Institute of Personnel Management. 1987

WICKENS P. *The Road to Nissan*. London, Macmillan. 1987

WILLIAMS A, DOBSON P AND WALTERS M. *Changing Culture: New organisational approaches*. London, Institute of Personnel Management. 1989

Appendix 1

Investors in People

(Extract from the Investing in People *tool kit, 1991; Crown copyright, by permission of the Department of Employment)*

An *Investor in People* makes a public commitment from the top to develop all employees to achieve its business objectives.

- Every employer should have a written but flexible plan which sets out business goals and targets, considers how employees will contribute to achieving the plan and specifies how development needs in particular will be assessed and met.
- Management should develop and communicate to all employees a vision of where the organisation is going and the contribution employees will make to its success, involving employee representatives as appropriate.

An *Investor in People* regularly reviews the training and development needs of all employees.

- The resources for training and development employees should be clearly identified in the business plan.
- Managers should be responsible for regularly agreeing training and development needs with each employee in the context of business objectives, setting targets and standards linked, where appropriate, to the achievement of National Vocational Qualifications (or relevant units) and, in Scotland, Scottish Vocational Qualifications.

An *Investor in People* takes action to train and develop individuals on recruitment and throughout their employment.

- Action should focus on the training needs of all new recruits and continually developing and improving the skills of existing employees.

- All employees should be encouraged to contribute to identifying and meeting their own job-related development needs.

An *Investor in People* evaluates the investment in training and development to assess achievement and improve future effectiveness.

- The investment, the competence and commitment of employees, and the use made of skills learned should be reviewed at all levels against business goals and targets.
- The effectiveness of training and development should be reviewed at the top level and lead to renewed commitment and target setting.

Appendix 2

The six NVET strategic objectives

(From A Strategy for Skills, *1991, pp. 33–6; Crown copyright, by permission of the Department of Employment)*

1 Employers must invest more effectively in the skills their businesses need

TECS to address in their Business Plans:

- National targets, related local targets and progress towards convening local strategic forums
- Awareness by employers of the business benefits of training and the new Standard for Investors in People
- Provision of consistent assessment of employers against the IIP Standard
- Becoming IIPs themselves
- Training in essential business skills and other support for owner-managers of new and small firms
- Adoption of more effective measures to meet employers' skill needs at all levels, in particular through:
  Management Development
  Collaboration with other employers
  Most cost-efficient and effective learning techniques, such as flexible learning
  Coherent information and advisory services to help employers to take informed decisions about training and development

2 Young people must have the motivation to achieve their full potential and to develop the skills the economy needs

TECs to address in their Business Plans:

- National targets and related local targets
- Skill needs of the local and national economy, including to NVQ Level 111 and above

- Increasing employer involvement in and contibutions to Youth Training
- The curriculum in secondary, further and higher education such as to ensure that all young people are helped to achieve their full potential
- Greater access, flexibility, quality and relevance to working life in the education of young people
- Links between employers and education
- Providing teachers with experience of business and an understanding of employers' needs
- Greater participation in FE and training by those who leave school at 16
- The introduction of credits (11 Pilot schemes by November, 1991, and new rounds to be introduced until by 1996 all 16- and 17-year-olds leaving full-time education will have the offer of a training credit)
- Advice and counselling to individuals to make better informed decisions (e.g. using Careers Service Partnerships and supporting up-dating of Careers libraries)

3 Individuals must be persuaded that training pays and that they should take more responsibility in their own development

TECs to address in their Business Plans:

- Individual awareness of the benefits of education and training in order to change attitudes and increase personal motivation
- Improving access to information, advice and guidance so that individuals know what is available and can make informed choices
- Access to education, training and development, including the promotion of open and flexible learning
- Assessment and accreditation of skills
- Financial assistance (e.g. vouchers, training credits, tax relief – new, for those who finance their own training – Career Development Loans for people to gain new skills or update existing ones, etc.) to help and encourage people to make a greater personal commitment to education and training

4 People who are unemployed and those at a disadvantage in the jobs market must be helped to get back to work and to develop their abilities to the full

TECs to address in their Business Plans:

- Help for long-term unemployed people, people with disabilities and others with specific needs, to acquire the skills they need to get jobs and qualifications including, where appropriate, training for professional and other higher level skills (e.g. through tailoring ET and Employment Action to meet differing needs of the unemployed in a cost-effective way)
- The requirement that training and temporary work activities match the needs of the local market
- Increasing employer involvement in and contributions to Employment Training

5 The providers of education and training must offer high quality and flexible provision which meets the needs of individuals and employers

TECs to address in their Business Plans:

- Marketing and adoption of NVQs
- Securing more flexible access to assessment, education and training
- Support for education and training providers in making their provision more responsive and open to individual needs
- Assuring the quality of its programmes, including the selection of competent suppliers and the maintenance of quality standards
- The supply of competent trainers and assessors, and plans to fulfil those needs

6 Enterprise must be encouraged throughout the economy, particularly through the continued growth of small business and self-employment.

TECs to address in their Business Plans:

- The need for a strategic focus for local economic development
- Assistance to the survival and growth of small businesses
- Assistance to the growth of self-employment
- Provision of quality, coherent and accessible business information and counselling services
- Development of enterprise awareness and skills

Appendix 3

An introduction to the National Standards

(extracted from the National Standards for Training and Development, *1992; Crown copyright, by permission of the Department of Employment)*

The National Standards for Training and Development describe:

- the overall contribution of Training and Development to the UK economy – this is the key purpose statement and is equivalent to a corporate mission statement.
- what has to be achieved to fulfil the key purpose – that is, the main *areas of competence* which together will accomplish the *key purpose*
- the contributions individuals can be expected to make within each area, analysed into the results or outcomes individuals are expected to achieve in making each contribution. Each outcome is defined as a *standard or element of competence.*

The Key Purpose Statement describes what Training and Development is expected to achieve in the most general terms. The Standards

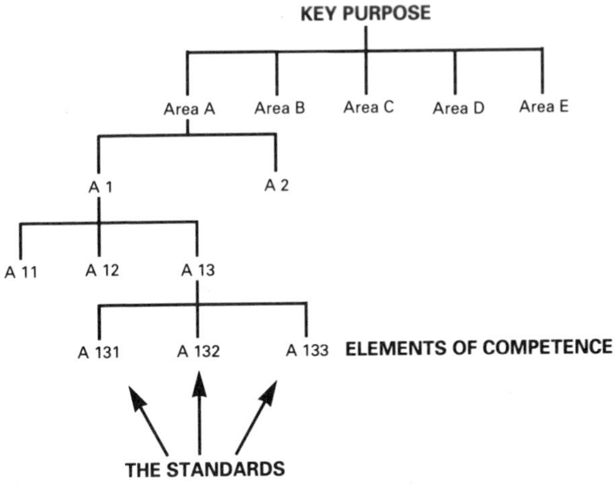

describe what individuals are expected to achieve in their work roles. This diagram shows the link between the Standards and the Key Purpose.

Key Purpose

The Lead Body has defined the Key Purpose of Training and Development as:

TO DEVELOP HUMAN POTENTIAL TO ASSIST ORGANIZATIONS AND INDIVIDUALS TO ACHIEVE THEIR OBJECTIVES.

This statement reflects Training and Development's dual role – to assist both organizations and individuals. It does not assume, of course, that achieving one will achieve the other.

Areas of Competence

What has to be done to achieve the Key Purpose? To answer this question the Lead Body has used the systematic training cycle to define areas of competence.

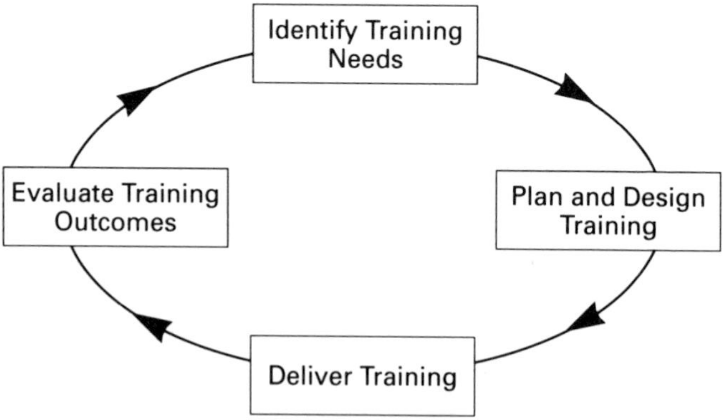

The Systematic Training Cycle

The cycle was chosen because:

- it describes systematically and comprehensively the whole training and development process
- it is familiar in all sectors and to all parts of the training community
- most training and development roles can be located within it.

Each of the Areas of Competence (A-E) corresponds to a stage in the training cycle. They have been split into 12 sub-areas, as shown in the diagram below:

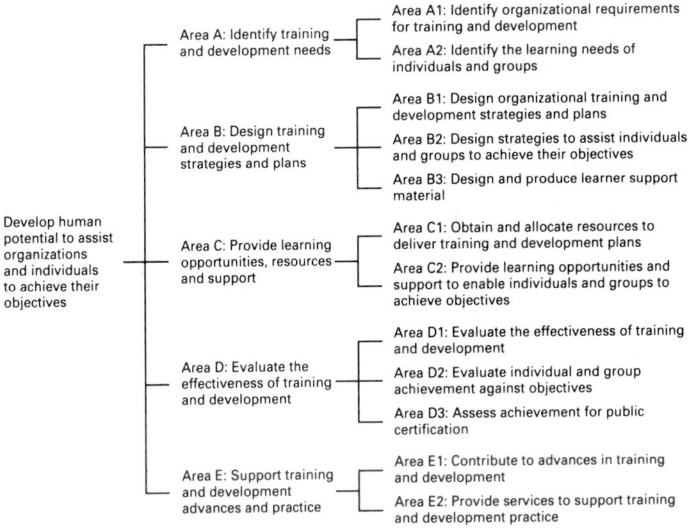

The distinction between Training and Development in support of organizations and in support of individuals is reflected in the difference between Areas A1 and A2, C1 and C2, etc.

Each sub-area is analysed into a number of elements of competence. For example:

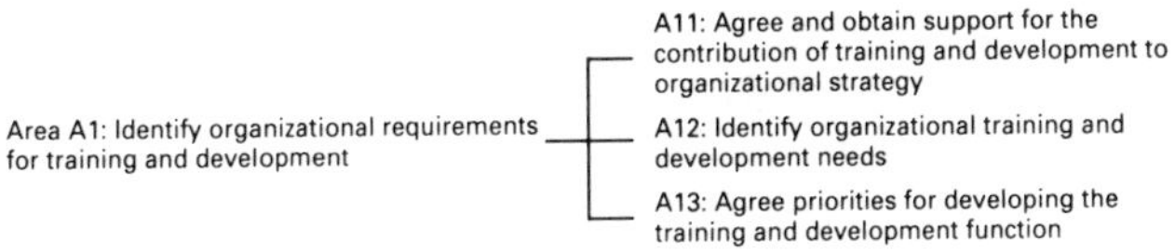

Elements of competence are grouped to form Units of competence, which in turn form the 'building blocks' of National and Scottish Vocational Qualifications (NVQs and SVQs). Each Unit is the smallest sub-division of an NVQ/SVQ which is worthy of separate accreditation, and comprises a title and the standards or elements of competence (and their performance criteria and range statements) to which the Unit refers.

The TDLB also offers these Units to other Lead Bodies for use in their qualifications and will welcome suggestions and proposals from Lead Bodies and Awarding Bodies on this.

Because the process of qualifications design is not yet complete, not all the standards have been formed into Units for accreditation. Again, the TDLB welcomes proposals on this subject.

Some roles expected of practitioners cannot be located within the training cycle. Responsibility for the development of training itself – both theory and practice – is a role that underpins the whole cycle. The effect is to add a fifth area to the Standards Framework – *E Support training and development advances and practice.*

Many Training and Development jobs also require competence in occupational areas other than training. The TDLB has not attempted to define standards for these areas of competence. For roles such as training manager, training administrator and training centre manager, the appropriate standards from other Lead Bodies should be combined with relevant Units from the TDLB's framework to define the requirements of these roles. This process results in the identification of 'hybrid' NVQs and SVQs (see the Qualifications Structure for further information).

What does a National Standard look like?

The standards describe what is expected of an individual performing a particular Training and Development role in a working environment. They do this by defining the outcomes expected of a competent performance in the role – that is, what a competent person would be expected to achieve. Like any other standard – for electrical safety for instance – they are a specification of what is acceptable. However they are used, they must distinguish acceptable from unacceptable performance.

Each standard has three components:

- an element title
- a set of performance criteria
- range statements.

The performance criteria apply to each element. They enable you to distinguish satisfactory from unsatisfactory performance. Each criterion defines one characteristic of satisfactory performance of the element. All the criteria attached to an element have to be met – because they are essential to a satisfactory performance.

The range statements describe the range of contexts and applications in which a competent person would be expected to achieve the outcome or element.

Each standard is accompanied by an evidence specification which describes what information is required to assess competence. The type of evidence required has been specified for each standard. The nature of the evidence is determined by the performance criteria. Range statements are used to determine what samples of evidence are required to assess someone's achievement of the standards.

Appendix 4

The IPD Code of Continuous Development: People and Work

Introduction and Aims

'Continuous Development' is self-directed, lifelong learning. Continuous development policies are policies first to allow and then to facilitate such learning at work, through work itself.

An organization's success depends upon its people. If the organization is to grow (become more effective and efficient), its people must be nurtured in order that they can grow (learn). Thus, employee learning should be managed continuously – not specially and separately but constantly in relation to all work activities. Continuous development focuses on results.

The Code, *Continuous Development: People and Work*, was drawn up to help senior managers, not just personnel professionals, to broaden their views about learning and training, to help them firmly to anchor their learning activity in the organization's business activities, and most important of all, to emphasize that learning within the organization must be managed on a continuous basis. The IPD considered that such a Code was necessary because, in the UK, training is not thought of as a continuous process, rather as a series of short term expedients.

If learning activity in an organization is to be fully beneficial both to the organization and its employees, the following conditions must be met:

- the organization must have some form of strategic business plan. It is desirable that the implications of the strategic plan, in terms of skills and knowledge of the employees who will achieve it, should be spelled out
- managers must be ready and willing (and able) to define and meet needs as they appear; all learning needs cannot be anticipated; organizations must foster a philosophy of continuous development
- as far as practicable, learning and work must be integrated. This

means that encouragement must be given to all employees to learn from the problems, challenges and successes inherent in their day-to-day activities

- the impetus for continuous development must come from the chief executive and other members of the top management team (the board of directors, for example). The top management team must regularly and formally review the way the competence of its management and workforce is being developed. It is important too that one senior executive is charged with responsibility for ensuring that continuous development activity is being effectively undertaken
- investment in continuous development must be regarded by the top management team as being as important as investment in research, new product development or capital equipment. It is not a luxury which can be afforded only in the 'good times'. Indeed, the more severe the problems an organization faces the greater the need for learning on the part of its employees and the more pressing the need for investment in learning. Money spent within the organization on research and development into human resource development itself is money well spent. An evaluation of current human resource development procedures can confirm the effectiveness of current practice or point the way towards necessary change. Such research is as valuable as technical research.

Successful continuous development demands:

- rapid and effective communication of priority operational needs
- the availability of appropriate learning facilities and resources as a normal part of working life
- recognition by each employee that he or she is able to create some personal development plan
- all strategic and tactical operational plans fully take into account the learning implications for the employees affected
- clear understanding, by everyone, of their responsibilities.

These issues are covered in greater detail in the Code under seven key headings:

Policies

Responsibilities and roles

The identification of learning opportunities and needs

Learner involvement

The provision of learning resources

Benefits

Results

Policies

Most organizations find written statements of policy useful. Any statement of general policy relating to the management of people should indicate:

- a firm corporate commitment to continuous development
- that self development is a responsibility of every individual within the organization
- the need for all employees, clients and customers to understand as much as possible about how individuals and groups of people learn, and why it is important
- the organization's commitment to acknowledge improved performance, to use enhanced skills operationally and to provide appropriate rewards
- 'who carries responsibility for what?' in the identification of learning aims and the promotion of learning activity
- ways in which operational aims and objectives are communicated to employees
- agreed procedures and methods for performance appraisal and assessment
- avenues, procedures and processes for career development and progression
- facilities provided for learning during work time, including any policy on paid or unpaid leave for this purpose
- the organization's policy on employee involvement, especially that relating to involvement in reviewing education and training facilities and resources.

If the statement of general policy is not to be a sterile document of mere good intentions:

- the Board and chief executive must be committed to it and demand periodic activity reports
- senior executives and middle and junior level managers must be given the opportunity to suggest amendments to the statement in line with what they regard as 'current operational reality'
- the document must regularly be discussed with trade union representatives and/or other representatives of the workforce
- the organization must satisfy itself that it is making best use of the latest information relating to research and development findings in the human resource development field (and perhaps get involved with such research activity).

Responsibilities and roles

All members in the organization should be able to view the operational life of the organization as a continuous learning process – and one in which they all carry responsibilities.

Senior executives have the responsibility to ensure that policy statements and practices promote continuous development (as set out elsewhere in this Code) and that forward plans incorporate future management needs, particularly to improve performance, taking into account the impact of key changes in legal requirements, technology, work patterns and (not least) ideas. They must encourage managers to plan learning activities to facilitate the process of change.

Managers as part of their responsibilities for getting the best out of their staff, must give regular and ongoing attention to subordinates' continuous development, that is, discussing needs, creating plans, coaching, introducing changes which make learning easier and/or more effective. Managers must promote their own 'learning about learning'.

Personnel professionals have various responsibilities. They should provide an ongoing information service on resources and continuously monitor the extent and quality of learning activity in the organization. If they feel the learning activity is inadequate to support the operational needs of the business, they should take the initiative in generating strategic and/or tactical discussions, recommending appropriate action as necessary. They should ensure that review discussions happen at least once a year within the senior executive group and within any consultative groups. Internal personnel department review discussions should take place frequently.

All learners (including the three groups above) should appreciate that they are responsible for clarifying their own learning goals within the framework established by forward plans and discussions with management. They should raise their problems with management; seek new information without waiting for it to be delivered; and demonstrate new learning whenever possible. The ultimate aim is for continuous development to become fully integrated into work, with learners managing most of the activity for themselves and everyone contributing to the identification of learning opportunities.

Identification of Learning Opportunities and Needs

It is worth repeating that everyone needs to contribute to the identification of learning opportunities. But some sources are stronger than others, for example:

Operational plans: every proposal for a new operational element or instrument, that is, a new product, a new item of plant, a new procedure, a new department, a new member of staff, a new accounting convention, a new *anything*, should be accompanied by an estimate of:

- which employees need to learn something
- what needs to be learned
- how the learning can happen.

If these things cannot be defined with confidence, the proposal should include a plan which allows this to be completed later. Some needs are indirectly related; new technical systems, for example, may demand not merely instruction in the system itself, but also new levels and types of maintenance. Removing existing resources (machines, materials, or perhaps people) may also demand a learning plan.

Job descriptions and specifications: documents outlining management responsibilities should normally include references to:

- the roles of appraisor, counsellor, tutor
- the responsibility to develop understanding of learning processes
- the manager's inclusion of learning elements in operational plans.

Separately, all job descriptions and specifications (regardless of level or type) should emphasize the job holder's responsibilities for self development on a continuous basis.

Appraisal: appraisal forms and guidance notes should explicitly demand reports on improved performance goals and hence learning needs. Appraisal interviews should normally include joint appraisor/appraisee discussions on the extent to which self development takes place, and again on the frequency of management-inspired learning plans. Ideally informal appraisal discussions will happen continuously; a standard question on these occasions should be 'how long is it since we/you/I learned something new at work?'

Special reviews and audits: parts of the learning system should be specially reviewed from time to time. Diagonal-slice (that is, various employees from various departments) working parties, joint consultative committees, trainee groups and, not least, particular individuals, can be charged with collecting data, analysing it and reporting to senior executives or to personnel management. These reviews are particularly useful in those parts of the learning system where knowledge or awareness needs to be renewed from time to time, as for example, in health and safety.

Learner Involvement

Learners need to be motivated to want to learn. This motivation may be lacking if they feel that learning activities are imposed, especially if they seem unrelated to personal aspirations. It is necessary therefore to encourage learners' involvement in the creation of any training plans that will involve them.

To that end:

- joint appraisor/appraisee decisions should aim at joint definition of objectives and the means to achieve them

- standing committees should include in their agenda, at regular, periodic intervals, an item demanding review of their achievements and future aims
- special organizational groupings (e.g. quality circles, briefing groups) should explicitly contain 'improved performance' and 'management of change' aims, and should devote time to discussing the learning aspects of any proposals for future activity
- when new plant or equipment is introduced, contracts with suppliers should explicitly contain reference to the early involvement of staff during the commissioning process. It is normally desirable that suppliers should provide more than written manuals; active dialogue between them and those who are to operate and maintain the new equipment (including contract maintenance staff where appropriate) is needed
- work teams should encourage a 'multi-skills' approach to their future operations, minimizing divisions between jobs and maximizing the flexibility that goes with increased versatility
- where unionized and/or joint consultative arrangements exist, policies relating to training should regularly be discussed with employee representatives at all levels
- reference should be made to training policies, and to any current learning priorities, in progress reports, house magazines and through other available communication channels. Incentives towards self development are as useful in this area as in others.

The Provision of Learning Resources

Self development, team learning, and continuous operation development, all require resource material and facilities. The organization should clarify its policies and practices on the following:

- training/learning budgets
- authorities to approve training/learning plans and expenditure
- facilities for study during standard working hours, including paid/unpaid leave
- financial assistance with travel, books, tapes, and other facilities
- awards and/or scholarships
- coaching and tutorial resources
- management's responsibility to create an environment in which continuous development can prosper.

All employees, and especially management, should have access to documents detailing these policies.

Benefits

Strategic plans, or research and development expenditure, are not expected directly to yield precisely quantifiable benefits. They are means to ends. In the same way, expenditure on education, training and development should be regarded as a necessary and calculated investment yielding consequent pay off in terms of enhanced business performance. The following benefits can be expected:

- strategic plans are more likely to be achieved
- ideas can be expected to be generated, in a form which relates to operational needs
- everyone in the organization will recognize the need for learning effort on their part if the organization is to survive and their jobs made more secure
- and, in general, fewer mistakes, fewer accidents, less waste, higher productivity, higher morale, lower staff turnover, better industrial relations, better customer service, and hence, greater returns to the organization.

The major benefits are, first, improved operational performance, and second, the joint development of people and work.

Results

How do you spot the 'continuous development' team? Its characteristics are many and varied, but here is a list of the key ones:

- all members, management and non-management, appear to understand and share ownership of operational goals
- immediate objectives exist and are understood by all
- new developments are promoted; change is constructive and welcomed and enjoyed, not forced and resisted
- managers are frequently to be heard discussing learning methods with their subordinates and colleagues

- managers frequently ask subordinates what they have learned recently
- time is found by all the team to work on individual members' problems
- reference documents (manuals, dictionaries, specification sheets and the like) are available to all without difficulty, and are used
- members use other members as resources
- members do not just swap information; they tackle problems and create opportunities
- all members share responsibility for success or failure; they are not dependent upon one or more leaders
- members appear to learn while they work, and to enjoy both.

The latest edition of this Code, now entitled *The IPD Statement on Continuous Development: People and Work* can be obtained from the Communications Department, the Institute of Personnel and Development, IPD House, Camp Road, Wimbledon, London SW19 4UX (0181-971 9000)

Appendix 5

Job Description and Job Training Specification: Key Task Analysis

(Example from 1988, reproduced by permission of C Gray and the then North Eastern Electricity Board)

JOB DESCRIPTION

1 Organizational Context

1.1 Organization
The North Eastern Electricity Board (5000 employees, comprising approximately 500 professional electrical engineers, 500 professional and administrative staff, 1000 clerical staff and 3000 industrial staff at Headquarters, 5 District Offices, 47 Electricity showrooms and various other small locations.)

1.2 Unit
Cleveland District (540 employees, split proportionately as above, located at District Headquarters and 2 Depots.)

1.3 Nature of Business
Electricity Distribution.

1.4 Job
Head of District Personnel Section, based at District Headquarters.

2 Job Context

2.1 Job Title
Principal Assistant (Personnel and Training)

2.2 Department
Manager's Department (Cleveland District)

2.3 Section
Personnel and Training

2.4 Responsible to
Senior Executive Officer (Administration)

2.5 Subordinates
One Senior Clerical Assistant
One Clerical Assistant

2.6 Purpose of job

a To assist the SEO (Administration) in the supervision and control of the Personnel function throughout the District.

b To plan, control and coordinate the work of the staff under his control and to ensure that their efforts are continually directed towards the improvements of work standards and methods.

3 Duties and Responsibilities

3.1 Industrial Relations
*KEY TASKS
The implementation and control of National Agreements

The implementation and control of Statutory Instruments and Board Instructions as they relate to the Personnel function

To give advice on the above, insofar as they govern Pay and Conditions of Service

*OTHER TASKS
Act in the absence of the SEO (Administration) as Board Side Secretary of all Negotiating and Local Joint Coordinating Council (including Health & Safety) Committees

3.2 Training
*KEY TASK
Prepare annual Training Budget

*OTHER TASKS

To advise line management on a quarterly basis of training courses planned in the future, and to assist in the nomination of appropriate staff

To control and coordinate the District's involvement in a Work Experience Programme involving local schools and colleges

To ensure that the Industry's requirements and obligations are met in respect of Apprentice and Clerical Training in the District

3.3 Recruitment

*KEY TASKS

To assist in the recruitment and selection of clerical staff throughout the District, and represent the Personnel Section at selection interviews

To carry out craft apprentice and clerical trainee selection tests

*OTHER TASKS

To advise line management on various sources of recruitment available for clerical and industrial staff

3.4 Welfare

*KEY TASKS

On matters of sickness/staff welfare to carry out visits and demonstrate the interest the Board has in the well-being of its staff

To liaise closely with the Board's Nursing Officer in cases of long-term sickness or serious injury involving any District employee

*OTHER TASKS

To discuss with employees concerned, and to ensure that they fully understand, the provisions of the Industry's Pension Scheme in cases of ill-health retirement, and the financial terms applicable in cases of redundancy

3.5 Manpower

*KEY TASK

To assist as required in the preparation of manpower proposals and manpower budgets

3.6 General
*KEY TASKS
To give advice and information as requested to all staff on all matters covered by the Personnel function

Reasons for Choosing Key Task Analysis

The job under analysis is a Junior Managerial/Supervisory job and a KTA approach has been adopted. A variety of separate tasks are involved under several headings, covering a wide range of Personnel specialisms, and I feel the best way to analyse the job is by establishing the *key* tasks (those tasks which are crucial to overall effectiveness) and identifying the knowledge, skills and attitudes required to fulfil those tasks, together with measures of performance. The level of the job would suggest that the job-holder does not require training in minor tasks, but that his training needs and priorities would be best isolated by establishing and analysing *key* tasks.

An extract from the key task analysis appears overleaf

KEY TASK ANALYSIS (Extract)

Task	Knowledge	Skills
INDUSTRIAL RELATIONS *The Implementation and Control of National Agreements*	a Range, scope and content of each Agreement b Constitutions of the Negotiating Bodies. c Local custom and practice. d I.R. Theory.	a Ability to recognize principles in Agreements, rather than adopting an over-literal approach. b Judgemental skill in anticipating I.R. implications of changes or new interpretations of Agreements. c Verbal skill in drafting staff information sheets on I.R. matters. d Ability to think logically so that all relevant factors are taken into account (e.g. precedent, custom and practice, local circumstances etc) in implementing Agreements. e Apply I.R. Theory within context of Agreements and NEEB policy.
The Implementation and Control of Statutory Instruments and Board Instructions as they relate to the Personnel function	a Range, scope and content of S.I.'s, especially those parts affecting the Board in relation to its employees and vice-versa. b Range, scope and content of all Personnel Instructions.	a As above.

Attitude	Measures of Performance
a Firm, but not legalistic.	a Agreed terms and conditions applied consistently and fairly throughout District.
a As above, but always aware of *legal* requirements.	a NEEB's statutory obligations in the Employment field fully met throughout District. b Spirit and intentions of Personnel Instructions fulfilled in District.

Appendix 6

Example of a Problem-Centred Job Training Analysis

(Reproduced by permission of M. Mullen, now Assistant Director, O. and R., Northumberland County Council)

A Job Information

Designation: Management Services Assistant.

Department: Personnel and Management Services, M.B.C.

Accountable to: Team Leader in charge of 2–3 assistants.

Liaising with: Middle/Senior management of administrative departments.
Middle/Line management of craft departments.
Other support services staff, e.g. Finance, Legal, Computers.

B Notes of Guidance

(i) I have tried, as far as possible, to follow the same methodology as Warr and Bird, but obviously without a large sample this is difficult to achieve.

(ii) Without going into great detail one cannot 'group' problems as Warr and Bird did, so the problems listed on the analysis sheets relate to specific instances. However, these could just as easily be classified under headings such as 'relationships with subordinates' etc. (See Warr and Bird).

(iii) The frequencies used in the examples relate more to the type of problem rather than to the specific examples quoted – e.g. in example 1B it is likely that the practitioner would experience interpersonal problems almost constantly.

(iv) The 'organizational factors' column indicates where problems can become endemic to the organization, although the link between the specific problem quoted and the general problem intimated may not appear to be very clear.

(v) Even under the job specific problems, an attempt has been made to indicate the type of person to be or not to be at risk.

(vi) The biographical information could be culled using a form very similar to Warr and Bird's with one or two amendments or additions, and therefore it was not felt necessary to include an example as such.

The examples are given on page 510 overleaf.

[Note: This piece of work was carried out as an Assignment by Mullen while a student on an IPM Stage 2 Course in 1985. Often the problem-centred approach is used to analyse the needs of large numbers of personnel, but here, as observed in B(i), the sample was very small. Nonetheless, important needs could be identified]

Examples of Critical Incident Forms

1A

DAY 1

What was the most difficult job or situation that you had to deal with today?

'Joe Bloggs the Foreman at – Depot phoned me to ask if I would have a word with one of his chargehands who was having difficulty completing his paperwork and in particular his bonus and time sheets. I had already been out to see this chap when he started 3 weeks ago and I didn't see it as my job to interfere in a situation where I had no direct control or authority. Nevertheless I did it because we are supposed to be providing a service to management – aren't we?'

Approximately how often do you have to deal with a difficulty of this kind?

a Daily

b Weekly

c Monthly

d Every three months ✓

e Yearly

f Other (please specify)

1B

DAY 2

'I had to go out this morning to study a tarmac gang laying a new type of material. When I arrived on site I was not happy about the number of men on the job nor the type of roller they were going to use to consolidate the tarmac. I informed the chargehand concerned in no uncertain manner about my misgivings and threatened to report the whole gang to senior management for trying to 'con' me. At this point the men laid down their tools and refused to be studied by me. I returned to the office and informed my team leader of what had happened.'

Frequency: weekly-monthly.

1C

DAY 3

'I had a meeting this afternoon with senior management of the – Department, i.e. the Deputy Director, the Assistant Director (Admin.) and the ——— ——— ——— to discuss my report and recommendations on my investigation into the organization, structure and practices of the ——— Section of the ——— Department. I came back seething because although they agreed in principle with my recommendations and could not dispute my figures they could not agree to the implementation of my report due to 'external' factors which had recently arisen and which could not be discussed at this stage. When I protested vehemently I was told quite clearly by the Deputy that it was his department and he would organize it the way he liked. What's the point? I ask myself.'

Frequency: whenever the recommendations are in any way controversial or liable to cause departmental management too many headaches.

Problem centred analysis

Problem	Type of Person *Likely* to be at Risk	Type of Person *Unlikely* to be at Risk
1 Tendency for one's concept of standard performance to err far away from the ideal and thus affect the accuracy of any resulting data particularly when using techniques such as time study and activity sampling.	b,c,d,e	a
2 Dissatisfaction with the level and quality of work being given by the Team leader – generally boring, routine and mundane.	a,b	d,e
3 Lack of clarity of role/function in relation to line supervision	b,c	

Type of Problem *i.e. Job Specific or Job General*	**Possible Training Solutions**	**Organizational Factor**
Job General – a technical problem of skill liable to affect almost all practitioners at some time.	a Regular (monthly) in-house 'rating' clinics using bought-in films so that individual's performance can be measured. b Give those whose concept of standard is off beam more experience in the field to sharpen up their rating skill.	
Job Specific – liable to lead to low motivation and therefore poor performance. Problem probably stems from individual's lack of success/initiative in previous assignments.	a Course in creative/ lateral thinking techniques to try to increase ingenuity and initiative. b Secondment to other teams engaged in different types of projects for a certain period to give the individual a 'wider' experience.	The problem may be made more complex by the fact that the Team leader may need some training in leadership styles and motivational techniques
Job Specific	Awareness of organizational structures and relationships within the Authority.	Problems tend to indicate a need for a closer look at supervisory training or at least 'sideways' training to bring people in different departments doing similar level work together.

Problem	Type of Person *Likely* to be at Risk	Type of Person *Unlikely* to be at Risk
4 Lack of knowledge of health and safety regulations in general and in particular with regard to the type of work carried out by local authority DLO's i.e. maintenance and minor works.	b,c,d	a,e
5 Relationships with people from other departments involved in studies/investigations.	b,c,d	e
6 Frustration at not having these recommendations accepted by departmental management.	b,c,d	e

Biographical information (see analysis)

a = ex-tradesman
b = younger practitioners
c = graduates with little/no work experience
d = practitioners from outside industry with no local government experience
e = experienced practitioners/administrators

Type of Problem *i.e. Job Specific or Job General*	Possible Training Solutions	Organizational Factor
Job General	In house training course for all management services assistants on the HASAWA and its provisions followed by more detailed analysis of type of safety problems likely to be encountered in local authority work e.g. eye protection, abrasive wheel regulations, ladder work etc.	Would be useful to involve the men's representatives/ chargehands and line and middle management of the Public Works Department.
Job Specific – maybe an attitude problem which is difficult to remedy and should perhaps have been noticed at the selection stage.	Interpersonal skills training either by attendance at a course and/or close supervision on the job.	Again perhaps a need to look at training information throughout the organization as a whole on the purpose/ role of a management services investigation.
Job General	Greater emphasis on negotiating skills and ways of implementation of schemes – probably in-house but could benefit from an IR Course in such skills.	The problem may not have a training solution *per se* but requires a clarification of function/ role/power by the Management Team or Committee. Again a lateral and vertical problem.

Appendix 7

Personnel Specification

Principal Assistant (Personnel Dept), North Eastern Electricity Board, 1988
(Example from 1988, reproduced by permission of C Gray and the then North Eastern Electricity Board)

PERSONAL QUALITIES	**ESSENTIAL**
IMPACT ON OTHERS	
APPEARANCE	Clean and well-dressed; must be acceptable to others both within and outside NEEB.
SPEECH	Clear speech.
MANNER	Friendly, pleasant but also business-like when appropriate.
SELF-CONFIDENCE	Sufficient to deal face to face with all levels of staff, and to take initiative where appropriate in dealing with Senior Management.
COMPETENCE IN DEALING WITH SITUATIONS INVOLVING OTHER PEOPLE	Good interpersonal skills. Must be tactful and discreet where necessary.
QUALIFICATIONS	
GENERAL EDUCATION	4 'O' levels or equivalent, including Maths and English Language.

DESIRABLE

Very well-presented, certain to create good impression.

Good fluency in speech. Voice sufficiently powerful to address group, meeting or audience on public occasions.

Very good social skills and manner, able to mix well and communicate with all types of people.

Sufficient to make own decisions within sphere of competence and responsibility without always seeking approval.

Self-confidence necessary in exercising purposeful leadership of section.

High degree of tact and discretion required in dealing with matters of a confidential nature.

Able to demonstrate authoritative approach where dealing with others.

Persuasive skills to gain agreement of others to various courses of action.

Degree or equivalent. Evidence of ability to carry out a course of study successfully.

Potential for gaining further qualifications (IPM or ICSA).

PERSONAL QUALITIES	ESSENTIAL
OCCUPATIONAL TRAINING	None
OCCUPATIONAL EXPERIENCE	At least 18 months within ESI, prefe NEEB, including at least 6 months in Personnel work.
ABILITIES	
APTITUDES	Numerate, good written and oral ski Able to apply information intelligent Must be potentially good Supervisor Ability to meet deadlines.
I.Q.	Above average intelligence.
MOTIVATION	
ABILITY TO ORGANIZE OWN WORK AND WORK OF SUBORDINATES	Ability to plan ahead and assess priorities.
ABILITY TO SET SELF GOALS AND SET SUBORDINATES' GOALS	Must recognize main purpose of ow and of subordinates in order that rea and appropriate goals may be set.
ABILITY TO WORK ALONE OR IN A TEAM	Ability to work alone or in a team as appropriate.

ESIRABLE

IEEB Clerical Supervisory Skills Course (1 week). ESI Introduction to Management Course (3 weeks).

t least 1–2 years experience of Personnel work within NEEB.

ome District experience.

ome supervisory experience.

xcellent written style – skill in drafting and minute-writing.

bility to plan ahead and control and organize work of section.

ublic speaking skill.

ligh I.Q. Quick, perceptive thinker. Ability to absorb and analyse large mounts of written information.

bility to relate all tasks within section to each other and establish efficient vorking practices.

bility to identify priorities and delegate duties where necessary to oncentrate on own priorities and goals and aid development of subordinates.

bility to gain agreement of staff to goals set.

bility to work effectively in role of team leader of section and to ensure eam work of section is good.

bility to work as part of team in Working Parties, Project Groups etc.

bility to work alone where necessary and to motivate self to meet time and standard targets.

PERSONAL QUALITIES	ESSENTIAL
ADJUSTMENT	
RESPONSIBILITY AND RELIABILITY	Responsible, mature approach. Reliable in handling confidential ma meeting important deadlines and providing information to Senior Management.
LEADERSHIP	Must be potentially a good supervis leader.
ACCEPTABILITY	Appearance and manner should be acceptable to all levels of staff, and people from outside NEEB.

(Using 5-Point Plan format: see J M Fraser, Employment Interviewing; *5th ed. London Macdonald and Evans, 1978)*

ESIRABLE

igh degree of responsibility required to work increasingly without upervision, and occasionally as stand-in for SEO (Admin).

ery responsible and reliable in dealing with all personnel matters, specially own Key tasks.

ood leadership skills. Some supervisory experience.

ppearance and manner should at all times create a good impression.

hould be able to communicate effectively in a friendly, open way with all taff and outsiders.

Appendix 8

Form for a Developmental Appraisal Scheme

Employee's name ______________________________

Position ______________________________

Date this position/level ______________________________

Date last appraisal ______________________________

Date this appraisal ______________________________

A. JOB DESCRIPTION

Any changes in the Job Description since last year? If so, what?

B. REVIEW OF APPRAISEE'S PERFORMANCE SINCE LAST APPRAISAL

THE JOB Key tasks/objectives appraisee had to achieve in the past year	CRITERIA FOR MEASURING PERFORMANCE How performance related to each objective has been/can be measured	NOTES ON PERFORMANCE Any comments on how far objectives were, or were not, achieved

Any job-related training/development done in the past year, and the use to which it has been put?

Generally, what do you see as your main achievements last year? And were there any areas where you were less satisfied?

FINAL RATING OF LAST YEAR'S PERFORMANCE IN THE JOB.

(A. Results far exceeded requirements of the job in all areas.
B. Results achieved consistently exceeded the requirements of the job in most areas.
C. Results achieved met the requirements of the job, and exceeded them in some areas.
D. Results achieved met the requirements of the job.
E. Results achieved did not meet the requirements of the job.)

THE JOB Key tasks/objectives for coming year (classified as before)	CRITERIA How performance related to each key task/objective will be measured	NOTES Any special help/resources needed to achieve tasks/objectives (except training – see below)

Training/development (e.g. formal courses, internal staff development activities, changes in responsibilities) needed in relation to the coming year's work targets.

If none, then how will appraisee keep 'fresh' in the job?

D. CAREER PLANNING AND DEVELOPMENT

The appraisee's general career plan.

Any steps taken in relation to overall career development in the past year.

Anything proposed for the coming year to contribute to appraisee's overall career development.

E. ACTION PLANS AGREED AT END OF DISCUSSION

Action related to job description

If any changes have been agreed at the end of the discussion, note these, and how and when they will be achieved.

Action related to helping appraisee to achieve targets in coming year
Note here anything agreed to meet job-related needs: training and development, extra resources, etc. Also note who will be responsible for action; when it will occur; when and by whom it will be evaluated.

Action related to career development needs
Note here anything agreed to meet career-related needs; who will be responsible for ensuring the action/s materialize; when each action will occur; when and by whom action will be monitored and evaluated.

Signature of appraiser ______________________ Date ____________________

Signature of appraisee ______________________ Date ____________________

Appendix 9

The Training and Development Problem: Brief for the Head of the Engineering Department

You have been appraising the performance of your Quality Assurance Manager, and have reached the stage of discussing his skills in appraising and developing his staff (seven inspectors). You both work in a small light engineering group which is part of a national engineering company. The Group is virtually autonomous, with a young and very able Managing Director who, over the past five years, has built up a strong task culture and team-based structure, taking the Group into a leading market position. There are 23 managers (including supervisors of shop floor workers) and about 100 other employees. (The organization chart for your Department follows this brief.)

Three and a half years ago the company brought in a consultant who worked with the management team to design a simple appraisal scheme, with a self-appraisal strategy and focusing on key result areas and targets of performance. It aims to help with the appraisal of current work performance, work planning, and the diagnosis of training and development needs leading to individual development plans. The scheme has been running successfully for three years, and covers the whole Group, not just the management team. The team chose the design themselves, and piloted the scheme for a year, before it was extended to the rest of the organization in the second and third years.

The QA Manager is 43, married, with one son who is an apprentice in the company. He has been in his present job for ten years (you yourself have only been here for three years, and are 34, a graduate recruit from another engineering firm and with – you have been led to believe – top management potential). He has been with the company since himself being an apprentice. At the personal level you don't particularly care for him, and feel that he has no real liking for you either. You have never had an outright dispute with him, but find him unresponsive to views that do not coincide with his own, and unlikely to admit easily to weaknesses. Generally his performance in his job is good although without signs of any real potential which could take him higher in the organization. He achieves his technical targets, and is meticulous in carrying out his duties. His staff seem effective too, although not achieving much above adequate performance (judging from his own appraisal of them).

The problem with the QA Manager is, you feel, his poor record in appraising and developing his inspector team. Although he holds annual appraisal interviews, and appropriate forms are completed and action plans carried out relating to training and development, nevertheless his staff have spent less time on training and development activities than most others in the Group – on average, about two days each per year, compared with an overall average of eight days per person in the rest of the Group. Furthermore, the training that they have been given is entirely technical, yet you would expect some developmental activities which would enable them to show potential for promotion, and generally aid their longer-term development.

You have also noticed (because there is a space on the appraisal form which asks the appraiser to note how long the appraisal interview lasted) that his appraisal interviews last on average no more than an hour, whereas the overall average in the Group is two hours. Furthermore, on at least two of the forms completed last year the Inspector concerned registered failure to agree with the QA Manager on matters related to areas which the QA Manager saw as weaknesses. The comments made by the appraisees showed that they had not been convinced by the QA Manager's reasons when he judged their performance as inadequate. They had put forward counter-arguments, which they felt he had dismissed without adequate discussion, and stalemate had been reached. In neither case had a final Appeal been made, but clearly this could come if such clashes were to recur and you wish to ensure that such an outcome does not occur.

It is difficult to know whether the QA Manager could be helped by skills training related to all the above issues or not. He did go through a two-day Workshop on Appraisal Skills three years ago, run by the same consultant who worked with the management team in the design of the appraisal scheme, but perhaps some form of short course which would give him help specifically related to the weaknesses you believe he has would be appropriate now. Or is there some other form of training or development that might work? Or is some other solution altogether more likely to succeed? You intend to go into the whole matter at some length with him, since the basic issues of appraisal, training and development of his team are so crucial to the longer-term effectiveness of his unit. You are not looking forward to this part of the interview, and have therefore planned it particularly carefully in order to try to achieve positive outcomes.

Appendix 10

The Training and Development Problem: Organization Chart

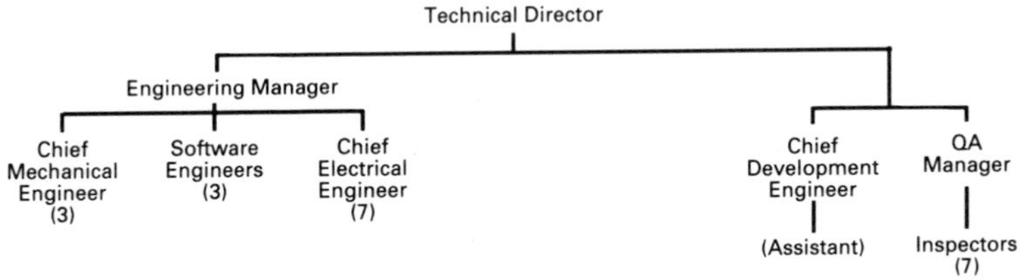

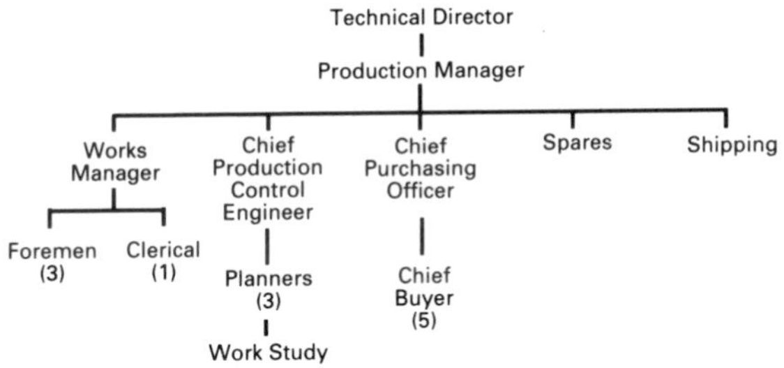

Appendix 11

The Training and Development Problem: Brief for the Quality Assurance Manager

You are nearing the end of the 'appraisal of performance' part of your annual appraisal interview carried out by your manager, the Head of the Engineering Department. You are pleased with the outcome of the discussion so far but hope that it will soon be over as there is the usual build-up of work over in your area and you need to get back as soon as possible.

You both work in a small light engineering group which is part of a national engineering company. The Group is virtually autonomous, with a young and very able Managing Director who, over the past five years, has built up a strong task culture and team-based structure, taking the Group into a leading market position. There are 23 managers (including supervisors of shop floor workers) and about 100 other employees. (The organization chart for your Department precedes this brief.)

You are 43, married, with one son who is an apprentice in the company. You have been in your present job for ten years. You have been with the company since being an apprentice, and feel considerable loyalty to it. Although you would like to be at least one step higher up the management ladder than you are now, you are prepared to take things steadily and wait, confident in the belief that promotion will come before too long. Your Manager is 34, a graduate recruit from another engineering firm, and has been in the company for three years as Head of Department. He is very bright, and is talked of as a future top manager. Personally you don't like him, and sense that the feeling is mutual. You work together well enough – well, you have never had an outright dispute with him – but find him unresponsive to views that do not coincide with his own, and unlikely to admit easily to weaknesses. You therefore avoid him as much as possible, and try to do your job in such a way as to make sure that you can't be criticized for anything.

Three and a half years ago the company brought in a consultant who worked with the management team (including yourself) to design a simple appraisal scheme, with a self-appraisal strategy, focusing on key result areas and targets of performance. It aims to help with the appraisal of current work performance, work planning, and the diagnosis of training and development needs leading to individual development plans. The scheme has been running successfully for three years, and covers the whole Group, not just the management team. The team chose the design themselves, and piloted the scheme for a year, before it was extended to the rest of the organization in the second and third years. In that first (pilot) year you and the rest of the management team attended an Appraisal Skills Workshop specially designed for all of you and run by the Consultant, and you found it very useful. You have tried hard to apply the skills of appraisal to your own task of appraising your seven Inspectors annually. You have done that task twice now – once last year, and once this.

You know that your performance in your job is generally rated as good, even though you never seem to get particularly enthusiastic comments from your manager. You achieve all your technical targets, and are acknowledged as being meticulous in carrying out your duties. As to your Inspectors, they're pretty good men, if with no obvious potential to get any higher. They do what they are told and never cause any real problems, and that is as much as you can hope for in work where everything has to be done so accurately and under so many pressures.

You never need to spend more than an hour on their appraisal interviews (you remember that, because you have to write on each appraisal interview form how long the discussion has taken), which is all the time you and they can ever spend on this task. You always see that the appraisal forms are very carefully completed, and that any action plans relating to training and development are carried out exactly as agreed – you are conscientious in this, as in all your duties. Your staff actually do well on training and development, spending about two days each per year in some kind of formal refresher training activities (since all are adequate performers, they never need more than that), and coming to you for discussions whenever they hit problems in their jobs. In other words, you try to develop them in their daily work as well as you can, using their mistakes as learning points. They can always ask you if they want anything more – initiative, you feel, is very important in these matters – but so far they never have.

It was a pity that on two of the forms completed last year the Inspectors concerned registered failure to agree with you on matters related to areas where they clearly had weaknesses (although neither ended up making any formal Appeal). The comments they made showed that they did not accept that their performance *was* inadequate: they had put forward counter-arguments, which they said you had dismissed without sufficient discussion, and stalemate had been reached. However, in both cases the problem was their poor interpersonal skills, which had caused difficulties, minor but repeated, with a small group of shopfloor workers. It's always difficult to get anyone to accept that they are not good at dealing with people, and these two Inspectors, both into their fifties, are never going to change their ways: lengthy discussion would have only made matters worse, so in the end you had to simply instruct them in a few procedures to use in such situations, and warn them about the need to observe these if problems with the Union were to be avoided.

They didn't like it, but at least there had been no further outbreaks and in every other respect their performance was quite satisfactory. Afterwards you had wondered whether training or development of any kind could have made any difference to this area of their work, but had come to the conclusions that to have even suggested it would have got their backs up: both are steady, reliable men, looking forward to their retirement, and very set in their ways. Procedures are something they understand, but some form of 'interpersonal skills' training would be just seen as a threat, and would cause more problems than it would resolve.

Appendix 12

The IPD Self-assessment Exercise

Introduction

The exercise is divided into three parts:

1 Assessment
The 3-page Questionnaire. This can be completed either on your own, or after discussion with someone else – anyone who is interested in your career development and willing to give up about an hour to help you think through your answers to the various questions.

2 Diagnosis
The 'Assessment of Learning Needs' sheet. This is filled in after the self-assessment exercise has been completed, using the insights generated by that exercise.

3 Action planning
One sheet, which should be copied and used for each component of the overall Plan. The Plan should tackle whichever learning needs (listed on your diagnostic sheet) you feel need the most immediate attention. Thus should you decide to tackle three areas of need in the forthcoming period, three separate sheets should be drawn up.

Please note, when completing your Action Plans, that there is an extra page in the Appendix that shows a range of possible developmental methods. Before completing the Assessment, please write a brief introduction, in which you explain who 'you' are: your job, role and level in the organization; your overall life goals and your career aspirations in the light of those goals; any barriers and/or aids to learning and development that currently exist in your work situation, and in your non-work situation, and how you carried out the self-assessment exercise (by yourself, or with the help of someone else). When considering barriers and aids to learning, think of the learning process in the way it was described in Chapter 7, as consisting of four stages in continuous interaction:

1 Experiencing something – a problem, a need, a situation.
2 Observing and reflecting – suspending judgment whilst gathering information, making comparisons, looking for patterns, similarities and differences to previous experiences.
3 Conceptualizing – analysing the information, forming a set of concepts about it, and/or trying to fit it into some existing body of theory in order to 'learn' from the experience; diagnosing the crucial issues.
4 Experimenting – trying out a different or amended approach to this sort of experience, suggested by the processes of reflecting and theorizing.

In *Continuous Development: A Teaching Pack for IPM Course Tutors* (IPM, 1985), Pike and colleagues explain that the sort of barriers to learning and development you might experience at work could include the structural and cultural barriers listed below.

Barriers to Learning and Problem-Solving

Barriers to EXPERIENCING
Structural barriers: Activities are closely defined and specialized. They are routine, predictable, undemanding, low in variability, uninvolving, not stimulating.
Cultural barriers: General preference for distance and detachment. People tend to be reserved, non-expressive, impersonal. Code of behaviour that stresses 'Don't get your hands dirty or muck in'; 'Don't get involved', etc.

Barriers to REFLECTING AND OBSERVING
Structural barriers: Poor communications and information flow. Inadequate feedback. Geographical or structural isolation. Fast pace of work and other pressures.
Cultural barriers: The organization/department is preoccupied with the present. Tendency to be secretive and distrustful. Norms of behaviour include 'Let's get cracking'; 'What's next?'; 'That's just history – live for today'; 'Keep your opinions to yourself'; 'Don't wash your dirty linen in public'; 'Keep your cards close to your chest', etc.

Barriers to THEORIZING/ANALYSING
Structural barriers: Emphasis on results at work. Interruptions and short time-scales. Lack of reviews. Lack of procedures for 'post-mortems', policy-making, planning and 'think-tanks'.
Cultural barriers: Action oriented. Pragmatic. Over-responsive. Typical views are 'Thinking is for academics'; 'Ignorance is bliss'; 'No use sitting around on your backside', etc.

Barriers to EXPERIMENTING
Structural barriers: Over-prescribed duties, methods, rules and procedures. Red tape. High costs of failure. Lack of encouragement to experiment or innovate.
Cultural barriers: Cautious. Conservative, traditional, conforming. Often heard phrases include 'Tread carefully'; 'Don't rock the boat'; 'We don't do it that way here', etc.

When you have finished the exercise, write a brief note on how each Action Plan will be monitored and reviewed, when, and by whom.

Self-assessment Exercise

(Reproduced by permission of the Institute of Personnel and Development)

Self-Assessment Sheet for Continuous Development

Current work performance

(i) Professional knowledge of present job

A	☐	Inadequate
	☐	Tendency to A
	☐	Tendency to B
B	☐	Thorough knowledge of job

(ii) Quantity of work (speed and consistency in producing required results)

A	☐	Fair
	☐	Tendency to A
	☐	Tendency to B
B	☐	Unusually high output

(iii) Quality of work (extent to which results meet requirements of accuracy, thoroughness and neatness)

A	☐	Passable
	☐	Tendency to A
	☐	Tendency to B
B	☐	High quality

(iv) Attitude towards job

A	☐	Not always interested/enthusiastic
	☐	Tendency to A
	☐	Tendency to B
B	☐	High willingness and enthusiasm

(v) Judgement and Analytical Ability (extent to which decisions or actions based on a sound appraisal of the situation and reached by logical reasoning)

A		Conclusions sometimes inaccurate
		Tendency to A
		Tendency to B
B		Sound judgement

Personal characteristics in relation to the job

(i) Personality and acceptability

A		Impact and effect on others not always favourable
		Tendency to A
		Tendency to B
B		Make a very good impression

(ii) Ability to communicate

(a) Verbal (at meetings, discussions, interviews)

A		Verbal communication not always effective
		Tendency to A
		Tendency to B
B		High standard of presentation

(b) Written (reports, memoranda, letters)

A		Limited basic writing skills
		Tendency to A
		Tendency to B
B		Writes very well

(iii) Mental alertness and initiative (initiative, grasp of new ideas, with problem solving, etc.)

A		Tend to follow precedent
		Tendency to A
		Tendency to B
B		Constructive and creative thinker

Only complete this section if responsibility is held for planning and organizing the work of subordinates

(i) Planning and organizing (devising programmes, budgets, schedules, as required)

A		Need some assistance
		Tendency to A
		Tendency to B
B		Above average organizing ability

(ii) Delegating (assigning and monitoring responsibility for work)

A		Find difficulty in delegating work
		Tendency to A
		Tendency to B
B		Highly successful in delegating

(iii) Controlling and co-ordinating (keeping group working toward objectives, measure performance, interpreting results, initiating correcting action)

A		Finding difficulty in controlling work
		Tendency to A
		Tendency to B
B		Very successful in controlling work

(iv) Leadership (securing full and willing response from subordinates, both individually and as a team)

A		Ineffectual
		Tendency to A
		Tendency to B
B		Effective leader

(v) Development of subordinates (recognition and development of ability)

A		Somewhat lacking
		Tendency to A
		Tendency to B
B		Competent developing talent

Assessment of learning needs/objectives for continuous development

Rate your ability in:	**High** Low	**Learning Needs** *(tick as appropriate)*
Assessing other people's capabilities	☐	☐
Decision making	☐	☐
Delegating	☐	☐
Giving instructions	☐	☐
Problem solving	☐	☐
Judgement	☐	☐
Leadership/initiative	☐	☐
Listening	☐	☐
Planning	☐	☐
Public speaking	☐	☐
Running meetings	☐	☐
Self discipline/coping with stress	☐	☐
Selling ideas	☐	☐
Thinking/creativity	☐	☐
Understanding other people	☐	☐
Use of time	☐	☐
OTHER AREAS ____________	☐	☐

Action Plan **No.** **Continuous Development**

(A separate sheet should be completed for each action plan)

1 Objective

---

2 Factors helping **Actions**

---

3 Factors hindering **Actions**

---

4 Itemized plan of action **Timetable**

---

5 Others to be involved

Some Suggested Sources of Learning/Information for Continuous Development

1 Professional

Journals/publications – (e.g. IPD Journal, Employment Gazette)
Technical information services (IPD Library, Industrial Society, etc.)
Colleges of Further and Higher Education
Courses/Seminars
The media
'Others'
Job rotation
Job exchange
Development of new aspects of one's own job
Work-related projects

2 Social

Evening classes – non-professional subjects
Committee membership
Community work

Index

Other titles in the Management Studies series

Management Studies 1

The Corporate Environment

David Farnham

Effective managers need the clearest possible picture of the environment within which their organisations operate. David Farnham's essential student text examines the different sectors of the economy, the nature of markets and price mechanisms, the impact of interest groups and the ways that the political and legal systems impinge on both the private and the public sector. This second edition has been fully revised and updated throughout to take account of the new-look Labour Party, changing population patterns, social trends and employment rights, moves towards European integration, and on-going developments within local government and the NHS.

Second Edition 1995 336pp Pbk ISBN 0 85292 605 7 **£15.95**

Management Processes and Functions

Michael Armstrong

Managers decide what to do and get it done – against a background of interruptions, pressure and uncertainty. The basic pillars of management – planning, organising, motivating and controlling – provide the framework to bring order out of chaos. In this major book, Michael Armstrong shows how successful managers manage their own time and work, and use the key interpersonal skills of communicating, delegating, counselling and leadership to get the best from others. Yet they also form part of a larger team – the whole organisation. Armstrong therefore provides students with invaluable insights into the structure of typical organisations and shows how the different functions interact to serve corporate strategies and goals.

1990 304pp Pbk ISBN 0 85292 438 0 **£15.95**

Managing Human Resources

Jane Weightman

All effective managers need to know how to work with and through people to achieve business results. Jane Weightman sets out the main theories of individual and group psychology, communications and learning, and then proceeds to show how they can be applied in practice. Later sections consider recruitment and selection, developing competence, and dealing with problem people. This second edition includes a completely new chapter on reward systems and expanded coverage of both motivation and performance management.

'A handy frame of reference for those who wish to introduce themselves to the subject or brush up on fundamentals' – Training and Development

'A cost and time-effective route to examination competence' – SOCPO News

Second Edition 1993 184pp Pbk ISBN 0 85292 520 4 **£12.95**

Management Information Systems and Statistics

Roland Bee and Frances Bee

Managers need a constant flow of information – available at the right time and in the right form. All organisations must therefore establish a Management Information System tailored to their particular circumstances. Roland and Frances Bee describe in detail how this can be done and then look at the basic sources of data and the statistical techniques, such as probability, sampling, correlation and decision-analysis, which can be used to convert raw data into real information. Detailed worked examples are provided to illustrate the techniques and the result is a thorough and accessible text which assumes no specialist mathematical training. The book concludes with a clear survey of the advantages of computerising management information, and the best ways of selecting and setting up the right system.

1990 264pp Pbk ISBN 0 85292 435 6 **£15.95**

Finance and Accounting for Managers

David Davies

All managers need to understand money and use financial information systems to ensure effective planning, decision-making and control. In this excellent step-by-step student text for non-specialists, David Davies examines the sources and uses of money, assets and liabilities, and how these are recorded on the balance sheet, cash statement, and profit and loss account. For this thoroughly revised second edition, following consultation with course tutors, he has extended the coverage of management accounting, particularly in the areas of costing and budgeting, and provided far greater detail about the financial implications of personnel decisions. Exercises and worked examples, some based on recent Marks and Spencer accounts, cash flow tables, a glossary and bibliography complete this clear and comprehensive introduction to finance and accounting.

Second Edition 1994 208pp Pbk ISBN 0 85292 527 1 **£12.95**

Management Studies 2

Employee Resourcing

Derek Torrington, Laura Hall, Isabel Haylor and Judith Myers

Employee resourcing – from corporate manpower planning to individual contracts of employment – is at the very heart of modern personnel management. Here, Professor Torrington and his colleagues provide full accounts of communications, computing and organisational structures; selection, appraisal and termination; the principles of payment; and health and safety. Other chapters give a vital framework of knowledge, enhanced by study themes combining further reading, plausible management problems and personal organisation-based learning. The result is a superb book, one which is ideally suited to educational needs yet which never neglects practical applications in the real world.

1991 392pp Pbk ISBN 0 85292 464 X **£18.95**

Employee Relations

David Farnham

In both unionised and non-unionised organisations, managers have constant contact, collective and individual, with their staff. Making the most of such contact is the essence of employee relations. In this book, David Farnham – author of the IPD's highly successful *The Corporate Environment* and *Personnel in Context* – examines the concepts and contexts, parties and processes, which form the cornerstones of employee relations. Part 2 turns to the key management issues: collective bargaining; employee involvement and representation; industrial action; and the role of the state. Throughout, assignments help students deepen their knowledge and apply their skills to practical examples. The result is a superb textbook which never neglects the problems of the real world.

1993 484pp Pbk ISBN 0 85292 474 7 **£18.95**

Passing Your IPM Exams

Elaine Crosthwaite

Elaine Crosthwaite draws on IPM syllabuses, examiners' reports, and past papers to offer everyone studying personnel management exactly what they need. She shows in detail how to:

- make the most of your tutor
- learn how you learn
- improve your reading, note-taking and case-study skills
- revise, get ready for exams and eradicate nerves
- work through model questions
- prepare and present assignments
- write up your management report
- get the results you deserve.

1993 208pp Pbk ISBN 0 85292 515 8 **£9.95**